CRITICAL APPROACHES TO LITERATURE

DAVID DAICHES

Second edition

LONGMAN

London and New York

Longman Group UK Limited,
Longman House, Burnt Mill, Harlow, Essex CM20 2JE England
and Associated Companies throughout the world

*Published in the United States of America
by Longman Inc., New York*

© David Daiches 1981

First published 1956
Thirteenth impression 1977
Second edition 1981
Fifth impression 1986

British Library Cataloguing in Publication Data
Daiches, David
Critical approaches to literature. — 2nd ed.
1. Criticism
I. Title
801'.95   PN81
ISBN 0-582-49180-0

Library of Congress Cataloging in Publication Data
Daiches, David, 1912 —
Critical approaches to literature.
Includes index.
1. Criticism. 2. Poetry. I. Title.
PN81.D3 1981   801   81-8180
ISBN 0-582-49180-0 (pbk)   AACR2

Produced by Longman Singapore Publishers (Pte) Ltd.
Printed in Singapore.

Contents

Preface to Second Edition

LOOKING THROUGH this book twenty-four years after it first appeared, I realise that while there is nothing significant that I should want to change in the discussion of older critics, recent trends in criticism demand some consideration. I realize also that the discussion of Marxist criticism does not adequately take account of the more sophisticated kinds of Marxist criticism that have been made available over the last quarter century. I have therefore added a section on Georg Lukács to the previous brief account of Marxist criticism, and I have also added sections on what seem to me to be the two most significant developments in criticism during the period since the book was written. These are new ideas about 'archetypal' criticism stemming from the seminal work of Northrop Frye, and the influence on criticism of linguistics and anthropology as manifested in the movement known as structuralism. I have also made some relatively minor changes in the text of the original chapters.

DAVID DAICHES

Edinburgh

We are grateful to the following for permission to reproduce copyright material:

The English Association for extracts from *Contemporary Approaches to English Studies* by Jonathan Culler edited by Hilda Schiff; The Merlin Press Ltd for extracts from *Studies In European Realism* by Georg Lukács; Princeton University Press for extracts from pp. 11, 74, 163, 238 and 341 *Anatomy of Criticism: Four Essays* by Northrop Frye Copyright © 1957 by Princeton University Press; Princeton Paperback 1971. Reprinted by permission of Princeton University Press.

Whilst every effort has been made, we are unable to trace the copyright holder of a poem by William Carlos Williams and would appreciate any information which would enable us to do so.

Introduction

TO ILLUMINATE both the nature of literature and the nature of criticism, this book presents some of the more important ways in which literature has been discussed. It is neither a history of criticism nor an annotated anthology of significant critical works. The critical pieces quoted and discussed represent examples of a method and a point of view—and their implications in both theory and practice.

The division into three parts is dictated by both logic and convenience. Part One considers how various critics have answered the question "What is the nature of imaginative literature; what is its use and value?" Part Two deals with the practical critic, and the different ways in which specific works of literary art have been and can be evaluated. Part Three takes up those fields of inquiry in which the literary critic touches other kinds of investigation, such as the psychological and the sociological; it inquires into the relationship between literary criticism and these other disciplines. True, many critics move freely from philosophic criticism to practical criticism, and the practical critic frequently advances and retreats around the area discussed in Part Three: further, a definition of the nature of poetry often has practical consequences in description and evaluation. There is bound to be some overlapping between the Parts—but the reader will have no difficulty in recognizing the different kinds of critical activity involved at any given point.

Many important critics are not discussed at all: Horace, Quintilian, Vida, Boileau, for instance, will not be found here, although each is important in the history of criticism. None of them, however, illustrates a method of approaching a literary work which is fundamentally different from that of some other critic who is discussed.

Where possible, I have taken my examples of methods and approaches from critics who wrote in English, to avoid the problems that inevitably arise when a critic's thought is translated. Plato, Aristotle, and Longinus had to be included because of the unique importance of the contribution of each, even though this has meant giving more than one key passage whose original meaning is problematical.

I have used individual critical essays to illustrate ways in which works of literature can be discussed, or points of view about the nature and value of works of literary art. The modern critical works quoted and discussed are not meant to represent a complete conspectus of modern criticism. Nor has it been my intention to give a full account of the thought of any individual critic—it has been no part of my aim to provide a full account of the philosophy of Plato or the history of the opinions of John Crowe Ransom. A passage cited might even be untypical of its author: the point in which I am interested is whether it represents a significant method or attitude, not whether it represents its author's total thought.

In short, my aim has been to provide an aid to the intelligent study of literary criticism, and of literature, of a kind that none of the standard histories or anthologies provide: *I am concerned with methodology, with the varying ways in which the art of literature and works of literature can be profitably discussed; I am not here concerned with critics as such or with the history of criticism as such.*

Clear conceptions concerning the different things the literary critic can do and has done seem to me the primary requisite for a serious interest in literary criticism. It is little use stuffing one's head with ideas of what this critic said or that critic believed if one cannot see clearly in what area of critical activity each critic is operating. Or, to put it another way, it is no use learning a series of answers if one does not know what the questions were.

What kinds of question can the literary critic ask? We must surely know this before we can profitably discuss his answers. We must know, too, what kinds of answer can be given before we can begin to compare one critic's answers with another's. This book's purpose is to help the reader obtain this sort of information: its primary object is clarification. Lest any reader imagine that I expect too much from this or any other kind of literary criticism, he is advised to turn to the *Epilogue* before, rather than after, he has gone through the book.

Cambridge   DAVID DAICHES

PART ONE

The Philosophical Inquiry

1

The Platonic dilemma

LITERARY CRITICISM concerns itself with any of
several questions. It can ask the philosophical question concerning the
nature of imaginative literature, and in a logical sense this question
should precede all others—for how can we discuss anything at all
unless we know in the first place what we are talking about? Yet
inquirers have often asked other questions about literature before they
have defined its nature, and asked them profitably, too, for the road
to understanding does not always follow the most obvious logical
route.

The major critical questions

We can ask what literature *does*, which is to define it in terms of its
function and at the same time to suggest its value. We can ask norma-

tive rather than descriptive questions, seeking to discover how to distinguish the good from the less good and the bad among literary works. And in the realm of description we can develop all kinds of special techniques of demonstration and analysis in such a way as to include or imply a value judgment. We may tackle the psychological problem of how the literary mind operates in creation. Finally, criticism may ask no questions at all, but simply seek to increase appreciation on the reader's part by any one of a great variety of methods, ranging from objective demonstration of certain qualities to impressionistic (or even autobiographical) revelation of how the work affects the critic. The critic's activity may thus be ontological, functional, normative, descriptive, psychological, or appreciative. Each of these activities has its place and its usefulness, and the many questions involved can be and have been asked in many different ways.

The philosophical inquiry into the nature of literature—what are its distinguishing features? how does it differ from other kinds of discourse?—has been going on in the Western world for well over two thousand years, and it continues today as actively as ever. This is the kind of question each generation prefers to answer in its own way, for literature is a complex phenomenon different aspects of which are seen and emphasized by different ages. Yet, though the answers differ from age to age, there are family resemblances among groups of answers, and it is not difficult to make some general classifications among them. Further, some answers, however much bound up with the problems of a particular literature in a particular time, have been especially germinal, later critics have accepted them or re-interpreted them or built on them or made use of them in some other way. Perhaps the most fruitful of all critical discussions devoted to inquiry into the nature and value of imaginative literature has been the *Poetics* of Aristotle, written in the fourth century before the birth of Christ—and, as we have it, an incomplete and fragmentary work—but still basic to any discussion of the question. Aristotle's definition of literature brings out its special, differentiating qualities, demonstrates its function and assesses value in terms of that function, and vindicates it against those who consider it useless or immoral.

Literature, as we are here using the term, refers to any kind of composition in prose or verse which has for its purpose not the communication of fact but the telling of a story (either wholly invented or given new life through invention) or the giving of pleasure through some use of the inventive imagination in the employment of words. This is not, of course, a definition of literature, for to give one at this stage would be to anticipate the whole argument of this book, but simply an indication of how the term is being used. There is, oddly enough, no single word in English that corresponds to the Greek *poesis* or the German *Dichtung*, terms which refer to products of the literary imagination and do not include, as the term *literature* does, anything at all that is written. The term *poetry* as used by some earlier writers—by Sir Philip Sidney, for example, in his *Apologie for Poetrie*—has the wider meaning of *poesis* or *Dichtung*, but it has since narrowed in meaning, just as *literature* has become too wide. Thus it is impossible to translate the title of Goethe's great work *Dichtung und Wahrheit* into English simply and neatly: it does not mean "Poetry and Truth," but rather "Imaginative Writing and Truth" or perhaps even (if one must do it in three words) "Fiction and Fact."

Poetry and the moralists

The use of language for other purposes than to communicate literal truth was bound to come under suspicion as soon as moral ideas were organized and philosophic systems developed. At an earlier stage in civilization the distinction between poetic and literal truth is often blurred, since all discourse in language is conducted through a kind of spontaneous symbolism, all statement is metaphorical, and the imagination is always on hand to describe and interpret the real world. That is what Shelley meant when, in *A Defence of Poetry* (1821), he claimed that "in the youth of the world" all discourse was in a sense poetry. "Their (primitive men's) language is vitally metaphorical; that is, it marks the before unapprehended relations of things and perpetuates their apprehension, until the words which represent them, become, through time, signs for portions or classes of thoughts instead of pictures of integral thoughts; and then if no new poets should arise to create afresh the associations which have been thus disorganized, language will be dead to all the nobler purposes of human intercourse."

The kind of naive poetry that Shelley was talking about was not consciously distinguished from other uses of language. As soon as poetry became self-conscious it became suspect. If poetry does not tell the truth, is it not immoral, or at best useless? It is perhaps strange that the idea that the poetic imagination may reveal profound truths of its own was nothing new or startling to man in a very primitive state of civilization and that as civilization advanced this awareness disappeared and had to be rediscovered by the conscious effort of critics. The vindication of the poetic imagination—which needed no vindication for primitive man—thus became one of the most important functions of literary critics in a self-conscious civilization.

The poet as divinely inspired

An obvious way of achieving this vindication was to differentiate sharply between imaginative literature (or poetry, in Sidney's sense) and all other forms of discourse. The poet was a possessed creature, not using language in the way that normal human beings do, but speaking in a divinely inspired frenzy. Such a view removed the poet from ordinary canons of judgment, and made him something between a prophet and a madman—sometimes one, sometimes the other, and sometimes both. There was, of course, a very primitive element in this view—the prophet working himself up into a frenzy before becoming possessed and delivering the word of God is a common enough notion in early stages of civilization—but nevertheless the view could be developed with deliberate sophistication in order to put the poet beyond the reach of philosophic censure. Plato suggests this view in a passage in his *Phaedrus:*[1]

The third kind is the madness of those who are possessed by the Muses; this enters into a delicate and virgin soul, and there inspiring frenzy, awakens lyrical and all other numbers; with these adorning the myriad actions of ancient heroes for the instruction of posterity. But he who, having no touch of the Muses' madness in his soul, comes to the door and thinks that he will get into the temple by the help of art—he, I say, and his poetry are not admitted; the sane man is nowhere at all when he enters into rivalry with the madman.

Plato develops this view at greater length in his *Ion*, in which the poet is presented as the inspired rhapsodist through whom God

[1] The quotations from Plato are Jowett's translation, with some minor alterations.

speaks, a man lacking art and volition of his own, a passive vehicle merely. In this dialogue, Socrates is speaking to Ion:

The gift which you possess . . . is not an art, but, as I was just saying, an inspiration; there is a divinity moving you, like that contained in the stone which Euripides calls a magnet, but which is commonly known as the stone of Heraclea. This stone not only attracts iron rings, but also imparts to them a similar power of attracting other rings; and sometimes you may see a number of pieces of iron and rings suspended from one another so as to form quite a long chain: and all of them derive their power of suspension from the original stone. In like manner the Muse first of all inspires men herself; and from these inspired persons a chain of other persons is suspended, who take the inspiration from them. For all good poets, epic as well as lyric, compose their beautiful poems not by art, but because they are inspired and possessed. And as the Corybantian revellers when they dance are not in their right mind, so the lyric poets are not in their right mind when they are composing their beautiful strains: but when falling under the power of music and metre they are inspired and possessed; like Bacchic maidens who draw milk and honey from the rivers when they are under the influence of Dionysus, but not when they are in their right mind. And the soul of the lyric poet does the same, as they themselves say; for they tell us that they bring songs from honeyed fountains, culling them out of the gardens and dens of the Muses; winging their way there from flower to flower like the bees. And this is true. For the poet is a light and winged and holy thing and there is no invention in him until he has been inspired and is out of his senses, and the mind is no longer in him: when he has not attained to this state, he is powerless and is unable to utter his oracles. Many are the noble words in which poets speak concerning the actions of men; but like yourself when speaking about Homer, they do not speak of them by any rules of art: they are simply inspired to utter that to which the Muse impels them, and that only; and when inspired, one of them will make dithyrambs, another hymns of praise, another choral strains, another epic or iambic verses—and he who is good at one is not good at any other kind of verse: for not by art does the poet sing, but by power divine. Had he learned by rules of art, he would have known how to speak not of one theme only, but of all; and therefore God takes away the minds of poets, and uses them as his ministers, as he also uses diviners and holy prophets, in order that we who hear them may know them to be speaking not of themselves who utter these priceless words in a state of unconsciousness, but that God himself is the speaker, and that through them he is conversing with us. And Tynnichus the Chalcidian affords a striking instance of what I am saying: he wrote nothing that anyone would care to remember but the famous paean which is in every one's mouth, one of the finest poems ever written, simply an invention of the Muses, as he himself says. For in this way the God would seem to indicate to us and not allow us to doubt that these beautiful poems are not human, or the work of man, but divine and the work of God: and that the poets are only the interpreters of the Gods by whom they are severally possessed. Was not this the lesson which the God intended to teach when by the mouth of the worst of poets he sang the best of songs?

Ion is a rhapsodist who recites and embellishes the works of the great poets. The poet is inspired by the God, and the rhapsodist is inspired by the poet, and so the magnetic chain develops. There is a certain amount of irony in the way Socrates makes Ion admit that he is not in his right mind when he recites and interprets Homer. "Are you not carried out of yourself, and does not your soul in an ecstasy seem to be among the persons or places of which she is speaking, whether they are in Ithaca or in Troy or whatever may be the scene of the poem?" And Ion replies, "That proof strikes home to me, Socrates. For I must confess that at the tale of pity my eyes are filled with tears, and when I speak of horrors, my hair stands on end and my heart throbs." "Well, Ion," Socrates replies, "and what are we to say of a man who at a sacrifice or festival, when he is dressed in holiday attire, and has gold crowns upon his head, of which nobody has robbed him, appears weeping or panic-stricken in the presence of more than twenty thousand friendly faces, when there is no one spoiling or wronging him;—is he in his right mind or is he not?" "No indeed, Socrates," Ion has to concede; "I must say that strictly speaking he is not his right mind." Socrates then points out that Ion's performance produces a similar effect on the spectators, who thus also become inspired:

Do you know that the spectator is the last of the rings which, as I am saying, derive their power from the original magnet; and the rhapsode like yourself and the actors are intermediate links, and the poet himself is the first link of all? And through all these the God sways the soul of men in any direction which he pleases, and makes one man hang down from another. There is also a chain of dancers and masters and under-masters of bands, who are suspended at the side, and are the rings which hang from the Muse. And every poet has a Muse from whom he is suspended, and by whom he is said to be possessed, which is nearly the same thing; for he is taken possession of.

Socrates then discusses whether the inspired reciter and interpreter of the poets can judge better of any given matter treated by the poet than the expert in that subject can (for example, can the rhapsodist or the general judge more effectively whether Homer correctly presents the art of war?) and after confusing poor Ion badly on this subject (and no wonder, for in putting the question thus, Socrates begs the fundamental question concerning the difference between *Dichtung* and *Wahrheit*, between poetry and science) forces him to choose between accepting the charge of dishonesty or admitting that he knows nothing himself but recites and interprets through a process of inspiration.

The *Ion* is the most elaborate presentation in the ancient world of the notion of poetry as pure inspiration—a notion which has had a long history, has gone through many modifications, and which survives today. "Great wits are sure to madness near alli'd," wrote Dryden in his *Absalom and Achitophel* two thousand years later, and nearly a hundred years before Dryden Shakespeare had noted that

> The lunatic, the lover and the poet
> Are of imagination all compact. . . .

It is possible, of course, that Plato wrote the *Ion* as well as the passage in the *Phaedrus* with his tongue in his cheek. Certainly, the view of poetry he presented in Book X of the *Republic* is very different, though this fact does not mean much, for a philosopher, like anybody else, has a perfect right to change his mind. But the note of irony which is sustained throughout the *Ion* and the way in which Socrates makes a fool out of Ion suggests that Plato was emphasizing the difference between the poet and the philosopher, wholly to the advantage of the latter. Further meditation on this distinction may well have led him to the position he maintains in the *Republic*.

It is significant that the theory of inspiration which Plato presents in the *Ion* says nothing about the poet's lying: he is speaking divine truths, but Plato does not go on to say that divine truths may sometimes appear to the ordinary human mind as literal untruths. The *Ion* assumes, indeed, that what the poet speaks of is the true and the beautiful, so that we can hardly say that Plato takes refuge in the theory of inspiration in order to vindicate the poet against the charge of lying or irresponsibility. As Plato developed his moral ideas further, he may well have come to ponder more and more the poet's moral responsibility, and some such development of his thought, together with further meditation on the war between poet and philosopher, may be the explanation of the famous charges brought against the poet in Book X of the *Republic*.

Plato's view of the place of the poet in the good society

The *Republic* is an elaborately reasoned discussion of the general principles of the good society and the means by which it is to be attained. Any discussion of poetry in this context is bound to be in a sense incidental: the subject is brought in only in a discussion of the means by which the good society is to be attained and preserved. Our definition of the good society depends on our notions of God and of justice; education for the good society will be education in the proper notions of these subjects.

This is made clear in Book II where Plato is discussing the education of the good citizen. He insists that all stories told to children should be morally edifying; they should never suggest wrong ideas. (One must remember that the poets, especially Homer, were a chief medium of education in ancient Greece.) Here is a characteristic passage from Book II, part of a dialogue between Socrates and Adeimantus:

Literature may be either true or false?
Yes.
And the young should be trained in both kinds, and we begin with the false?
I do not understand your meaning, he said.
You know, I said, that we begin by telling the children stories which, though not wholly destitute of truth, are in the main fictitious; and these stories are told them when they are not of an age to learn gymnastics.
Very true.
That was my meaning when I said that we must teach music [which includes literature] before gymnastics.
Quite right, he said.

You know also that the beginning is the most important part of any work, especially in the case of a young and tender thing; for that is the time at which the character is being formed and the desired impression is more readily taken.

Quite true.

And shall we just carelessly allow children to hear any casual tales which may be devised by casual persons, and to receive into their minds ideas for the most part the very opposite of those which we should wish them to have when they are grown up?

We can not.

Then the first thing will be to establish a censorship of the writers of fiction, and let the censors permit any tale of fiction which is good, and reject the bad; and we will desire mothers and nurses to tell their children the authorized ones only. Let them fashion the mind with such tales, even more fondly than they mould the body with their hands; but most of those which are now in use must be discarded. . . .

But which stories do you mean, he said; and what fault do you find with them?

A fault which is most serious, I said; the fault of telling a lie, and, what is more, a bad lie. . . .

If we mean our future guardians[2] to regard the habit of quarrelling among themselves as of all things the basest, no word should be said to them of the wars in heaven, or of the plots and fightings of the gods against one another, for they are not true. . . . If they would only believe us we would tell them that quarrelling is unholy, and that never up to this time has there been any quarrelling between citizens: this is what old men and old women should begin by telling children; and when they grow up, the poets also should be told to compose for them in a similar spirit. But the narrative of Hephaestus binding Here his mother, or of how on another occasion Zeus sent him flying for taking her part when she was beaten, and all the battles of the gods in Homer—these tales must not be admitted into our State, whether they are supposed to have an allegorical meaning or not. For a young person can not judge what is allegorical and what is literal; anything that he receives into his mind at that age is likely to become indelible and unalterable; and therefore it is most important that the tales which the young first hear should be models of virtuous thoughts.

This is a remarkable presentation of a naively pedagogical view of literature. And note that while stories about the gods quarrelling are to be forbidden both because they are unedifying and because they are not true, Plato has no objection to children being told untrue

---

[2] *Guardian* is Plato's name for a member of the ruling caste of the ideal state.

stories if they are edifying—stories, for example, that there never has been any quarrelling between citizens.

In a later passage in Book II Plato makes Socrates distinguish between the "true lie"—"ignorance in the soul of him who is deceived" —and the "lie in words," which is "only a kind of imitation and shadowy picture of a previous affection of the soul, not pure un-adulterated falsehood." The true lie is hated by gods and men, but "the lie in words is in certain cases useful and not hateful; in dealing with enemies—that would be an instance; or again, when those whom we call our friends in a fit of madness or illusion are going to do some harm, then it is useful and is a sort of medicine or preventive; also in the tales of mythology, of which we were just now speaking—be-cause we do not know the truth about ancient times, we make false-hood as much like truth as we can, and so turn it to account."

Here Plato touches on a point which, if developed, might have led him to a position close to Aristotle's view of the *probable* as in a deep sense more true than the *actual*. But, as so often the case with Plato, he only touches this point in passing, and goes on at once to make a distinction between the poet, who may occasionally tell a use-ful or probable lie, and God, who can never have any reason to lie.

Plato's references to poetry in Book II of the *Republic* do not constitute a full-scale examination of the nature and value of imagi-native literature, and it would be unfair, as well as unwise, to de-velop a complete theory of poetry from them. In Book X, however, he discusses the nature of poetry more fully—though still in the con-text of the ideal state—and brings against it charges which have been taken up, in many different ways, again and again in subsequent gen-erations. The passage is worth quoting at length, for it constitutes a major document in the history of criticism and is the fullest statement of an approach to imaginative literature which is natural to some kinds of philosophic minds and which is therefore always with us. Socrates is talking with Glaucon.

Of the many excellences which I perceive in the order of our State, there is none which upon reflection pleases me better than the rule about poetry.

To what do you refer?

To the rejection of imitative poetry, which certainly ought not to be received; as I see far more clearly now that the parts of the soul have been distinguished.

What do you mean?

Speaking in confidence, for I should not like to have my words repeated to the tragedians and the rest of the imitative tribe—but I do not mind saying to you, that all poetical imitations are ruinous to the understanding of the hearers, and that the knowledge of their true nature is the only antidote to them. . . . Can you tell me what imitation is? for I really do not know.

A likely thing, then, that I should know. . . .

Well then, shall we begin the enquiry in our usual manner: Whenever a number of individuals have a common name, we assume them to have also a corresponding idea or form:—do you understand me?

I do.

Let us take any common instance; there are beds and tables in the world —plenty of them, are there not?

Yes.

But there are only two ideas or forms of them—one the idea of a bed, the other of a table.

True.

And the maker of either of them makes a bed or he makes a table for our use, in accordance with the idea—that is our way of speaking in this and similar instances—but no artificer makes the ideas themselves: how could he?

Impossible.

And there is another artist,—I should like to know what you would say of him.

Who is he?

One who is the maker of all the works of all other workmen.

What an extraordinary man!

Wait a little, and there will be more reason for your saying so. For this is he who is able to make not only vessels of every kind, but plants and animals, himself and all other things—the earth and heaven, and the things which are in heaven or under the earth; he makes the gods also.

He must be a wizard and no mistake.

Oh! you are incredulous, are you? Do you mean that there is no such maker or creator, or that in one sense there might be a maker of all these things but in another not? Do you see that there is a way in which you could make them all yourself?

What way?

An easy way enough; or rather, there are many ways in which the feat might be quickly and easily accomplished, none quicker than that of turning a mirror round and round—you would soon enough make the sun and the heavens, and the earth and yourself, and other animals and plants, and all the other things of which we were just now speaking, in the mirror.

Yes, he said; but they would be appearances only.

Very good, I said, you are coming to the point now. And the painter too is, as I conceive, just such another—a creator of appearances, is he not?

Of course.

But then I suppose you will say that what he creates is untrue. And yet there is a sense in which the painter also creates a bed?

Yes, he said, but not a real bed.

And what of the maker of the bed? were you not saying that he too makes, not the idea which, according to our view, is the essence of the bed, but only a particular bed?

Yes, I did.

Then if he does not make that which exists he cannot make true existence, but only some semblance of existence; and if any one were to say that the work of the maker of the bed, or of any other workman, has real existence, he could hardly be supposed to be speaking the truth.

At any rate, he replied, philosophers would say that he was not speaking the truth.

No wonder, then, that his work too is an indistinct expression of truth.

No wonder.

Suppose now that by the light of the examples just offered we enquire who this imitator is?

If you please.

Well, then, here are three beds: one existing in nature, which is made by God, as I think that we may say—for no one else can be the maker?

No.

There is another which is the work of the carpenter?

Yes.

And the work of the painter is a third?

Yes.

Beds, then, are of three kinds, and there are three artists who superintend them: God, the maker of the bed, and the painter?

Yes, there are three of them.

God, whether from choice or from necessity, made one bed in nature and one only; two or more such ideal beds neither ever have been nor ever will be made by God.

Why is that?

Because even if He had made but two, a third would still appear behind them which both of them would have for their idea, and that would be the ideal bed and not the two others.

Very true, he said.

God knew this, and He desired to be the real maker of a real bed, not a particular maker of a particular bed, and therefore He created a bed which is essentially and by nature one only.

So we believe.

Shall we, then, speak of Him as the natural author or maker of the bed?

Yes, he replied; inasmuch as by the natural process of creation He is the author of this and of all other things.

And what shall we say of the carpenter—is not he also the maker of the bed?

Yes.

But would you call the painter a creator and maker?

Certainly not.

Yet if he is not the maker, what is he in relation to the bed?

I think, he said, that we may fairly designate him as the imitator of that which the others make.

Good, I said; then you call him who is third in the descent from nature an imitator?

Certainly, he said.

And the tragic poet is an imitator, and therefore, like all other imitators, he is thrice removed from the king and from the truth?

That appears to be so.

Then about the imitator we are agreed. . . . Now do you suppose that if a person were able to make the original as well as the image, he would seriously devote himself to the image-making branch? Would he allow imitation to be the ruling principle of his life, as if he had nothing higher in him?

I should say not.

The real artist, who knew what he was imitating, would be interested in realities and not in imitations; and would desire to leave as memorials of himself works many and fair; and, instead of being the author of encomiums, he would prefer to be the theme of them. . . .

Then must we not infer that all these poetical individuals, beginning with Homer, are only imitators; they copy images of virtue and the like, but the truth they never reach? . . .

Here is another point: The imitator or maker of the image knows nothing of true existence; he knows appearances only. Am I not right?

Yes.

Then let us have a clear understanding, and not be satisfied with half an explanation.

Proceed.

Of the painter we say that he will paint reins, and he will paint a bit?

Yes.

And the worker in leather and brass will make them?

Certainly.

But does the painter know the right form of the bit and reins? Nay, hardly even the workers in brass and leather who make them; only the horseman who knows how to use them—he knows their right form.

Most true.

And may we not say the same of all things?

What?

That there are three arts which are concerned with all things: one which uses, another which makes, a third which imitates them? . . .

Just so.

Thus far we are pretty well agreed that the imitator has no knowledge worth mentioning of what he imitates. Imitation is only a kind of play or sport, and the tragic poets, whether they write in Iambic or in Heroic verse, are imitators in the highest degree?

Very true.

And now tell me, I conjure you, has not imitation been shown by us to be concerned with that which is thrice removed from the truth? . . .

This was the conclusion at which I was seeking to arrive when I said that painting or drawing, and imitation in general, when doing their own proper work, are far removed from truth, and the companions and friends and associates of a principle within us which is equally removed from reason, and that they have no true or healthy aim.

Exactly.

The imitative art is an inferior who marries an inferior, and has inferior offspring.

Very true.

And is this confined to the sight only, or does it extend to the hearing also, relating in fact to what we term poetry?

Probably the same would be true of poetry. . . .

We may state the question thus:—Imitation imitates the actions of men, whether voluntary or involuntary, on which, as they imagine, a good or bad result has ensued, and they rejoice or sorrow accordingly. . . .

Were we not saying that a good man, who has the misfortune to lose his son or anything else which is most dear to him, will bear the loss with more equanimity than another?

Yes.

But will he have no sorrow, or shall we say that although he cannot help sorrowing, he will moderate his sorrow? . . . There is a principle of law and reason in him which bids him resist, as well as a feeling of his misfortune which is forcing him to indulge his sorrow?

True. . . .

The law would say that to be patient under suffering is best, and that we should not give way to impatience, as there is no knowing whether such things are good or evil; and nothing is gained by impatience; also, because no human thing is of serious importance, and grief stands in the way of that which at the moment is most required.

What is most required? he asked.

That we should take counsel about what has happened, and when the dice have been thrown order our affairs in the way which reason deems best; not, like children who have had a fall, keeping hold of the part struck and wasting time in setting up a howl, but always accustoming the soul forthwith to apply a remedy, raising up that which is sickly and fallen, banishing the cry of sorrow by the healing art.

Yes, he said, that is the true way of meeting the attacks of fortune.

Yes, I said; and the higher principle is ready to follow this suggestion of reason?

Clearly.

And the other principle, which inclines us to recollection of our troubles and to lamentation, and can never have enough of them, we may call irrational, useless, and cowardly?

Indeed, we may.

And does not the latter—I mean the rebellious principle—furnish a great variety of materials for imitation? Whereas the wise and calm temperament, being always nearly equable, is not easy to imitate or to appreciate when imitated, especially at a public festival when a promiscuous crowd is assembled in a theatre. For the feeling represented is one which they are strangers.

Certainly.

Then the imitative poet who aims at being popular is not by nature made, nor is his art intended, to please or to affect the rational principle in the soul; but he will prefer the passionate and fitful temper, which is easily imitated?

Clearly.

And now we may fairly take him and place him by the side of the painter, for he is like him in two ways: first, inasmuch as his creations have an inferior degree of truth—in this, I say, he is like him; and he is also like him in being concerned with an inferior part of the soul; and therefore we shall be right in refusing to admit him into a well-ordered State, because he awakens and nourishes and strengthens the feelings and impairs the reason. As in a city when the evil are permitted to have authority and the good are put out of the way, so in the soul of man, as we maintain, the imitative poet implants an evil constitution, for he indulges the irrational nature which has no discernment of greater and less, but thinks the same thing at one time great and at another small—he is a manufacturer of images and is very far removed from the truth.

Exactly.

But we have not yet brought forward the heaviest count in our accusation:—the power which poetry has of harming even the good (and there are very few who are not harmed), is surely an awful thing?

Yes, certainly, if the effect is what you say.

Hear and judge: The best of us, as I conceive, when we listen to a passage of Homer, or one of the tragedians, in which he represents some pitiful hero who is drawling out his sorrows in a long oration, or weeping, and smiting his breast—the best of us, you know, delight in giving way to sympathy, and are in raptures at the excellence of the poet who stirs our feelings most.

Yes, of course I know.

But when any sorrow of our own happens to us, then you may observe that we pride ourselves on the opposite quality—we would fain be quiet and patient; this is the manly part, and the other which delighted us in the recitation is now deemed to be the part of a woman.

Very true, he said.

Now can we be right in praising and admiring another who is doing that which any one of us would abominate and be ashamed of in his own person?

No, he said, that is certainly not reasonable.

Nay, I said, quite reasonable from one point of view.

What point of view?

If you consider, I said, that when in misfortune we feel a natural hunger and desire to relieve our sorrow by weeping and lamentation, and that this feeling which is kept under control in our own calamities is satisfied and delighted by the poets;—the better nature in each of us, not having been sufficiently trained by reason or habit, allows the sympathetic element to break loose because the sorrow is another's; and the spectator fancies that there can be no disgrace to himself in praising and pitying any one who comes telling him what a good man he is, and making a fuss about his troubles; he thinks that the pleasure is a gain, and why should he be supercilious and lose this and the poem too? Few persons ever reflect, as I should imagine, that from the evil of other men something of evil is communicated to themselves. And so the feeling of sorrow which has gathered strength at the sight of the misfortunes of others is with difficulty repressed in our own. . . . And does not the same hold also of the ridiculous? There are jests which you would be ashamed to make yourself, and yet on the comic stage, or indeed in private, when you hear them, you are greatly amused by them, and are not at all disgusted at their unseemliness;—the case of pity is repeated;—there is a principle in human nature which is disposed to raise a laugh, and this which you once restrained by reason, because you were afraid of being thought a buffoon, is now let out again; and having stimulated the risible faculty at the theatre, you are betrayed unconsciously to yourself into playing the comic poet at home.

Quite true, he said.

And the same may be said of lust and anger and all the other affections, of desire and pain and pleasure, which are held to be inseparable from every action—in all of them poetry feeds and waters the passions instead of drying them up; she lets them rule, although they ought to be controlled, if mankind are ever to increase in happiness and virtue.

I cannot deny it.

Therefore, Glaucon, I said, whenever you meet with any of the eulogists of Homer declaring that he has been the educator of Hellas, and that he is profitable for education and for the ordering of human things, and that you should take him up again and again and get to know him and regulate your whole life according to him, we may love and honour those who say these things—they are excellent people, as far as their lights extend; and we are ready to acknowledge that Homer is the greatest of poets and first of tragedy writers; but we must remain firm in our conviction that hymns to the gods and praises of famous men are the only poetry which ought to be admitted into our State. For if you go beyond this and allow the honeyed muse to enter, either in epic or lyric verse, not law and the reason of mankind, which by common consent have ever been deemed best, but pleasure and pain will be the rulers in our State.

That is most true, he said.

And now since we have reverted to the subject of poetry, let this our defence serve to show the reasonableness of our former judgment in sending away out of our State an art having the tendencies which we have described; for reason constrained us. But that she may not impute to us any harshness or want of politeness, let us tell her that there is an ancient quarrel between philosophy and poetry; of which there are many proofs. . . . Notwithstanding this, let us assure our sweet friend and the sister arts of imitation, that if she will only prove her title to exist in a well-ordered State we shall be delighted to receive her—we are very conscious of her charms; but we may not on that account betray the truth. I dare say, Glaucon, that you are as much charmed by her as I am, especially when she appears in Homer?

Yes, indeed, I am greatly charmed.

Shall I propose, then, that she be allowed to return from exile, but upon this condition only—that she make a defence of herself in lyrical or some other metre?

Certainly.

And we may further grant to those of her defenders who are lovers of poetry and yet not poets the permission to speak in prose on her behalf: let them show not only that she is pleasant but also useful to States and to human life, and we will listen in a kindly spirit; for if this can be proved we shall surely be the gainers—I mean, if there is a use in poetry as well as a delight?

Certainly, he said, we shall be the gainers.

If her defence fails, then, my dear friend, like other persons who are enamoured of something, but put a restraint upon themselves when they think their desires are opposed to their interests, so too must we after the manner of lovers give her up, though not without a struggle. We too are inspired by that love of poetry which the education of noble States has implanted in us, and therefore we would have her appear at her best and truest; but so long as she is unable to make good her defence, this argument of ours shall be a charm to us, which we will repeat to ourselves while we listen to her strains; that we may not fall away into the childish love of her which captivates the many. At all events we are well aware that poetry being such as we have described is not to be regarded seriously as attaining to the truth; and he who listens to her . . . should be on his guard against her seductions and make our words his law.

Yes, he said, I quite agree with you.

Yes, I said, my dear Glaucon, for great is the issue at stake, greater than appears, whether a man is to be good or bad. And what will any one be profited if under the influence of honour or money or power, aye, or under the excitement of poetry, he neglect justice and virtue?

Yes, he said; I have been convinced by the argument, as I believe that any one else would have been.

The significance of Plato's objections to poetry

Plato's primary objection to poetry might be called an epistemological one—it stems from his theory of knowledge. If true reality consists of the *ideas* of things, of which individual objects are but reflections or imitations, then anyone who imitates those individual objects is imitating an imitation, and so producing something which is still further removed from ultimate reality. It is significant that Plato develops this argument first with reference to the painter, and that he takes a simple representational view of painting. Here the point is clear enough: representational painting *is* an imitation of a specific object or groups of objects, and if it is nothing but that, if reality lies not in individual objects but in general ideas or forms, then, from the point of view of the philosopher whose main interest is in apprehending reality, the painter is not doing anything particularly valuable—though on the other hand what he is doing is not necessarily vicious. (Why it did not occur to Plato that the painter, by painting the *ideal* object, could suggest the ideal form and thus make direct contact with reality in a way denied to ordinary perception, is not easy to see: presumably because he could not conceive of reality as being apprehensible through the senses at all.)

Just as the painter, furthermore, only imitates what he sees and does not know how to make or to use what he sees (he could paint a bed, but not make one), so the poet imitates reality without necessarily understanding it. Not only, therefore, are the arts imitations of imitations and thus thrice removed from the truth: they are also the product of a futile ignorance. The man who imitates or describes or represents without really knowing what he is imitating is demonstrating both his lack of useful purpose and his lack of knowledge. "The real artist, who knew what he was imitating, would be interested in realities and not in imitations; and would desire to leave as memorials of himself works many and fair; and, instead of being the author of encomiums, he would prefer to be the theme of them." If Homer had understood what makes men behave well, instead of merely describing men behaving well, he would have been at the second instead of the third remove from ideal truth and have been a much more useful citizen.

This emphasis on practicality and utility is perhaps surprising in a philosopher (something very like Plato's objections to art, though not deriving from his particular theory of knowledge, constitutes the standard Philistine argument against taking art seriously) but one must remember always that in these passages from the *Republic* Plato is discussing the proper environment for producing the good citizen, the "guardian" of the ideal state. This emphasis on practicality goes even further, however, than it would ever do in the normal Philistine argument, for Plato is not content with putting the "imitator" of something below its maker (as the man who paints reins and a bit is inferior to the maker of them); he puts the maker below the user. "There are three arts which are concerned with all things: one which uses, another which makes, a third which imitates them." The user teaches the maker, whose product is then imitated (painted or described) by the artist. Presumably the philosopher who by meditation is led to an understanding of the ideal form of the thing made is far above both user and maker, but Plato does not say so here. If he had, it might have led him to the notion that the artist might be the one to suggest or indicate the ideal form. After all, as has been many times pointed out, it is by every kind of poetic device—metaphor, symbol, fiction—that Plato puts his own philosophy across, and Book X itself, in the words of Lord Lindsay, "begins with an attack on poetry and ends with a poem."

The artist, then, is but an imitator of an imitation and in addition he is ignorant of the true use and nature of what he imitates. This is Plato's main objection to poetry, but there are two further objections closely related to it. Not only is artistic imitation, whether in painting or in literature, far removed from the truth; it both employs and appeals to an inferior part of the human faculties. "The imitative poet who aims at being popular is not by nature made, nor is his art intended, to please or to affect the rational principle in the soul; but he will prefer the passionate and fitful temper, which is easily imitated." The poet does not deal calmly, wisely, and equably with the essential truth of things but excitedly with their changing surfaces. This leads to the third and more serious charge—that "poetry feeds and waters the passions instead of drying them up." Plato the philosopher naturally opposes (as certain Christian thinkers were to do later) the reason to the passions: it is the duty of the wise man to control passion by reason; poetry, by exciting and strengthening the passions, makes this task more difficult. There is no trace in Plato —or indeed anywhere in Greek thought—of the modern romantic notion that self-indulged emotion is itself good or valuable, or that sensibility as such—the capacity to be easily moved—is a sign of superior character. Plato would have been equally astonished at Henry Mackenzie's admiration of "the man of feeling" and at Wordsworth's defense of poetry as "the spontaneous overflow of powerful feeling," to say nothing of more extravagant romantic defenses of emotional self-indulgence.

Poetry, therefore, according to Plato, is far removed from truth, and springs from improper knowledge and lack of understanding of both how to use and how to make what it describes; it is the product of an "inferior part of the soul"; and it harms by nourishing the passions, which ought to be controlled and disciplined. Any defense of poetry against Plato would have to tackle first the epistemological argument, that poetry is inferior because it is an imitation of an imitation, proceed to show that the poetic gift derives from a uniquely significant human faculty, and finally demonstrate that if poetry arouses passion it is only in order in the long run to allay it or discipline it. This triple task is brilliantly achieved by Aristotle in his *Poetics*. Perhaps Plato was not unaware of the possibility of defending poetry along the lines that Aristotle was to take: his final remarks on poetry in the *Republic* suggest that he has presented only the brief for the prosecution and is awaiting the arguments of the defense.

2

The Aristotelian solution

THE PLATONIC DILEMMA is at once the dilemma of
the metaphysician and of the practical moralist; it reflects what Plato
himself calls the "ancient quarrel between philosophy and poetry"
and at the same time appeals to the man of affairs to whom any activity is suspect if it cannot be directly related to an obvious pragmatic goal. Any effective solution to the dilemma would have to take
both aspects into account.

Clarification by classification

Aristotle undertakes to examine the nature and differentiating qualities of imaginative literature with a view to demonstrating that it is

true, serious, and useful (whereas Plato had shown it to be false, trivial, and harmful). His argument proceeds in the characteristically Aristotelian fashion of distinguishing between different species of literature in order to show both what they have in common and wherein they differ from each other. This leads him into some fairly detailed discussion of the different types of Greek literature, which is less important for our purposes than those remarks he makes either about imaginative literature generally or about one species or another which illuminate the nature, function, and value of imaginative literature as such. His classification is naturally based on the varieties of literature with which he was familiar—Aristotle's method is essentially one of examining observed phenomena with a view to noting their qualities and characteristics. His concern is the ontological one of discovering what in fact literature is rather than the normative one of describing what it should be. He is describing, not legislating; yet his description is so organized as to make an account of the nature of literature involve an account of its function, and its value emerges in terms of its function.

All the kinds of poetry, says Aristotle—epic, tragic, comic, and dithyrambic, listing the kinds known to him in Greek literature—involve *mimesis*, imitation or representation; and one can represent various aspects of real or imaginary situations through any one of a variety of means or media. The kinds of poetry—and Aristotle is using the term in the general sense we have discussed earlier—are therefore distinguished according to the medium of representation they use, what aspects of real or imagined life they represent, and the way in which the presentation (or communication, embodiment and presentation in language) is effected. The difference in medium between the painter and the poet, for example, is obvious: the former uses color and form, the latter uses words in their denotative, connotative, rhythmic, and musical aspects. Differences can also be noted between the different kinds of use of language employed by writers of different kinds of literature.

Aristotle points out that in his day there was no common term applicable to all the ways of employing language, both in prose and metrically—no term, that is, comparable to the modern meaning of the word *literature*. Clearly meter alone is not the distinguishing feature of poetry, for medical and scientific treatises have been written in verse (a practice commoner in ancient Greece than today). "There is no common term we could apply to the mimes of Sophron and

Xenarchus and the Socratic dialogues on the one hand; and, on the other, to poetic imitations in iambic, elegiac, or any similar meter. People do, indeed, add the word 'maker' or 'poet' to the name of the meter, and speak of elegaic poets, or epic (that is, hexameter) poets, as if it were not the imitation that makes the poet, but the verse that entitles them all indiscriminately to the name. Even when a treatise on medicine or natural science is brought out in verse, the author is usually called a poet; and yet Homer and Empedocles [a fifth century philosopher who expressed his philosophical and religious notions in hexameter verse] have nothing in common but the meter, so that it would be right to call the one poet, the other physicist rather than poet."

If poetry is an art of imitation or representation, and the objects of imitation are "men doing or experiencing something"—men in action—one can classify poetry according to the kinds of people it represents—they are either better than they are in real life, or worse, or the same. One could present characters, that is, on the grand or heroic scale; or one could treat ironically or humorously the petty follies of men; or one could aim at naturalism, presenting men neither heightened nor trivialized.

Third, the poet can tell a story partly in narrative form and partly through the speeches of the characters (as Homer does), or it can all be done in third-person narrative, or the story can be presented dramatically, with no use of third-person narrative at all.

These, then, are the three ways in which Aristotle, at the beginning of his treatise, distinguishes between kinds of representational art—they can differ in the representative medium employed, in the kinds of objects represented, and in the way in which a given medium is handled; in medium, subject-matter, and technique, as we might put it. Comedy and tragedy differ in the second respect: tragedy deals with men on a heroic scale, men "better" (not necessarily in the simple moral sense but in terms of impressiveness and dignity) than they are in everyday life, whereas comedy deals with the more trivial aspects of human nature, with characters "worse" than they are in real life, but again not in the simple moral sense. Epic or heroic poetry is like tragedy in this respect (differing in technique but not in the kind of characters represented) and satirical poetry is like comedy. Aristotle spends some time speculating on the human faculty for imitation or representation and on its development. He then embarks on a full-length discussion of tragedy in which he really comes to grips with the nature of imaginative literature and in doing so finds a way out of Plato's dilemma.

The nature of tragedy

Reserving epic poetry and comedy for later discussion, Aristotle examines the nature of tragedy:[1]

A tragedy is the imitation of an action that is serious and also, as having magnitude, complete in itself; in language with pleasurable accessories, each kind brought in separately in the parts of the work; in a dramatic, not in a narrative form; with incidents arousing pity and fear, wherewith to accomplish its catharsis of such emotions. Here by 'language with pleasurable accessories' I mean that with rhythm and harmony or song superadded; and by 'the kinds separately' I mean that some portions are worked out with verse only, and others in turn with song.

I. As they act the stories, it follows that in the first place the Spectacle (or stage-appearance of the actors) must be some part of the whole; and in the second Melody and Diction, these two being the means of their imitation. Here by 'Diction' I mean merely this, the composition of the verses; and by 'Melody,' what is too completely understood to require explanation. But further: the subject represented also is an action; and the action involves agents, who must necessarily have their distinctive qualities both of character and thought, since it is from these that we ascribe certain qualities to their actions. There are in the natural order of things, therefore, two causes, Character and Thought, of their actions, and consequently of their success or failure in their lives. Now the action (that which was done) is represented in the play by the Fable or Plot. The Fable, in our present sense of the term, is simply this, the combination of the incidents, or things done in the story; whereas Character is what makes us ascribe certain moral qualities to the agents; and Thought is shown in all they say when proving a particular point or, it may be, enunciating a general truth. There are six parts consequently of every tragedy, as a whole, that is, of such or such quality, viz. a Fable or Plot, Characters, Diction, Thought, Spectacle and Melody; two of them arising from the means, one from the manner, and three from the objects of the dramatic imitation; and there is nothing else besides these six. Of these, its formative elements, then, not a few of the dramatists have made due use, as every play, one may say, admits of Spectacle, Character, Fable, Diction, Melody, and Thought.

[1] *Ars Poetica*, translated by Ingram Bywater (Oxford: Clarendon Press).

II. The most important of the six is the combination of the incidents of the story. Tragedy is essentially an imitation not of persons but of action and life, of happiness and misery. All human happiness or misery takes the form of action; the end for which we live is a certain kind of activity, not a quality. Character gives us qualities, but it is in our actions—what we do —that we are happy or the reverse. In a play accordingly they do not act in order to portray the Characters; they include the Characters for the sake of the action. So that it is the action in it, i.e. its Fable or Plot, that is the end and purpose of the tragedy; and the end is everywhere the chief thing. Besides this, a tragedy is impossible without action, but there may be one without Character. The tragedies of most of the moderns are characterless —a defect common among poets of all kinds, and with its counterpart in painting in Zeuxis as compared with Polygnotus; for whereas the latter is strong in character, the work of Zeuxis is devoid of it. And again: one may string together a series of characteristic speeches of the utmost finish as regards Diction and Thought, and yet fail to produce the true tragic effect; but one will have much better success with a tragedy which, however inferior in these respects, has a Plot, a combination of incidents, in it. And again: the most powerful elements of attraction in Tragedy, the Peripeties[2] and Discoveries, are parts of the Plot. A further proof is in the fact that beginners succeed earlier with the Diction and Characters than with the construction of a story; and the same may be said of nearly all the early dramatists. We maintain, therefore, that the first essential, the life and soul, so to speak, of Tragedy is the Plot; and that the Characters come second—compare the parallel in painting, where the most beautiful colours laid on without order will not give one the same pleasure as a simple black-and-white sketch of a portrait. We maintain that Tragedy is primarily an imitation of action, and that it is mainly for the sake of the action that it imitates the personal agents. Third comes the element of Thought, i.e. the power of saying whatever can be said, or what is appropriate to the occasion. This is what, in the speeches in Tragedy, falls under the arts of Politics and Rhetoric; for the older poets make their personages discourse like statesmen, and the moderns like rhetoricians. One must not confuse it with Character. Character in a play is that which reveals the moral purpose of the agents, i.e. the sort of thing they seek or avoid, where that is not obvious—hence there is no room for Character in a speech on a purely indifferent subject. Thought, on the other hand, is shown in all they say when proving or disproving some particular point, or enunciating some universal proposition. Fourth among the literary elements is the Diction of the personages, i.e. as before explained, the expression of their thoughts in words, which is practically the same thing with verse as with prose. As for the two remaining parts, the Melody is the greatest of the pleasurable

2 See page 33.

accessories of Tragedy. The Spectacle, though an attraction, is the least artistic of all the parts, and has least to do with the art of poetry. The tragic effect is quite possible without a public performance and actors; and besides, the getting-up of the Spectacle is more a matter for the costumier than the poet.

The significance of plot

Aristotle is considering tragedy as a literary form rather than as a theatrical presentation, and he does not, therefore, regard the "spectacle" as an integral part of the dramatist's medium. "The tragic effect is quite possible without a public performance and actors." Actual stage presentation can, of course, immeasurably increase the impact of a play, and there are certain aspects of the action and language of a play written for the stage which can only be justified and fully appreciated if we take into account the particular kind of stage representation intended (as Granville-Barker has shown in his *Prefaces to Shakespeare*). Aristotle is concerned with the essential meaning and value of a play, not with the techniques of getting that meaning and value across to an audience. The most important thing for him is the action, the arrangement of the events, by which he does not mean of course the mere summarizable epitome of events (though he sometimes talks as though he does) but the way in which the action proceeds at each point. Thus the "plot" (in Aristotle's sense) of a Shakespeare play is not to be identified with the story he found in his source—in Holinshed or in an Italian *novella* or in an earlier play— even though the summarizable plots may be almost identical: if that were so, then one could not at the same time maintain Shakespeare's greatness as a dramatist and hold that "the plot is the life and soul of tragedy." Similarly, the plots of Aeschylus or Sophocles are not identical with the myths on which they based their tragedies, even though the tragedies did in fact use the stories as known in the myths. Plot is something fuller and subtler than this; it is the way in which the action works itself out, the whole causal chain which leads to the final outcome.

In this sense, plot can be said to be the "soul" of tragedy as well as of certain kinds of novel. Character is important, too, but important as a causal element in the plot. In a dramatic monologue by Browning character is interesting for its own sake; Browning is spotlighting a psychological situation; he is not interested in character as contributing to a pattern of action but in character as revealing a certain kind of approach to life, a certain way of reacting to experience. Many of the unactable "closet dramas" of the nineteenth century are simply collections of dramatic monologues rather than true dramas whose essential life consists in their action. But a novel like Jane Austen's *Emma*, no less than tragedies like Sophocles' *Oedipus the King* and Shakespeare's *Hamlet*, develops its meaning through the progression of the action; what Emma *does* illustrates what she *is*, and the way in which her actions affect other people and interact with other people's actions not only helps to reveal character but also provides the essence of the novel: the interactions of different characters result in a plot pattern in which lies the nature of Jane Austen's ironic contemplation of the social scene. If *Emma* consisted of a series of self-revelations of the characters in conversation, without any plot, or if *Hamlet* were only a series of soliloquies by the hero in which he revealed his soul and discussed his dilemma without anything taking place, these works would doubtless possess a certain interest but not the kind of interest proper to a novel or a drama. So Aristotle's arrangement of the elements of tragedy in an order of importance which puts plot first and character second, with thought[3] third and diction fourth, seems logical enough.[4]

[3] The term *dianoia*, which is here rendered *thought*, is not easy to translate. Bywater comments: "*Dianoia* in the sense it bears in the Poetics is, like *ethos* (character), an element in the personality of the dramatis personae. It is their intellectual capacity, as evinced in their language (or it may be, in their actions), and it is to be seen whenever they argue or make an appeal to the feelings of their hearers, in other words when they reason or plead with one of the other dramatis personae in the same sort of way as a rhetor might do. Hence it is that the general theory of the *dianoia* in a play is said to belong to Rhetoric rather than Poetry; and a speech with a great display of *dianoia* in it is a rhetorical speech." (*Aristotle on the Art of Poetry*, with critical introduction, translation and commentary, by Ingram Bywater, Oxford, 1909, p. 164.) An obvious example of *dianoia* in Shakespearean tragedy would be Antony's funeral speech in *Julius Caesar*. The famous speech on "degree" by Ulysses in *Troilus and Cressida* would also be pure *dianoia*.
[4] The modern critic of poetic drama would be inclined to put diction higher up in the scale, for he would consider it to mean more than the most effective expression of a required point, but the whole way of bodying forth a situation in a language full of suggestion and evocation. Indeed, the poetry of a poetic drama can hardly be separated from the other significant elements, for it is largely what creates these elements or at least what gives them meaning. Aristotle here shows no interest in the exploratory aspects of poetic language, those aspects which, by the effective use of image and symbol, help to create a whole world of echoing meaning. His approach is analytic; his are the notes of an observer and a thinker who is accustomed to clarify knowledge in the first instance by classification; and he has nothing to say of the organic relation of the various elements to each other and to the whole, except in so far as they are all related to plot.

So far, Aristotle has not touched on those aspects of tragedy which differentiate it from other kinds of drama, nor, except for the almost casual mention of melody and spectacle, on those which differentiate it from other kinds of narrative, such as the epic or the modern novel. And he has said nothing yet that is at all relevant to the charges brought against poetry by Plato. He has much more to say about the nature of plot in general before he comes to specify the nature of a tragic plot, and only when he has done that does he proceed to draw conclusions about the nature and value of tragedy, where, without mentioning Plato or his arguments, he answers Plato's charges.

Having thus distinguished the parts, let us now consider the proper construction of the Fable or Plot, as that is at once the first and the most important thing in Tragedy. We have laid it down that a tragedy is an imitation of an action that is complete in itself, as a whole of some magnitude; for a whole may be of no magnitude to speak of. Now a whole is that which has beginning, middle, and end. A beginning is that which is not itself necessarily after anything else, and which has naturally something else after it; an end is that which is naturally after something itself, either as its necessary or usual consequent, and with nothing else after it; and a middle, that which is by nature after one thing and has also another after it. A well-constructed Plot, therefore, cannot either begin or end at any point one likes; beginning and end in it must be of the forms just described. Again: to be beautiful, a living creature, and every whole made up of parts, must not only present a certain order in its arrangement of parts, but also be of a certain definite magnitude. Beauty is a matter of size and order, and therefore impossible either (1) in a very minute creature, since our perception becomes indistinct as it approaches instantaneity; or (2) in a creature of vast size—one, say, 1,000 miles long—as in that case, instead of the object being seen all at once, the unity and wholeness of it is lost to the beholder. Just in the same way, then, as a beautiful whole made up of parts, or a beautiful living creature, must be of some size, a size to be taken in by the eye, so a story or Plot must be of some length, but of a length to be taken in by the memory. As for the limit of its length, so far as that is relative to public performances and spectators, it does not fall within the theory of poetry. If they had to perform a hundred tragedies, they would be timed by water-clocks, as they are said to have been at one period. The limit, however, set by the actual nature of the thing is this: the longer the story, consistently with its being comprehensible as a whole, the finer it is by reason of its magnitude. As a rough general formula, 'a length which allows of the hero passing by a series of probable or necessary stages from misfortune to happiness, or from happiness to misfortune,' may suffice as a limit for the magnitude of the story.

The Unity of a Plot does not consist, as some suppose, in its having one man as its subject. An infinity of things befall that one man, some which it is impossible to reduce to unity; and in like manner there are many actions of one man which cannot be made to form one action. One sees, therefore, the mistake of all the poets who have written a *Heracleid*, a *Theseid*, or similar poems; they suppose that, because Heracles was one man, the story also of Heracles must be one story. Homer, however, evidently understood this point quite well, whether by art or instinct, just in the same way as he excels the rest in every other respect. In writing an *Odyssey*, he did not make the poem cover all that ever befell his hero—it befell him, for instance, to get wounded on Parnassus and also to feign madness at the time of the call to arms, but the two incidents had no probable or necessary connexion with one another—instead of doing that, he took an action with a Unity of the kind we are describing as the subject of the *Odyssey*, as also of the *Iliad*. The truth is that, just as in the other imitative arts one imitation is always of one thing, so in poetry the story, as an imitation of action, must represent one action, a complete whole, with its several incidents so closely connected that the transposal or withdrawal of any one of them will disjoin and dislocate the whole. For that which makes no perceptible difference by its presence or absence is no real part of the whole.

From what we have said it will be seen that the poet's function is to describe, not the thing that has happened, but a kind of thing that might happen, i.e. what is possible as being probable or necessary. The distinction between historian and poet is not in the one writing prose and the other verse—you might put the work of Herodotus into verse, and it would still be a species of history; it consists really in this, that the one describes the thing that has been, and the other a kind of thing that might be. Hence poetry is something more philosophic and of graver import than history, since its statements are of the nature rather of universals, whereas those of history are singulars. By a universal statement I mean one as to what such or such a kind of man will probably or necessarily say or do—which is the aim of poetry, though it affixes proper names to the characters; by a singular statement, one as to what, say, Alcibiades did or had done to him. In Comedy this has become clear by this time; it is only when their plot is already made up of probable incidents that they give it a basis of proper names, choosing for the purpose any names that may occur to them, instead of writing like the old iambic poets about particular persons. In Tragedy, however, they still adhere to the historic names; and for this reason: what convinces is the possible; now whereas we are not yet sure as to the possibility of that which has not happened, that which has happened is manifestly possible, else it would not have come to pass. Nevertheless even in Tragedy there are some plays with but one or two known names in them, the rest being inventions; and there are some without a single known name, e.g. Agathon's *Antheus*, in which both incidents and names are of the poet's invention; and it is no less delightful on that account. So that one must not aim at a rigid adherence to the traditional stories on which tragedies are based. It would be absurd, in fact, to do so, as even the known stories are only known to a few, though they are a delight none the less to all.

It is evident from the above that the poet must be more the poet of his stories or Plots than of his verses, inasmuch as he is a poet by virtue of the imitative element in his work, and it is actions that he imitates. And if he should come to take a subject from actual history, he is none the less a poet for that; since some historic occurrences may very well be in the probable and possible order of things; and it is in that aspect of them that he is their poet.

Of simple Plots and actions the episodic are the worst. I call a Plot episodic when there is neither probability nor necessity in the sequence of its episodes. Actions of this sort bad poets construct through their own fault, and good ones on account of the players. His work being for public performance, a good poet often stretches out a Plot beyond its capabilities, and is thus obliged to twist the sequence of incident.

Tragedy, however, is an imitation not only of a complete action, but also of incidents arousing pity and fear. Such incidents have the very greatest effect on the mind when they occur unexpectedly and at the same time in consequence of one another; there is more of the marvellous in them then than if they happened of themselves or by mere chance. Even matters of chance seem most marvellous if there is an appearance of design as it were in them; as for instance the statue of Mitys at Argos killed the author of Mitys' death by falling down on him when a looker-on at a public spectacle; for incidents like that we think to be not without a meaning. A Plot, therefore, of this sort is necessarily finer than others.

Plots are either simple or complex, since the actions they represent are naturally of this twofold description. The action, proceeding in the way defined, as one continuous whole, I call simple, when the change in the hero's fortunes takes place without Peripety or Discovery; and complex, when it involves one or the other, or both. These should each of them arise out of the structure of the Plot itself, so as to be the consequence, necessary or probable, of the antecedents. There is a great difference between a thing happening *propter hoc* and *post hoc*.

A Peripety is the change from one state of things within the play to its opposite of the kind described, and that too in the way we are saying, in the probable or necessary sequence of events; as it is for instance in *Oedipus:* here the opposite state of things is produced by the Messenger, who, coming to gladden Oedipus and to remove his fears as to his mother, reveals the secret of his birth. And in *Lynceus:* just as he is being led off for execution, with Danaus at his side to put him to death, the incidents preceding this bring it about that he is saved and Danaus put to death. A Discovery is, as the very word implies, a change from ignorance to knowledge, and thus to either love or hate, in the personages marked for good or evil fortune. The finest form of Discovery is one attended by Peripeties, like that which goes with the Discovery in *Oedipus.* There are no doubt other forms of it; what we have said may happen in a way in reference to inanimate things, even things of a very casual kind; and it is also possible to discover whether some one has done or not done something. But the form most directly connected with the Plot and the action of the piece is the first-mentioned. This, with a Peripety, will arouse either pity or fear—actions of that nature being what Tragedy is assumed to represent; and it will also serve to bring about the happy or unhappy ending. The Discovery, then, being of persons, it may be that of one party only to the other, the latter being already known; or both the parties may have to discover themselves. Iphigenia, for instance, was discovered to Orestes by sending the letter; and another Discovery was required to reveal him to Iphigenia.

Two parts of the Plot, then, Peripety and Discovery, are on matters of this sort. A third part is Suffering; which we may define as an action of a destructive or painful nature, such as murders on the stage, tortures, woundings, and the like. The other two have been already explained. . . .

The next points after what we have said above will be these: (1) What is the poet to aim at, and what is he to avoid, in constructing his Plots? and (2) What are the conditions on which the tragic effect depends?

We assume that, for the finest form of Tragedy, the Plot must be not simple but complex; and further, that it must imitate actions arousing pity and fear, since that is the distinctive function of this kind of imitation. It follows, therefore, that there are three forms of Plot to be avoided. (1) A good man must not be seen passing from happiness to misery, or (2) a bad man from misery to happiness. The first situation is not fear-inspiring or piteous, but simply odious to us. The second is the most untragic that can be; it has no one of the requisites of Tragedy; it does not appeal either to the human feeling in us, or to our pity, or to our fears. Nor, on the other hand, should (3) an extremely bad man be seen falling from happiness into misery. Such a story may arouse the human feeling in us, but it will not move us to either pity or fear; pity is occasioned by undeserved misfortune, and fear by that of one like ourselves; so that there will be nothing either piteous or fear-inspiring in the situation. There remains, then, the inter- mediate kind of personage, a man not pre-eminently virtuous and just, whose misfortune, however, is brought upon him not by vice and depravity but by some error of judgement, of the number of those in the enjoyment of great reputation and prosperity: e.g. Oedipus, Thyestes, and the men of note of similar families. The perfect Plot, accordingly, must have a single, and not (as some tell us) a double issue; the change in the hero's fortunes must be not from misery to happiness, but on the contrary from happiness to misery; and the cause of it must lie not in any depravity, but in some great error on his part; the man himself being either such as we have de- scribed, or better, not worse, than that. Fact also confirms our theory. Though the poets began by accepting any tragic story that came to hand, in these days the finest tragedies are always on the story of some few houses, on that of Alcmeon, Oedipus, Orestes, Meleager, Thyestes, Tele- phus, or any others that may have been involved, as either agents or sufferers, in some deed of horror. The theoretically best tragedy, then, has a Plot of this description. The critics, therefore, are wrong who blame Euripides for taking this line in his tragedies, and giving many of them an unhappy ending. It is, as we have said, the right line to take. The best proof is this: on the stage, and in the public performances, such plays, properly worked out, are seen to be the most truly tragic; and Euripides, even if his execution be faulty in every other point, is seen to be nevertheless the most tragic certainly of the dramatists. After this comes the construction of Plot which some rank first, one with a double story (like the *Odyssey*) and an opposite issue for the good and the bad personages. It is ranked as first only through the weakness of the audiences; the poets merely follow their public, writing as its wishes dictate. But the pleasure here is not that of Tragedy. It belongs rather to Comedy, where the bitterest enemies in the piece (e.g. Orestes and Aegisthus) walk off good friends at the end, with no slaying of any one by any one.

The tragic fear and pity may be aroused by the Spectacle; but they may also be aroused by the very structure and incidents of the play—which is the better way and shows the better poet. The Plot in fact should be so framed that, even without seeing the things take place, he who simply hears the account of them shall be filled with horror and pity at the in- cidents; which is just the effect that the mere recital of the story in *Oedipus* would have on one. To produce this same effect by means of the Spectacle is less artistic, and requires extraneous aid. Those, however, who make use of the Spectacle to put before us that which is merely monstrous and not productive of fear, are wholly out of touch with Tragedy; not every kind of pleasure should be required of a tragedy, but only its own proper pleasure.

The tragic pleasure is that of pity and fear, and the poet has to produce it by a work of imitation; it is clear, therefore, that the causes should be included in the incidents of his story. Let us see, then, what kinds of incident strike one as horrible, or rather as piteous. In a deed of this description the parties must necessarily be either friends, or enemies, or indifferent to one another. Now when enemy does it on enemy, there is nothing to move us to pity either in his doing or in his meditating the deed, except so far as the actual pain of the sufferer is concerned; and the same is true when the parties are indifferent to one another. Whenever the tragic deed, however, is done within the family—when murder or the like is done or meditated by brother on brother, by son on father, by mother on son, or son on mother—these are the situations the poet should seek after. The traditional stories, accordingly, must be kept as they are, e.g. the murder of Clytaemnestra by Orestes and of Eriphyle by Alcmeon. At the same time even with these there is something left to the poet himself; it is for him to devise the right way of treating them. Let us explain more clearly what we mean by 'the right way.' The deed of horror may be done by the doer knowingly and consciously, as in the old poets, and in Medea's murder of her children in Euripides. Or he may do it, but in ignorance of his relationship, and discover that afterwards, as does the Oedipus in Sophocles. Here the deed is outside the play; but it may be within it, like the act of the Alcmeon in Astydamas, or that of the Telegonus in *Ulysses Wounded*. A third possibility is for one meditating some deadly injury to another, in ignorance of his relationship, to make the discovery in time to draw back. These exhaust the possibilities, since the deed must necessarily be either done or not done, and either knowingly or unknowingly.

The worst situation is when the personage is with full knowledge on the point of doing the deed, and leaves it undone. It is odious and also (through the absence of suffering) untragic; hence it is that no one is made to act thus except in some few instances, e.g. Haemon and Creon in *Antigone*. Next after this comes the actual perpetration of the deed meditated. A better situation than that, however, is for the deed to be done in ignorance, and the relationship discovered afterwards, since there is nothing odious in it, and the Discovery will serve to astound us. But the best of all is the last; what we have in *Cresphontes*, for example, where Merope, on the point of slaying her son, recognizes him in time; in *Iphigenia*, where sister and brother are in a like position; and in *Helle*, where the son recognizes his mother, when on the point of giving her up to her enemy. . . .

In the Characters there are four points to aim at. First and foremost, that they shall be good. There will be an element of character in the play, if (as has been observed) what a personage says or does reveals a certain moral purpose; and a good element of character, if the purpose so revealed is good. Such goodness is possible in every type of personage, even in a woman or a slave, though the one is perhaps an inferior, and the other a wholly worthless being. The second point is to make them appropriate. The Character before us may be, say, manly; but it is not appropriate in a female Character to be manly, or clever. The third is to make them like the reality, which is not the same as their being good and appropriate, in our sense of the term. The fourth is to make them consistent and the same throughout; even if inconsistency be part of the man before one for imitation as presenting that form of character, he should still be consistently inconsistent. . . . The right thing, however, is in the Characters just as in the incidents of the play to endeavour always after the necessary or the probable; so that whenever such-and-such a personage says or does such-and-such a thing, it shall be the probable or necessary outcome of his character; and whenever this incident follows on that, it shall be either the necessary or the probable consequence of it. From this one sees (to digress for a moment) that the Dénouement also should arise out of the plot itself, and not depend on a stage-artifice, as in *Medea*, or in the story of the (arrested) departure of the Greeks in the *Iliad*. The artifice must be reserved for matters outside the play—for past events beyond human knowledge, or events yet to come, which require to be foretold or announced; since it is the privilege of the Gods to know everything. There should be nothing improbable among the actual incidents. If it be unavoidable, however, it should be outside the tragedy, like the improbability in the *Oedipus* of Sophocles. But to return to the Characters. As Tragedy is an imitation of personages better than the ordinary man, we in our way should follow the example of good portrait painters, who reproduce the distinctive features of a man, and at the same time, without losing the likeness, make him handsomer than he is. The poet in like manner, in portraying men quick or slow to anger, or with similar infirmities of character, must know how to represent them as such, as Agathon and Homer have represented Achilles. . . .

A great deal of this discussion seems far removed from the general question of the nature and value of imaginative literature. But we must remember that Aristotle is proceeding by an inductive method; he gathers his data before he proceeds to draw any inferences; and his account of the different elements that go to make up a tragedy are part of his search for the essential nature of tragedy. Only by discovering its essential nature in this way can he infer both what is good and what is bad tragedy (and it should be noted how in the course of his discussion standards of judgment arise naturally out of the description of the nature of tragedy—tragedy being *this*, then the more its elements are organized and chosen so as to help it to become precisely this, the better the tragedy) and also what its value and function are. Tragedy, of course, is chosen as the most impressive literary form known to him: he discusses epic later on, and apparently discussed comedy in the lost second book of the *Poetics*.

Imitation and probability

Most of Aristotle's remarks on the proper construction of a tragedy need little comment; they show him moving logically between discussion of what a tragedy essentially *is* and what makes a tragedy good of its kind. His treatment of unity and organization is significant as showing that he was sensitive to poetic form, and aware of the pleasure to be derived from the working of different elements into a proper literary whole. (Plato, though he must have been sensitive to this aspect of literary art, studiously avoided discussing the satisfaction to be derived from the contemplation of structure and pattern in literature or the possible psychological value of such satisfaction.) But it is when he comes to discuss the relationship between poetry and history that Aristotle deals Plato's attack on poetry as an imitation of an imitation its most damaging blow. The poet does not simply imitate or represent particular events or situations which he happens to have noted or invented; he handles them in such a way that he brings out their universal and characteristic elements, thus illuminating the essential nature of some event or situation whether or not what he is telling is historically true. The poet works "according to the law of probability or necessity," not according to some chance observation or random invention. He is thus more fundamentally scientific and serious than the historian, who must restrict himself to what happened to have occurred and cannot arrange or invent his facts in order to present what, in terms of human psychology and the nature of things, is more inherently probable. Because the poet invents or arranges his own story, he creates a self-sufficient world of his own, with its own compelling kind of probability, its own inevitability, and what happens in the poet's story is both "probable" in terms of that world and, because that world is itself a formal construction based on elements in the real world, an illumination of an aspect of the world as it really is.

As soon as one denies that the poet is a passive imitator and proceeds to raise the whole question of formal probability, literary criticism is on another level. Two new notions are involved. First, there is the notion that a historical falsehood may be an ideal truth, that a "probable impossibility" may reflect a more profound reality than an "improbable possibility"; and, second, there is the perception that a literary artist produces a work which has a unity and a formal perfection of its own, a work which thus creates its own world of probability within which truth can be recognized and appreciated. All kinds of developments of each of these two notions are possible. From the first we can develop a view of the cognitive aspects of the artistic imagination and so regard art as a means of exploring the nature of reality. On this view a literary work becomes in the last analysis a form of knowledge, a unique way of presenting a kind of insight into a phase of the human situation which cannot be expressed or communicated in any other way. From the second implication of the Aristotelian view of literary probability we can develop a theory of literary form and structure, investigating the kinds of unity a poem or other literary work can achieve and the kinds of satisfaction afforded by recognition and appreciation of that unity. Putting both implications together, we can see the unique part played by form in presenting the special kinds of insight achieved by the artistic imagination, the relation between art as pattern and art as knowledge, and we can see, too, how different kinds of literary art can stress one or other aspect—the cognitive or the purely formal—until we reach the point at which we can construct a normative scale of values, according to which the work which combines the communication of profound insight with the satisfaction of formal perfection (*Hamlet* or *King Lear*, for example) is greater than a work which demonstrates only the latter quality (such as a perfect detective story). One might add that no work could have the former without the latter quality, because the kind of insight communicated by art is achieved in large measure through form; but one can have the latter without the former, since form need not necessarily be used cognitively. This is the difference between art and craft, between the work which puts technique at the service of the ultimate vision—where indeed the vision seems to be bound up with the technique so that form and content imply each other—and the work which demonstrates craftsmanship and nothing else: all art implies craftsmanship but all craftsmanship does not necessarily produce art.

The exploration of such lines of critical discussion can yield a mature and flexible body of critical principles which handles not only the philosophical questions of the nature and value of poetry but also the normative problem of how to discriminate between different poetic works. We shall see later how positions implicit in these remarks of Aristotle are developed by later critics, and of what practical assistance they can be in discussing particular works of literary art. For the moment let us be content with noting that Aristotle's remarks about probability are perhaps the most germinal sentences in the history of literary criticism. The modern critic who finds in Shakespeare's plays archetypal patterns which reflect the dramatist's profound understanding of elemental human emotions and his feeling for what Yeats considered the universal poetic language of symbols, and the perceptive producer who notes that there are two levels of probability in *The Merchant of Venice*—the amoral fairy tale of the three caskets, and the psychological realism of, say, the court scene—which can only be kept from interfering with each other on the stage by very careful stylization of certain parts of the acting: both are working with a development of the Aristotelian tradition.

"*Katharsis*"

One can fairly maintain that a whole view of the *value* of imaginative literature is implicit in Aristotle's discussion of the relation between poetry and history and the nature of literary probability. But he is not content with answering Plato's contention that art is but an imitation of an imitation, three removes from truth; he wishes also to answer specifically Plato's notion that art corrupts by nourishing the passions. His reply to this charge is simple and remarkable. Far from nourishing the passions, he asserts, it gives them harmless or even useful purgation; by exciting pity and fear in us, tragedy enables us to leave the theater "in calm of mind, all passion spent." There is considerable disagreement among scholars and critics over what Aristotle really meant by *katharsis*, purgation, but it seems clear that he was claiming some kind of therapeutic value for tragedy. A tragedy not only communicates its own special insight (being more "probable" and "universal" than history) and provides the satisfaction to be got from observing structural unity, but it also provides a safe outlet for disturbing passions which it effectively siphons off. Tragedy gives new knowledge, yields esthetic satisfaction, and produces a better state of mind. This triumvirate of values effectively disposes of Plato's attack.

Aristotle's remarks on plot show his awareness of the importance of structure, of artistic unity, and his understanding of the relation between structure and "truth." Some of his remarks on specific devices commonly employed in Greek tragedy—recognition, for example, where the identity of the hero is finally discovered, as it is, most conspicuously and tragically, in *Oedipus the King*—have less universal application than Aristotle perhaps thought; but it is natural that in examining literature as he found it he should occasionally have confused casual with essential features. The remarkable thing is that he did it so rarely and saw so clearly the central facts about the nature of literary truth and literary form.

The epic

In his discussion of epic poetry, Aristotle develops some of the points he makes in discussing tragedy and goes into further detail on the important question of the nature of poetic truth and its relation to literal truth of historical fact. He almost seems here to be deliberately answering Plato's charges that poets are liars or imitators of imitations, and he disposes, too, of Plato's argument that the user of a thing knows most about it, the maker of a thing comes next, and the poet, who talks about it without using or making, a poor third. The poet, says Aristotle, can make an error of fact that "is not in the essentials of the poetic art" and does not affect the poetic truth of his work. He distinguishes clearly between practical knowledge and literal truth on the one hand, and imaginative understanding and poetic truth on the other, and in doing so shows much of Plato's discussion of this aspect of the matter to be thoroughly confused.

Aristotle's account of the epic is of special interest to us today because the epic was the nearest approach among the literary forms of the ancient world to the modern novel. It was, of course, written in verse, and it seemed inevitable to Aristotle that it should be so written: hexameter or heroic verse he considered "the gravest and weightiest of metres" and hence "no one has ever written a long story in any but heroic verse; nature herself . . . teaches us to select the metre appropriate to such a story." Prose fiction was unknown in Aristotle's day, and so he takes verse to be an essential medium for narrative. But his main concern is with the nature and organization of the story, and here he says much that is relevant to criticism of the modern novel:

> As for the poetry which merely narrates, or imitates by means of versified language (without action), it is evident that it has several points in common with Tragedy.
>
> I. The construction of its stories should clearly be like that in a drama; they should be based on a single action, one that is a complete whole in itself, with a beginning, middle, and end, so as to enable the work to produce its own proper pleasure with all the organic unity of a living creature. Nor should one suppose that there is anything like them in our usual histories. A history has to deal not with one action, but with one period and all that happened in that to one or more persons, however disconnected the several events may have been. Just as two events may take place at the same time, e.g. the sea-fight off Salamis and the battle with the Carthaginians in Sicily, without converging to the same end, so too of two consecutive events one may sometimes come after the other with no one end as their common issue. Nevertheless most of our epic poets, one may say, ignore the distinction.
>
> Herein, then, to repeat what we have said before, we have a further proof of Homer's marvellous superiority to the rest. He did not attempt to deal even with the Trojan war in its entirety, though it was a whole with a definite beginning and end—through a feeling apparently that it was too long a story to be taken in in one view, or if not that, too complicated from the variety of incident in it. As it is, he has singled out one section of the whole; many of the other incidents, however, he brings in as episodes, using the Catalogue of the Ships, for instance, and other episodes to relieve the uniformity of his narrative. As for the other epic poets, they treat of one man, or one period; or else of an action which, although one, has a multiplicity of parts in it. . . .
>
> II. Besides this, Epic poetry must divide into the same species as Tragedy; it must be either simple or complex, a story of character or one of suffering. Its parts, too, with the exception of Song and Spectacle, must be the same, as it requires Peripeties, Discoveries, and scenes of suffering just like Tragedy. Lastly, the Thought and Diction in it must be good in their way. All these elements appear in Homer first; and he has made due use of them. His two poems are each examples of construction, the *Iliad* simple and a story of suffering, the *Odyssey* complex (there is Discovery throughout it) and a story of character. And they are more than this, since in Diction and Thought too they surpass all other poems.
>
> There is, however, a difference in the Epic as compared with Tragedy,

(1) in its length, and (2) in its metre. (1) As to its length, the limit already suggested will suffice: it must be possible for the beginning and end of the work to be taken in in one view—a condition which will be fulfilled if the poem be shorter than the old epics, and about as long as the series of tragedies offered for one hearing. For the extension of its length epic poetry has a special advantage, of which it makes large use. In a play one cannot represent an action with a number of parts going on simultaneously; one is limited to the part on the stage and connected with the actors. Whereas in epic poetry the narrative form makes it possible for one to describe a number of simultaneous incidents; and these, if germane to the subject, increase the body of the poem. This then is a gain to the Epic, tending to give it grandeur, and also variety of interest and room for episodes of diverse kinds. Uniformity of incident by the satiety it soon creates is apt to ruin tragedies on the stage. (2) As for its metre, the heroic has been assigned it from experience. . . .

Homer, admirable as he is in every other respect, is especially so in this, that he alone among epic poets is not unaware of the part to be played by the poet himself in the poem. The poet should say very little *in propria persona*, as he is no imitator when doing that. Whereas the other poets are perpetually coming forward in person, and say but little, and that only here and there, as imitators, Homer after a brief preface brings in forthwith a man, a woman, or some other Character—no one of them characterless, but each with distinctive characteristics.

The marvellous is certainly required in Tragedy. The Epic, however, affords more opening for the improbable, the chief factor in the marvellous, because in it the agents are not visibly before one. The scene of the pursuit of Hector would be ridiculous on the stage—the Greeks halting instead of pursuing him, and Achilles shaking his head to stop them; but in the poem the absurdity is overlooked. The marvellous, however, is a cause of pleasure, as is shown by the fact that we all tell a story with additions, in the belief that we are doing our hearers a pleasure. . . .

A likely impossibility is always preferable to an unconvincing possibility. The story should never be made up of improbable incidents; there should be nothing of the sort in it. If, however, such incidents are unavoidable, they should be outside the piece, like the hero's ignorance in *Oedipus* of the circumstances of Laius' death; not within it, like the report of the Pythian games in *Electra*, or the man's having come to Mysia from Tegea without uttering a word on the way, in *The Mysians*. So that it is ridiculous to say that one's Plot would have been spoilt without them, since it is fundamentally wrong to make up such Plots. If the poet has taken such a Plot, however, and one sees that he might have put it in a more probable form, he is guilty of absurdity as well as a fault of art. Even in the *Odyssey* the improbabilities in the setting-ashore of Ulysses would be clearly intolerable in the hands of an inferior poet. As it is, the poet conceals them, his other excellences veiling their absurdity. Elaborate Diction, however, is required only in places where there is no action, and no Character or Thought to be revealed. Where there is Character or Thought, on the other hand, an over-ornate Diction tends to obscure them.

As regards Problems and their Solutions, one may see the number and nature of the assumptions on which they proceed by viewing the matter in the following way. (1) The poet being an imitator just like the painter or other maker of likenesses, he must necessarily in all instances represent things in one or other of three aspects, either as they were or are, or as they are said or thought to be or to have been, or as they ought to be. (2) All this he does in language, with an admixture, it may be, of strange words and metaphors, as also of the various modified forms of words, since the use of these is conceded in poetry. (3) It is to be remembered, too, that there is not the same kind of correctness in poetry as in politics, or indeed any other art. There is, however, within the limits of poetry itself a possibility of two kinds of error, the one directly, the other only accidentally connected with the art. If the poet meant to describe the thing correctly, and failed through lack of power of expression, his art itself is at fault. But if it was through his having meant to describe it in some incorrect way (e.g. to make the horse in movement have both right legs thrown forward) that the technical error (one in a matter of, say, medicine or some other special science), or impossibilities of whatever kind they may be, have got into his description, his error in that case is not in the essentials of the poetic art. These, therefore, must be the premises of the Solutions in answer to the criticisms involved in the Problems.

I. As to the criticisms relating to the poet's art itself. Any impossibilities there may be in his descriptions of things are faults. But from another point of view they are justifiable, if they serve the end of poetry itself—if (to assume what we have said of that end) they make the effect of some portion of the work more astounding. The Pursuit of Hector is an instance in point. If, however, the poetic end might have been as well or better attained without sacrifice of technical correctness in such matters, the impossibility is not to be justified, since the description should be, if it can, entirely free from error. One may ask, too, whether the error is in a matter directly or only accidentally connected with the poetic art; since it is a lesser error in an artist not to know, for instance, that the hind has no horns, than to produce an unrecognizable picture of one.

II. If the poet's description be criticized as not true to fact, one may urge perhaps that the object ought to be as described—an answer like that of Sophocles, who said that he drew men as they ought to be, and Euripides as they were. If the description, however, be neither true nor of the thing as it ought to be, the answer must be then, that it is in accordance with opinion. The tales about Gods, for instance, may be as wrong as Xenophanes thinks, neither true nor the better thing to say; but they are certainly in accordance with opinion. Of other statements in poetry one may perhaps say, not that they are better than the truth, but that the fact was so at the time; e.g. the description of the arms: 'Their spears stood upright, butt-end upon the ground'; for that was the usual way of fixing them then, as it is still with the Illyrians. As for the question whether something said or done in a poem is morally right or not, in dealing with that one should consider not only the intrinsic quality of the actual word or deed, but also the person who says or does it, the person to whom he says or does it, the time, the means, and the motive of the agent—whether he does it to attain a greater good, or to avoid a greater evil. . . .

Speaking generally, one has to justify (1) the Impossible by reference to the requirements of poetry, or to the better, or to opinion. For the purposes of poetry a convincing impossibility is preferable to an unconvincing possibility; and if men such as Zeuxis depicted be impossible, the answer is that it is better they should be like that, as the artist ought to improve on his model. (2) The Improbable one has to justify either by showing it to be in accordance with opinion, or by urging that at times it is not improbable; for there is a probability of things happening also against probability. (3) The contradictions found in the poet's language one should first test as one does an opponent's confutation in a dialectical argument, so as to see whether he means the same thing, in the same relation, and in the same sense, before admitting that he has contradicted either something he has said himself or what a man of sound sense assumes as true. But there is no possible apology for improbability of Plot or depravity of character, when they are not necessary and no use is made of them, like the improbability in the appearance of Aegeus in *Medea* and the baseness of Menelaus in *Orestes*.

The question may be raised whether the epic or the tragic is the higher form of imitation. It may be argued that, if the less vulgar is the higher, and the less vulgar is always that which addresses the better public, an art addressing any and every one is of a very vulgar order. . . .

The answer to this is twofold. In the first place, one may urge (1) that the censure does not touch the art of the dramatic poet, but only that of his interpreter; for it is quite possible to overdo the gesturing even in an epic recital, as did Sosistratus, and in a singing contest, as did Mnasitheus of Opus. (2) That one should not condemn all movement, unless one means to condemn even the dance, but only that of ignoble people—which is the point of the criticism passed on Callippides and in the present day on others, that their women are not like gentlewomen. (3) That Tragedy may produce its effect even without movement or action in just the same way as Epic poetry; for from the mere reading of a play its quality may be seen. So that, if it be superior in all other respects, this element of inferiority is no necessary part of it.

In the second place, one must remember (1) that Tragedy has everything that the Epic has (even the epic metre being admissible), together with a not inconsiderable addition in the shape of the Music (a very real factor in the pleasure of the drama) and the Spectacle. (2) That its reality of presentation is felt in the play as read, as well as in the play as acted. (3) That the tragic imitation requires less space for the attainment of its end; which is a great advantage, since the more concentrated effect is more pleasurable than one with a large admixture of time to dilute it—consider the *Oedipus* of Sophocles, for instance, and the effect of expanding it into the number of lines of the *Iliad*. (4) That there is less unity in the imitation of the epic poets, as is proved by the fact that any one work of theirs supplies matter for several tragedies; the result being that, if they take what is really a single story, it seems curt when briefly told, and thin and waterish when on the scale of length usual with their verse. In saying that there is less unity in an epic, I mean an epic made up of a plurality of actions, in the same way as the *Iliad* and *Odyssey* have many such parts, each one of them in itself of some magnitude; yet the structure of the two Homeric poems is as perfect as can be, and the action in them is as nearly as possible one action. If, then, Tragedy is superior in these respects, and also besides these, in its poetic effect (since the two forms of poetry should give us, not any or every pleasure, but the very special kind we have mentioned), it is clear that, as attaining the poetic effect better than the Epic, it will be the higher form of art.

The most remarkable paragraph in this discussion is Aristotle's extension and illustration of his earlier remarks about probability. That "a likely impossibility is always preferable to an unconvincing possibility" is, as we have seen, a perception of the highest importance to literary criticism. Once one sees this, the whole Platonic dilemma fades away. Criticism has grown up. In fact, it took a long time before it progressed any farther, and some would maintain that at best it has only marked time. But, after all, the *Poetics* is incomplete and sketchy, and many of the ideas Aristotle throws out in it are not fully developed or properly illustrated. There is a whole line of literary criticism which simply develops and re-interprets and rounds out (and sometimes perverts) Aristotle's notions. Let us take a look at some of the later answers to the questions raised by Aristotle, and see whether there are any basically different approaches to the description and evaluation of imaginative literature.

Longinus on the Sublime: a new approach

Before we do so, however, something must be said about another, and much later, Greek critic whose treatise *On the Sublime* shows a radically different approach from either Plato's or Aristotle's. The author, whose identity is uncertain but who may have been Cassius Longinus of Palmyra, who lived in the third century A.D., or may have been somebody else who lived perhaps two centuries earlier, is generally referred to as Longinus and his work has long been known simply as *Longinus on the Sublime*. His importance lies in the fact that he asked quite different questions about literature from those asked by Plato or Aristotle. Taking for granted Aristotle's demonstration that poetry yielded a peculiar pleasure of its own, Longinus turned his attention to its pleasurable effect on the reader or audience and produced the first "affective" theory of literature. (It is true that classical theories of rhetoric, the art of persuasion, were "affective" in that they concerned the ways in which words could be made to "move" listeners or readers, but this "moving" was merely one of several means of achieving persuasion, not, as with Longinus, an instantaneous effect and one valuable in itself.) The value of a work of literature can be assessed, according to Longinus, by introspection on the part of the reader or hearer: if he is carried away, transported, moved to ecstasy by the grandeur and passion of the work, then the work is good. Whether it is a good thing to be carried away and moved to ecstasy, Longinus does not explicitly discuss; but he does not simply assume that because the sensation is enjoyable it is therefore valuable, for by insisting that it is nobility and grandeur which are the sources of this enjoyment he links the pleasures of literature to the highest human faculties. The Greek word which it has become traditional to translate as *sublime* in English means literally *height* or *elevation*, and Longinus refers to those qualities in a work of literature which instantaneously create in the reader a sense of being carried to new heights of passionate experience; sublimity is the greatest of all the literary virtues, the one which makes a work, whatever its minor defects, truly impressive. The ultimate function of literature, and its ultimate justification, is to be sublime

and to have on its readers the effect of ecstasy or transport that
sublimity has.

The author, the work and the reader

Longinus, for all his insistence on the importance of the reader's
response, is not a mere impressionist,[5] who judges literature in purely
autobiographical terms. He insists that it takes much experience of
literature to respond to it properly—"judgment of literature is the
final fruit of ripe experience"—and he is concerned to distinguish
those elements of style and structure which contribute to the effect
of sublimity. His treatise—or what exists of it: only portions of it
survive—is a careful inquiry into the elements which produce sublimity, illustrated by much quotation, in which successful and unsuccessful attempts are compared and discussed; and it really, therefore, properly belongs to the second section of this book, where we
discuss not the philosophical inquiry into the nature and value of
literature but the various kinds of practical inquiry into the relative
virtues of this and that particular work. We take it up here, however,
because in spite of the fact that Longinus' inquiry into what constitutes sublimity in literature is essentially practical criticism, his whole
method assumes an answer to the philosophical inquiry wholly different from any other given in the ancient world and not easily paral-
lelled in later times. True, Longinus was known and admired in the
Renaissance and the eighteenth century; but, for all that, and for all
the influence he had in the eighteenth century, the implications concerning the nature and function of literature which his work contains were not realized or accepted. (The eighteenth century critics
tended to interpret Longinus rhetorically and to see him as the great
investigator into the emotional effects of particular uses of language,
rather than as a critic who saw the quality of sublimity as at once the

[5] Gibbon has a frequently-quoted remark on Longinus in his *Journal*. "Till now, I
was acquainted only with two ways of criticizing a beautiful passage, the one to show
by an exact anatomy of it the distinct beauties of it and whence they sprung; the other
an idle exclamation or a general encomium, which leaves nothing behind it. Longinus
has shown me that there is a third. He tells me his own feelings upon reading it, and
tells them with such energy that he communicates them." But this is not accurate.
Longinus does not merely "tell his own feelings on reading"; he discusses the proper
equipment of the writer and the necessary qualities in the work for producing on the
reader the effect of ecstasy or transport. Though introspection is involved in discovering the effect, and though the ultimate test and value of literature lie in its producing
this effect, Longinus is far from reducing criticism to impressionist confession.

mark of the truly great writer and the true source of the reader's pleasure.) Longinus' interest for us in our endeavor to classify some of the more important answers which critics have given to the question concerning the nature and value of literature is that he answers this question by identifying those qualities in an author (impressive thought and passion), that quality in the work (sublimity), and that effect on the reader (excitement, transport, ecstasy) which indicate greatness in literature. The true nature of literature is defined by a discussion of the criteria of *great* literature (the essence of a thing being determined by its highest manifestation) and the definition takes in moral and intellectual qualities of authors and reactions of readers as well as the make-up of the work. Throughout the discussion the argument moves freely between the author, the work, and the reader.

For Longinus, great literature is that which excites and arouses the reader not only once but repeatedly; if it produces this impression after repeated readings, and among men "of different pursuits, lives, ambitions, ages and languages," then its greatness is beyond question. To produce this effect on his readers the author must possess certain qualities as a man as well as certain skills as a writer. As a man he must have impressiveness of thought[6] and vehemence of emotion. As a writer, he must possess three qualities which are "partly the product of art" (the previous two being innate); these are the ability to handle "figures" (both of speech and of thought), nobility of diction, and the ability to put the whole composition together so as to produce dignity and elevation. Longinus has much that is interesting to say under each of these heads—discussing, for example, with many illustrations, imagery, metaphor, and what modern critics call *empathy*, the author's ability to feel himself into the midst of the situation he is describing. But he comes back continually to his main point: if the work is to be considered great, its effect on the reader must be to move him to passionate excitement. "I would confidently affirm that nothing makes so much for grandeur as true emotion in the right place, for it inspires the words, as it were, with a wild gust of mad enthusiasm and fills them with divine frenzy." The purpose of literature is to be moving, exciting, elevating, transporting, and the critic's duty is to see how this is achieved by showing which elements best conduce to this result. Neither the Plato of the *Ion* nor the Plato of the *Republic* would have seen any force or relevance in Longinus' arguments; they would

have been, to Plato, all beside the point. Aristotle, though he would
have had some sympathy with Longinus' analyses of individual passages in order to demonstrate how certain means produce certain
effects (he would have treated them as minor questions of rhetoric),
would on the whole have been puzzled by Longinus' premises and
have thought that he was asking and answering the wrong questions.

[6] At this point Longinus comes near the view that Milton was later to express: "He
who would not be frustrate of his hope to write well . . . ought himself to be a true
poem; that is, a composition and pattern of the best and honorablest things." The
great writer, says Longinus, must have genuine nobility of soul. "It is impossible that
those whose lives are trivial and servile should flash out anything wonderful and
worthy of immortality."

3

The poet as
moral teacher

I N 1595, after its author's death, appeared Sir Philip
Sidney's critical essay, *The Defence of Poesie*,[1] which had been
written over ten years before. Sidney was concerned to defend
poetry—by which term, as we have seen, he meant imaginative
literature in general—against the charge brought against it by the
Puritans that it was immoral, debilitating, lying, and provocative of
debauchery. He was thus faced with a problem similar to that of
Aristotle in meeting Plato's charges, though the arguments to which
Sidney was replying were less coherent and less well argued than
Plato's had been. Nevertheless, the knowledge that Plato had ex-
pelled poets from his ideal republic was used by the Puritans in their

---

[1] Two editions appeared in the same year, one entitled *The Defence of Poesie* and
the other *An Apologie for Poetrie*.

attack, and Plato's prestige, which was formidable in the Renaissance, lent weight to his opinion even though the reasons underlying it were not fully appreciated.

The Defence of Poesie

If Aristotle in his *Poetics* had demonstrated the essential truth, seriousness, and usefulness of imaginative literature, one might have thought that Sidney had arguments ready to hand with which to demolish the Puritan opposition. However, the circumstances under which the *Poetics* was rediscovered and used in the Renaissance, as well as the whole Christian tradition of defense of works of imagination by treating them allegorically which had intervened between classical times and the editing and translating of the *Poetics* by sixteenth century Italian humanists, meant that for Sidney Aristotle's arguments were available in a context which gave them a meaning rather different from anything Aristotle had intended. We are not here concerned with the sources of Sidney's *Defence*, but with its method and the critical position it takes up: to demonstrate that Sidney was putting together a host of arguments common to renaissance critics and through them deriving from a variety of classical and Christian sources is not necessarily to show their critical significance, which is our present purpose. By what arguments, then, does Sidney defend poetry?

Verse and fable

His opening arguments strike us at first sight as singularly irrelevant. He stresses the antiquity of poetry and its early civilizing function. The first philosophers and scientists wrote in verse. But is not this to ignore Aristotle's warning that "Homer and Empedocles have nothing in common but the metre, so that it would be right to call the one poet, the other physicist rather than poet"? Indeed, Sidney cites Empedocles among the early Greek philosophers who "durst not a long time appeare to the worlde but under the masks of Poets." It soon becomes clear, however, that Sidney does not call them poets merely because they write metrically. "For that wise *Solon* was

directly a Poet it is manifest, hauing written in verse the notable fable
of the Atlantick Iland, which was continued by *Plato*."

"Hauing written in *verse* the notable *fable"*—we see two criteria
of poetry here, with the latter clearly the more important. Solon
conveyed his wisdom not only in verse but through a fable, through
an invented story; and he shrewdly adds (for later he has to deal
with Plato's embarrassing attack on poets) that this same invented
story was also used by Plato. Poetry is verse, but, more important, it
is invention, the telling of a story which is not literally true. The
reference to Solon, the great Greek lawgiver, in this context thus
suggests that untruths may be valuable as means of communicating
wisdom. This is not Aristotle's position; he never suggests that
poetry is an effective way of communicating a kind of knowledge
that could also be communicated (but less effectively) by other kinds
of discourse. But for Sidney lies can be shown to be good and valuable if they are used as allegorical ways of teaching moral doctrine.

This is in essence the old doctrine of allegory which goes back to
Philo, the Jew of Alexandria, who in the first century A.D. endeavored
to reconcile the Hebrew Bible with Platonic philosophy by interpreting parts of the biblical narrative allegorically. It is perhaps an obvious way of defending imaginative literature, and one eagerly
seized on by Christian writers who wanted to keep parts of pagan
classical literature from ecclesiastical proscription. But Sidney goes
further than this. He proceeds to point out that Plato himself used
invented situations in his philosophical works:

And truely, even *Plato*, whosoever well considereth, shall find that in the
body of his work, though the inside and strength were Philosophy, the
skinne as it were and beautie depended most of Poetrie: for all standeth
vpon Dialogues, wherein he faineth many honest Burgesses of Athens to
speake of such matters, that, if they had been sette on the racke, they
would neuer haue confessed them. Besides, his poetical describing the
circumstances of their meetings, as the well ordering of a banquet, the
delicacie of a walke, with enterlacing meere tales, as *Giges* Ring, and
others, which who knoweth not to be flowers of Poetrie did neuer walke
into *Apollos* Garden.

Poetry is the record of imaginary events, but it is more: the events
must be described in a lively and persuasive style. And when Sidney
goes on to cite the historian Herodotus as a poet because "both he and
all the rest that followed him either stole or vsurped of Poetrie

their passionate describing of passions, the many particularities of battailes, which no man could affirme" he is adding passion, forceful and moving expression, to his criteria, so that by poetry he now means fiction plus liveliness plus passion. If a lively and passionately expressed invention can be employed as a means of conveying historical or moral truths, then poetry is justified—but not as an art in itself so much as one among many ways of communicating kinds of knowledge which are themselves known independently to be valuable. At this stage in Sidney's argument, poetry is simply a superior means of communication, and its value depends on what is communicated. And to determine that value we have to go to other arts—to history or moral philosophy.

Sidney is here expressing a view that has long been popular and is still very common among lay readers of poetry. Imaginative literature can be justified if it communicates historical or philosophical or moral truths in a lively and pleasing manner, and if this means telling things which are not literally true, the untruths can either be interpreted allegorically as ways of representing an underlying general truth, or, in the case of the historical poet, as plausible reconstructions of what might well have occurred. This latter point brings us fairly close to Aristotle's notion of probability, but it stops short of it. Sidney does not go on to say that the "fained" speeches of the historian can give a more fundamental insight into the truth of the human situation than the factual historical record; he does not, in fact, at this stage in his argument go further than to say that the historian, in his search for a means of communicating what he has to say in a lively and convincing manner, is led to draw on his own invention and thus to become a poet. When Herodotus describes "the many particularities of battailes, which no man could affirme" he is behaving like a poet, but the only conclusion Sidney seems to be drawing from this fact is that if historians use poetry then poetry must be a good thing. This is a curious kind of *argumentum ad hominem*— the worth of an art depends on the intentions and purposes of its user—and is far from a justification of poetry (in the sense of fiction plus liveliness plus passion) for its own sake. One can only begin to justify poetry for its own sake if one can isolate its differentiating qualities and consider what unique function poetry serves. Are fiction plus liveliness plus passion good in themselves, or good only if they serve as means to communicate kinds of knowledge which are known independently to be good? Sidney does not here answer this question, and although the tone of his argument suggests that they *are* good in themselves he does not tell us why. Later on, however, he gives this argument a new turn.

The argument from antiquity

Before he does so he pauses to remind us of the universality of poetry. He has already mentioned its antiquity, and now he points out—with illustrations from Ireland and Wales, and from Romans, Saxons, Danes, and Normans—that it is to be found in every nation. The universality and antiquity of an art is perhaps no necessary proof of its value—many patently harmful activities are both long established and widespread—but some notion of the implications of this kind of argument can be seen if we put beside Sidney's remarks some observations made nearly two hundred years later by Dr Johnson in his preface to his edition of Shakespeare:

> To works . . . of which the excellence is not absolute and definite, but gradual and comparative; to works not raised upon principles demonstrative and scientifick, but appealing wholly to observation and experience, no other test can be applied than length of duration and continuance of esteem. What mankind have long possessed they have often examined and compared; and if they persist to value the possession, it is because frequent comparisons have confirmed opinion in its favour. . . . The reverence due to writings that have long subsisted arises therefore not from any credulous confidence in the superior wisdom of past ages, or gloomy persuasion of the degeneracy of mankind, but is the consequence of acknowledged and indubitable positions, that what has been longest known has been most considered, and what is most considered is best understood.

The appeal to antiquity and universality may thus be considered as the appeal to the verdict of many different kinds of people over a long period of time. This kind of argument is not, of course, drawn from any further insight into the special nature of poetry, but is general and *prima facie:* it is not likely that what has been long and widely esteemed should be worthless. It is rather a further reason for pursuing the investigation into the nature and value of poetry than a further step in that investigation. It is nevertheless a point of some importance in that it implies (however indirectly) an underlying humanist position. The appeal is to what all sorts of men have always done and have always considered valuable: this makes poetry an activity essentially appropriate to man, what the Greeks called ἀνθρώπινον and the Romans, translating the Greek term, *humanum*. If one takes the Christian position on Original Sin, one cannot of course take the view that what is *humanum* is good—the Latin proverb *humanum est errare*, "to err is human," would be the appropriate one there rather than the famous declaration "*homo sum, et nihil humani a me alienum puto*," "I am a man, and nothing human is alien to me"—certainly there is no overt suggestion in Sidney that he accepts the complete humanist position. But he does make the appeal to human nature, which later critics were to develop much further. That could only be done by an age which had become much more optimistic about the nature of man.

Sidney then proceeds to consider the significance of the title given to the poet by the Greeks and Romans. The Romans called him *vates* "which is as much as a Diviner, Fore-seer, or Prophet," and that poetry can be (but not that it must be) "divine" is shown by the Psalms of David. The Psalms are songs, written in meter, argues Sidney. But meter alone does not make poetry; we must have the lively invention. So he reminds us that the Psalms are full of vigorous figures of speech—David tells "of the Beastes joyfulness and hills leaping," which is to tell literal untruths—and can so be considered poetry in the sense of his earlier discussion. Again, however, it is the non-poetic objective which gives the poetry its ultimate value. This is simply an extension of what he had said earlier about the philosopher and the historian.

The poet as "maker"

When he comes to the name the Greeks gave to the poet, *Poietes*, maker, he has found a channel that leads to an important new argument, and a new justification for poetry. The poet is indeed a "maker," and this distinguishes him from the practitioners of other arts and sciences:

There is no Arte deliuered to mankinde that hath not the workes of Nature for his principall obiect, without which they could not consist, and on which they so depend, as they become Actors and Players, as it were, of what Nature will haue set foorth. So doth the Astronomer looke vpon the starres, and, by that he seeth, setteth downe what order Nature hath taken therein. So doe the Geometrician and Arithmetician in their diuerse sorts of quantities. So doth the Musitian in times tel you which by nature agree, which not. The naturall Philosopher thereon hath his name, and the Morall Philosopher standeth vpon the naturall vertues, vices, and passions of man. . . . The Lawyer sayth what men haue determined. The Historian what men haue done. The Grammarian speaketh onely of the rules of speech; and the Rhetorician and Logitian, considering what in Nature will soonest proue and perswade, thereon giue artificial rules, which still are compassed within the circle of a question, according to the proposed matter. The Phisition waigheth the nature of a mans bodie, and the nature of things helpefull or hurtefull vnto it. And the Metaphysick, though it . . . be counted supernaturall, yet doth hee indeede builde vpon the depth of Nature. Onely the Poet, disdayning to be tied to any such subiection, lifted vp with the vigor of his own inuention, dooth growe in effect another nature, in making things either better than Nature bringeth forth, or, quite a newe, formes such as neuer were in Nature, as the *Heroes, Demigods, Cyclops, Chimeras, Furies* and such like: so as hee goeth hand in hand with Nature, not inclosed within the narrow warrant of her guifts, but freely ranging onely with the Zodiack of his owne wit.

The poet does not imitate or represent or express or discuss things which already exist: he *invents* new things. We have already seen that Sidney, in an earlier stage of his argument, stressed the fact that the poet made things up, so that philosophers turn poet when they use illustrative fables or imaginary dialogues in order to bring home their points, and historians turn poet when they draw on their imagination for details of events they could not have known. Here he is approaching this point more directly. Invention is the distinguishing character of the poet; he creates new things by drawing on "his owne wit." Is this an exaltation of the inventive imagination? Is Sidney claiming that the creative aspect of the poet's art is in itself valuable? Is there a splendor in the very process of creation, in the exercise of the imagination, without any ulterior motive? Sidney certainly seems to be emphasizing this differentiating quality of the poet and holding it up to be admired. Is he then the first English protagonist of the imagination as such? Note how he proceeds:

Nature neuer set forth the earth in so rich tapistry as diuers Poets haue done, neither with plesant riuers, fruitful trees, sweet smelling flowers, nor whatsoeuer els may make the too much loued earth more louely. Her world is brasen, the Poets only deliuer a golden. But let those things alone and goe to man, for whom as other things are, so it seemeth in him her vttermost cunning is imployed, and knowe whether shee haue brought foorth so true a louer as *Theagines*, so constant a friende as *Pilades*, so valiant a man as *Orlando*, so right a Prince as *Xenophons Cyrus*, so excellent a man euery way as *Virgils Aeneas:* neither let this be iestingly conceiued, because the works of the one be essentiall, the other, in imitation or fiction; for any vnderstanding knoweth the skil of the Artificer standeth in that *Idea* or fore-conceite of the work, and not in the work it selfe. And that the Poet hath that *Idea* is manifest, by deliuering them forth in such excellencie as hee hath imagined them. Which deliuering forth also is not wholie imaginatiue, as we are wont to say by them that build Castles in the ayre: but so far substantially it worketh, not onely to make a *Cyrus*, which had been but a particular excellencie, as Nature mught haue done, but to bestow a *Cyrus* vpon the worlde, to make many *Cyrus's*, if they wil learne aright why and how that Maker made him.

Sidney is here making many interesting points. In the first place, he is saying that the world invented or created by the poet is a *better* world than the real one. It is not the mere exercise of his imagination that justifies the poet, but the exercise of his imagination in order to create this better world. The real world "is brasen, the Poets only deliuer a golden." Only the poet can, by his invention, produce something that goes beyond nature. The lovers of fiction are truer than those of real life; its friends are more constant, its warriors more valiant, its princes more "right," its heroes more "excellent in euery way." Note that for Sidney the poet's world is not better than the real world in some special poetic way, in that it is more probable in the Aristotelian sense, for example, but it is better on standards we apply in ordinary life. Flowers smell sweeter in the works of the poets than they do in real gardens.

The next point Sidney makes in the paragraph quoted above is one which might well have been used by Aristotle in an endeavor to turn Plato's own notions against his attack on the poets. In creating this better world, the poet has in view the *Idea* (in the Platonic sense, clearly) of the quality he is representing; he is not imitating the idea as reflected palely in real life, but is directly embodying his own vision of the ideal. The poet's embodiment can then in turn be imitated by the poet's readers, just as, for Plato, any human instance of constancy, courage, or any other virtue, represents an imitation of the idea of that virtue. The poet makes direct contact with the world of Platonic ideas, and thus Plato's charge against the poet, as someone who merely imitates an imitation, is dismissed. But Sidney does not seem to realize that he has here disposed of one of Plato's main charges against poets, and when, later on in his essay, he comes to defend the poet against Plato, he seems unaware of the relevance of this argument.

What is Sidney getting at here, and why does he not develop his second point much further? The answer seems to be that, fighting as he is on his enemy's ground (defending poetry against the Puritan charge that it is conducive to immorality) he is so anxious to prove the perfection (both moral and in every way) of the world created by the poets that he lays his main emphasis on the difference between the poet's world and the imperfect real world, slurring over the implication that what the poet creates is not so much different from reality as the very essence of it, the original undimmed Platonic idea of it. Aristotle had met Plato's charge that the poet painted imitations of imitations by showing how, by concerning himself with fundamental probabilities rather than with casual actualities, the poet reaches more deeply into reality than the historian. Sidney is on the point of answering Plato in more purely Platonic terms. But, carried away by his enthusiasm for *creation*, and anxious to vindicate the quality of the world created by the poets against the charges of the Puritans, he ends by striving to show that *the imagination does not give us insight into reality, but an alternative to reality*, the alternative being in every way superior.

A new notion of imitation

This development leads Sidney away from the Aristotelian notion of imitation; even though he uses the term "imitation" later on in his discussion, he is not really concerned to prove that poetry imitates anything—indeed, its glory is that it is the only one of the arts that does not imitate, but creates. He almost proceeds to develop a theory of "ideal imitation," the notion that the poet imitates not the mere appearances of actuality but the hidden reality behind them, but stops short of this to maintain the more naive theory that the poet creates a better world than the one we actually live in. He does not, however, rest content with a mere escapist position. The function of imaginative literature is not to provide us with an escape world in which our imaginations can seek consolation for the difficulties and imperfections of real life. It is true that this view of literature as simple escape is often held, and that the great majority of ordinary readers of popular magazine stories today have some such view of the function of fiction, but for Sidney this would be a far from adequate defense of poesy, and would certainly not meet the Puritan charge. No; for Sidney the ideal world of the poet is of value because it is both a better world than the real one and it is presented in such a way that the reader is stimulated to try and imitate it in his own practice. Thus the Aristotelian notion of imitation is transferred from the poet to the reader. The poet does not imitate but creates: *it is the reader who imitates what the poet creates.*

This is a most interesting development of the argument. Taking from the Roman poet Horace the view that the poet both delights and teaches, Sidney goes on to show that the poets "indeede doo meerely make to imitate, and imitate both to delight and teach, and delight to moue men to take that goodnes in hande, which without delight they would flye as from a stranger; and teach, to make them know that goodnes whereunto they are mooued, which being the noblest scope to which euer any learning was directed, yet want there not idle tongues to barke at them." He then proceeds to point out that verse "is but an ornament and no cause to Poetry" and "it is not riming and versing that maketh a Poet, no more than a long gowne maketh an Aduocate . . . But it is that fayning notable images of vertues, vices, or what els, with that delightful teaching which must be the right describing note to know a Poet by: although indeed the Senate of Poets hath chosen verse as their fittest rayment, meaning, as in matter they passed all in all, so in maner to goe beyond them: not speaking (table talke fashion or like men in a dreame) words as they chanceably fall from the mouth, but peyzing [weighing] each sillable of each worde by iust proportion according to the dignitie of the subiect."

The poet, then, teaches by presenting an ideal world for the imitation of the reader. But if the poet's world is, as he had earlier maintained, a perfect world, where all rivers are pleasant, all trees fruitful, all lovers faithful and all friends constant, how can the poet's activity be described as "fayning notable images of vertues, *vices, or what else*"? Should not they all be virtues? The answer to this is that when Sidney asked earlier where such perfect lovers, friends, princes, and heroes as one finds in the works of the poets were to be found in real life, he did not really mean that *all* characters in fiction were ideal; he meant that when they were good they acted in accordance with the full perfection of that kind of goodness, and when they were bad their badness was equally unmixed, obviously ugly, and inevitably leading to appropriate punishment. The perfection of the poet's world, it emerges later in Sidney's argument, does not consist in its being peopled with wholly virtuous characters, but in its heroes always being perfect in behavior and successful in fortune and its villains always thoroughly and obviously villainous and doomed to a certain bad end. In the poet's world the righteous always prosper and the wicked are never left unpunished. It is from this conception that we get the term "poetic justice."

Poetry, history, philosophy

In this lies the superiority of the poet to the historian who, sticking to what really happened, must often show us the wicked prospering and the righteous suffering. *That* is no way to teach people to be good, says Sidney. If we should reply that it is not the function of the poet to make people good, Sidney might retort that he is arguing against Puritans who held that no activity is justified unless it conduces directly to moral improvement—and he might add that Plato held this position also. Sidney accepts the assumption that unless we can show that poetry leads to moral improvement in its readers it cannot be really justified. Its two chief rivals in this claim (on the purely human level, excepting revealed religion and divinity) are moral philosophy and history:

. . . the ending end of all earthly learning being vertuous action, those skilles that most serue to bring forth that haue a most iust title to bee Princes ouer all the rest. Wherein if wee can shewe the Poets noblenes, by setting him before his other Competitors, among whom as principall challengers step forth the morall Philosophers, whom, me thinketh, I see comming towards mee with a sullen grauity, as though they could not abide vice by day light, rudely clothed for to witnes outwardly their contempt of outward things, with bookes in their hands agaynst glory, whereto they sette theyr names, sophistically speaking against subtility, and angry with any man in whom they see the foule fault of anger: these men casting larges [largesse, abundance] as they goe of Definitions, Diuisions, and Distinctions, with a scornefull interogatiue doe soberly aske whether it bee possible to finde any path so ready to leade a man to vertue

as that which teacheth what vertue is? and teacheth it not onely by deliuering forth his very being, his causes, and effects; but also by making
known his enemie vice, which must be destroyed, and his cumbersome
seruant Passion, which must be maistered; by shewing the generalities that
contayneth it, and the specialities that are deriued from it; lastly, by
playne setting downe, how it extendeth it selfe out of the limits of a
mans own little world to the gouernment of families, and maintayning of
publique societies.

The Historian scarcely giueth leysure to the Moralist to say so much,
but that he, loden with old Mouse-eaten records, authorising himselfe (for
the most part) vpon other histories, whose greatest authorities are built
vpon the notable foundation of Heare-say, hauing much a-doe to accord differing Writers and to pick trueth out of partiality, better acquainted with a thousande yeeres a goe then with the present age, and yet
better knowing how this world goeth then how his owne wit runneth,
curious for antiquities and inquisitiue of nouelties, a wonder to young
folkes and a tyrant in table talke, denieth, in a great chafe, that any man
for teaching of vertue, and vertuous actions, is comparable to him. . . .

'The Phylosopher' (sayth hee) 'teacheth a disputatiue vertue, but I doe
an actiue: his vertue is excellent in the dangerlesse Academie of *Plato*, but
mine sheweth foorth her honorable face in the battailes of *Marathon*,
Pharsalia, *Poitiers*, and *Agincourt*. Hee teacheth vertue by certaine abstract
considerations, but I onely bid you follow the footing of them that haue
gone before you. Olde-aged experience goeth beyond the fine-witted
Phylosopher, but I giue the experience of many ages. Lastly, if he make
the Songe-booke, I put the learners hande to the Lute: and if hee be the
guide, I am the light.'

Then woulde hee alledge you innumerable examples, conferring storie
by storie, how much the wisest Senatours and Princes haue been directed by
the credite of history, as *Brutus*, *Alphonsus* of *Aragon*, and who not, if
need be? At length the long lyne of theyr disputation maketh a point in
thys, that the one giueth the precept, and the other the example.

This is in Sidney's best style, and his vivacious and mocking portrait
of the historian (which is directed against the claims of history, then
being so strongly pressed in England as elsewhere in Europe, to be
the best "mirror for magistrates" and instructor of princes) is itself
a good example of that liveliness of presentation which he lists as
one of the qualities of a good work of literary art. But the attractive-
ness of the style must not distract our attention from what is happening to his argument here. He is making quite clear that the
arts are valuable only in so far as they are conducive to virtuous

action, and the claims of poetry must stand or fall on this criterion. Moral philosophy teaches virtue by abstract precept and theoretical argument, whereas the historian claims to do better since he teaches by concrete example, drawn from history. But both are defective:

> The Philosopher therfore and the Historian are they which would win the gole, the one by precept, the other by example. But both not hauing both, doe both halte. For the Philosopher, setting downe with thorny argument the bare rule, is so hard of vtterance, and so mistie to be conceiued, that one that hath no other guide but him shall wade in him till hee be olde before he shall finde sufficient cause to bee honest: for his knowledge standeth so vpon the abstract and generall, that happie is that man who may vnderstande him, and more happie that can applye what hee dooth vnderstand. On the other side, the Historian, wanting the precept, is so tyed, not to what shoulde bee but to what is, to the particuler truth of things and not to the general reason of things, that hys example draweth no necessary consequence, and therefore a lesse fruitfull doctrine.

The philosopher is too abstract to be persuasive, while the historian is tied to "the particuler truth of things" so that his examples are not always the most suitable for his purpose. There is an echo here of Aristotle's argument that poetry is more "probable" than history, but it is only an echo, and Sidney's argument is bound in a very different direction. Note how he proceeds:

> Nowe dooth the peerelesse Poet performe both: for whatsoeuer the Philosopher sayth shoulde be doone, hee giueth a perfect picture of it in some one, by whom hee presupposeth it was doone. So as hee coupleth the generall notion with the particuler example. A perfect picture I say, for hee yeeldeth to the powers of the minde an image of that whereof the Philosopher bestoweth but a woordish description: which dooth neyther stroke, pierce, nor possesse the sight of the soule so much as that other dooth.
>
> For as in outward things, to a man that had neuer seene an Elephant or a Rinoceros, who should tell him most exquisitely all theyr shapes, cullour, bignesse, and perticular markes, or of a gorgeous Pallace the Architecture, with declaring the full beauties, might well make the hearer able to repeate, as it were by rote, all hee had heard, yet should neuer satisfie his inward conceits with being witnes to it selfe of a true liuely knowledge: but the same man, as soone as hee might see those beasts well painted, or the house wel in moddel, should straightwaies grow, without need of any description,

to a iudicial comprehending of them: so no doubt the Philosopher with his learned definition, bee it of vertue, vices, matters of publick policie or priuat gouernment, replenisheth the memory with many infallible grounds of wisdom, which, notwithstanding, lye darke before the imaginatiue and iudging powre, if they bee not illuminated or figured foorth by the speaking picture of Poesie.

Tullie taketh much paynes, and many times not without poeticall helpes, to make vs knowe the force loue of our Countrey hath in vs. Yet vs but heare old *Anchises* speaking in the middest of Troyes flames, or see *Vlisses* in the fulnes of all *Calipso's* delights bewayle his absence from barraine and beggerly *Ithaca*. Anger, the *Stoicks* say, was a short madnes: let but *Sophocles* bring you *Aiax* on a stage, killing and whipping Sheepe and Oxen, thinking them the Army of Greeks, with theyr Chiefetaines *Agamemnon* and *Menelaus*, and tell mee if you haue not a more familiar insight into anger then finding in the Schoolemen his *Genus* and difference. See whether wisdome and temperance in *Vlisses* and *Diomedes*, valure in *Achilles*, friendship in *Nisus* and *Eurialus*, euen to an ignoraunt man carry not an apparent shyning: and, contrarily, the remorse of conscience in *Oedipus*, the soone repenting pride of *Agamemnon*, the selfe-deuouring crueltie in his Father *Atreus*, the violence of ambition in the two *Theban* brothers, the sowre-sweetnes of reuenge in *Medæa*, and, to fall lower, the *Terentian Gnato* and our *Chaucers Pandar* so exprest that we nowe vse their names to signifie their trades: and finally, all vertues, vices, and passions so in their own naturall seates layd to the viewe, that wee seeme not to heare of them, but cleerely to see through them. But euen in the most excellent determination of goodnes, what Philosophers counsell can so redily direct a Prince, as the fayned *Cyrus* in *Xenophon?* or a vertuous man in all fortunes, as *Aeneas* in *Virgill?* or a whole Common-wealth, as the way of Sir *Thomas Moores Eutopia?* . . . Certainly, euen our Sauiour Christ could as well haue giuen the morrall common places of vncharitablenes and humblenes as the diuine narration of *Diues* and *Lazarus;* or of disobedience and mercy, as that heauenly discourse of the lost Child and the gratious Father; but that hys through-searching wisdom knewe the estate of *Diues* burning in hell, and of *Lazarus* being in *Abrahams* bosome, would more constantly (as it were) inhabit both the memory and iudgment. Truly, for my selfe, mee seemes I see before my eyes the lost Childes disdainefull prodigality, turned to enuie a Swines dinner: which by the learned Diuines are thought not historicall acts, but instructing Parables. For conclusion, I say the Philosopher teacheth, but he teacheth obscurely, so as the learned onely can vnderstande him, that is to say, he teacheth them that are already taught; but the Poet is the foode for the tenderest stomachs, the Poet is indeed the right Popular Philosopher, whereof *Esops* tales giue good proofe: whose pretty Allegories, stealing vnder the formall

tales of Beastes, make many, more beastly then Beasts, begin to heare the
sound of vertue from these dumbe speakers.

But now may it be alledged that if this imagining of matters be so fitte for
the imagination, then must the Historian needs surpasse, who bringeth you
images of true matters, such as indeede were doone, and not such as fan-
tastically or falsely may be suggested to haue been doone. Truely, *Aristotle*
himselfe, in his discourse of Poesie, plainely determineth this question,
saying that Poetry is *Philosophoteron* and *Spoudaioteron*, that is to say, it
is more Philosophicall and more studiously serious than history. His reason
is, because Poesie dealeth with *Katholon* that is to say, with vniuersall consideration; and the history with *Kathekaston*, the perticuler: 'nowe,' sayth
he, 'the vniuersall wayes what is fit to bee sayd or done, eyther in likelihood or necessity, (which the Poesie considereth in his imposed names),
and the perticuler onely marks whether *Alcibiades* did, or suffered, this or
that.' Thus farre *Aristotle:* which reason of his (as all his) is most full of
reason. For indeed, if the question were whether it were better to haue a
perticular acte truly or falsly set down, there is no doubt which is to be
chosen, no more then whether you had rather have *Vespasians* picture
right as hee was, or at the Painters pleasure nothing resembling. But if the
question be for your owne vse and learning, whether it be better to haue it
set downe as it should be, or as it was, then certainely is more doctrinable
the fained *Cirus* in *Xenophon* then the true *Cyrus* in *Iustine*, and the fayned
Aeneas in *Virgil* then the right *Aeneas* in *Dares Phrigius*. As to a Lady that
desired to fashion her countenance to the best grace, a Painter should more
benefite her to portraite a most sweet face, wryting *Canidia* vpon it, then
to paynt *Canidia* as she was, who, *Horace* sweareth, was foule and ill
fauoured.

Poetry, Sidney claims, is superior as a moral teacher to both
philosophy and history, because it does not deal with mere abstract
propositions, as philosophy does, but with the concrete example, and
as its examples are not tied to fact it can make them more apt and
convincing than anything found in history. The true nature of virtue
is painted vividly and attractively, while vice, with equal vividness, is
made to appear always ugly and unattractive. Though he cites
Aesop's fables as examples of effective moral teaching by the poet, it
would be unfair to Sidney to say that his argument implies that the
beast fable is the highest form of literature, for, in the first place,
he has already emphasized the importance of liveliness and passion,
which are no necessary qualities of a fable, and, second, he has also,
more than once, cited the epic as an especially effective kind of
poetry since it gives us, in the persons of its heroes and villains, those

"notable images of vertues, vices, or what els, with that delightful teaching which must be the right describing note to know a Poet by."

Sidney and Aristotle

In the last of the paragraphs quoted above, Sidney refers to Aristotle, quoting his famous dictum that poetry is more philosophical and more serious than history because it deals with the universal rather than with the particular. Nevertheless, Sidney's position is not Aristotelian at all. When he argues that the fictitious rendering of the poet is more effective than the true report of the historian, his point is that the ideal world of the poet shows things as they *ought* to be rather than as they *are* and is thus more conducive to virtuous action in the reader. "If the question be for your owne vse and learning, whether it be better to haue it set downe as it should be, or as it was, then certainely is it more doctrinable the fained *Cirus* in *Xenophon* then the true *Cyrus* in *Iustine*." The key word here is "should." *Sidney has changed Aristotle's probable "should" to a moral "should."* To Aristotle, the poet wrote of what "should" be in the sense of what was most probable; his "should" was a "should" of probability. To Sidney, the poet wrote of what ought to be, in a purely moral sense. The world created by Sidney's poet is more edifying than the the real world, not more true to the fundamental probabilities of the human situation or probable in terms of the self-consistent world which it creates.

Thus though Sidney, like Aristotle, is concerned with replying to the kind of arguments against poetry that Plato brought forward, his defense is basically different from Aristotle's. For Sidney the poet is the creator of a world which leads those who view it to follow virtue and shun vice:

If the Poet doe his part a-right, he will shew you in *Tantalus*, *Atreus*, and such like, nothing that is not to be shunned; in *Cyrus*, *Aeneas*, *Vlisses*, each thing to be followed; where the Historian, bound to tell things as things were, cannot be liberall (without hee will be poeticall) of a perfect patterne, but, as in *Alexander* or *Scipio* himselfe, shew dooings, some to be liked, some to be misliked. . . .

For see wee not valiant *Milciades* rot in his fetters? The iust *Phocion* and the accomplished *Socrates* put to death like Traytors? The cruell *Seuerus* liue prosperously? The excellent *Seuerus* miserably murthered? *Sylla* and *Marius* dying in theyr beddes? *Pompey* and *Cicero* slaine then when they would haue thought exile a happinesse? See wee not vertuous *Cato* driuen to kyll himselfe? and rebell *Caesar* so aduanced that his name yet, after 1600 yeares, lasteth in the highest honor? . . . I conclude, therefore, that hee [the poet] excelleth Historie, not onely in furnishing the minde with knowledge, but in setting it forward to that which deserueth to be called and accounted good: which setting forward, and moouing to well dooing, indeed setteth the Lawrell crowne vpon the Poet as victorious, not onely of the Historian, but ouer the Phylosopher, howsoeuer in teaching it may bee questionable.

The poet not only exceeds the philosopher in his ability to create the perfect example, but also in his ability to move the reader to follow that example. "I thinke that no man is so much *Philophilosophos* [a lover of philosophy] as to compare the philosopher, in moouing, with the Poet." This comes close to identifying poetry with rhetoric, the art of persuasion, as Sidney himself realizes later on in his argument. But at the same time it enables Sidney to find room in his didactic theory of poetry for the qualities of liveliness and vigor which he had already commended. However ideal the poet's world may be, however virtuous its heroes and however much "poetic justice" may prevail in the course of the action, no reader is going to be "moved" to imitate that world in his own behavior unless it be presented with such life and passion that he finds it irresistible. The delight which the reader has in reading of this ideal world and in responding to its vitality depends not on content but on form and style. Thus by his theory of moving Sidney finds a way of including the purely esthetic qualities of form and style in his criteria of the good work of literary art.

Form and content

It is perhaps question-begging at this stage to use the word "esthetic" at all, for are we not concerned to discover what kinds of meaning can be given to this term? But all that is meant by the term here is those qualities which provide for the reader pleasure in the reading regardless of the content—qualities which derive from the way in which language is handled. (Whether in the last analysis form and content can be distinguished in this way is a profound question, which will arise later: Sidney's critical thought was hardly sophisticated enough to reach this question.) The point to be made here is the important one that Sidney frames a didactic theory of poetry in such a way that he includes *style* among his interests and "good style" among his criteria for a good work of literature, though he does not use the actual word. In doing so he makes it possible to separate a purely stylistic judgment from a total judgment of the value of a poem as something which both teaches and delights and teaches by delighting; when, later on in his essay, he condemns the love poetry of his day because it is written in too cold and artificial a style, he is being perfectly consistent. What is cold and artificial can never carry conviction, can never be, in Wordsworth's much later phrase, "carried alive into the heart by passion." "The Poet binds together by passion and knowledge the vast empire of human society," Wordsworth was to claim more than two hundred years after Sidney, and Sidney would have at least agreed that the poet combines passion and knowledge, the knowledge being moral knowledge and the passion manifesting itself in the vigor and liveliness of the style.

One can hardly emphasize too much Sidney's insistence that the poet's world should be presented delightfully, and that the delight comes from the passionate vitality of the expression, for this gives him a criterion which, if necessary, he can abstract altogether from his total view of poetry as the most effective way of moving to virtue and apply to a work of literary art whatever its subject matter and whether it has a moral purpose or not. If you say that poetry both teaches and delights, and have separate criteria for what is good doctrine and what constitutes delight in the way of expression, then you have prepared the way for the emergence of a purely esthetic point of view. You have also, however, oversimplified the relation between form and content and paved the way for the kind of criticism which talks about "a bad book, but so well written"—an approach which, as we shall see, involves a far too mechanical view of the nature of literary form.

We have seen that for Sidney the world created by the poet is not an "imitation," in any sense, of the real world we live in, but an improvement on it, presented so persuasively that the reader will wish to imitate that improvement. The limitations of this point of view come out most clearly when Sidney uses the sister art of painting as an analogy. "As to a Lady that desired to fashion her countenance to the best grace, a Painter should more benefite her to portraite a most sweet face, wryting *Canidia* vpon it, then to paint *Canidia* as she was, who, *Horace* sweareth, was foule and ill fauoured." The implication here is clearly that it is the function of portrait painting to help people to improve their own faces by imitating the portrait. This is the difficulty one gets into if one transfers the Aristotelian notion of imitation from the artist to his public, so that the artist does not imitate the world but invents a better one for the public to improve itself by imitating. On the other hand, later critics who maintained that the function of art *was* to imitate human nature and who at the same time demanded that art be morally instructive were caught up in another kind of dilemma if they were honest enough to admit that human nature as we know it in real life is far from edifying. If poetic justice does not prevail in life as it is and men in their actual lives are far from models of moral perfection, how can one at the same time imitate nature (which, to the seventeenth and much of the eighteenth century, meant human nature) and lead your readers to the paths of virtue? Dr Johnson, who had no illusions about life as it is and men as they are, at the same time praised Shakespeare for knowing and imitating human nature and blamed him for not having sufficient poetic justice in his plays. You cannot have it both ways, and it is more consistent, if you wish the poet's picture of man to be morally edifying, to insist (unless you want to edify solely by a series of awful warnings) that the poet is not concerned with the real world at all. There is, of course, a third way, which is to maintain that the "real" world is not the everyday world but the patterns underlying that world as seen by the poet's imagination. Only in this last way can an imitative theory of art be reconciled with a didactic one, and, though there are (as we have noted) traces of such an argument in Sidney, he never really develops it.

Teaching and "moving"

We have seen that for Sidney the world created by the poet can be "golden" in more than one way. It can present ideal heroes so vividly that one will wish to imitate their virtues. It can present a world in which virtue always triumphs and vice is always punished. Or it can present a world in which evil, whether it triumphs or not, is made to appear so ugly that the reader will in future always wish to avoid it. In the latter part of his essay, in which he discusses the objections made by the Puritans to the different kinds of literature, he suggests other ways in which the poet can "move to virtue." The satirist "sportingly neuer leaueth, vntil hee make a man laugh at folly, and, at length ashamed, to laugh at himselfe." Similarly, "Comedy is an imitation of the common errors of our life, which he representeth in the most ridiculous and scornefull sort that may be; so as it is impossible that any beholder can be content to be such a one." And tragedy "openeth the greatest wounds, and sheweth forth the Vlcers that are couered with Tissue; that maketh Kinges feare to be Tyrants, and Tyrants manifest their tirannical humors; that, with sturring the affects of admiration and commiseration, teacheth the vncertainety of this world, and vpon how weake foundations guilden roofes are builded"—a definition which, using some of Aristotle's terminology ("admiration and commiseration" represent a modification of Aristotle's fear and pity, admiration being used in its earlier sense of mingled wonder and reverence), changes Aristotle's psychological explanation of the therapeutic function of tragedy to a straight moral theory.

It is in his discussion of lyric poetry that Sidney places such emphasis on the importance of "moving"—whose relation to the moral function of poetry we have already discussed—that he seems for the moment almost to be resting his case on this quality alone:

Is it the Liricke that most displeaseth, who with his tuned Lyre, and wel accorded voyce, giueth praise, the reward of vertue, to vertuous acts? who giues morrall precepts, and naturall Problemes, who sometimes rayseth vp his voice to the height of the heauens, in singing the laudes of the immortall God. Certainly I must confesse my own barbarousness: I neuer heard the olde song of *Percy* and *Duglas* that I found not my heart mooued more than with a Trumpet; and yet is it sung by some blinde Crouder, with no rougher voyce then rude stile. . . .

Earlier, Sidney had emphasized the poet's ability to "move" as the factor which contributed most to the didactic effect of a poem: not only was the reader shown the ideal world, but, in virtue of the way in which it was presented, he was moved to imitate it. But the word "move" is ambiguous, and while most of the time Sidney uses it to

mean "spur on" or even simply "persuade," in the passage just quoted
he seems to be talking of emotion without any regard to its results in
action; the thrilling sounds of a trumpet affect the hearer emotionally,
and though of course the implication is that he is stirred to acts of
greater courage the immediate suggestion here is that the "affective
quality" (to borrow a term from some modern critics) in itself is what
matters. At any rate, later critics have seen such an implication in this
passage and have based on it a claim for Sidney to be a "romantic"
critic in the sense that he is interested in the arousing of emotion for
its own sake. But if virtue results from the subduing of passion by
reason—a point agreed by both Plato and the Christian Platonists of
Sidney's day—to say that poetry arouses passion is to concede one of
Plato's main objections and to yield an important point to the Puritans. Sidney, then, cannot have intended any overt suggestion of the
kind we cannot help seeing in the passage quoted. His whole case depends on his enlisting passion on the side of virtue: he shows how by
a passionate picture of an embodied ideal the poet can move men to
follow it. We have noted that this means that he has a criterion of
style, that "passionate describing" becomes important for him, and we
have seen that Sidney is content to keep his criteria of style and of
moral content separate. But nowhere does he come right out and say
that passionate describing *of anything* is poetically valuable, even
though we may sometimes feel that if he had not been constrained to
fight on his enemy's ground he might have said something like this.
The most he does in the argument he overtly presents is to show that
passion need not be on the Devil's side—"I don't see why the Devil
should have all the good tunes," as a later moralist was to put it—but
could be enlisted in the cause of virtue to make poetry, by its passionate teaching, the most effective of all didactic instruments. Richardson, said Dr Johnson in a later century, talking of the mixture of
psychological realism and moral teaching in the former's novels,
"taught the passions to move at the command of virtue." Sidney might
have reversed this, and said that the poet teaches virtue to move at the
command of the passions. One must not forget that, while Sidney was
replying to a Puritan attack on poetry, he, like Spenser, was a Puritan
himself. He was also, like Spenser, a neo-Platonist, a humanist, and a
poet. His defense of poetry was a noble attempt to combine all these
positions.

If the rhetorical side of Sidney's theory enables him to lay such emphasis on "moving" and thus insist on the importance of a lively and passionate style, it should also be noted that his insistence that the function of poetry is to show forth an ideal golden world instead of imitating the brazen one of actuality enables him to construct a hierarchy of literary forms. He can defend satire as the kind of poetry that laughs a man out of his folly, comedy as making the common errors of life seem ridiculous, and tragedy as showing the awful consequences of tyranny so that kings will fear to be tyrants (this last being perhaps the most inadequate of all Sidney's definitions), but the kind of poetry which paints directly the kind of virtue to which the readers are to be drawn will be the highest kind. That is heroic or epic poetry, "for by what conceit can a tongue be directed to speake euill of that which draweth with it no lesse Champions than *Achilles, Cyrus, Aeneas, Turnus, Tideus,* and *Rinaldo?* who not onely teach and moue to a truth, but teacheth and mooueth to the most high and excellent truth; who maketh magnanimity and iustice shine throughout all misty fearefulness and foggy desires. . . . But if any thing be already sayd in the defence of sweete Poetry, all concurreth to the maintaining the Heroicall, which is not only a kinde, but the best and the most accomplished kinde of Poetry."

Sidney, then, is able to answer the Platonic and the Puritan objections, he can find room for a criterion of style while insisting on a didactic content, and he has some ideas of a hierarchy of literary *genres.* He does all this, however, at the expense of making a dangerously clear-cut division between manner and matter and by making the ultimate objective and function of poetry not something unique, with a "peculiar pleasure" (in Aristotle's phrase) of its own and differentiating qualities in terms of which its very essence is to be recognized and valued, but as something shared with all other worthy human activities. Unlike Aristotle, Sidney does not justify poetry by singling out and justifying what is uniquely poetic and like Plato he applies a single value standard to all products of the human mind and imagination. He gets out of the Platonic dilemma by showing that passion is not the Devil's prerogative but can be used to implement virtue and by insisting that what the poet creates, if like nothing in the world of actuality, is morally better than the world of actuality and portrayed in such a way that the reader will want to try to bring it into being. But his triumph is won at the cost of poetry's independence. Though poetry for Sidney is a more effective moral teacher than philosophy or history, the critic of poetry has to wait for the moral philosopher or the man of religion to tell him what is morally good and what is morally bad before he can proceed to judge a poem. Aristotle's *Poetics* had been a declaration of independence for poetry as well as a justification of it; Sidney is content to achieve the latter at the expense of the former. And if—with some justice—we think Sidney's position naive, we might remember that from his day to ours the vast majority of readers of imaginative literature have taken substantially his view and generally applied it with less cunning and sensitivity.

4

Imitation and instruction

FOR PLATO, the poet's world was a second-hand imitation of reality, and therefore of no value; for Aristotle, the poet could, by the proper selection and organization of incident, achieve a reality more profound than that represented by the casual surface of things which we meet in ordinary experience; for Sidney, the poet created a world morally better than the real world, for the moral edification and improvement of the reader. None of these critics suggests that the poet would do well to describe life merely as he finds it; for Plato, that is to imitate shadows; for Aristotle and Sidney, for different reasons, it is simply not worth considering.

Dryden and the imitation of human nature

In 1668, however, John Dryden published his *Essay of Dramatic Poesie*, a dialogue on the nature of poetic drama and the respective merits of classical, modern French, Elizabethan, and restoration plays, in which everybody agrees to define a play as "A just and lively image of human nature, representing its passions and humours, and the changes of fortune to which it is subject, for the delight and instruction of mankind." Here, a hundred years after Sidney, a great English poet and critic is maintaining a principle utterly at variance with Sidney's view that the poet does not imitate the world as it is but invents a "golden" world which is better. Do we have here another solution to the Platonic dilemma?

Let us first note just what it is that Dryden is saying. A play—it is agreed in the essay that this definition really applies to imaginative literature in general, whether in the form of drama or not—in the first place gives us an image of human nature. It shows people acting in such a way as to reveal what they are like. By the use of the word *image* Dryden seems to be emphasizing the appearance, to be quite untroubled by Plato's notion that to do so is simply to imitate an imitation. Dryden makes no distinction, in fact, between an *image* of human nature and the *truth* about human nature: the former, if it is "just," gives the latter. The image is not only to be just; it must also be lively. Sidney would have agreed with the necessity for liveliness. It is the basis of a criterion of style, and provides also a further criterion by which to judge plot, whose first requirement is that it should be so organized as to give a just image of human nature. We have so far discussed four terms in the definition—"just," "lively," "image," and "human nature." They are all important and each one contributes materially to the definition. A just account of human nature could be given by a psychologist, but it would be neither lively nor an image. Similarly, an image could be lively without being just, while a just image of human nature could be dull rather than lively. All four elements are necessary.

The next phrase in Dryden's definition is more an elaboration of what he means by the first phrase than the addition of new requirements. You obtain a just and lively image of human nature by representing its "passions and humours" ("humours" meaning states of mind or mental characteristics), and by representing the changes of fortune to which men are subject. It is only when we see a character's reactions to changes of fortune that we get a real view of his "passions and humours." If Hamlet's father had not been murdered by his uncle and his mother had not married that same uncle, Hamlet would never have been driven to exhibit the true image of his nature. It is the testing circumstance that illuminates character.

Is Dryden, then, demanding that the writer of fiction, whether in plays or in other forms, indulge in what we today might call psychological realism? Is it the duty of the writer to show us men involved in actions which exhibit their fundamental characteristics and so tell us something about human nature? This would be a perfectly logical defense of poetry. The function of poetry would then be to inform the reader, in a lively and agreeable way, of what human nature is like. Literature would be a form of knowledge, and it would bear the same relation to psychology as in Sidney it does to ethics. That is, while for Sidney the poet makes vivid and impressive, by his imaginary examples, the ideas of the moral philosopher, so for Dryden the poet makes vivid and impressive, by his imaginary examples, the knowledge of the psychologist.

Instruction and recognition

It might be maintained that the concluding phrase of Dryden's definition confirms this interpretation. It is all to be done for the delight and instruction of mankind. The delight comes from the liveliness with which human nature is represented, and from the pleasure which comes from recognizing in fictional characters fundamental psychological truths; while the instruction is not moral instruction, but instruction in the facts of human nature. The reader is instructed in psychology, in fact. For why should we restrict the term "instruction" to mean only moral instruction? There can be any kind of instruction: we send children to school to be instructed in arithmetic without any expectation that their sums will make them morally better. So could we not argue that Dryden is here pleading for a lively psychological realism, on the grounds that it gives pleasure and at the same time provides instruction in human psychology? Would not that be an adequate solution of the Platonic dilemma, and an adequate defense of poetry?

It might well be that Dryden had some such notion in mind, although it must be admitted that the word "instruction" is ambiguous, and it generally carried the meaning of moral teaching in its use by critics of the period. We might note, however, that if Dryden meant that the function of drama was to delight and instruct by providing lively images of human nature in action under testing circumstances, the delight cannot have been supposed to come from *recognizing* what we already know about human nature if at the same time the play is to *instruct* us in human nature, which is to say, to tell us what we did not know before. "Poetry," wrote Keats in one of his letters, "should strike the reader as a wording of his own highest thoughts, and appear almost a Remembrance." It is not simple recognition, but *almost* a remembrance. Dr Johnson, arguing with William Pepys about Pope's definition of "true wit" in poetry as "what oft was thought but ne'er so well expressed," objected strongly: "That, sir, is a definition both false and foolish. . . . 'What oft was thought' is all the worse for being often thought, because to be wit, it ought to be newly thought." It is clearly not enough to recognize what we already know. Nevertheless, one can recognize as "just" what one did not know before. Keats' phrase "almost a Remembrance" is suggestive because it indicates that there is a middle ground between recognition and new knowledge and it is on that middle ground that imaginative literature operates. If, therefore, "a just and lively imitation of human nature" delights and instructs us, the delight is not simply a matter of recognizing examples of what we already knew to be true, nor, on the other hand, are we "instructed" in what we had never known before: there is a kind of recognition at work, but it is only apparently recognition —it is new knowledge, operating through an impression of the familiar.

The implication of Dryden's definition is that literature is a form of knowledge rather than a technique of persuasion. The knowledge pleases partly because it is pleasant to increase our awareness and partly because of the delightful manner in which it is conveyed: both the "justness" and the "liveliness" of the imitation of human nature contribute to the pleasure given by the work. Such a position, of course, ignores as meaningless the Platonic objection that what the poet imitates is itself an imitation of an imitation. The poet describes men as they are, that is, as they are found to be by observation and introspection and by reading the reports of the observations of others. To object that direct experience does not yield knowledge is, in the age of John Locke, to play the willful obscurantist.

Which aspects of human nature?

There are none the less difficulties in this point of view. What in fact is human nature? we might ask. Men acting and suffering, the reply would be. But what men, and what are they acting and suffering?

Human nature is illustrated by a man swearing when he hits his finger with a hammer as well as by Hamlet going to pieces on learning the truth about his father's death and his uncle's guilt. What aspects of human nature in action are most fit for the poet to describe? It will be seen at once that even to raise such a question is to pave the way for a hierarchy of more and less appropriate kinds of theme. Ambition represented by Alexander the Great is different from ambition as represented by a draper's assistant working and scheming to have a store of his own. Cleopatra in love is different from Jenny being tousled by Jock behind the cowshed. Yet both illustrate human nature. Which theme is more appropriate to literature? The modern critic would probably refuse to admit the validity of this question. Why should one be more appropriate than the other? Whichever it may be, if it is done effectively, if it is "just and lively," if, in virtue of the way the story is put together and presented, it both pleases and instructs, providing that combination of recognition of what we think we knew and awareness of new insight which we have already discussed, then it is justified. But to concede that any aspect of human nature, illustrated by any kind of person, is equally suitable for literature is to assume that we can get equal "delight" from an account of Cleopatra's passion for Antony and from a picture of a farm hand's seduction of a milk-maid. In a democratic age like ours such an assumption may seem obvious, but it was far from obvious to earlier ages, and neither Dryden nor Pope nor Dr Johnson would have accepted as material for the literary imagination characters and situations which were not dignified by a symbolic external impressiveness. The "passions" of men were indeed the subject of poetry, but in the highest form of literature they were to be illustrated in people whose fate involved more than their own domestic fortunes. Both the Greeks and the Elizabethans also felt this (though the Elizabethans had their humbler kind of tragedy too) and part of the significance of Oedipus, as of Hamlet and Lear, is that, being rulers, their inner conflicts involve a large outer world, and at the same time, possessing "great" natures (not necessarily naturalistically presented), they are more representative of the total human possibilities than, say, a farmhand.

Poetry illuminates human nature, and pleases and instructs by so doing. By choosing for its chief characters persons sufficiently exalted in position for their fate to affect whole countries one can, without blurring the picture of human nature, make the story more arresting and more far-reaching in its implications. Thus if for Sidney heroic poetry is at the top of the hierarchy because it shows us directly the virtuous actions the reader is to be inspired to imitate, in those later critics who saw as the poet's task not the creation of an ideal world to be imitated but the projection of a lively image of the real world of men for the reader's pleasure and instruction, heroic poetry is likewise at the top because it deals with characters whose fortunes are more interesting since they involve the fortunes of so many others. In each case, a theory of the nature and value of poetry has led to a hierarchy of poetic "kinds," and though the theories differ the hierarchy is the same.

"Expression"

There is more even than this, however, hidden in Dryden's definition. If poetic fiction provides "a just and lively image of human nature," we can choose, while demanding both, to lay chief emphasis on either the justness or the liveliness. We might ignore the whole question of whether we can receive instruction from what we already know, take the "justness" for granted, and insist that the peculiar pleasure of poetry (still using this term in its larger sense) lies in the polish, wit, grace, liveliness, or some such qualities, with which familiar truths are presented. That, as we have noted, was Pope's view, represented in his famous phrase "what oft was thought but ne'er so well expressed." But even Pope did not mean that poetry was merely the polished expression of well-known abstract truths. His own "Rape of the Lock," for example, is very far from that. He must have meant to include in the verb *expressed* the imaginative way in which the general truths are illustrated: in other words, expression must include plot as well as style, invention as well as diction. The epigram, even for Pope, was not the highest form of poetry. For Pope, the good poet uses his reason and his common sense—to both of which faculties he gives the name "Nature"—to discover what the general truths about human character and behavior (also called "Nature") are; notes how the great poets of Greece and Rome have embodied *their* observations about human character in poetry; and, profiting both by the example of the ancient poets and his own observation (which, he insists, yield the same conclusions), proceeds to illustrate those truths in as polished, witty, and generally delightful a way as possible. This might involve a story, it might involve the author moralizing or satirizing in his own person, it might involve an elegy, or an apostrophe to some person or idea, or a number of other things, but whatever is involved will be included in the *expression*. As in Sidney, form and content are separable, and the latter comes first. You decide what you want to say, and then, profiting by the example of your greatest predecessors, decide on how to say it.

Dr Johnson and "general nature"

Pope's "Essay on Criticism" (1711) is not, as Sidney's *Defence of Poesie* is, an inquiry into the nature and value of poetry, but a series of generalizations about good taste, the difficulties of criticizing impartially and justly, and the characteristics of the good critic. It takes the major questions for granted, and we cannot learn from it, for example, whether the instruction we receive from poetry is instruction in the facts of human nature or moral instruction, or indeed whether he would agree with Dryden at all in including instruction as one of the functions of poetry (though we know from other remarks he makes that he would agree), nor does he tell us whether the pleasure in effective expression is the main joy and value of poetry. For further inquiry along the lines laid down by Dryden's definition we must, among major English critics, turn to Dr Johnson.

In his preface to his edition of Shakespeare, Dr Johnson praises the playwright because he fulfills precisely Dryden's requirement of "a just and lively image of human nature":

Nothing can please many, and please long, but just representations of general nature. Particular manners can be known to few, and therefore few only can judge how nearly they are copied. The irregular combination of fanciful invention may delight a-while, by that novelty of which the common satiety of life sends us all in quest; but the pleasures of sudden wonder are soon exhausted, and the mind can only repose on the stability of truth.

Shakespeare is above all writers, at least above all modern writers, the poet of nature; the poet that holds up to his readers a faithful mirrour of manners and of life. His characters are not modified by the customs of particular places, unpractised by the rest of the world; by the peculiarities of studies or professions, which can operate but upon small numbers; or by the accidents of transient fashions or temporary opinions: they are the genuine progeny of common humanity, such as the world will always supply, and observation will always find. His persons act and speak by the influence of those general passions and principles by which all minds are agitated, and the whole system of life is continued in motion. In the writings of other poets a character is too often an individual; in those of *Shakespeare* it is commonly a species.

It is from this wide extension of design that so much instruction is derived. It is this which fills the plays of *Shakespeare* with practical axioms and domestick wisdom. It was said of *Euripides*, that every verse was a precept; and it may be said of *Shakespeare*, that from his works may be collected a system of civil and œconomical prudence. Yet his real power is not shewn in the splendour of particular passages, but by the progress of his fable, and the tenour of his dialogue; and he that tries to recommend him by select quotations, will succeed like the pedant in *Hierocles*, who, when he offered his house for sale, carried a brick in his pocket as a specimen.

It will not easily be imagined how much *Shakespeare* excells in accommodating his sentiments to real life, but by comparing him with other authours. It was observed of the ancient schools of declamation, that the more diligently they were frequented, the more was the student disqualified for the world, because he found nothing there which he should ever meet in any other place. The same remark may be applied to every stage but that of *Shakespeare*. The theatre, when it is under any other direction, is peopled by such characters as were never seen, conversing in a language which was never heard, upon topicks which will never arise in the commerce of mankind. But the dialogue of this authour is often so evidently determined by the incident which produces it, and is pursued with so much ease and simplicity, that it seems scarcely to claim the merit of fiction, but to have been gleaned by diligent selection out of common conversation, and common occurrences. . . .

Other dramatists can only gain attention by hyperbolical or aggravated characters, by fabulous and unexampled excellence or depravity, as the writers of barbarous romances invigorated the reader by a giant and a dwarf; and he that should form his expectations of human affairs from the play, or from the tale, would be equally deceived. *Shakespeare* has no heroes; his scenes are occupied only by men, who act and speak as the reader thinks that he should himself have spoken or acted on the same occasion: Even where the agency is supernatural the dialogue is level with life. Other writers disguise the most natural passions and most frequent incidents; so that he who contemplates them in the book will not know them in the world: *Shakespeare* approximates the remote, and familiarizes the wonderful; the event which he represents will not happen, but if it were possible, its effects would probably be such as he has assigned; and it may be said, that he has not only shewn human nature as it acts in real exigencies, but as it would be found in trials, to which it cannot be exposed.

This therefore is the praise of *Shakespeare*, that his drama is the mirrour of life; that he who has mazed his imagination, in following the phantoms which other writers raise up before him, may here be cured of his delirious extasies, by reading human sentiments in human language, by scenes from which a hermit may estimate the transactions of the world, and a confessor predict the progress of the passions.

Though this is a discussion of Shakespeare and not a theoretical treatise on poetics, it is by implication also a statement of the nature and value of drama and of literary fiction generally. Shakespeare is praised for doing what a dramatist ought to do and few dramatists have done. The terms in which he is praised deserve careful consideration.

"Nothing can please many, and please long, but just representations of general nature." The implication of this sentence is clear: it is the duty of the poet (again, using the term in its wider sense) to please and the giving of pleasure is a—if not *the*—criterion of worth in poetry. The way to please the greatest number over the longest period of time is to provide accurate pictures of general human nature. Dryden had said "a just and lively image of human nature," but Johnson insists on *general* nature. Is anything new being added to the theory of the nature and value of poetry with this word?

Aristotle, it will be remembered, had pointed out that the poet represents the universal, the general. ". . . Poetry is more philosophical and more serious than history because poetry tends to render the general truths while history gives the particular facts." "Poetry"—to quote again Sidney's paraphrase of Aristotle—"dealeth with *Katholon*, that is to say, with the universall consideration; and the history with *Kathekaston*." Johnson is similarly contrasting the general and the particular. He does not mean, however, quite the same thing Aristotle meant. General nature is for Johnson what is found in most people in most ages—it is, one might almost say, a statistical rather than a philosophical concept. Its opposite is the idiosyncratic, the behavior of only a few people in few times or places. Yet it would be unfair to say that this statistical concept is not at the same time philosophical, for, Dr Johnson would maintain, what is most common is most typical and most revealing of human nature as it really is. Reality and generality are in a sense identified: what is most general is what is most real.

The implication here is, of course, that human nature does not change. If the poet represents those aspects of human nature which are common to all times and places, and in doing so presents to us the reality about human nature, then men must be fundamentally the same at all times and places and they must differ only in trivialities. Indeed, any theory of literary value which sees literature as some kind of illumination of the nature of man is committed to the position that that nature is unchanging, unless it is prepared to concede that the literature of past ages has ceased to be of value. When Pope tells us that the Greek and Roman writers found out the best way of "imitating Nature" and that therefore to copy Homer is to copy Nature, he is naturally assuming that men in Homer's day were, in those aspects of their nature which are of interest to the poet, identical with the men of his own day. And that assumption was certainly shared by Johnson.

In the second paragraph quoted above Johnson praises Shakespeare for holding up to his readers "a faithful mirrour of manners and of life" and for not allowing his characters to be modified "by the customs of particular places, unpractised by the rest of the world" or "by the peculiarities of studies or professions, which can operate but upon small numbers." We might set beside this the remarks on poetry which Johnson had earlier put into the mouth of Imlac in his moral tale, *Rasselas:*

"The business of a poet," said Imlac, "is to examine, not the individual, but the species; to remark general properties and large appearances; he does not number the streaks of the tulip, or describe the different shades in the verdure of the forest. He is to exhibit in his portraits of nature such prominent and striking features as recall the original to every mind, and must neglect the minuter discriminations, which one may have remarked and another have neglected, for those characteristics which are alike obvious to vigilance and carelessness.

"But the knowledge of nature is only half the task of a poet; he must be acquainted likewise with all the modes of life. His character requires that he estimate the happiness and misery of every condition; observe the power of all the passions in all their combinations, and trace the changes of the human mind, as they are modified by various institutions and accidental influence of climate or custom, from the sprightliness of infancy to the despondence of decrepitude. He must divest himself of the prejudices of his age or country; he must consider right and wrong in their abstracted and invariable state; he must disregard present laws and opinions, and rise to general and transcendental truths, which will always be the same. He must, therefore, content himself with the slow progress of his name, contemn the applause of his own time, and commit his claims to the justice of posterity. He must write as the interpreter of nature and legislator of mankind, and consider himself as presiding over the thoughts and manners of future generations, as a being superior to time and place."

The poet must know the manners and customs of men of all times and conditions, not because it is his duty to make vivid to the reader the different ways in which men have lived and behaved, but so that he is not taken in by surface differences and is able to penetrate to the common humanity underlying these. But, it will be objected, to give a picture of a generalized man is impossible; philosophers may talk about such a concept but the poet cannot embody him in a concrete creation, for a concrete creation must be particularized to carry any conviction at all. Does not the poet reach out to the universal *through the particular?* And can a poet at the same time present a picture of general human nature and be lively and realistic, as Johnson also claims that Shakespeare is? Johnson claims that Shakespeare's characters are not unreal abstractions but "men who act and speak as the reader thinks that he should himself have spoken or acted on the same occasion." In fact, he goes so far as to say that Shakespeare's dialogue "is pursued with so much ease and simplicity, that it seems scarcely to claim the merit of fiction, but to have been gleaned by diligent selection out of common conversation, and common occurrence."

We must note, however, that Johnson is not claiming that Shakespeare is what would later have been called "naturalistic." His dialogue does not report the actual speech of men; it *seems* to have been gleaned by *diligent selection* out of common conversation, which is something very different. Johnson knew perfectly well that people do not speak blank verse in daily life. When he says that Shakespeare's dialogue is "level with life" he does not mean that it is mere reporting; he is talking about the impression created by the dialogue, about the vitality and the psychological plausibility of the characters as they create themselves by speech and action. That is why it is useless to recommend Shakespeare "by select quotations" and why he must be judged "by the progress of his fable [plot] and the tenour of his dialogue"—by the total effect, that is. If it were the simple naturalism of his dialogue that pleased Johnson, then of course he *could* be recommended by select quotations. Style and plot contribute to the effect of reality, to the illusion that here are real people acting as they do in real life, while at the same time their behavior illuminates those general aspects of human nature which, Johnson insists, are the true concern of the poet. When Johnson says that "Shakespeare has no heroes" he does not mean that none of his characters are heroic in character or behavior or impressive in the strength of their personality: he means that his heroes illustrate and act according to the general laws of human nature. They are not demigods or supermen, but men, whom we recognize as fellow human beings.

If, therefore, one might be inclined to believe that Johnson's insistence on the general, on not numbering the streaks of the tulip, on avoidance of particularizing differences between men, would lead him to defend the cold and the abstract in literature and to remove both the "lively" and the "image" from Dryden's phrase "a just and lively image of human nature" so as to produce simply just generalizations about human nature, one has only to go on to read his list of reasons for praising Shakespeare to see that this does not follow; an air of lively realism is an all-important quality in a good play and such an air cannot be produced by making characters into generalized abstractions. In other words, Johnson's praise of Shakespeare's psychological realism is by implication a recognition of the importance of the particular, through which the general must be presented. No character in a work of fiction or drama can appear real if he is not individualized.

For Johnson, then, as for Dryden, literature is a form of knowledge; it is valuable for its illustration and illumination of human nature. We derive pleasure from seeing human nature thus illustrated and illuminated, and, Johnson would add, from the incidental beauties of expression which the poet employs. Johnson is clearer than Dryden on the question of whether what we learn about human nature is new knowledge or simply a lively illustration of what we already know. It is in essence what observant and thoughtful people already know, though often conveyed through examples of a kind hitherto unknown to the reader. Imlac insists that the poet must study all kinds of men of different ages and countries; the poet, that is, must have a greater store of particulars through which to illustrate the known generalities. The pleasure the reader gets derives from his recognition in these different characters of general human nature as he knows it.

Recognition, even through unfamiliar examples, is not, however, instruction, and it would be difficult to obtain from Johnson's criticism any notion that the didactic effect of literature lies in its teaching us new things about human nature. From Shakespeare's plays, he says, "a hermit may estimate the transactions of the world, and a confessor predict the progress of the passions." The plays would give instruction to a hermit, because he has lived removed from the world and is therefore ignorant of it; to the reasonably observant man who has lived in the world Shakespeare would provide, through lively and pleasing fictions, illustrations and confirmations of what he knows human nature to be like.

Dr Johnson's dilemma

Is recognition, then, the sole value of literature? Even if we add to it the pleasure we get from the aptness, liveliness, and effective expression of the example which provides the recognition, will this exhaust the functions of literature? Johnson is quite specific on this point. Poetry has in addition the higher function of moral instruction. "The end of writing is to instruct; the end of poetry is to instruct by pleasing," he tells us further on in the Shakespeare preface, and again: "The greatest graces of a play, are to copy nature and instruct life." That by instruction Johnson means moral instruction is made quite clear when he comes to that part of the preface which discusses Shakespeare's faults:

His first defect is that to which may be imputed most of the evil in books or in men. He sacrifices virtue to convenience, and is so much more careful to please than to instruct, that he seems to write without any moral purpose. From his writings indeed a system of social duty may be selected, for he that thinks reasonably must think morally; but his precepts and axioms drop casually from him; he makes no just distribution of good or evil, nor is always careful to shew in the virtuous a disapprobation of the wicked; he carries his persons indifferently through right and wrong, and at the close dismisses them without further care, and leaves their examples to operate by chance. This fault the barbarity of his age cannot extenuate; for it is always a writer's duty to make the world better, and justice is a virtue independant on time and place.

. . . He omits opportunities of instructing and delighting which the train of his story seems to force upon him, and apparently rejects those exhibitions which would be more affecting, for the sake of those which are more easy.

If a poet's duty is both to represent human nature accurately and vividly and to arrange his story so that it provides moral instruction for the reader, then it must follow that human nature in itself must be edifying. Sidney agreed that poetry should be morally instructive, but, well aware that life as it is does not convey a moral lesson to the observer, he insisted that the poet create a new and better world. Johnson wants to have it both ways. As we have seen, this is fair enough if he believes that the real world is in fact edifying, but he knows very well that it is not. In a review which he had written earlier of Soame Jenyns' *Free Enquiry into the Origin and Nature of Evil* he had eloquently protested against the facile theory that the world as it is, is a happy and perfectly conducted place, with no un-deserved suffering and with the apparent misfortunes of the virtuous neatly compensated, so that, for example, the poor man has more hopes, fewer fears, and greater health than the rich. Johnson thun-dered against this facile optimism, and showed how much more plausi-bly the facts could be turned the other way. Jenyns raised the possi-bility that just as men hunt animals for their pleasure, so there may be beings who deceive and torment or destroy men for their own pleas-ure and utility, and this would 'justify' the divine order. Johnson commented grimly:

I cannot resist the temptation of contemplating this analogy, which, I think, he might have carried further, very much to the advantage of his argument. He might have shown, that these "hunters, whose game is man," have many sports analogous to our own. As we drown whelps and kittens, they amuse themselves, now and then, with sinking a ship, and stand round the fields of Blenheim, or the walls of Prague, as we encircle a cockpit. As we shoot a bird flying, they take a man in the midst of his business or pleasure, and knock him down with an apoplexy. Some of them, perhaps, are virtuosi, and delight in the operations of an asthma, as a human philoso-pher in the effects of an air-pump. To swell a man with a tympany is as good sport as to blow a frog. Many a merry bout have these frolick beings at the vicissitudes of an ague, and good sport it is to see a man tumble with an epilepsy, and revive and tumble again, and all this he knows not why. As they are wiser and more powerful than we, they have more exquisite di-versions; for we have no way of procuring any sport so brisk and so lasting, as the paroxysms of the gout and stone, which, undoubtedly, must make high mirth, especially if the play be a little diversified with the blunders and puzzles of the blind and deaf. We know not how far their sphere of observation may extend. Perhaps, now and then, a merry being may place himself in such a situation, as to enjoy, at once, all the varieties of an epi-demical disease, or amuse his leisure with the tossings and contortions of every possible pain, exhibited together.

For Johnson, the only hope came from revealed religion, not from life as lived on this earth, which was neither edifying nor in itself suggestive of a benign providence. The spectacle of men behaving as they do is not conducive to moral uplift. If this is so, it is surely illogical to demand at the same time that the poet show life as it is and that his picture of life must lead men to be better. Sidney, in claiming that the poet created a golden world superior to the brazen world of reality, was more logical. Literature cannot be both "a just and lively imitation of human nature" and a means of moral instruction and improvement unless one holds the optimistic view that the world as it is provides an edifying and improving exhibition. In other words, to hold a view of literature which is at once imitative and didactic one must be a very special kind of optimist. Some eighteenth century writers may have had this kind of optimism, but Johnson certainly did not.

"Almost a Remembrance"

We have seen that for Johnson the imitation of human nature which the poet provided gave to the reader a recognition of what he was likely to have known already. The poet illustrates rather than reveals. But we have also noticed that Johnson criticized Pope's view that wit in poetry consists in presenting "what oft was thought but ne'er so well expressed" arguing that it ought to be newly thought. Does that mean that, in spite of his insistence that great poets are known by the way in which they reveal and illustrate recognizable human nature, he felt that they also in some way instruct us in aspects of human nature we had not known before? The fact is, neither Dryden nor Pope nor Johnson is very explicit on this issue, and all of them seem sometimes to talk as though the poet provides new exploration of the human situation and at other times as though he simply illustrated effectively and convincingly what we know to be true. Both poetry as exploration and poetry as providing recognition, as cognitive and as illustrative, seem to be included in their views. Johnson, however, is most emphatic on the illustrative aspect. In his life of Gray, he remarks:

In the character of his *Elegy* I rejoice to concur with the common reader; for by the common sense of readers uncorrupted with literary prejudices, after all the refinements of subtility and the dogmatism of learning, must be finally decided all claim to poetical honours. The *Church-yard* abounds with images which find a mirrour in every mind, and with sentiments to which every bosom returns an echo. The four stanzas beginning *Yet even these bones,* are to me original: I have never seen the notions in any other place; yet he that reads them here, persuades himself that he has always felt them . . .

"Images which find a mirrour in every mind" and "sentiments to which every bosom returns an echo" are phrases which clearly suggest that the function of the poet is to render "what oft was thought but ne'er so well expressed." And there are many similar statements throughout Johnson's criticism, many of them most emphatic. Yet we cannot fail to observe that in the very next sentence he introduces a new note: "I have never seen the notions in any other place; yet he that reads them here, persuades himself that he has always felt them." This surely leads us again to Keats' "almost a Remembrance." We can recognize what we had not previously known. When we see new knowledge rendered in the special way the poet employs we see it both as new and as familiar, and our reaction combines recognition with insight. A claim for poetry as conveying a special kind of awareness which, while new, comes with the force of recognition, is never explicitly made in any of the critical passages we have been considering in this chapter; yet some such notion is more than once hinted at.

5

The vindication of pleasure

THE QUESTION of what poetry is and what kind of value it possesses can be answered by an examination of the products of the poet's activity (of poems, that is to say) or by an inquiry into how the poet operates. Instead of asking "What is poetry?" we can ask "What is a poet?" This latter question will often lead to the former, and critics have quite frequently approached the whole problem of the nature and value of poetry through a study of the psychology of poetic creation. In his famous preface to the second edition of *Lyrical Ballads* Wordsworth proceeds to give his view of what poetry is and wherein its value lies by asking first "What is a Poet? To whom does he address himself? And what language is to be expected from him?" Poetry is an activity as well as a species of art object, and the basic critical questions can be approached by looking at the activity as well as by examining the product. This kind of critical inquiry will be discussed in a later chapter, for it raises questions of its own which are quite distinct from these we have so far been considering. Wordsworth, the first important English poet to explain, defend, and define poetry by asking how it was produced, thus belongs with those modern critics who are chiefly concerned with the process of creation, and he will be discussed with them. Nevertheless, it is worth taking out of their context at this point some of his generalizations about the nature of poetry which are comparable to those we have quoted from Dryden and Johnson.

"Truth general and operative"

We have noted Aristotle's distinction between the universal and the particular, Sidney's un-Aristotelian interpretation of this, Dryden's insistence that poetry is an imitation of human nature, and Dr Johnson's emphasis on the *general* nature of that imitation. We have raised, too, the question whether poetry, if it is a representation of human nature, pleases us because it illustrates what we already know, and so recognize, or by giving us a new illumination, or by somehow doing both simultaneously. We have noted Johnson's remark about a passage in Gray's "Elegy" ("I have never seen the notions in any other place; yet he that reads them here persuades himself that he has always felt them") and compared Keats' statement that poetry strikes us as "almost a Remembrance." Let us put beside these the following quotation from Wordsworth's preface:

Aristotle, I have been told, has said, that Poetry is the most philosophic of all writings: it is so: its object is truth, not individual and local, but general, and operative; not standing upon external testimony, but carried alive into the heart by passion; truth which is its own testimony, which gives competence and confidence to the tribunal to which it appeals, and receives them from the same tribunal. Poetry is the image of man and nature. The obstacles which stand in the way of the fidelity of the Biographer and Historian, and of their consequent utility, are incalculably greater than those which are to be encountered by the Poet who comprehends the dignity of his art. The Poet writes under one restriction only, namely, the necessity of giving immediate pleasure to a human Being possessed of that information which may be expected from him, not as a lawyer, a physician, a mariner, an astronomer, or a natural philosopher, but as a Man. Except this one restriction, there is no object standing between the Poet and the image of things; between this, and the Biographer and Historian, there are a thousand.

The distinction that Wordsworth makes between truth "individual and local" and truth "general and operative" is similar to Aristotle's distinction between historical and poetic truth, and it is linked also to the question of recognition. Poetic truth for Wordsworth is "operative"—it works on us, it carries its own conviction with it, so that we cannot but acknowledge it as true. "Individual and local" truth does not carry its own conviction: before we could be sure that a historian or a biographer were telling the truth we should have to know what his sources were and how honestly he used them. The poet's truth is general in the sense that it needs no authentication to be recognized as true: it does not "stand upon external testimony" but is "carried alive into the heart by passion" and is thus its own testimony. Our hearts recognize it as true—not necessarily because we have known it before, but because the psychological structure of our minds assents to it; it makes contact somehow with the basic mental laws which determine human perception and emotion. The reaction is thus not literal recognition, but it is recognition in a profounder sense. Again, it is reminiscent of Keats' later phrase "almost a Remembrance."

The mind of man and the workings of nature

Wordsworth is thus here tying up a number of concepts which had previously exercised critics; his point of view is not strictly Aristotelian, though it has elements in common with Aristotle (Wordsworth and Aristotle would certainly not have agreed, for example, on the nature and value of passion); and he attempts to probe deeper than either Dryden or Johnson into the reasons why general representation of human nature pleases us. It must be general and *operative*, it must carry its own passionate conviction with it, and the pleasure we derive from it comes from our having our basic psychological structure touched and illuminated. Wordsworth goes further: he believed that our psychological structure is paralleled in the workings of the universe as a whole, and one reason why the poet is able to express truths which are general and operative is that he is "a man pleased with his own passions and volitions, and who rejoices more than other men in the spirit of life that is in him; delighting to contemplate similar volitions and passions as manifested in the goings-on of the Universe, and habitually impelled to create them where he does not find them." That is why the poet gives pleasure "to a human Being possessed of that information which may be expected from him, not as a lawyer, a physician, a mariner, an astronomer, or a natural philosopher, but as a Man." The function of poetry, and its value, lies in its giving this kind of pleasure:

Nor let this necessity of producing immediate pleasure be considered as a degradation of the Poet's art. It is far otherwise. It is an acknowledgement of the beauty of the universe, an acknowledgement the more sincere, because not formal, but indirect; it is a task light and easy to him who looks at the world in the spirit of love: further, it is a homage paid to the native and naked dignity of man, to the grand elementary principle of pleasure, by which he knows, and feels, and lives, and moves. We have no sympathy but what is propagated by pleasure: I would not be misunderstood; but wherever we sympathise with pain, it will be found that the sympathy is produced and carried on by subtle combinations with pleasure. We have no knowledge, that is, no general principles drawn from the contemplation of particular facts, but what has been built up by pleasure, and exists in us by pleasure alone. The Man of science, the Chemist and Mathematician, whatever difficulties and disgusts they may have had to struggle with, know and feel this. However painful may be the objects with which the Anatomist's knowledge is connected, he feels that his knowledge is pleasure: and where he has no pleasure he has no knowledge. What then does the Poet? He considers man and the objects that surround him as acting and re-acting upon each other, so as to produce an infinite complexity of pain and pleasure; he considers man in his own nature and in his ordinary life as contemplating this with a certain quantity of immediate knowledge, with certain convictions, intuitions, and deductions, which from habit acquire the quality of intuitions; he considers him as looking upon this complex scene of ideas and sensations, and finding everywhere objects that immediately excite in him sympathies which, from the necessities of his nature, are accompanied by an over-balance of enjoyment.

To this knowledge which all men carry about with them, and to these sympathies in which, without any other discipline than that of our daily life, we are fitted to take delight, the Poet principally directs his attention. He considers man and nature as essentially adapted to each other, and the mind of man as naturally the mirror of the fairest and most interesting properties of nature. And thus the Poet, prompted by this feeling of pleasure, which accompanies him through the whole course of his studies, converses with general nature, with affections akin to those, which, through labour and length of time, the Man of science has raised up in himself, by conversing with those particular parts of nature which are the objects of his studies. The knowledge both of the Poet and the Man of science is pleasure; but the knowledge of the one cleaves to us as a necessary part of our existence, our natural and unalienable inheritance; the other is a personal and individual acquisition, slow to come to us, and by no habitual and direct sympathy connecting us with our fellow-beings. The Man of science seeks truth as a remote and unknown benefactor; he cherishes and loves it in his solitude: the Poet, singing a song in which all human beings join with him, rejoices in the presence of truth as our visible friend and hourly companion. Poetry is the breath and finer spirit of all knowledge; it is the impassioned expression which is in the countenance of all Science. Emphatically may it be said of the Poet, as Shakespeare hath said of man, 'that he looks before and after.' He is the rock of defence for human nature; an upholder and preserver, carrying everywhere with him relationship and love. In spite of difference of soil and climate, of language and manners, of laws and customs: in spite of things silently gone out of mind, and things violently destroyed; the Poet binds together by passion and knowledge the vast empire of human society, as it is spread over the whole earth, and over all time. The objects of the Poet's thoughts are everywhere; though the eyes and senses of man are, it is true, his favourite guides, yet he will follow wheresoever he can find an atmosphere of sensation in which to move his wings. Poetry is the first and last of all knowledge—it is as immortal as the heart of man. If the labours of Men of science should ever create any material revolution, direct or indirect, in our condition, and in the impressions which we habitually receive, the Poet will sleep then no more than at present; he will be ready to follow the steps of the Man of science, not only in those general indirect effects, but he will be at his side, carrying sensation in the midst of the objects of the science itself. The remotest discoveries of the Chemist, the Botanist, or Mineralogist, will be as proper objects of the Poet's art as any upon which it can be employed, if the time should ever come when these things shall be familiar to us, and the relations under which they are contemplated by the followers of these respective sciences shall be manifestly and palpably material to us as enjoying and suffering beings. If the time should ever come when what is now called science, thus familiarised to men, shall be ready to put on, as it were, a form of flesh and blood, the Poet will lend his divine spirit to aid the transfiguration, and will welcome the Being thus produced, as a dear and genuine inmate of the household of man. . . .

"Relationship and love"

This passionate statement carries us as far from Aristotle as from Sidney. Aristotle, it is true, had spoken of the "peculiar pleasure" of each kind of poetry, but he was far from raising pleasure to a moral principle in the universe. And though there is some relation between Sidney's notion of "moving" and Wordsworth's "carried alive into the heart by passion," there is nothing in common between Sidney's view that the poet creates an ideal world so persuasively that the reader wishes to imitate it in his own behavior and Wordsworth's description of the poet as paying "homage to the native and naked dignity of man." Nor is Wordsworth's view of pleasure any more closely related to Dryden's view of the delight which poetry should give or to Dr Johnson's notion of pleasing. For Wordsworth it is neither the edifying nature of the poet's world, nor the accuracy of his psychological observations, nor the smoothness and agreeableness of his versification, which gives pleasure: it is his ability to body forth in concrete and sensuous terms those basic principles illustrated alike in the mind of man and the workings of nature. The poet "considers man and nature[1] as essentially adapted to each other, and the mind of man as naturally the mirror of the fairest and most interesting properties of nature." Further, "Poetry is the breath and finer spirit of all knowledge; it is the impassioned expression which is in the countenance of all Science." The poet "is the rock of defence for human nature; an upholder and preserver, carrying everywhere with him relationship and love." "The Poet binds together by passion and knowledge the vast empire of human society. . . . he will follow wheresoever he can find an atmosphere of sensation in which to move his wings." He talks of the poet "carrying sensation into the midst of the objects of the science itself." The poet relates men to each other and to the world of external nature through an account of illustrative situations sensuously apprehended and concretely described, and in doing so both demonstrates and increases the pleasure which lies at the heart of all

---

[1] *Nature* being used here, of course, not in Dryden's or Pope's sense, to mean human nature or common sense, but in the modern sense of the non-human physical world and of the universe as a whole.

activity, human and natural. The poet can follow after the particular discoveries of the scientist and relate them to the world of basic human and natural values in a spirit of "relationship and love."

The modern reader may at times feel a certain impatience with Wordsworth's way of putting things. What, he may ask, are those "fairest and most interesting properties of nature" of which the mind of man is a mirror? What is meant by saying that the poet is "the rock of defence for human nature" and how does the poet "bind together the vast empire of human society"? The answer to these questions can be obtained by putting Wordsworth's theories side by side with his practice, by reading his preface in the light of his achievement in his best and most characteristic poems. The "fairest and most interesting properties of nature" are not the most beautiful and most picturesque aspects of natural scenery, but those aspects of the physical world which, when they react on the sensitive mind of the poet, produce, either immediately or, more profoundly, in subsequent recollection, an awareness of some of the basic laws of the human mind, laws which derive from the essential structure of the mind and personality and which are in turn part of the larger pattern of the structure of the universe. These sudden and passionate glimpses into human nature begin with sensation, the sensation of one whose physical senses are peculiarly alert, and proceed through involuntary recollection through conscious meditation and introspection to achieve the final and full awareness which is recorded in the poem. As for the poet being the "rock of defence for human nature," this would seem to mean that the poet, in virtue of his achievement of this kind of awareness, redeems man from triviality and from selfishness by demonstrating the importance of sympathy and the relation of the individual experience to the sum of life. And the poet "binds together the vast empire of human society" by revealing the common psychological laws which underlie all sensation and all sensitivity, and revealing it not by abstract discussion but by showing through the persuasive concrete illustration—which may be drawn from the experience of a humble or even half-witted person, a shepherd, a leech-gatherer, or an idiot boy —the primary laws of human nature. The poet thus reveals the relationship of men both to each other and to the external world.

For Wordsworth, "relationship" is the keyword, rather than "general" or "universal." He is not concerned with Aristotelian probability, in either its psychological or its formal interpretation, but with correspondences and sympathies concretely and passionately illustrated. Further, passion for him is not acquired by stylistic devices but arises from the nature of the poet's perception of his subject, and of the subject itself. The essential quality of the poet's utterance does not depend on its being in verse rather than prose (he would agree with Sidney there) and he is not convincing when he goes on to argue, later in the essay, that by "superadding" meter he gives an additional charm to poetry. From his presentation of his theory one might imagine that for the true poet expression takes care of itself. If only the poet has the right kind of perception, what he has to say will be poetry. This is very different from Pope's "what oft was thought but ne'er so well expressed" (or at least from the popular understanding of that phrase) and, odd though it may seem at first sight, if anything somewhat more closely akin to Johnson's position. Wordsworth could not have taken exception to anybody's praising a poem, as Johnson did Gray's "Elegy," because "it abounds with images which find a mirrour in every mind, and with sentiments to which every bosom returns an echo." It is true, he would have interpreted these phrases differently, but he would have agreed that true poetry strikes an immediate response in the reader—provided, at least, that the reader had had sufficient experience of true poetry to have had his perceptions educated or redeemed from corruption.

The poet "is a man speaking to men," wrote Wordsworth in an earlier part of the preface, and Dryden and Johnson would have immediately agreed. They would not have agreed, however, with Wordsworth's view of the relation of man to the natural world or with his stress on the primary importance of that relationship and the significance of the pleasure with which its recognition was accompanied. Wordsworth removes the instruction from the "instruction and delight" formula of many seventeenth and eighteenth century critics, but saves himself from falling into a simple hedonistic theory by insisting on the moral dignity of pleasure and its universal significance in man and nature. He resolves the Platonic dilemma in a quite new way. Poetry is not an imitation of an imitation, but a concrete and sensuous illustration of both a fact and a relationship which provides pleasure and at the same time shows the universal importance of pleasure. It does not debase men by nourishing their passions, for passions are not debasing but a means of knowledge. Passion, sensation, and pleasure are, under the proper conditions, good and helpful things, conducive to knowledge and to love. It is an answer curiously Platonic in tone though so un-Platonic in its assumptions.

6

Form and the imagination

Wordsworth was clear enough in expressing his view of what the poet did and why what he did was valuable, but he was not clear on the question of how the poet's aim affected his way of writing and of how a poem, as an individual work of literary art, differs from other forms of expression. The metrical element in poetry he tended to regard as an optional adornment, and as for the question of poetic diction, his famous pronouncement there seemed to boil down simply to asserting that since poetry concerns itself with grand elemental facts about man and nature, the poet should avoid "transitory and accidental ornaments" and use simple and elemental language. The old problem of the relation of form and content was thus still unresolved. While not maintaining, as Pope and Dr Johnson would have, that a poem is the handling of a paraphraseable con-

tent in skillful and pleasing versification, and insisting on the uniqueness of the poet's kind of perception, he did not make clear how that
unique perception inevitably sought its uniquely appropriate form—
indeed, he seemed to be content to regard the form as in greater or
less degree suitable rather than uniquely appropriate. For Sidney, it
will be recalled, poetry was the creation of an ideal world, but that
ideal world had to be presented in a persuasive manner so that the
reader would be moved to imitate it: thus though Sidney made a
clear difference between form and content he assigned a definite role
to each. Similarly, Dryden insisted that the poet present "a just and
lively image of human nature," and if the justness was a matter of
content or plot, the liveliness could only be guaranteed by the proper
kind of style or form. For Wordsworth the vitality of the poet's perception seemed to guarantee both its own justness and liveliness, and
the whole form-content problem is left in the air.

Coleridge's inquiry into the peculiar qualities of a poem

In attempting to remedy this defect in Wordsworth's argument, Coleridge put the philosophical inquiry into the nature and value of
poetry on an entirely new footing.

Unfortunately, Coleridge conducted his argument in an elaborate
and ambitiously conceived chain of reasoning which embraced all his
general philosophical principles and proceeded through a series of
what, to the inexpert reader, often appear the most casual digressions.
He never summed up his view of the nature and value of poetry in a
brief and cogent essay, but wound into his argument in a manner
which, though brilliant and exciting to the careful and sympathetic
reader, is disconcerting to anybody who wants to get at his argument
quickly, or to expound and illustrate it briefly. The nearest we can
get to a single short essay summing up his view of poetry is the famous
fourteenth chapter of his *Biographia Literaria* (published in 1817)
and the succinct and somewhat cryptic paragraph on the imagination
in chapter thirteen; but in both these discussions we miss a great deal
if we have not followed carefully the previous winding argument.
With this warning, therefore, we proceed to quote from the fourteenth chapter of the *Biographia:*

The office of philosophical *disquisition* consists in just *distinction;* while it is the priviledge of the philosopher to preserve himself constantly aware, that distinction is not division. In order to obtain adequate notions of any truth, we must intellectually separate its distinguishable parts; and this is the technical *process* of philosophy. But having so done, we must then restore them in our conceptions to the unity, in which they actually co-exist; and this is the *result* of philosophy. A poem contains the same elements as a prose composition; the difference therefore must consist in a different combination of them, in consequence of a different object being proposed. According to the difference of the object will be the difference of the combination. It is possible, that the object may be merely to facilitate the recollection of any given facts or observations by artificial arrangement; and the composition will be a poem, merely because it is distinguished from prose by metre, or by rhyme, or by both conjointly. In this, the lowest sense, a man might attribute the name of a poem to the well-known enumeration of the days in the several months;

"Thirty days hath September,
April, June, and November," &c.

and others of the same class and purpose. And as a particular pleasure is found in anticipating the recurrence of sounds and quantities, all compositions that have this charm super-added, whatever be their contents, *may* be entitled poems.

So much for the superficial *form.* A difference of object and contents supplies an additional ground of distinction. The immediate purpose may be the communication of truths; either of truth absolute and demonstrable, as in works of science; or of facts experienced and recorded, as in history. Pleasure, and that of the highest and most permanent kind, may *result* from the *attainment* of the end; but it is not itself the immediate end. In other works the communication of pleasure may be the immediate purpose; and though truth, either moral or intellectual, ought to be the *ultimate* end, yet this will distinguish the character of the author, not the class to which the work belongs. Blest indeed is that state of society, in which the immediate purpose would be baffled by the perversion of the proper ultimate end. . . .

But the communication of pleasure may be the immediate object of a work not metrically composed; and that object may have been in a high degree attained, as in novels and romances. Would then the mere super-addition of metre, with or without rhyme, entitle *these* to the name of poems? The answer is, that nothing can permanently please, which does not contain in itself the reason why it is so, and not otherwise. If metre be superadded, all other parts must be made consonant with it. They must be such, as to justify the perpetual and distinct attention to each part, which an exact correspondent recurrence of accent and sound are calculated to excite. The final definition, then, so deduced, may be thus worded. A poem is that species of composition, which is opposed to works of science, by proposing for its *immediate* object pleasure, not truth; and from all other species (having *this* object in common with it) it is discriminated by proposing to itself such delight from the *whole*, as is compatible with a distinct gratification from each component *part*.

Controversy is not seldom excited in consequence of the disputants attaching each a different meaning to the same word; and in few instances has this been more striking, than in disputes concerning the present subject. If a man chooses to call every composition a poem, which is rhyme, or measure, or both, I must leave his opinion uncontroverted. The distinction is at least competent to characterize the writer's intention. If it were subjoined, that the whole is likewise entertaining or affecting, as a tale, or as a series of interesting reflections, I of course admit this as another fit ingredient of a poem, and an additional merit. But if the definition sought for be that of a *legitimate* poem, I answer, it must be one, the parts of which mutually support and explain each other; all in their proportion harmonizing with, and supporting the purpose and known influences of metrical arrangement. The philosophic critics of all ages coincide with the ultimate judgement of all countries, in equally denying the praises of a just poem, on the one hand, to a series of striking lines or distiches, each of which, absorbing the whole attention of the reader to itself, disjoins it from its context, and makes it a separate whole, instead of an harmonizing part; and on the other hand, to an unsustained composition, from which the reader collects rapidly the general result, unattracted by the component parts. The reader should be carried forward, not merely or chiefly by the mechanical impulse of curiosity, or by a restless desire to arrive at the final solution; but by the pleasurable activity of mind excited by the attractions of the journey itself. Like the motion of a serpent, which the Egyptians made the emblem of intellectual power; or like the path of sound through the air; at every step he pauses and half recedes, and from the retrogressive movement collects the force which again carries him onward. "Praecipitandus est *liber* spiritus" ["the *free* spirit must be hastened along"], says Petronius Arbiter most happily. The epithet, *liber*, here balances the preceding verb; and it is not easy to conceive more meaning condensed in fewer words.

What Coleridge is inquiring into here are the differentiating qualities of poetry and the *raison d'être* of these differentiating qualities. Philosophy begins by making just distinctions and ends by discovering

how these distinguished characteristics form a unity among themselves. How does a poem differ from other ways of handling language? What is the point of its so differing? How are these points of
difference justified by the function and nature ("object and contents") of a poem? This is what might be called the ontological approach: let us look at this phenomenon and see what it *is* and then see
if we can account for what it is in terms of what it does. Sidney
talked about what poetry might be made to do; Dryden of what it
should do; Wordsworth of what went on in the poet's mind: but Coleridge, using Aristotle's method though not looking in quite the same
way at quite the same phenomena, restores philosophical responsibility to the esthetic inquiry.

"A poem contains the same elements as a prose composition." Both
use words. The difference between a poem and a prose composition
cannot, then, lie in the medium, for each employs the same medium,
words. It must therefore "consist in a different combination of them, in
consequence of a different object being proposed." A poem combines
words differently, because it is seeking to do something different. Of course, all it may be seeking to do may be to facilitate memory. You may take a piece of prose and cast it into rhymed and metrical form in order to remember it better. And rhyming tags of that
kind, with their recurring "sounds and quantities," yield a particular
pleasure too, though not of a very high order. If one wants to give the
name of poem to a composition of this kind, there is no reason why
one should not. It is a question of semantics, as we would put it today.
But we should note that, though such rhyming tags have the charm of
meter and rhyme, meter and rhyme have been "superadded" (Coleridge is ironically using Wordsworth's term); they do not arise from
the nature of the content but have been imposed on it in order to
make it more easily memorized.

The "superficial form," the externalities, provide however no profound logical reason for distinguishing between different ways of
handling language. "A difference of object and contents supplies an
additional ground of distinction." The philosopher will seek to differentiate between two ways of handling language by asking what each
seeks to achieve and how that aim determines its nature. The immediate purpose may be the communication of truth, or the communication of pleasure. The communication of truth might in turn yield a
deep pleasure (we may get a profound pleasure from reading a work
of science or history), but, Coleridge insists, one must distinguish be-

tween the ultimate and the immediate end. Similarly, if the immediate aim be the communication of pleasure, truth may nevertheless be the ultimate end, and while in an ideal society nothing that was not truth could yield pleasure, in society as it has always existed a literary work might communicate pleasure without having any concern with "truth, either moral or intellectual." The proper kinds of distinction between different kinds of writing can thus be most logically discussed in terms of the difference in the immediate aim, or function, of each. The immediate aim of poetry is to give pleasure.

Clearly this is not going far enough. "The communication of pleasure may be the immediate object of a work not metrically composed" —in novels, for example. Do we make these into poems simply by superadding meter with or without rhyme? To which Coleridge replies by emphasizing a very important principle: you cannot derive true and permanent pleasure out of any feature of a work which does not arise naturally from the total nature of that work. To "superadd" meter is to provide merely a superficial decorative charm. "Nothing can permanently please, which does not contain in itself the reason why it is so, and not otherwise. If meter be superadded, all other parts must be made consonant with it." Rhyme and meter involve "an exact correspondent recurrence of accent and sound" which in turn "are calculated to excite" a "perpetual and distinct attention to each part." A poem, therefore, must be an organic unity in the sense that, while we note and appreciate each part, to which the regular recurrence of accent and sound draw attention, our pleasure in the whole develops cumulatively out of such appreciation, which is at the same time pleasurable in itself and conducive to an awareness of the total pattern of the complete poem.

Thus a poem differs from a work of scientific prose in having as its immediate object pleasure and not truth, and it differs from other kinds of writing which have pleasure and not truth as their immediate object by the fact that in a poem the pleasure we take from the whole work is compatible with and even led up to by the pleasure we take in each component part. You can if you like, Coleridge repeats, call anything in rhyme or in meter or in both a poem, but a *legitimate* poem is a composition in which the rhyme and the meter bear an organic relation to the total work; in it "the parts mutually support and explain each other, all in their proportion harmonizing with, and supporting the purpose and known influences of metrical arrangement." A true poem is neither a striking series of lines or verses, each complete in it-self and bearing no necessary relation to the rest of the work, nor the kind of loosely knit work where we gather the general gist from the conclusion without having been led into the unique reality of the work by the component parts as they unfolded. The differentiating quality of a poem is thus its special kind of form, and it is this which provides both its function and its justification. What sort of a justifica-tion is this?

"Poems" and "poetry"

Before we investigate this question any further, we might interrupt the argument to note that, unlike Sidney and some of the other critics we have been discussing, Coleridge is not here talking about imagina-tive literature in general, but about poems. Is Coleridge's view of what constitutes a poem then unrelated to any larger view of the nature of imaginative literature? Does Coleridge's contribution to critical the-ory consist simply of the notion that in a "legitimate" poem the rela-tion between the parts and the whole is so intimate, so "organic," that a total harmony of expression results, and form and content become different aspects of the same thing? That, indeed, is what many mod-ern critics have made of Coleridge's position, as we shall see; but in fact Coleridge's view was much more comprehensive than this. The clue to Coleridge's general theory is to be found in a distinction he proceeds to make immediately after his definition of a legitimate poem. It is a distinction between "a poem" and "poetry."

But if this should be admitted as a satisfactory character of a poem, we have still to seek for a definition of poetry. The writings of PLATO, and Bishop TAYLOR, and the "Theoria Sacra" of BURNET, furnish undeniable proofs that poetry of the highest kind may exist without metre, and even without the contra-distinguishing objects of a poem. The first chapter of Isaiah (indeed a very large portion of the whole book) is poetry in the most emphatic sense; yet it would be not less irrational than strange to as-sert, that pleasure, and not truth, was the immediate object of the prophet. In short, whatever *specific* import we attach to the word, poetry, there will be found involved in it, as a necessary consequence, that a poem of any length neither can be, or ought to be, all poetry. Yet if an harmonious whole is to be produced, the remaining parts must be preserved *in keeping* with the poetry; and this can be no otherwise effected than by such a studied selection and artificial arrangement, as will partake of *one*, though not a *peculiar* property of poetry. And this again can be no other than the property of exciting a more continuous and equal attention than the language of prose aims at, whether colloquial or written.

My own conclusions on the nature of poetry, in the strictest use of the word, have been in part anticipated in the preceding disquisition on the fancy and imagination.* What is poetry? is so nearly the same question with, what is a poet? that the answer to the one is involved in the solution of the other. For it is a distinction resulting from the poetic genius itself, which sustains and modifies the images, thoughts, and emotions of the poet's own mind.

The poet, described in *ideal* perfection, brings the whole soul of man into activity, with the subordination of its faculties to each other, according to their relative worth and dignity. He diffuses a tone and spirit of unity, that blends, and (as it were) *fuses*, each into each, by that synthetic and magical power, to which we have exclusively appropriated the name of imagination. This power, first put in action by the will and understanding, and retained under their irremissive, though gentle and unnoticed, controul (*laxis effertur habenis*) reveals itself in the balance or reconciliation of opposite or discordant qualities: of sameness, with difference; of the general, with the concrete; the idea, with the image; the individual, with the representative; the sense of novelty and freshness, with old and familiar objects; a more than usual state of emotion, with more than usual order; judgement ever awake and steady self-possession, with enthusiasm and feeling profound or vehement; and while it blends and harmonizes the natural and the artificial, still subordinates art to nature; the manner to the matter; and our admiration of the poet to our sympathy with the poetry. "Doubtless," as Sir John Davies observes of the soul (and his words may

* The IMAGINATION then, I consider either as primary, or secondary. The primary IMAGINATION I hold to be the living Power and prime Agent of all human Perception, and as a repetition in the finite mind of the eternal act of creation in the infinite I AM. The secondary Imagination I consider as an echo of the former, co-existing with the conscious will, yet still as identical with the primary in the *kind* of its agency, and differing only in *degree*, and in the *mode* of its operation. It dissolves, diffuses, dissipates, in order to re-create; or where this process is rendered impossible, yet still at all events it struggles to idealize and to unify. It is essentially *vital*, even as all objects (*as* objects) are essentially fixed and dead.

Fancy, on the contrary, has no other counters to play with, but fixities and definites. The Fancy is indeed no other than a mode of Memory emancipated from the order of time and space; while it is blended with, and modified by that empirical phenomenon of the will, which we express by the word CHOICE. But equally with the ordinary memory the Fancy must receive all its materials ready made from the law of association.—*Biographia Literaria*, Chapter XIII.

with slight alternation be applied, and even more appropriately, to the
poetic IMAGINATION)

> "Doubtless this could not be, but that she turns
>   Bodies to spirit by sublimation strange,
> As fire converts to fire the things it burns,
>   As we our food into our nature change.
>
> From their gross matter she abstracts their forms,
>   And draws a kind of quintessence from things;
> Which to her proper nature she transforms,
>   To bear them light on her celestial wings.
>
> Thus does she, when from individual states
>   She doth abstract the universal kinds;
> Which then re-clothed in divers names and fates
>   Steal access through our senses to our minds."

Finally, GOOD SENSE is the BODY of poetic genius, FANCY its DRAPERY, MO-
TION its LIFE, and IMAGINATION the SOUL that is everywhere, and in each;
and forms all into one graceful and intelligent whole.

This is not an easy argument to follow, and it has puzzled many
commentators. Shawcross, in his standard edition of the *Biographia*,
comments: "It is doubtful whether the distinction [between 'poem'
and 'poetry'], as here drawn, makes for clearness, or indeed whether it
can be fairly drawn at all. Coleridge gives no real justification of the
bold statement that 'a poem of any length neither can be or ought to
be, all poetry,' and instead of reaching a clear definition of poetry he
contents himself with a description of the *poet*, which in its turn resolves into an enumeration of the characteristics of the Imagination."
But there is a logic in Coleridge's development of the argument, and if
we can follow it, it becomes clear why a definition of poetry turns
into a description of the poet which in turn becomes a discussion of
Imagination. Poetry for Coleridge is a wider category than that of
"poem"; that is, poetry is a kind of activity which can be engaged in
by painters or philosophers or scientists and is not confined to those
who employ metrical language, or even to those who employ language
of any kind. Poetry, in this larger sense, brings "the whole soul of
man" into activity, with each faculty playing its proper part according to its "relative worth and dignity." This takes place whenever the
"secondary imagination" comes into operation. We can only under-

stand what poetry in this larger sense really is, if we appreciate the way in which the human faculties are employed together in its production. Thus Coleridge (like Wordsworth in his method, though differing from him in premises and conclusions) defines poetry through an account of how the poet works: the poet works through the exercise of his Imagination. Whenever the synthesizing, the integrating, powers of what Coleridge calls the secondary imagination are at work, bringing all aspects of a subject into a complex unity, then poetry in this larger sense results. Poetry in the narrower sense—that is, a *poem*—may well use the same elements as a work of poetry in the larger sense (the first chapter of the book of Isaiah, for example) but it differs from the work of poetry in the larger sense by combining its elements in a different way, "in consequence of a different object being proposed." That different object is the immediate communication of pleasure. But since a poem is also poetry, the communication of pleasure may be its immediate object but is not its whole function. A poem is distinguished from the other arts (which also have as their immediate object the communication of pleasure) by the fact that its medium is language; it is distinguished from works of literature that are not poems "by proposing to itself such delight from the *whole,* as is compatible with a distinct gratification from each component part." But though a poem is to be distinguished from science, from the non-literary arts, and from other kinds of literature, and its uniqueness can be seen only when we have made these distinctions, it is, like other kinds of poetry (in the larger sense), a product of the secondary imagination, of the "esemplastic power," the unifying power which enables all the faculties to be brought into play simultaneously, each playing its proper part, to produce a complex synthesis of comprehension. And that, of course, is a significant part of its function.

It might have been easier for the reader if Coleridge had first defined Imagination, then discussed the various kinds of activities which can be undertaken by the "secondary imagination," which would involve a discussion of "poetry" in the wider sense he gives the term, and only then gone on to discuss a "poem," which, however much it requires to be distinguished from things that are not poems, must also be seen as one kind of "poetry" in this larger sense. The reasons why he preferred a more circuitous method of approach are bound up with his whole purpose in writing the *Biographia Literaria,* and it would take us too far afield to discuss them here. Suffice it to note that for

Coleridge "poetry" is a wider category than "poem" and is to be explained in terms of the way the imagination functions.

The imagination

Coleridge begins, then, with the imagination, which in its primary manifestation is the great ordering principle—or rather, an agency which enables us both to discriminate and to order, to separate and to synthesize, and thus makes perception possible (for without it we should have only a collection of meaningless sense data). If the act of creation is conceived as being essentially and perpetually the bringing of order out of chaos, destroying chaos by making its parts intelligible by the assertion of the identity of the designer, as it were, then the primary imagination is essentially creative and "a repetition in the finite mind of the eternal act of creation in the infinite I AM."

The secondary imagination is the conscious human use of this power. When we employ our primary imagination in the very act of perception we are not doing so with our conscious will but are exercising the basic faculty of our awareness of ourselves and the external world; the secondary imagination is more conscious and less elemental, but it does not differ in kind from the primary. It projects and creates new harmonies of meaning. The employment of the secondary imagination is, in the larger sense, a poetic activity, and we can see why Coleridge is led from a discussion of a poem to a discussion of the poet's activity when we realize that for him the poet belongs to the larger company of those who are distinguished by the activity of their imagination. A poem is always the work of a poet, of a man employing the secondary imagination and so achieving the harmony of meaning, the reconciliation of opposites, and so on, which Coleridge so stresses; but a poem is also a specific work of art produced by a special handling of language. The harmony and reconciliation resulting from the special kind of creative awareness achieved by the exercise of the imagination cannot operate over an extended composition: one could not sustain that blending and balance, that reconciliation "of sameness, with difference; of the general, with the concrete; the idea, with the image; the individual, with the representative; the sense of novelty and freshness, with old and familiar objects" and so on, for an indefinite period. In a long poem, therefore, which would not be all poetry, a style appropriate to poetry though not the peculiar property of poetry should be used throughout: the style to choose should be one which has "the property of exciting a more continuous and equal attention than the language of prose aims at, whether colloquial or written." Thus we come back to the definition of a "legitimate" poem as a work "the parts of which mutually support and explain each other; all in their proportion harmonizing with, and supporting the purpose and known influences of metrical arrangement." Rhyme and meter are appropriate to a poem considered in the larger sense of poetry, because they are means (though not the only means) of achieving harmonization, reconciliation of opposites, and so forth, which, as we have seen, are objects of poetry in its widest imaginative meaning; being a means of achieving poetry, and also capable of being used on their own, as it were, without necessarily producing or being produced by poetry, they can appropriately be employed in long works both in the parts that are poetry and in the parts that are not.

The immediate object of a poem is pleasure, not truth; the immediate object of poetry in the larger sense may be truth (as in the case of the first chapter of Isaiah) or it may be pleasure. The criterion of a poem *qua* poem is the degree to which it provides immediate pleasure by "proposing to itself such delight from the *whole*, as is compatible with a distinct gratification from each component *part*." This special kind of unity, which makes rhyme and meter no mere ornaments but an essential part of the cumulative achievement, is both pleasing and valuable. But the pleasure lies in the poem's special qualities as a poem while its value derives from its qualities as poetry. Ideally, the good poet always achieves the special kind of pleasure to be derived from a poem by using language in the appropriate way, and that use of language, in producing a work which pleases by proposing to itself such delight from the whole as is compatible with a distinct gratification from each component part, is also the means of diffusing "a tone and spirit of unity, that blends, and (as it were) *fuses*, each into each, by that synthetic and magical power, to which we have exclusively appropriated the name of imagination." Ideally, that is to say, the qualities which make a poem a "legitimate" poem at the same time result from and illustrate the working of the imagination. And the working of the imagination, which is the achievement of poetry, at its highest and most ideal organizes into a harmony and employs simultaneously all the faculties together. "The poet, described in *ideal* perfection, brings the whole soul of man into activity, with the subordination of its faculties to each other, according to their relative worth and dignity." The ideal poet in producing a poem is also using his imagination and producing poetry of the highest kind. The value of a poem, then, must derive partly from its qualities as poetry (so that its value would be that it achieves and communicates that great imaginative synthesis which is both valuable in itself and a special kind of awareness or insight).

Unity and form

The notion of organic unity is common to Coleridge's view of poetry in the larger sense and of a poem as a special handling of language. "Nothing can permanently please, which does not contain in itself the reason why it is so, and not otherwise," he remarked in discussing the place of rhyme and meter in a poem. Nothing that is "super-added," merely stuck on for ornament or decoration, can really please in a poem: every one of its characteristics must *grow out* of its whole nature and be an integral part of it. (It is true that in a long poem, which for Coleridge "neither can be, or ought to be, all poetry" a "harmonious whole" is produced by keeping the non-poetic parts in the same general style and tone as the rest and thus it can hardly be said that all the characteristics of the whole poem develop organically from its essential nature.) This is related to Coleridge's distinction between imagination and fancy. The former is more fitted to achieve true unity of expression: "it dissolves, diffuses, dissipates, in order to re-create . . . It is essentially *vital*. . . ." But fancy "has no other counters to play with but fixities and definites." Fancy constructs surface decorations out of new combinations of memories and perceptions, while the imagination "generates and produces a form of its own." The operation of the imagination can be compared to organic or biological growth and the forms it produces are organic forms, developing under its "shaping and modifying power" which is contrasted with "the aggregative and associative power" of the fancy. The imagination enables the poet to achieve design which is described not in mechanistic but in biological terms, not a fitting together of a number of separable parts but a flowering forth of central unity.

These biological metaphors are used by Coleridge when discussing the nature and function of the imagination rather than in describing the structure of a poem, and thus belong more properly to his definition of "poetry" than to that of "a poem." They help him to describe that unifying and harmonizing activity which is the essence of the poetic process in the larger sense. But it is not difficult to see a connection between this and his definition of a "legitimate" poem. His objection to mere "superadding," his insistence that nothing which does not contain in itself the reason why it is so and not otherwise, which form part of his definition of a "legitimate" poem, are, on a lower level, the same thing as his emphasis on the imagination as "essentially vital," as a faculty which "generates and produces a form of its own" and whose rules "are themselves the very powers of growth and production." The general activity of the imagination which he calls poetry, and the particular structure of words which he calls a poem, are related not only in that the latter (if successful) is a special case of the former, but also in that the kind of pleasure produced by a poem derives from an ordering of language comparable to that larger ordering and harmonizing of "opposite or discordant qualities" which is the great function of the secondary imagination.

We remarked earlier that for Coleridge the differentiating quality of a poem is its special kind of form, and it is this which provides both its function and its justification; and we asked "What sort of a justification is this?" To answer that question we had to follow Coleridge into his difficult discussion of the difference between poetry and a poem, which in turn led us to his view of the nature and function of the imagination. The question has, we hope, been answered in the process of this further discussion. To see all that a poem is, on Coleridge's view, one must take into account both the special characteristics of a poem and the general nature of poetic activity. The latter (which embraces more than the writing of poems) is bound up with the imagination, and on the creative, unifying, and regenerative powers of the imagination the case must finally rest. Form may yield pleasure and pleasure may in itself be valuable; but true organic form is an achievement of the imagination and as such (at least ideally) "brings the whole soul of man into activity." It is in the last analysis through his new definition of the imagination that Coleridge is able to escape completely from Plato's dilemma.

7

Platonism against Plato

SHELLEY's *Defence of Poetry*, written in 1821 and published in 1840, was originally conceived as the defense of the value of poetry against the arguments brought forward by Thomas Love Peacock in *The Four Ages of Poetry* that poetry had outlived its usefulness and in an age of knowledge, reason, and enlightenment appealed only to obscurantism and superstition. But as the work developed the polemic element disappeared and the essay emerged as a large theoretical statement of the nature and value of poetry modeled in general style on Sidney's *Defence* though lacking the simple didacticism so important to Sidney's position. Shelley's argument is conducted in terms of passionate abstractions, and in this respect is reminiscent of some of the great renaissance critical documents. It is in a sense an anachronism, for, though Shelley follows Coleridge in his stress on the function of the imagination, he is not developing Coleridge's position but re-interpreting it in the light of his own Platonic idealism. Shelley's interest as a critic, indeed, lies largely in his use of Platonic ideas to escape from the Platonic dilemma, and he does this by recognizing that the poet, through his use of the imagination, comes directly into contact with the world of Platonic ideas, and so with true reality, instead of simply imitating the reflections of those ideas, as Plato himself claimed.

Poetry and the Platonic idea

Such a view of the function of the imagination inevitably involved the defense of poetry in the defense of something larger than poetry, just as Coleridge in discussing a poem is led to consider the wider imaginative activity of which a poem is a special case. For Shelley any exercise of the imagination which brought one into contact with the Platonic idea underlying the ordinary phenomena of experience was, in the larger sense, poetry.

Poetry, in a general sense, may be defined to be "the expression of the imagination"; and poetry is connate with the origin of man. . . . In the youth of the world, men dance and sing and imitate natural objects, observing in these actions, as in all others, a certain rhythm or order. And, although all men observe a similar, they observe not the same order, in the motions of the dance, in the melody of the song, in the combinations of the language, in the series of their imitations of natural objects. For there is a certain order or rhythm belonging to each of these classes of mimetic representation, from which the hearer and the spectator receive an intenser and purer pleasure than from any other: the sense of an approximation to this order has been called taste by modern writers. Every man in the infancy of art observes an order which approximates more or less closely to that from which this highest delight results: but the diversity is not sufficiently marked, as that its gradations should be sensible, except in those instances where the predominance of this faculty of approximation to the beautiful (for so we may be permitted to name the relation between this highest pleasure and its cause) is very great. Those in whom it exists in excess are poets, in the most universal sense of the word; and the pleasure resulting from the manner in which they express the influence of society or nature upon their own minds, communicates itself to others, and gathers a sort of reduplication from that community. Their language is vitally metaphorical; that is, it marks the before unapprehended relations of things and perpetuates their apprehension, until the words which represent them become, through time, signs for portions or classes of thoughts instead of pictures of integral thoughts; and then if no new poets should arise to create afresh the associations which have been thus disorganized, language will be dead to all the nobler purposes of human intercourse. These similitudes or relations are finely said by Lord Bacon to be 'the same footsteps of nature impressed upon the various subjects of the world';[1] and he considers the faculty which perceives them as the storehouse of axioms common to all knowledge. In the infancy of society every author is necessarily a poet, because language itself is poetry; and to be a poet is to apprehend the true and the beautiful, in a word, the good which exists in the relation, subsisting, first between existence and perception, and secondly between perception and expression. Every original language near to its source is in itself the chaos of a cyclic poem: the copiousness of lexicography and the distinctions of grammar are the works of a later age, and are merely the catalogue and the form of the creations of poetry.

But poets, or those who imagine and express this indestructible order, are not only the authors of language and of music, of the dance, and architecture, and statuary, and painting; they are the institutors of laws, and the founders of civil society, and the inventors of the arts of life, and the teachers, who draw into a certain propinquity with the beautiful and the true, that partial apprehension of the agencies of the invisible world which is called religion. Hence all original religions are allegorical, or susceptible of allegory, and, like Janus, have a double face of false and true. Poets, according to the circumstances of the age and nation in which they appeared, were called, in the earlier epochs of the world, legislators, or prophets: a poet essentially comprises and unites both these characters. For he not only beholds intensely the present as it is, and discovers those laws according to which present things ought to be ordered, but he beholds the future in the present, and his thoughts are the germs of the flower and the fruit of latest time. Not that I assert poets to be prophets in the gross sense of the word, or that they can foretell the form as surely as they foreknow the spirit of events: such is the pretence of superstition, which would make poetry an attribute of prophecy, rather than prophecy an attribute of poetry. A poet participates in the eternal, the infinite, and the one; as far as related to his conceptions, time and place and number are not. The grammatical forms which express the moods of time, and the difference of persons, and the distinction of place, are convertible with respect to the highest poetry without injuring it as poetry; and the choruses of Aeschylus, and the book of *Job*, and Dante's *Paradise*, would afford, more than any other writings, examples of this fact, if the limits

[1] *De Augment. Scient.*, cap.i, lib.iii.

of this essay did not forbid citation. The creations of sculpture, painting, and music, are illustrations still more decisive.

Language and the imagination

Primitive language is poetic because it is used freshly by those who, through language, are discovering for themselves the nature of reality. Only when language has become worn and the "vital metaphors" of which it is composed have become dead metaphors, does it become "dead to all the nobler purposes of human intercourse." A correspondence with the ideal order of things, which is what we mean by beauty, is achieved by "a certain order or rhythm belonging to each of these classes of mimetic representation" (in dance, music, and poetry proper) and recognition of that achievement, or of an approach to it, is called taste. The achievement of a correspondence to the ideal order of things can be effected through any one of the arts or through lawmakers, politicians, and founders of religions. For there is an ideal legal order, an ideal social order, and an ideal moral order, as well as that more general ideal of order which we call beauty. And the legal, social, and moral orders are themselves bound up with beauty and part of it, so that "the institutors of laws, and the founders of civil society, and the inventors of the arts of life, and the teachers, who draw into a certain propinquity with the beautiful and the true" can all be called poets.

Language, colour, form, and religious and civil habits of action, are all the instruments and materials of poetry; they may be called poetry by that figure of speech which considers the effect as a synonyme of the cause. But poetry in a more restricted sense expresses those arrangements of language, and especially metrical language, which are created by that imperial faculty, whose throne is curtained within the invisible nature of man. And this springs from the nature itself of language, which is a more direct representation of the actions and passions of our internal being, and is susceptible of more various and delicate combinations, than colour, form, or motion, and is more plastic and obedient to the control of that faculty of which it is the creation. For language is arbitrarily produced by the imagination, and has relation to thoughts alone; but all other materials, instruments, and conditions of art, have relations among each other, which limit and interpose between conception and expression. The former is as a mirror which reflects, the latter as a cloud which enfeebles, the light of which both are mediums of communication. Hence the fame of sculptors, painters, and musicians, although the intrinsic powers of the great masters of these arts may yield in no degree to that of those who have employed language as the hieroglyphic of their thoughts, has never equalled that of poets in the restricted sense of the term; as two performers of equal skill will produce unequal effects from a guitar and a harp. The fame of legislators and founders of religions, so long as their institutions last, alone seems to exceed that of poets in the restricted sense; but it can scarcely be a question, whether, if we deduct the celebrity which their flattery of the gross opinions of the vulgar usually conciliates, together with that which belonged to them in their higher character of poets, any excess will remain.

Language is the most effective servant of the imagination because the imagination itself produces it for its own needs, while the media of the other arts exist in the external word independently of the artist and their position in the external world limits their effectiveness as means of expressing an imaginative vision. That gives the poet a superiority to other artists, including legislators and founders of religions. (This is hardly a fair argument of Shelley's. Language is also used, in the give and take of daily conversation, for non-imaginative purposes, and even if, as Shelley claims, language originally arose as an instrument of the imagination, Shelley also admitted earlier that it soon lost that metaphorical liveliness.)

If language is the ideal medium in which the imagination seeks expression, one must make a further distinction between metrical and unmetrical language:

We have thus circumscribed the word poetry within the limits of that art which is the most familiar and the most perfect expression of the faculty itself. It is necessary, however, to make the circle still narrower, and to determine the distinction between measured and unmeasured language; for the popular division into prose and verse is inadmissable in accurate philosophy.

Sounds as well as thoughts have relation both between each other and towards that which they represent, and a perception of the order of those relations has always been found connected with a perception of the order of the relations of thoughts. Hence the language of poets has ever affected a certain uniform and harmonious recurrence of sound, without which it were not poetry, and which is scarcely less indispensable to the communication of its influence, than the words themselves, without reference to that peculiar order. Hence the vanity of translation; it were as wise to cast a violet into a crucible that you might discover the formal principle of its colour and odour, as seek to transfuse from one language into another the creations of a poet. The plant must spring again from its seed, or it will bear no flower—and this is the burthen of the curse of Babel.

Harmony of utterance, achieved by the proper choice of words and the relation of sound to sense among the words, is part of the way in which the imagination achieves a correspondence with the ideal order, and thus translation from one language into another, which means loss of this unique relation, is well-nigh impossible. One might note also in Shelley's urging of this position that he uses a botanical metaphor in a very Coleridgean manner. Sound and sense come together as an organic whole, as the seed grows into a flower, and they cannot be put together mechanically.

Poetry, harmony, and truth

Shelley continues:

An observation of the regular mode of the recurrence of harmony in the language of poetical minds, together with its relation to music, produced metre, or a certain system of traditional forms of harmony and language. Yet it is by no means essential that a poet should accommodate his language to this traditional form, so that [so long as] the harmony, which is its spirit, be observed. The practice is indeed convenient and popular, and to be preferred, especially in such composition as includes much action: but every great poet must inevitably innovate upon the example of his predecessors in the exact structure of his peculiar versification. The distinction between poets and prose writers is a vulgar error. The distinction between philosophers and poets has been anticipated. Plato was essentially a poet—the truth and splendour of his imagery, and the melody of his language, are the most intense that it is possible to conceive. He rejected the measure of the epic, dramatic, and lyrical forms, because he sought to kindle a harmony in thoughts divested of shape and action, and he forbore to invent any regular plan of rhythm which would include, under determinate forms, the varied pauses of his style. Circero sought to imitate the cadence of his periods, but with little success. Lord Bacon was a poet.[2] His language has a sweet and majestic rhythm, which satisfies the sense, no less than the almost superhuman wisdom of his philosophy satisfies the intellect; it is a strain which distends, and then bursts the circumference of the reader's mind, and pours itself forth together with it into

[2] See the *Filum Labyrinthi*, and the Essay on Death particularly.

the universal element with which it has perpetual sympathy. All the authors of revolutions in opinion are not only necessarily poets as they are inventors, nor even as their words unveil the permanent analogy of things by images which participate in the life of truth; but as their periods are harmonious and rhythmical, and contain in themselves the elements of verse; being the echo of the eternal music. Nor are those supreme poets, who have employed traditional forms of rhythm on account of the form and action of their subjects, less capable of perceiving and teaching the truth of things, than those who have omitted that form. Shakespeare, Dante, and Milton (to confine ourselves to modern writers) are philosophers of the very loftiest power.

A poem is the very image of life expressed in its eternal truth. There is this difference between a story and a poem, that a story is a catalogue of detached facts, which have no other connexion than time, place, circumstance, cause and effect; the other is the creation of actions according to the unchangeable forms of human nature, as existing in the mind of the Creator, which is itself the image of all other minds. The one is partial, and applies only to a definite period of time, and a certain combination of events which can never again recur; the other is universal, and contains within itself the germ of a relation to whatever motives or actions have place in the possible varieties of human nature. Time, which destroys the beauty and the use of the story of particular facts, stripped of the poetry which should invest them, augments that of poetry, and for ever develops new and wonderful applications of the eternal truth which it contains. Hence epitomes have been called the moths of just history; they eat out the poetry of it. A story of particular facts is as a mirror which obscures and distorts that which should be beautiful: poetry is a mirror which makes beautiful that which is distorted.

The second of the two paragraphs just quoted shows an interesting combination of a purely Platonic position ("A poem is the very image of life expressed in its eternal truth" means that a poem reflects and embodies the Platonic idea of things) with Aristotle's view that poetry is more philosophical than history because it presents the probable and the universal rather than the possible and the particular. But Shelley's position is basically no more Aristotelian than Sidney's. He goes on to argue that "the parts of a composition may be poetical, without the composition as a whole being a poem. A single sentence may be considered as a whole, though it may be found in the midst of a series of unassimilated portions; a single word even may be a spark of inextinguishable thought." If poetry is the revelation of the Platonic idea, then it is possible to hold this position, though we may wonder what becomes of the harmony and order, which for Shelley is so essential a part of ideal truth, in a poetical utterance of only one word. Shelley's position here is equally far from Aristotle and from Coleridge, for Coleridge's distinction between a poem and poetry and his assertion that "a poem of any length neither can be, nor ought to be all poetry" means that the great harmonizing powers of the imagination cannot be sustained indefinitely, not that they can manifest themselves in a single word or phrase. (One remembers Coleridge's objection to "a series of striking lines or distiches, each of which, absorbing the whole attention of the reader to itself, becomes disjoined from its context, and forms a separate whole, instead of a harmonizing part.")

Poetry and pleasure

Shelley, however, agrees with both Wordsworth and Coleridge on the importance of pleasure to poetry: "Poetry is ever accompanied with pleasure: all spirits on which it falls open themselves to receive the wisdom which is mingled with its delight." He does not, as Wordsworth did, go into detail about the source of this pleasure or examine how and why it is bound up with poetry.[3] Shelley's whole method in this essay is sketchy and suggestive: he hurries with rapid eloquence from one point to another, throwing out passionate analogies and soaring generalizations, and sometimes one has to reconstruct his meaning from a knowledge of his views taken from his other works. Having made his point about pleasure, for instance, he hastens on to explain that a poet is rarely appreciated in his own lifetime: "A poet is a nightingale, who sits in darkness and sings to cheer its own solitude with sweet sounds; his auditors are as men entranced by the melody

---

[3] But he gives us a short paragraph on pleasure later in the essay: "It is difficult to define pleasure in its highest sense; the definition involving a number of apparent paradoxes. For, from an inexplicable defect of harmony in the constitution of human nature, the pain of the inferior is frequently connected with the pleasures of the superior portions of our being. Sorrow, terror, anguish, despair itself, are often the chosen expressions of an approximation to the highest good. Our sympathy in tragic fiction depends on this principle; tragedy delights by affording a shadow of the pleasure which exists in pain. This is the source also of the melancholy which is inseparable from the sweetest melody. The pleasure that is in sorrow is sweeter than the pleasure of pleasure itself. And hence the saying, 'It is better to go to the house of mourning, than to the house of mirth.' Not that this highest species of pleasure is necessarily linked with pain. The delight of love and friendship, the ecstasy of the admiration of nature, the joy of the perception and still more of the creation of poetry, is often wholly unalloyed."

of an unseen musician, who feel that they are moved and softened, yet know not whence or why." He is then led to a discussion of Homer's relation to his contemporaries and, somewhat unexpectedly, proceeds to take Sidney's position that Homer's characters embody ideals of human virtue to be imitated by his hearers and readers: "Homer embodied the ideal perfection of his age in human character; nor can we doubt that those who read his verses were awakened to an ambition of becoming like Achilles, Hector, and Ulysses: the truth and beauty of friendship, patriotism, and persevering devotion to an object, were unveiled to the depths in these immortal creations: the sentiments of the auditors must have been refined and enlarged by a sympathy with such great and lovely impersonations, until from admiring they imitated, and from imitation they identified themselves with the objects of their admiration."

Possibilities and limitations of Shelley's view

That Shelley is led to this Sidneyan view that the reader imitates the virtues of the characters described in poetry is some indication of the difficulty he finds in applying concretely his Platonic view of poetry as the embodiment of the Platonic idea. He assumes that the Platonic ideas are all ideas of virtues, so that he is denied even Sidney's defense of comedy as a holding up to scorn of human foibles so that people will not imitate them, and he is equally deprived of a satisfactory theory of tragedy. If his view of the imagination represents a more profound position than Sidney's naive didacticism, he is nevertheless helpless when he comes to apply it in particular instances. It is all very well for him to describe Greek drama, in a later passage, as the employment of "language, action, music, painting, the dance, and religious institutions, to produce a common effect in the representation of the highest idealisms of passion and of power" and to talk of the comic relief in *King Lear* as "universal, ideal, and sublime," but we want to know about the place of evil and suffering in tragedy. We want to know more about how the imagination in fact operates and how what it produces is related to the world of ideal order.

When he discusses the imagination as in itself an instrument of moral good, Shelley is sketching a theory which would emancipate himself from the simpler didacticism of his remark about Homer. His argument here is interesting, and might have been developed further:

The whole objection . . . of the immorality of poetry rests upon a misconception of the manner in which poetry acts to produce the moral improvement of man. Ethical science arranges the elements which poetry has created, and propounds schemes and proposes examples of civil and domestic life: nor is it for want of admirable doctrines that men hate, and despise, and censure, and deceive, and subjugate one another. But poetry acts in another and diviner manner. It awakens and enlarges the mind itself by rendering it the receptacle of a thousand unapprehended combinations of thought. Poetry lifts the veil from the hidden beauty of the world, and makes familiar objects be as if they were not familiar; it reproduces all that it represents, and the impersonations clothed in its Elysian light stand thenceforward in the minds of those who have once contemplated them as memorials of that gentle and exalted content which extends itself over all thoughts and actions with which it coexists. The great secret of morals is love; or a going out of our own nature, and an identification of ourselves with the beautiful which exists in thought, action, or person, not our own. A man to be greatly good, must imagine intensely and comprehensively; he must put himself in the place of another and of many others; the pains and pleasures of his species must become his own. The great instrument of moral good is the imagination; and poetry administers to the effect by acting upon the cause. Poetry enlarges the circumference of the imagination by replenishing it with thoughts of ever new delight, which have the power of attracting and assimilating to their own nature all other thoughts, and which form new intervals and interstices whose void for ever craves fresh food. Poetry strengthens the faculty which is the organ of the moral nature of man, in the same manner as exercise strengthens a limb. A poet therefore would do ill to embody his own conceptions of right and wrong, which are usually those of his place and time, in his poetical creations, which participate in neither. By this assumption of the inferior office of interpreting the effect, in which perhaps after all he might acquit himself but imperfectly, he would resign a glory in a participation in the cause. There was little danger that Homer, or any of the eternal poets, should have so far misunderstood themselves as to have abdicated this throne of their widest dominion. Those in whom the poetical faculty, though great, is less intense, as Euripides, Lucan, Tasso, Spenser, have frequently affected a moral aim, and the effect of their poetry is diminished in exact proportion to the degree in which they compel us to advert to this purpose.

Imagination, sympathy, and morality

The remark that it is not "for want of admirable doctrines that men hate, and despise, and censure, and deceive, and subjugate one another" reminds one of Sidney's arguments against the moral philosophers, who state ethical theories coldly and abstractly while the poet gives a passionate concrete embodiment of them. But here Shelley develops a subtler position than Sidney's. The poet for him does not provide a "speaking picture" of moralty; instead, he makes for moral good by strengthening the imagination. Shelley's argument is conducted through two syllogisms. Sympathy is an instrument of moral good; imagination conduces to sympathy: therefore imagination is an instrument of moral good. Then he takes this conclusion as the major premise of his second syllogism, thus: Imagination is the instrument of moral good; poetry strengthens the imagination: therefore poetry is an instrument of moral good. Poetry has moral effect by strengthening the imagination, which "is the organ of the moral nature of man" because it develops sympathy which is the great instrument of morality. This, if developed, might well have led to a theory of *Einfühlung,* of poetry as producing a reading of oneself *into* a situation, which is full of possibilities. As it is, it emancipates him from the more naive didacticism in which he seems to have got himself entangled earlier. Poetry does not teach directly, by providing concrete examples of good behavior. "A poet . . . would do ill to embody his own conceptions of right and wrong. . . . Those in whom the poetical faculty, though great, is less intense, as Euripides, Lucan, Tasso, Spenser, have frequently affected a moral aim, and the effect of their poetry is diminished in exact proportion to the degree in which they compel us to advert to this purpose." This is a strong statement, and the position it maintains is very far from Sidney's.

But Shelley leaves this point undeveloped and returns to more uncertain ground:

> The drama at Athens, or wheresoever else it may have approached to its perfection, ever co-existed with the moral and intellectual greatness of the age. The tragedies of the Athenian poets are as mirrors in which the spectator beholds himself, under a thin disguise of circumstance, stript of all but that ideal perfection and energy which every one feels to be the internal type of all that he loves, admires, and would become.

And then for a moment he returns to his point about the imagination as strengthening sympathy, to repeat what he had said earlier:

The imagination is enlarged by a sympathy with pains and passions so mighty, that they distend in their conception the capacity of that by which they are conceived; the good affections are strengthened by pity, indignation, terror and sorrow; and an exalted calm is prolonged from the satiety of this high exercise of them into the tumult of familiar life.

This is an interesting twist to an Aristotelian notion. Instead of tragedy *purging* the emotions through pity and fear, it *strengthens the good affections* by pity, indignation, terror, and sorrow. Shelley proceeds to account for the place of evil in tragedy:

Even crime is disarmed of half its horror and all its contagion by being represented as the fatal consequence of the unfathomable agencies of nature; error is thus divested of its wilfulness; men can no longer cherish it as the creation of their choice. In a drama of the highest order there is little food for censure or hatred; it teaches rather self-knowledge and self-respect. Neither the eye nor the mind can see itself, unless reflected upon that which it resembles. The drama, so long as it continues to express poetry, is as a prismatic and many-sided mirror, which collects the brightest rays of human nature and divides and reproduces them from the simplicity of these elementary forms, and touches them with majesty and beauty, and multiplies all that it reflects, and endows it with the power of propagating its like wherever it may fall.

The rush of ideas here is rather bewildering. Crime in drama loses its horror because it is shown as being "the fatal consequence of the unfathomable agencies of nature." One might question whether this is true of any other play than *Oedipus Rex;* but even if it is, one wonders how it is related to the notion he had expressed so eloquently earlier that poetry expresses the indestructible ideal order. Crime is tolerable in drama because it is shown as resulting from a mysterious fatalism: but what, we may ask, is the advantage of that? Shelley then rushes on to a quite new point: drama teaches self-knowledge and self-respect. This is a new justification for poetry, which might well have been developed. The final sentence of this paragraph seems to be a hasty attempt to combine his Platonic theory of poetry as imitating the divine idea with the notion of poetry as refraction through a "prismatic and many-sided mirror" of the elemental forms of life. The process of refraction adds "majesty and beauty" to the original white light, which is an interesting reversal of the position he maintains in "Adonais":

> Life, like a dome of many-coloured glass,
> Stains the white radiance of Eternity.

Poetry and social morality

Shelley then proceeds to show, to his own satisfaction, that drama declines as the morality of social life declines—that is, to make a simple equation of social morality with literary effectiveness. He chooses drama to illustrate his point because "the drama being that form under which a greater number of modes of expression of poetry are susceptible of being combined than any other, the connexion of poetry and social good is more observable in the drama than in whatever other form." His point that "it is indisputable that the highest perfection of human society has ever corresponded with the highest dramatic excellence" is a dubious one, and his development of it one of the most strained parts of the essay. But he concludes this discussion with an interesting echo of Plato's *Ion*:

> But corruption must utterly have destroyed the fabric of human society before poetry can ever cease. The sacred links of that chain have never been entirely disjoined, which descending through the minds of many men is attached to those great minds, whence as from a magnet the invisible effluence is sent forth, which at once connects, animates, and sustains the life of all. It is the faculty which contains within itself the seeds at once of its own and of social renovation.

He concludes this paragraph with a comprehensive view of all works of literature as contributions to one great harmony:

> And let us not circumscribe the effects of the bucolic and erotic poetry within the limits of the sensibility of those to whom it was addressed. They may have perceived the beauty of those immortal compositions, simply as fragments and isolated portions: those who are more finely organized, or, born in a happier age, may recognize them as episodes to that great poem, which all poets, like the co-operating thoughts of one great mind, have built up since the beginning of the world.

Shelley then returns to his earlier, comprehensive definition of poetry as the expression of the ideal order as apprehended by the imagination. "The true poetry of Rome lived in its institutions; for whatever of beautiful, true, and majestic, they contained, could have sprung only from the faculty which creates the order in which they consist." He continues:

The life of Camillus, the death of Regulus; the expectation of the senators, in their godlike state, of the victorious Gauls; the refusal of the republic to make peace with Hannibal, after the battle of Cannae, were not the consequences of a refined calculation of the probable personal advantage to result from such a rhythm and order in the shows of life, to those who were at once the poets and the actors of these immortal dramas. The imagination beholding the beauty of this order, created it out of itself according to its own idea; the consequence was empire, and the reward ever-living fame. These things are not the less poetry, *quia carent vate sacro* [because they lack the holy bard]. They are the episodes of that cyclic poem written by Time upon the memories of man. The Past, like an inspired rhapsodist, fills the theatre of everlasting generations with their harmony.

The place of the poet

Shelley sums up much of the thought of the essay in his final paragraphs, where, in his characteristic rhetorical manner, he pictures the poet as an inspired rhapsodist capturing in language the moments of his contact with the ideal world:

We have more moral, political, and historical wisdom than we know how to reduce into practice; we have more scientific and economical knowledge than can be accommodated to the just distribution of the produce which it multiplies. The poetry in these systems of thought is concealed by the accumulation of facts and calculating processes. There is no want of knowledge respecting what is wisest and best in morals, government, and political economy, or at least what is wiser and better than what men now practice and endure. But we let "*I dare not* wait upon *I would,* like the poor cat in the adage." We want the creative faculty to imagine that which we know; we want the generous impulse to act that which we imagine; we want the poetry of life: our calculations have outrun conception; we have eaten more than we can digest. The cultivation of those sciences which have enlarged the limits of the empire of man over the external world, has, for want of the poetical faculty, proportionally circumscribed those of the internal world; and man, having enslaved the elements, remains himself a slave. To what but a cultivation of the mechanical arts in a degree disproportioned to the presence of the creative faculty, which is the basis of all knowledge, is to be attributed the abuse of all invention for abridging and combining labor, to the exasperation of the inequality of mankind? From what other cause has it arisen that the discoveries which should have lightened have added a weight to the curse imposed on Adam? Poetry, and the principle of Self, of which money is the visible incarnation, are the God and Mammon of the world.

The functions of the poetical faculty are two-fold: by one it creates new materials of knowledge, and power, and pleasure; by the other it engenders in the mind a desire to reproduce and arrange them according to a certain rhythm and order which may be called the beautiful and the good. The cultivation of poetry is never more to be desired than at periods when, from an excess of the selfish and calculating principle, the accumulation of the materials of external life exceed the quantity of the power of assimilating them to the internal laws of human nature. The body has then become too unwieldy for that which animates it.

Poetry is indeed something divine. It is at once the centre and circumference of knowledge; it is that which comprehends all science, and that to which all science must be referred. It is at the same time the root and blossom of all other systems of thought; it is that from which all spring, and that which adorns all; and that which, if blighted, denies the fruit and the seed, and withholds from the barren world the nourishment and the succession of the scions of the tree of life. It is the perfect and consummate surface and bloom of all things; it is as the odor and the color of the rose to the texture of the elements which compose it, as the form and splendor of unfaded beauty to the secrets of anatomy and corruption. What were virtue, love, patriotism, friendship—what were the scenery of this beautiful universe which we inhabit; what were our consolations on this side of the grave—and what were our aspirations beyond it, if poetry did not ascend to bring light and fire from those eternal regions where the owl-winged faculty of calculation dare not ever soar? Poetry is not like reasoning, a power to be exerted according to the determination of the will. A man cannot say, "I will compose poetry." The greatest poet even cannot say it; for the mind in creation is as a fading coal, which some invisible influence, like an inconstant wind, awakens to transitory brightness; this power arises from within, like the color of a flower which fades and changes as it is developed, and the conscious portions of our natures are unprophetic either of its approach or its departure. Could this influence be durable in its original purity and force, it is impossible to predict the greatness of the results; but when composition begins, inspiration is already on the decline, and the most glorious poetry that has ever been communicated to the world is probably a feeble shadow of the original conceptions of the poet. I appeal to the greatest poets of the present day, whether it is not an error to assert that the finest passages of poetry are produced by labor and study. The toil and the delay recommended by critics can be justly interpreted to mean no more than a careful observation of the inspired moments, and an artificial connection of the spaces between their suggestions by the inter-texture of conventional expressions—a necessity only imposed by the limitedness of the poetical faculty itself; for Milton conceived the *Paradise Lost* as a whole before he executed it in portions. We have his own authority also for the muse having "dictated" to him the "unpremeditated song." And let this be an answer to those who would allege the fifty-six various readings of the first line of the *Orlando Furioso*. Compositions so produced are to poetry what mosaic is to painting. The instinct and intuition of the poetical faculty is still more observable in the plastic and pictorial arts; a great statue or picture grows under the power of the artist as a child in the mother's womb; and the very mind which directs the hands in formation is incapable of accounting to itself for the origin, the gradations, or the media of the process.

Poetry is the record of the best and happiest moments of the happiest and best minds. We are aware of evanescent visitations of thought and feeling sometimes associated with place or person, sometimes regarding our own mind alone, and always arising unforeseen and departing unbidden, but elevating and delightful beyond all expression: so that even in the desire and the regret they leave, there cannot but be pleasure, participating as it does in the nature of its object. It is, as it were, the interpenetration of a diviner nature through our own; but its footsteps are like those of a wind over the sea, which the morning calm erases, and whose traces remain only as on the wrinkled sand which paves it. These and corresponding conditions of being are experienced principally by those of the most delicate sensibility and the most enlarged imagination; and the state of mind produced by them is at war with every base desire. The enthusiasm of virtue, love, patriotism, and friendship is essentially linked with such emotions; and, whilst they last, self appears as what it is, an atom to a universe. Poets are not only subject to these experiences as spirits of the most refined organization, but they can color all that they combine with the evanescent hues of this ethereal world; a word, a trait in the representation of a scene or a passion will touch the enchanted chord, and reanimate, in those who have ever experienced these emotions, the sleeping, the cold, the buried image of the past. Poetry thus makes immortal all that is best and most beautiful in the world; it arrests the vanishing apparitions which haunt the interlunations of life, and veiling them, or in language or in form, sends them forth among mankind, bearing sweet news of kindred joy to those with whom their sisters abide—abide, because there is no portal of expression from the caverns of the spirit which they inhabit into the universe of things. Poetry redeems from decay the visitations of the divinity in man.

Poetry turns all things to loveliness; it exalts the beauty of that which is most beautiful, and it adds beauty to that which is most deformed; it marries exultation and horror, grief and pleasure, eternity and change; it subdues to union under its light yoke all irreconcilable things. It transmutes all that it touches, and every form moving within the radiance of its presence is changed by wondrous sympathy to an incarnation of the spirit which it breathes; its secret alchemy turns to potable gold the poisonous waters which flow from death through life; it strips the veil of familiarity from the world, and lays bare the naked and sleeping beauty which is the spirit of its forms. . . .

. . . In spite of the low-thoughted envy which would undervalue contemporary merit, our own will be a memorable age in intellectual achievements, and we live among such philosophers and poets as surpass beyond comparison any who have appeared since the last national struggle for civil and religious liberty. The most unfailing herald, companion, and follower of the awakening of a great people to work a beneficial change in opinion or institution, is poetry. At such periods there is an accumulation of the power of communicating and receiving intense and impassioned conceptions respecting man and nature. The persons in whom this power resides may often, as far as regards many portions of their nature, have little apparent correspondence with that spirit of good of which they are the ministers. But even whilst they deny and abjure, they are yet compelled to serve, the power which is seated on the throne of their own soul. It is impossible to read the compositions of the most celebrated writers of the present day without being startled with the electric life which burns within their words. They measure the circumference and sound the depths of human nature with a comprehensive and all-penetrating spirit, and they are themselves perhaps the most sincerely astonished at its manifestations; for it is less their spirit than the spirit of the age. Poets are the hierophants of an unapprehended inspiration; the mirrors of the gigantic shadows which futurity casts upon the present; the words which express what they understand not; the trumpets which sing to battle, and feel not what they inspire; the influence which is moved not, but moves. Poets are the unacknowledged legislators of the world.

"Poetry is the record of the best and happiest moments of the happiest and best minds." "Poets are the unacknowledged legislators of the world." These are grand—perhaps grandiose—claims for poetry. They are justifiable, but in a sense that needs more particularizing than

Shelley gives us. This high Platonic idealism turned against Plato's attack on poetry to defend the very activity which Plato valued most is curiously impressive though not perhaps very helpful to a critic looking for a careful philosophic definition of the nature and value of poetry and subtle discrimination between poetry and kindred phenomena. Yet Shelley is successful in conveying a sense of the immense significance of poetry even to those who disagree with his position, and his statement is valuable if only as the last of the great general defenses done in the spirit of the Renaissance and with the added enthusiasm of the Romantic movement.

8

Science and poetry

THE QUESTION whether, and in what sense, poetry, was *true* worried many of the earlier critics. Plato, as we have seen, attacked the poets for providing only a second-hand reflection of truth; Aristotle defended the poet as presenting a more significant kind of probability than the mere factual recording of the historian; Sidney, asserting that "the poet nothing lieth because he nothing affirmeth," saw the poet's task not as the literal telling of the truth but as the provision of vivid and lively examples conducive to moral behavior; and Shelley saw the poet as someone who was in touch with the eternal patterns of things that underlie all reality.

The truth of poetry

Between Sidney and Shelley the question of the truth of poetry was little debated; for when you have a flourishing contemporary literature its general value tends to be taken for granted and critical interest is likely to be centered on questions of craftsmanship and the evaluation of particular works. Shelley returned to the question of truth partly because he was influenced by renaissance thought and partly because Thomas Love Peacock had raised the question of whether, in a modern scientific age when philosophers and scientists can investigate reality systematically and vigorously and we have outgrown the myths of poetry, the poet has not become a "semi-barbarian in a civilized community."

Peacock wrote early in the nineteenth century. As Victorian science developed, the question of the relation between science and poetry became more and more urgent. The poet, wrote Peacock, "lives in the days that are past. . . . In whatever degree poetry is cultivated, it must necessarily be to the neglect of some branch of useful study: and it is a lamentable thing to see minds, capable of better things, running to seed in the specious indolence of these empty aimless mockeries of intellectual exertion. Poetry was the mental rattle that awakened the attention of intellect in the infancy of civil society: but for the maturity of mind to make a serious business of the playthings of its childhood, is as absurd as for a grown man to rub his gums with coral, and cry to be charmed asleep by the jingle of silver bells."

Arnold on poetry, religion, and science

These words of Peacock were quoted by I. A. Richards in 1926, because he felt that they represented a widely accepted point of view, and one which required refuting. The prestige of science grew steadily throughout the nineteenth century and it became more and more necessary for poetry to have its position vis-à-vis science clearly and precisely defined. Matthew Arnold had anticipated Richards in facing the modern implications of this question. Arnold saw—or thought he saw—the factual basis of religion threatened by modern knowledge and sought to find in poetry a source of values which could not be threatened by this new scientific knowledge. "Our religion has materialised itself in the fact, in the supposed fact; it has attached its emotion to the fact, and now the fact is failing it. But for poetry the idea is everything; the rest is a world of illusion, of divine illusion. Poetry attaches its emotion to the idea; the idea *is* the fact." So Arnold wrote in 1879, and again Richards quoted him in 1926. Both Arnold and Richards were concerned with finding for poetry (and here as earlier the term "poetry" is being used to mean imaginative literature in general) a kind of meaning and a kind of usefulness which differentiated it clearly from science and freed it from any direct responsibility to scientific truth.

Arnold was content to give his answer in very general terms. "More and more mankind will discover that they have to turn to poetry to interpret life for us, to console us, to sustain us. Without poetry, our science will appear incomplete; and most of what now passes with us for religion and philosophy will be replaced by poetry. Science, I say, will appear incomplete without it. For finely and truly does Wordsworth call poetry 'the impassioned expression which is in the countenance of all science'; and what is a countenance without its expression? Again, Wordsworth finely and truly calls poetry 'the breath and finer spirit of all knowledge': our religion, parading evidences such as those on which the popular mind relies now; our philosophy, pluming itself on its reasonings about causation and finite and infinite being; what are they but the shadows and dreams and false shows of knowledge? The day will come when we shall wonder at ourselves for having trusted to them, for having taken them seriously; and the more we perceive their hollowness, the more we shall prize 'the breath and finer spirit of knowledge' offered to us by poetry."[1]

This is an eloquent statement of the significance and value of poetry, but it is far too general to be of much help to the student who is concerned with finding out precisely what it is that poetry does and how it does it. When Arnold goes on to say that "the best poetry is what we want; the best poetry will be found to have a power of forming, sustaining, and delighting us, as nothing else can," we realize that he is more concerned with discovering the means of distinguishing the best poetry from inferior kinds than in describing in accurate detail what poetry indeed is and how it operates. This is not to belittle Arnold as a critic: as we shall see later, he made some extremely important contributions to criticism. But on this question of the relation of poetry to science and the difference between poetic expression and other kinds of discourse, he only comments in the most general terms.

Later critics have endeavored to discuss this question more particularly. They are not only anxious to make absolutely clear just

[1] Introduction to Ward's *English Poets*, 1880.

what it is that poetry does that is done by no other kind of handling of language, but they use modern science itself in an endeavor to analyze the precise nature of poetry and to distinguish it from scientific discourse. I. A. Richards has been one of the most influential of modern critics who have approached the study of poetry with these two purposes in mind. In his study of the nature and value of poetry he uses tools provided by modern psychology to investigate what actually goes on in a poem and how a poem affects the reader. His objective is both descriptive and normative: he is concerned, that is, both to describe accurately what a poem is and what it does, and to show how and why what it does is valuable.

A psychological theory of value

Richards' *Principles of Literary Criticism* appeared in 1924, as a volume in the "international library of psychology, philosophy and scientific method"—a fact which itself tells us something of Richards' point of view. Just as Shelley used Platonism to remove Plato's objections to poets, so Richards wished to use science to remove the scientist's objections. He called his book "a machine for thinking with," and the argument proceeded with scientific rigor. He will have no truck with vague generalizations about esthetic experience, and dismisses in an introductory section the belief in "the phantom aesthetic state," the view that there is a type of esthetic experience which is wholly unlike any other kind of experience and can only be described in its own terms. Art is a human activity which affects human beings, and it is therefore capable of analysis by anyone who investigates properly what human beings are and how they operate. The key to the proper critical method is the proper description of the psychological processes that take place in both writer and reader when a work is produced and appreciated. On such a basis unlimited progress is possible: Richards here shares the optimistic belief in progress that has been characteristic of scientists since the days of Francis Bacon. "It should be borne in mind," he says in his preface, "that the knowledge which the men of A.D. 3000 will possess, if all goes well, may make all our aesthetics, all our psychology, all our modern theory of value, look pitiful." Thus criticism is linked to those aspects of knowledge which advance with new discoveries, and the assumption is made that these discoveries will probably be constant and regular. The scientific nature of the endeavor is stressed; the aim is "to link even the commonplaces of criticism to a systematic exposition of psychology."

Psychology, then, is Richards' science. Qualities in objects are discussed not as independent facts, but in terms of their effects on persons who experience those objects. We may ask how Richards derives a theory of *value* from mere *description*, however accurate. Psychology is a descriptive and not a normative science. This problem is solved quite simply by assessing value strictly in terms of *function*. "Anything is valuable that satisfies an appetency," and the most valuable psychological state is that which involves the satisfaction of the greatest number of appetencies consistent with the least number of frustrations of other appetencies. A subtly balanced organization of impulses becomes the ideal. The first positive contribution, then, which Richards makes in his book is the formulation of this general psychological point of view—what might be termed psychological humanism. It embraces ethics, too, but ethics redefined with the help of a behaviorist psychology. What is good is what produces value, and a conception of value is arrived at through the harmonizing of functions within the organism.

Meaning and communication

A psychological theory of value having been arrived at, there remains the equally important task of applying it to literature. We observe functions in the human organism and arrive at a theory of value dependent on those functions: now we have to apply that theory to external things that "act on" the organism. But what do we mean by "act on"? Can literature really "cause" states of mind? To answer these questions Richards has to turn from considerations of value to a consideration of how literature can produce value, how words can communicate attitudes which result in a valuable psychological state in the reader. (We may note here that Richards denies that the mind is a separate entity: it is simply a part of the activity of the nervous system.) This raises the whole problem of meaning and communication which in turn leads Richards to outline his view of perception in order to explain the initial processes in reading, and to discuss the nature of "signs" and the other elements involved in communication. It is the necessity for showing how a work of literature can produce a certain state of mind in the reader that leads Richards to link literary criticism with semantics, which is the scientific study of how words operate in communicating meaning. Already in 1923 Richards had brought out, with C. K. Ogden, a book entitled *The Meaning of Meaning,* a pioneer study of language from this point of view, the first by a great variety of authors of a host of works on semantics which have affected not only literary criticism but also views of the relation between language and thought held by philosophers, logicians, psychologists, and students of techniques of propaganda.

Richards conducts these investigations in order to come to some clear conclusions about what imaginative literature is, how it employs language, how its use of language differs from the scientific use of language, and what is its special function and value. His conclusion, at this stage in the development of his critical ideas (for it should be noted that Richards developed his views in different directions in his later works), is that a satisfactory work of imaginative literature represents a kind of psychological adjustment in the author which is valuable for personality, and that the reader, if he knows how to read properly, can have this adjustment communicated to him by reading the work. The qualification, "if he knows how to read properly," is important, for Richards insists that only the properly perceptive kind of reading can receive the true value of a work. Training in reading with care and sensitivity is therefore insisted on by him, and again this has had a great influence on modern criticism, which has more and more come to insist on the importance of a proper reading of the text.

Poetry and the nervous system

Poetry differs from science both in its objective—to perpetuate and communicate a valuable kind of psychological adjustment—and in the kind of meaning it attributes to words, which is "emotive" rather than "scientific" or "referential." "A poem," say Ogden and Richards in *The Meaning of Meaning,* ". . . has no concern with limited and directed reference. *It tells us, or should tell us, nothing.* It has a different, though an equally important and far more vital function—to use an evocative term in connection with an evocative matter. What

it does, or should do, is to induce a fitting attitude to experience."[2]
The poet, said Sidney, does not tell the literal truth about the real
world, but presents a picture of an ideal world which stimulates us to
endeavor to copy it in our own behavior: the poet, says Richards, does
not tell the literal truth about the real world, but suggests attitudes
which represent a proper balance of the nervous system and which
are absorbed by the properly qualified reader.

The best general summary of Richards' position on the whole question of the nature and value of poetry and its relation to science is
contained in his *Science and Poetry*, 1926. The following extracts
from this work will give some indication of his procedure:[3]

Very much toil has gone to the endeavour to explain the high place
of poetry in human affairs, with, on the whole, few satisfactory or convincing results. This is not surprising. For in order to show how poetry is
important it is first necessary to discover to some extent what it is. Until
recently this preliminary task could only be very incompletely carried out;
the psychology of instinct and emotion was too little advanced; and, moreover, the wild speculations natural in pre-scientific enquiry definitely stood
in the way. Neither the professional psychologist, whose interest in poetry
is frequently not intense, nor the man of letters, who as a rule has no adequate
ideas of the mind as a whole, has been equipped for the investigation. Both
a passionate knowledge of poetry and a capacity for dispassionate psychological analysis are required if it is to be satisfactorily prosecuted.

It will be best to begin by asking "What *kind of a thing*, in the widest
sense, is poetry?" When we have answered this we shall be ready to ask
"How can we use and misuse it?" and "What reasons are there for thinking it valuable?"

Let us take an experience, ten minutes of a person's life, and describe it
in broad outline. It is now possible to indicate its general structure, to
point out what is important in it, what trivial and accessory, which
features depend upon which, how it has arisen, and how it is probably
going to influence his future experience. There are, of course, wide gaps
in this description, none the less it *is* at last possible to understand in general
how the mind works in an experience, and what sort of stream of events
the experience is.

Richards here quotes and analyzes Wordsworth's Westminster
Bridge sonnet, discussing "the sound of the words 'in the mind's ear,' "

---

[2] Professor Max Black accuses Richards of "the lack of a consistent and coherent
theory of 'emotive meaning' " and has some interesting and cogent criticisms of this
whole position. See "A Symposium on Emotive Meaning: Some Questions about
Emotive Meaning," *The Philosophical Review*, March 1948, pp. 111-126.

[3] Quoted by permission of the author.

the pictures that arise "in the mind's eye," and the division of the experience of reading into a minor branch "which we may call the intellectual stream" and a major branch "which we may call the active, or emotional, stream," and "is made up of the play of our interests."

The active branch is what really matters; for from it all the energy of the whole agitation comes. The thinking which goes on is somewhat like the play of an ingenious and invaluable "governor" run by, but controlling, the main machine. Every experience is essentially some interest or group of interests swinging back to rest.

To understand what an interest is we should picture the mind as a system of very delicately poised balances, a system which so long as we are in health is constantly growing. Every situation we come into disturbs some of these balances to some degree. The ways in which they swing back to a new equipoise are the impulses with which we respond to the situation. And the chief balances in the system are our chief interests.

Suppose that we carry a magnetic compass about in the neighbourhood of powerful magnets. The needle waggles as we move and comes to rest pointing in a new direction whenever we stand still in a new position. Suppose that instead of a single compass we carry an arrangement of many magnetic needles, large and small, swung so that they influence one another, some able only to swing horizontally, others vertically, others hung freely. As we move, the perturbations in this system will be very complicated. But for every position in which we place it there will be a final position of rest for all the needles into which they will in the end settle down, a general poise for the whole system. But even a slight displacement may set the whole assemblage of needles busily readjusting themselves.

One further complication. Suppose that while all the needles influence one another, some of them respond only to some of the outer magnets among which the system is moving. The reader can easily draw a diagram if his imagination needs a visual support.

The mind is not unlike such a system if we imagine it to be incredibly complex. The needles are our interests, varying in their importance, that is in the degree to which any movement they make involves movement in the other needles. Each new disequilibrium, which a shift of position, a fresh situation, entails, corresponds to a need: and the wagglings which ensue as the system rearranges itself are our responses, the impulses through which we seek to meet the need. Often the new poise is not found until long after the original disturbance. Thus states of strain can arise which last for years. . . .

This development [of a child, as he grows up] takes a very indirect course. It would be still more erratic if society did not mould and re-mould him at every stage, reorganising him incompletely two or three times over before he grows up. He reaches maturity in the form of a vast assemblage of major and minor interests, partly a chaos, partly a system, with some tracts of his personality fully developed and free to respond, others tangled and jammed in all kinds of accidental ways. It is this incredibly complex assemblage of interests to which the printed poem has to appeal. Sometimes the poem is itself the influence which disturbs us, sometimes it is merely the means by which an already existing disturbance can right itself. More usually perhaps it is both at once.

We must picture then the stream of the poetic experience as the swinging back into equilibrium of these disturbed interests. We are reading the poem in the first place only because we are in some way interested in doing so, only because some interest is attempting to regain its poise thereby. And whatever happens as we read happens only for a similar reason. We understand the words (the intellectual branch of the stream goes on its way successfully) only because an interest is reacting through that means, and all the rest of the experience is equally but more evidently our adaptation working itself out.

The rest of the experience is made up of emotions and attitudes. Emo-tions are what the reaction, with its reverberations in bodily changes, feels like. Attitudes are the impulses towards one kind of behaviour or another which are set ready by the response. They are, as it were, its outward going part. Sometimes, as here in *Westminster Bridge*, they are very easily over-looked. But consider a simpler case—a fit of laughter which it is absolutely essential to conceal, in Church or during a solemn interview, for example. You contrive not to laugh; but there is no doubt about the activity of the impulses in their restricted form. The much more subtle and elaborate im-pulses which a poem excites are not different in principle. They do not show themselves as a rule, they do not come out into the open, largely because they are so complex. When they have adjusted themselves to one another and become organized into a coherent whole, the needs concerned may be satisfied. *In a fully developed man a state of readiness for action will take the place of action when the full appropriate situation for action is not present.* The essential peculiarity of poetry as of all the arts is that the full appropriate situation is *not* present. It is an *actor* we are seeing upon the stage, not Hamlet. So readiness for action takes the place of actual behaviour. . . .

In its use of words poetry is just the reverse of science. Very definite thoughts do occur, but not because the words are so chosen as logically to bar out all possibilities but one. No. But because the manner, the tone of voice, the cadence and the rhythm play-upon our interests and make *them* pick out from among an indefinite number of possibilities the precise particular thought which they need. That is why poetical descriptions often seem so much more accurate than prose descriptions. Language logically and scientifically used cannot describe a landscape or a face. To do so would need a prodigious apparatus of names for shades and nuances, for precise particular qualities. These names do not exist, so other means have to be used. The poet, even when, like Ruskin or De Quincey, he writes in prose, makes the reader pick out the precise particular sense required from an indefinite number of possible senses which a word, phrase or sentence may carry. The means by which he does this are many and varied. . . .

Misunderstanding and under-estimation of poetry is mainly due to over-estimation of the thought in it. We can see still more clearly that thought is not the prime factor if we consider for a moment not the experience of the reader but that of the poet. Why does the poet use these words and no others? Not because they stand for a series of thoughts which in themselves are what he is concerned to communicate. It is never what a poem *says* which matters, but what it *is*. The poet is not writing as a scientist. He uses these words because the interests which the situation calls into play combine to bring them, just in this form, into his consciousness as a means of *ordering, controlling, and consolidating* the whole experience. The experience itself, the tide of impulses sweeping through the mind, is the source and the sanction of the words. They represent this experience itself, not any set of perceptions or reflections, though often to a reader who approaches the poem wrongly they will seem to be only a series of remarks about other things. But to a suitable reader the words— if they actually spring from experience and are not due to verbal habits, to the desire to be effective, to factitious excogitation, to imitation, to irrelevant contrivances, or to any other of the failings which prevent most people from writing poetry—the words will reproduce in his mind a similar play of interests putting him for the while into a similar situation and leading to the same response.

We can see here how closely criticism becomes linked to psychology —not in the eighteenth century sense, where the critic approved, say, a play if it showed "a knowledge of the human heart," if it was recognizably true to human psychology as we know it in daily experience, nor yet in Wordsworth's sense, where the value of poetry was related to a theory of poetic creation far more general and less particularized than that of Richards, but with specific reference to theories of perception, of semantics, and of the nervous system generally. Richards' position is in a sense more impressive than that of many of his predecessors; but it is also more vulnerable. For if one does not accept his system of psychology, if one denies that his description of what happens when we read a poem really represents what takes place, then the whole critical theory falls to the ground. Controversy about Richards' position has generally centered on whether his description of the kind of psychological poise achieved by the poet and communicated through a reading of the poem to the qualified reader is truth or myth.

Psychological humanism

The extracts from *Science and Poetry* quoted above show Richards' views of what goes on when a poem is written and read: it remains for him to show exactly why that is valuable. He therefore proceeds to develop a general theory of value—general in the sense that it applies to all human activities, and not uniquely to poetry—and then to show how poetry is valuable on this general standard. We have seen how Sidney, in developing an ethical theory of the value of poetry, showed how poetry was valuable on a general ethical standard which for him, and more especially for the Puritans whom he was answering, was the only standard that could be applied to human affairs and the products of the human mind. We have noted that in doing so Sidney was led in some degree to gloss over the unique and differentiating qualities of poetry. Richards is very much concerned with those unique and differentiating qualities: it remains to be seen what happens to them when he applies to poetry his general theory of value.

Enough perhaps as to the kind of thing a poem is, as to the general structure of these experiences. Let us now turn to the further question "Of what use is it?" "Why and how is it valuable?"

The first point to be made is that poetic experiences are valuable (when they are) in the same ways as any other experiences. They are to be judged by the same standards. What are these?

. . . Now that the mind is seen to be a hierarchy of interests, what will for this account be the difference between Good and Evil?

It is the difference between free and wasteful organization, between fullness and narrowness of life. For if the mind is a system of interests, and if an experience is their play, the worth of any experience is a matter of the degree to which the mind, through this experience, attains a complete equilibrium.

This is a first approximation. It needs qualifying and expanding if it is to become a satisfactory theory.

Richards now proceeds to consider the case of a person who has one hour in which to make the fullest possible use of his life, in which to lead "the fullest, keenest, most active and complete kind of life."

Such a life is one which brings into play as many as possible of the *positive* interests. We can leave out the negative interests. It would be a pity for our friend to be frightened or disgusted even for a minute of his precious hour.

But this is not all. It is not enough that many interests should be stirred. There is a more important point to be noted.

The Gods approve
The depth and not the tumult of the soul.

The interests must come into play and remain in play with as little conflict among themselves as possible. In other words, the experience must be organized so as to give all the impulses of which it is composed the greatest possible degree of freedom. . . .

. . . In the past, Tradition, a kind of Treaty of Versailles assigning frontiers and spheres of influence to the different interests, and based chiefly upon conquest, ordered our lives in a moderately satisfactory manner. But Tradition is weakening. Moral authorities are not as well backed by beliefs as they were; their sanctions are declining in force. We are in need of something to take the place of the old order. Not in need of a new balance of power, a new arrangement of conquests, but of a League of Nations for the moral ordering of the impulses; a new order based on conciliation, not on attempted suppression.

Only the rarest individuals hitherto have achieved this new order, and never yet perhaps completely. But many have achieved it for a brief while, for a particular phase of experience, and many have recorded it for these phases.

Of these records poetry consists.

"Poetry," wrote Shelley, "is the record of the best and happiest moments of the happiest and best minds." This is precisely Richards' position, though Richards would define "best" and "happiest" in his own way. Whether the psychological humanism on which Richards bases his view of what is good in poetry as in any other human activity is really adequate to account for the special nature and value of poetry is arguable. To many of his readers there seems to be a gap between his perceptive, detailed discussion of particular poems and his generalizations about the value of poetry, which are in large measure based on psychological notions which no important contemporary psychologist accepts.

Poetry and civilization

Richards concludes *Science and Poetry* with further discussion of the difference between scientific and poetic truth. The poet makes, not true statements, but "pseudo-statements." "A pseudo-statement is 'true' if it suits and serves some attitude or links together attitudes which on other grounds are desirable." He emphasizes "the fundamental disparity and opposition between pseudo-statements as they occur in poetry and statements as they occur in science. A pseudo-statement is a form of words which is justified entirely by its effect in releasing or organising our impulses and attitudes . . .; a statement, on the other hand, is justified by its truth, *i.e.* its correspondence, in a highly technical sense, with the fact to which it points." After a brief discussion of some modern poets, Richards concludes with a general statement which puts him among those who, like Arnold (whom he quotes more than once), saw in poetry a central means of saving civilization:

. . . It is very probable that the Hindenburg Line to which the defence of our traditions retired as a result of the onslaughts of the last century will be blown up in the near future. If this should happen a mental chaos such as man has never experienced may be expected. We shall then be thrown back, as Matthew Arnold foresaw, upon poetry. It is capable of saving us; it is a perfectly possible means of overcoming chaos. But whether man is capable of the reorientation required, whether he can loosen in time the entanglement with belief which now takes from poetry half its power and would then take all, is another question, and too large for the scope of this essay.

By a theory of value based on a psychological humanism which is in turn based on certain psychological theories about how the nervous system functions, Richards finds a means of not only "defending" poetry, but of proving it to be the salvation of civilization. By a theory of perception, of stimuli and responses, of how signs and symbols work, he made semantics a tool of literary analysis and endeavored to show how poetry operates and how in fact it is able to capture and transmit those states which he considers valuable. A scientific method is used in order to distinguish poetry from science. Poetry was saved for the modern world, and Peacock's mocking questions were answered.

That, at least, was the intention. And more important even than the intention was the method, or at least the tone, of the inquiry. Though claiming as high a destiny for poetry as Shelley or Arnold, Richards' tone was always that of the calm scientific investigator. If we wish to discover the true nature and value of poetry, let us discover what really goes on when a poem is produced and a poem is read. The tone of resolute inquiry, the emphasis on careful analysis and meticulously defined terminology, and the suggestion that the value of a work of art can be discovered by an investigation of how it *operates*, have had considerable influence on modern criticism. Critics who have not accepted Richards' theory of value—and it is worth noting that, in the last analysis, in order to prove the value of poetry in a scientific age Richards had to construct a completely new general value theory: no other critic had had that kind of temerity—have nevertheless learned from him to observe closely and to conduct their discourses with "scientific" care.

9

The proper sphere of poetry

PLATO, we recall, would have banished poets from his ideal republic because poetry was not, in his view, conducive to the shaping of the good citizen. Aristotle defended poetry by removing its discussion from this general ethical context and showing that the nature, the function, and the special kind of pleasure produced by poetry were each unique. If poetry is to be defended by showing that it is a different kind of thing from that which its attackers assumed it to be, with a different kind of value, then the question of course arises: What kind of thing is it?

The search for the "quiddity" of poetry

This question, as we have seen, has been often asked in the history of criticism, and many different answers have been given. The more the critic has to resist discussion of poetry as a kind of history or a kind of moral philosophy or a kind of science, the more likely he is to press the search for the differentiating qualities of poetry, its "quiddity," its unique and essential nature. We have seen how I. A. Richards, in his endeavor to distinguish poetic from scientific discourse, is led to distinguish between different kinds of meaning and different uses of language, each with its appropriate function and value. The more knowledge we accumulate, the more ethical, historical, psychological, and scientific kinds of truth and kinds of fact we have available, the more tempting it becomes to define poetry in their terms and therefore the more important it becomes to resist this temptation and concentrate on the proper, unique nature of poetry. Imaginative literature can be broken down into so much psychological insight, so much historical truth, so much agreeable sound, so much reflection of the author's personality, and so on, and a given work can be discussed as though it were the sum of these things. The more knowledge we have, the more likely we are to do this. But to do this is to avoid the central critical question, which concerns the special and unique nature of poetry.

What the poet does not do

It is thus not surprising that after a period of rapidly increasing knowledge, when critics have tended to see works of literature as the sum of what can be said about them by the historian, the biographer, the psychologist, and others, there is a reaction in favor of defining more closely the proper sphere of imaginative literature as such. That reaction has produced in our own century a number of influential statements about the nature of poetry all of which are concerned with pointing to what poetry is that nothing else is. Poetry, for example, is not, for these critics, the expression of personality or "the spontaneous overflow of powerful feeling." "Poetry," wrote T. S. Eliot in 1917, "is not a turning loose of emotion, but an escape from emotion; it is not the expression of personality, but an escape from personality."[1] It is an escape from life into art, one might say. But what is art, and what is its relation to life? Modern critics answer these questions in various ways, but many of them are agreed that whatever

[1] "Tradition and the Individual Talent."

art is—and whatever the art of poetry is, in particular—it is different from life. "The poet," to quote Eliot again, "has not a 'personality' to express, but a particular medium, which is only a medium and not a personality, in which impressions and experiences combine in peculiar and unexpected ways. Impressions and experiences which are important for the man may take no place in the poetry, and those which become important in the poetry may play quite a negligible part in the man, the personality."

Critics who agree with this point of view will not agree with Richards that a poem is a vehicle for transferring a valuable state of psychological balance from author to reader, for this is to apply the same standard of value to life as to art. This is the Platonic method, and the method of Sidney and Shelley as well as Richards; the method which takes a norm applicable to life as a whole and applies it to poetry. The difference between Plato and the later Platonic critics is that while Plato, in applying his general norm to poetry, found that poetry would not qualify on that standard, the other critics, having a different though a no less general norm, found that it would. The Aristotelian method is to look in poetry for its own kind of value, though of course that value, if it is really a value, must be ultimately related to a general normative scheme of things. (We cannot simply say, for example, that the function of this water-tap is to allow water to drip out at the rate of thirty drops per minute and conclude that we have thus shown the value of the tap: we must also have a scheme of things within which the dropping of water at a rate of thirty drops per minute is valuable.)

Ransom on physical, Platonic, and metaphysical poetry

If poetry is a special kind of thing with its special kind of value, how do we discover what it is and how do we demonstrate its value? One of the ways is to distinguish between kinds of poetry which have much in common with other forms of discourse and kinds of poetry which seem to be more uniquely poetic. The making of this kind of distinction might help us to see the really poetic thing about poetry. John Crowe Ransom investigates the true nature of poetry by this method of making distinctions:[2]

[2] From *The World's Body* by John Crowe Ransom; copyright 1938 by Charles Scribner's Sons. Reprinted by permission of the publishers.

A poetry may be distinguished from a poetry by virtue of its subject-matter, and subject matter may be differentiated with respect to its ontology, or the reality of its being. An excellent variety of critical doctrine arises recently out of this differentiation, and thus perhaps criticism leans again upon ontological analysis as it was meant to do by Kant. The recent critics remark in effect that some poetry deals with things, while some other poetry deals with ideas. The two poetries will differ from each other as radically as a thing differs from an idea. . . .

I. PHYSICAL POETRY

The poetry which deals with things was much in favor a few years ago with the resolute body of critics. And the critics affected the poets. . . . The Imagists were important figures in the history of our poetry, and they were both theorists and creators. It was their intention to present things in their thinginess, or *Dinge* in their *Dinglichkeit;* and to such an extent had the public lost its sense of *Dinglichkeit* that their redirection was wholesome. What the public was inclined to seek in poetry was ideas, whether large ones or small ones, grand ones or pretty ones, certainly ideas to live by and die by, but what the Imagists identified with the stuff of poetry was, simply, things. . . .

For the purpose of this note I shall give to such poetry, dwelling as exclusively as it dares upon physical things, the name Physical Poetry. It is to stand opposite to that poetry which dwells as firmly as it dares upon ideas.

But perhaps thing *versus* idea does not seem to name an opposition precisely. Then we might phrase it a little differently: image *versus* idea. The idealistic philosophies are not sure that things exist, but they mean the equivalent when they refer to images.

. . . It can hardly be argued, I think, that the arts are constituted automatically out of original images, and arise in some early age of innocence. . . . Art is based on second love, not first love. In it we make a return to something which we had wilfully alienated. The child is occupied mostly with things, but it is because he is still unfurnished with systematic ideas, not because he is a ripe citizen by nature and comes along already trailing clouds of glory. Images are clouds of glory for the man who has discovered that ideas are a sort of darkness. Imagism, that is, the recent historical movement, may resemble a naive poetry of mere things, but we can read the theoretical pronouncements of Imagists, and we can learn that Imagism is motivated by a distaste for the systematic abstractedness of thought. It presupposes acquaintance with science; that famous activity which is "constructive" with respect to the tools of our economic role in this world, and destructive with respect to nature. Imagists wish to escape from science by immersing themselves in images.

Not far off the simplicity of Imagism was, a little later, the subtler simplicity of Mr. George Moore's project, shared with several others, in behalf of "pure poetry." In Moore's house on Ebury Street they talked about poetry, with an after-dinner warmth if not an early-morning discretion, and their tastes agreed almost perfectly and reinforced one another. The fruit of these conversations was the volume *Pure Poetry*. It must have been the most exclusive anthology of English poetry that had yet appeared, since its room was closed to all the poems that dallied visibly with ideas, so that many poems that had been coveted by all other anthologists do not appear there. Nevertheless the book is delicious, and something more deserves to be said for it.

First, that "pure poetry" is a kind of Physical Poetry. Its visible content is a thing-content. Technically, I suppose, it is effective in this character if it can exhibit its material in such a way that an image or set of images and not an idea must occupy the foreground of the reader's attention. Thus:

> Full fathom five thy father lies
> Of his bones are coral made.

Here it is difficult for anybody (except the perfect idealist who is always theoretically possible and who would expect to take a return from anything whatever) to receive any experience except that of a very distinct image, or set of images. It has the configuration of image, which consists in being sharp of edges, and the modality of image, which consists in being given and non-negotiable, and the density, which consists in being full, a plenum of qualities. What is to be done with it? It is pure exhibit; it is to be contemplated; perhaps it is to be enjoyed. The art of poetry depends more frequently on this faculty than on any other in its repertory; the faculty of presenting images so whole and clean that they resist the catalysis of thought. . . .

As critics we should have every good will toward Physical Poetry: it is the basic constituent of any poetry. But the product is always something short of a pure or absolute existence, and it cannot quite be said that it consists of nothing but physical objects. The fact is that when we are more than satisfied with a Physical Poetry our analysis will probably disclose that it is more than usually impure.

II. PLATONIC POETRY

The poetry of ideas I shall denominate: Platonic Poetry. This also has grades of purity. A discourse which employed only abstract ideas with no images would be a scientific document and not a poem at all, not even a Platonic poem. Platonic Poetry dips heavily into the physical. If Physical Poetry tends to employ some ideation surreptitiously while still looking innocent of idea, Platonic Poetry more than returns the compliment, for it tries as hard as it can to look like Physical Poetry, as if it proposed to conceal its medicine, which is the idea to be propagated, within the sugar candy of objectivity and *Dinglichkeit*. As an instance of this, it is almost inevitable that I quote a famous Victorian utterance:

> The year's at the spring
> The day's at the morn;
> Morning's at seven;
> The hill-side's dew-pearled;
> The lark's on the wing;
> The snail's on the thorn:
> God's in his heaven—
> All's right with the world!

which is a piece of transparent homiletics; for in it six pretty, co-ordinate images are marched, like six little lambs to the slaughter, to a colon and a powerful text. . . .

The ablest arraignment of Platonic Poetry that I have seen, as an exercise which is really science but masquerades as poetry by affecting a concern for physical objects, is that of Mr. Allen Tate in a series of studies recently in *The New Republic*. I will summarize. Platonic Poetry is allegory, a discourse in things, but on the understanding that they are translatable at every point into ideas. (The usual ideas are those which constitute the popular causes, patriotic, religious, moral, or social.) Or Platonic Poetry is the elaboration of ideas as such, but in proceeding introduces for ornament some physical properties after the style of Physical Poetry; which is rhetoric. It is positive when the poet believes in the efficacy of ideas. It is negative when he despairs of their efficacy, because they have conspicuously failed to take care of him, and utters his personal wail:

> I fall upon the thorns of life! I bleed!

This is "Romantic Irony," which comes at occasional periods to interrupt the march of scientific optimism. But it still falls under the category of Platonism; it generally proposes some other ideas to take the place of those which are in vogue. . . .

There must be a great deal of genuine poetry[3] which started in the poet's mind as a thesis to be developed, but in which the characters and the situa-

---

[3] The reader might note that Ransom has not yet defined the term "genuine poetry," and an implicit assumption is suddenly here thrust at him.

tions have developed faster than the thesis, and of their own accord. The thesis disappears; or it is recaptured here and there and at the end, and lodged sententiously with the reader, where every successive reading of the poem will dislodge it again. Like this must be some plays, even some plays out of Shakespeare, whose thesis would probably be disentangled with difficulty out of the crowded pageant; or some narrative poem with a moral plot but much pure detail; perhaps some "occasional" piece by a Laureate or official person, whose purpose is compromised but whose personal integrity is saved by his wavering between the sentiment which is a public duty and the experience which he has in his own right; even some proclaimed allegory, like Spenser's, unlikely as that may seem, which does not remain transparent and everywhere translatable into idea but makes excursions into the territory of objectivity. These are hybrid performances. They cannot possess beauty of design, though there may be a beauty in detailed passages. But it is common enough, and we should be grateful. The mind is a versatile agent, and unexpectedly stubborn in its determination not really to be hardened in Platonism. Even in an age of science like the nineteenth century the poetic talents are not so loyal to its apostolic zeal as they and it suppose, and do not deserve the unqualified scorn which it is fashionable to offer them, now that the tide has turned, for their performance is qualified.

But this may not be stern enough for concluding a note on Platonic Poetry. I refer again to that whose Platonism is steady and malignant. This poetry is in imitation of Physical Poetry, and not really a poetry. Platonists practise their bogus poetry in order to show that an image will prove an idea, but the literature which succeeds in this delicate mission does not contain real images but illustrations.

Ransom is conducting his investigation of the nature of poetry by making a preliminary weeding out of false claimants. Poetry is not merely a meticulous rendering in language of the physical appearance of things, for as soon as you begin to use language at all, other elements than the merely "physical" emerge. And poetry is certainly not the handling of images in such a way that the reader is exhorted to accept or follow a certain truth. This latter view he calls Platonism, and defends his definition in a paragraph (omitted here) in which he quotes a "high authority" as saying that "Two great forces are persistent in Plato: the love of truth and zeal for human improvement." Ransom comments: "The forces are one force. We love to view the world under universal or scientific ideas to which we give the name truth; and this is because the ideas seem to make not for righteousness but for mastery. The Platonic view of the world is ultimately the predatory, for it reduces to the scientific, which we know." The moral indignation here seems curiously out of place in a discussion of the nature of poetry. That we should not consider strictly as poetry the kind of discourse which, while using some of the devices of poetry, nevertheless does not seek a uniquely poetic objective—that is a tenable position; but that there should be moral blame attached to a writer who employs poetic devices in this way is a very strange assumption. In other words, it is reasonable to hold that a kind of writing might be good without its being good *poetry*, or that it might use some of the devices appropriate to poetry without being poetry in the fullest sense, and yet be an agreeable and valuable kind of writing. But Ransom's assumption is that a hybrid of this kind tends to corrupt both poetry and criticism.

Certainly, if what Ransom calls "Platonic Poetry" did not exist, the task of the critic seeking to discover the essential nature of poetry would be easier. But in fact there is a "Platonic" element in almost all poetry ever written: the problem is to discover what exactly its relation is to those other elements which are more purely characteristic of poetry as such. The true characteristics of poetry as such, the use of language which differentiates the poet from all other users of language, are to be found in what Ransom calls "Metaphysical Poetry."

. . . The mind does not come unscathed and virginal out of Platonism. Ontological interest would have to develop curiously, or wastefully and discontinuously, if men through their youth must cultivate the ideas so passionately that upon its expiration they are done with ideas forever and ready to become as little (and pre-logical) children. Because of the foolishness of idealists are ideas to be taboo for the adult mind? And, as critics, what are we to do with those poems (like *The Canonization* and *Lycidas*) which could not obtain admission by Moore into the anthology but which very likely are the poems we cherish beyond others?

The reputed "innocence" of the aesthetic moment, the "knowledge without desire" which Schopenhauer praises, must submit to a little scrutiny, like anything else that looks too good to be true. We come into this world as aliens come into a land which they must conquer if they are to live. For native endowment we have an exacting "biological" constitution which knows precisely what it needs and determines for us our inevitable desires. There can be no certainty that any other impulses are there, for why should they be? They scarcely belong in the biological picture. Perhaps we are simply an efficient animal species, running smoothly, working fast, finding the formula of life only too easy, and after a certain apprenticeship piling up power and wealth far beyond the capacity of our appetites to use. What will come next? Perhaps poetry, if the gigantic effort of science begins to seem disproportionate to the reward, according to a sense of the diminishing returns. But before this pretty event can come to pass, it is possible that every act of attention which is allowed us is conditioned by a gross and selfish interest.

Where is innocence then? The aesthetic moment appears as a curious moment of suspension; between the Platonism in us, which is militant, always sciencing and devouring, and a starved inhibited aspiration towards innocence which, if it could only be free, would like to respect and know the object as it might of its own accord reveal itself.

The poetic impulse is not free, yet it holds out stubbornly against science for the enjoyment of its images. It means to reconstitute the world of perception. Finally there is suggested some such formula as the following:

Science gratifies a rational or practical impulse and exhibits the minimum of perception. Art gratifies a perceptual impulse and exhibits the minimum of reason.

Now it would be strange if poets did not develop many technical devices for the sake of increasing the volume of the percipienda or sensibilia. I will name some of them:

First Device: metre. Metre is the most obvious device. A formal metre impresses us as a way of regulating very drastically the material, and we do not stop to remark (that is, as readers) that it has no particular aim except some nominal sort of regimentation. It symbolizes the predatory method, like a sawmill which intends to reduce all the trees to fixed unit timbers, and as business men we require some sign of our business. But to the Platonic censor in us it gives a false security, for so long as the poet appears to be working faithfully at his metrical engine he is left comparatively free to attend lovingly to the things that are being metered, and metering them need not really hurt them. Metre is the gentlest violence he can do them, if he is expected to do some violence.

Second Device: fiction. The device of the fiction is probably no less important and universal in poetry. Over every poem which looks like a poem is a sign which reads: This road does not go through to action; fictitious. Art always sets out to create an "aesthetic distance" between the object and the subject, and art takes pains to announce that it is not history. The situation treated is not quite an actual situation, for science is likely to have claimed that field, and exiled art; but a fictive or hypothetical one, so that science is less greedy and perception may take hold of it. . . . But in being called fictive or hypothetical the art-object suffers no disparagement. It cannot be true in the sense of being actual, and therefore it may be despised by science. But it is true in the sense of being fair or representative, in permitting the "illusion of reality"; just as Schopenhauer discovered that music may symbolize all the modes of existence in the world; and in keeping with the customary demand of the readers of fiction proper, that it shall be "true to life." The defenders of art must require for it from its practitioners this sort of truth, and must assert of it before the world this dignity. If jealous science succeeds in keeping the field of history for its own exclusive use, it does not therefore annihilate the arts, for they reappear in a field which may be called real though one degree removed from actuality. There the arts perform their function with much less interference, and at the same time with about as much fidelity to the phenomenal world as history has.

Third Device: tropes. I have named two important devices; I am not prepared to offer the exhaustive list. I mention but one other kind, the kind which comprises the figures of speech. A proper scientific discourse has no intention of employing figurative language for its definitive sort of utterance. Figures of speech twist accidence away from the straight course, as if to intimate astonishing lapses of rationality beneath the smooth surface of discourse, inviting perceptual attention, and weakening the tyranny of science over the senses. But I skip the several easier and earlier figures, which are timid, and stop on the climactic figure, which is the metaphor; with special reference to its consequence, a poetry which once in our history it produced in a beautiful and abundant exhibit, called Metaphysical Poetry.

And what is Metaphysical Poetry? The term was added to the official vocabulary of criticism by Johnson, who probably took it from Pope, who probably took it from Dryden, who used it to describe the poetry of a certain school of poets, thus: "He [John Donne] affects the metaphysics, not only in his satires, but in his amorous verses, where nature only should reign. . . . In this Mr. Cowley has copied him to a fault." But the meaning of metaphysical which was common in Dryden's time, having come down from the Middle Ages through Shakespeare, was simply: supernatural; *miraculous.* The context of the Dryden passage indicates it. . . .

Specifically, the miraculism arises when the poet discovers by analogy an identity between objects which is partial, though it should be considerable, and proceeds to an identification which is complete. It is to be contrasted with the simile, which says "as if" or "like," and is scrupulous to keep the identification partial. In Cowley's passage above,[4] the lover is say-

---

[4] The paragraph including it has been omitted here. The passage runs:

> Oh take my Heart, and by that means you'll prove
> Within, too stor'd enough of love:
> Give me but yours, I'll by that change so thrive
> That Love in all my parts shall live.
> So powerful is this my change, it render can
> My outside Woman, and your inside Man.

ing, not for the first time in this literature: "She and I have exchanged our hearts." What has actually been exchanged is affections, and affections are only in a limited sense the same as hearts. Hearts are unlike affections in being engines that pump blood and form body; and it is a miracle if the poet represents the lady's affection as rendering her inside into man. But he succeeds, with this mixture, in depositing with us the image of a very powerful affection.

From the strict point of view of literary criticism it must be insisted that the miraculism which produces the humblest conceit is the same miraculism which supplies to religions their substantive content. (This is said to assert the dignity not of the conceits but of the religions.) It is the poet and nobody else who gives to the God a nature, a form, faculties, and a history; to the God, most comprehensive of all terms, which, if there were no poetic impulse to actualize or "find" Him, would remain the driest and deadest among Platonic ideas, with all intension sacrificed to infinite extension. The myths are conceits, born of metaphors. Religions are periodically produced by poets and destroyed by naturalists. Religion depends for its ontological validity upon a literary understanding, and that is why it is frequently misunderstood. The metaphysical poets, perhaps like their spiritual fathers the mediaeval Schoolmen, were under no illusions about this. They recognized myth, as they recognized the conceits, as a device of expression; its sanctity as the consequence of its public or social importance.

But whether the topics be Gods or amorous experiences, why do poets resort to miraculism? Hardly for the purpose of controverting natural fact or scientific theory. Religion pronounces about God only where science is silent and philosophy is negative; for a positive is wanted, that is, a God who has his being in the physical world as well as in the world of principles and abstractions. Likewise with the little secular enterprises of poetry. Not now are the poets so brave, not for a very long time have they been so brave, as to dispute the scientists on what they call their "truth"; though it is a pity that the statement cannot be turned around. Poets will concede that every act of science is legitimate, and has its efficacy. The metaphysical poets of the seventeenth century particularly admired the methodology of science, and in fact they copied it, and their phrasing is often technical, spare, and polysyllabic, though they are not repeating actual science but making those metaphorical substitutions that are so arresting.

The intention of Metaphysical Poetry is to complement science, and improve discourse. Naturalistic discourse is incomplete, for either of two reasons. It has the minimum of physical content and starves the sensibility, or it has the maximum, as if to avoid the appearance of evil, but is laborious and pointless. Platonic poetry is too idealistic, but Physical Poetry too realistic, and realism is tedious and does not maintain interest. The poets therefore introduce the psychological device of the miracle. The predication which it permits is clean and quick but it is not a scientific predication.

For a scientific predication concludes an act of attention but miraculism initiates one. It leaves us looking, marvelling, and revelling in the thick *dinglich* substance that has just received its strange representation.

Let me suggest as a last word, in deference to a common Puritan scruple, that the predication of Metaphysical Poetry is true enough. It is not true like history, but no poetry is true in that sense, and only a part of science. It is true in the pragmatic sense in which some of the generalizations of science are true: it accomplishes precisely the sort of representation that it means to. It suggests to us that the object is perceptually or physically remarkable, and we had better attend to it.

The end of poetry

It will be seen that Ransom shares Richards' concern to differentiate poetic from scientific discourse, and that he shares also Arnold's view that the way poetry operates is the way that religion operates or should operate. But Ransom's view of three kinds of poetry, of which, in his view, only the last is truly and properly poetry, springs from a critical method equally different from that of Richards and that of Arnold. Physical Poetry would be the real thing, but it is really scarcely possible, and if it were it would be tedious; Platonic Poetry is poetry usurping the function of science and ethics; Metaphysical Poetry, because it uses "miraculism," the extended metaphor, the partial analogy treated as an identity, is truest poetry because it initiates attention, it startles into new awareness of the *dinglichkeit,* the "thingishness," of its subject. The function of poetry is thus seen to be to compel attention: poetry is a special way of drawing attention to things. But Ransom does not start by asserting this, and then go on to discuss which kind of poetry best achieves this function. He does not investigate the merits of what he calls physical, Platonic, and metaphysical poetry from this point of view. Physical poetry is inadequate, Platonic poetry is "malevolently" something else than poetry, and metaphysical poetry provides devices to make physical poetry arresting; it makes poetry arresting by startling us into a special kind of perception through its "miraculism." Therefore the startling into perception, the invitation to perceptual or physical awareness, is the function of poetry. The function of poetry is to persuade us that its subject is worth attending to, and is discovered at the *end* of a discussion of the kinds of poetry.

It is interesting that the more limited the function which the critic assigns to poetry, the more scrupulous he is in removing rival functions. Ransom gets much more heated in disposing of Platonic poetry than, say, Sidney does anywhere in the *Defence of Poesie*, yet the function which Sidney assigns to poetry—that of leading men to the good life—was the highest possible one. Yet for Sidney, to lead men to the good life was the function of *all* worthy human activities: poetry could only be defended if it also achieved this, and it could be exalted only if it achieved it better than anything else. For Ransom, as for many modern critics, the limitation of poetry's function is also its prime justification. Nothing else does what poetry does, and *that* is why poetry is so valuable—not simply for what it does, but because what it does is unique. Poetry invites attention, in a way no other kind of discourse can.

Of course, earlier critics had also claimed a special function for poetry. Coleridge too had made a careful distinction between the function of poetry and the function of historical or scientific discourse. Nevertheless, for Coleridge the poetic faculty operated in wider fields than in just poetry: that was his reason for making the distinction between a poem and poetry. For Ransom, the "miraculism" which is the sign of true poetry also operates in myths and religions: but that is not because poetry, mythology, and religion are reflections of one wider activity but simply because myths and religions, where they are of any interest and value at all, *are* poetry. Poetry is not exalted by making it religion: religion is saved by showing that it is poetry.

The mode of existence of a literary work [5]

What, it might be asked, *is* the poem that Ransom, or, for that matter, that Richards talks about? Is it a collection of words on paper, a collection of sounds in the ear, the state of mind of the author at the time of writing or of the reader at the time of reading, or what? It is clearly not merely the series of marks on paper which constitute the printed or written work, for a poem or a story may be recited orally and never written down. The visual shape of a poem may contribute an element to the total meaning, but it clearly cannot be equated with the poem. (Perhaps it should be mentioned that the term *poem* is being used here, as so often throughout this book, to mean any work of imaginative literature.) Again, while the sound of words often plays

---

[5] For a suggestive discussion of this question see René Wellek, "The Mode of Existence of a Literary Work," *Southern Review*, Spring 1942, reprinted as chapter 12 of *Theory of Literature*.

an important part in the total significance of a poem, no poem is simply a series of sounds; if it were, then translation would be impossible. Nor can the poem be identified with the state of mind, or intention, of the writer, because that is primarily a biographical question and it is obviously absurd to maintain that we cannot know what, say, "Lycidas" really is unless and until we can answer the biographical question of whether Milton was really upset about the death of Edward King. But again, the state of mind of the author clearly has some connection with the nature and significance of the work he creates. As for the state of mind of the reader, it is notorious that that varies between one reader and another, and if the "real" poem were the reader's experience in reading it, then every poem would exist in as many numbers as it had readers.

The answer to this question—what is the mode of existence of a work of literary art?—is not easy to give, though we might feel that the question is an academic one or even that the answer is obvious though not easily formulated. What is a Greek poem to someone who knows no Greek? Is it possible to write a great poem in a language invented by the poet and known only to him? One has only to pose these questions to realize that, whatever else a poem may be, it is a complex of meanings, and as meanings are conveyed through language, and language as a means of communication can only exist if it is used in common by a number of people, a poem in a completely unknown language[6] is not a poem to us. A poem exists as a group of words (spoken or written or both or actually one and potentially the other) capable, in view of public agreement as to what the words mean, in view of the additional shades and tones of meaning the words have acquired through their use in previous literature and through the special way the author combines them in this poem, and in view of certain common experiences or attitudes or mental or imaginative potentialities linking poet and reader, of producing in the reader a set of significant interacting meanings (one need not add "and emotions," because while an emotion or set of emotions may result from one's grasp of the meaning of a poem, and while rhythmic and other sound effects may contribute to the totality of meaning grasped by the reader, these emotions result from the reading of the poem and are

[6] So unknown, that is, that one cannot even guess at the sounds, and can see it only as a pattern of marks on paper. A poem communicated orally in an unknown language can have some sort of meaning as sound, but that would certainly not be the total meaning of the poem and perhaps, without any other meaning to interpret it, no part of the meaning of the poem at all.

not part of its essence). Might we not, then, say that a poem exists as a complex of potential meaning? If the human race were wiped out tomorrow, Shakespeare's plays would still exist as complexes of potential meaning, though the meaning would never become actual. What did the world look like before there were any seeing creatures on it? A meaningless question, perhaps; a thing must be seen, or capable of being seen, before it can be said to look like anything. A poem must have an audience, at least a potential audience, before it can have a meaning. The ideal of the modern analytic critic, with his concern to identify every element in the total complex of meaning, is to be every member of that potential audience at once. The reason—or one reason —why the experience of the reader cannot be taken to be the "real" poem is that the real poem is larger than the experience of any given reader, it contains the possibility of more experiences than any one reader could get from it. The total complex of potential meaning which is a poem can never be made actual by any given reader (which is one important difference between a poem and, say, a piece of journalistic prose). Modern analytic criticism, of the kind discussed in the following chapter and in chapter 15, tries by deliberate investigation to dig out the whole complex of potential meaning and thus to act the part of many different "partial" readers simultaneously.

10

The poet and his medium

Wᴇ ǫᴜᴏᴛᴇᴅ T. S. Eliot in the previous chapter: "The poet has not a 'personality' to express, but a particular medium, . . ." The poet's medium is, of course, language, and all critics agree that poets use language rather differently from those who write simply to convey factual information. But not all critics have agreed that the poet's way of using language constitutes his sole or his major distinguishing quality.

The potentialities of language

For Sidney the content was at least equally important: the poet was one who used language so as to present an edifying world persuasively;

to Dryden, at least the dramatic poet had the duty of presenting a just and lively image of human nature, and his use of language was a means of making lively what knowledge and observation had already made just; to Wordsworth, the state of the poet's mind was more important than his way of handling words. Coleridge, with his belief in organic unity, saw the poet's use of language as essentially bound up with the way his imagination worked and his production came into existence, and Shelley saw primitive language as the exercise of the creative imagination, but neither of them went so far as to say that fascination with the potentialities of words is the mark of the true poet. Even Pope, who maintained that the poet's duty was to produce "what oft was thought but ne'er so well expressed" did not see the poet as a man primarily haunted by words. But in the process of differentiating poetic statement from scientific statement, and of removing poetry from the realm of what Ransom called the "Platonic," many modern critics have been led to some such position.

But this does not mean that poetry is merely an ingenious game played with words. Poetry is not science, or rhetoric, or moral philosophy, but it is equally if not more important. W. H. Auden once wrote:

"Why do you want to write poetry?" If the young man answers: "I have important things to say," then he is not a poet. If he answers: "I like hanging around words listening to what they say," then maybe he is going to be a poet.[1]

But Auden also wrote in the same essay:

Two theories of poetry. Poetry as a magical means for inducing desirable emotions and repelling undesirable emotions in oneself and others, or Poetry as a game of knowledge, a bringing to consciousness, by naming them, of emotions and their hidden relationships.

The first view was held by the Greeks, and is now held by MGM, Agit-Prop, and the collective public of the world. They are wrong.

On this view poetry is a form of cognition; the poet uses language as a method of discovery. To quote Auden again:

How can I know what I think till I see what I say? A poet writes "The chestnut's comfortable root" and then changes this to "The chestnut's cus-

---

[1] "Squares and Oblongs" from *Poets at Work*, copyright, 1948, by Harcourt, Brace and Company, Inc.

tomary root." In this alteration there is no question of replacing one emotion by another, or of strengthening an emotion, but of discovering what the emotion is. The emotion is unchanged, but waiting to be identified like a telephone number one cannot remember. "8357. No, that's not it. 8557, 8457, no, it's on the tip of my tongue, wait a moment, I've got it, 8657. That's it."

And again:

If I understand what Aristotle means when he speaks of catharsis, I can only say he is wrong. It is an effect produced, not by works of art, but by bull-fights, professional football matches, bad movies and, in those who can stand that sort of thing, monster rallies at which ten thousand girl guides form themselves into the national flag.

For John Crowe Ransom, metaphysical poetry—which he takes to be the highest form of poetry—"suggests to us that the object is perceptually or physically remarkable, and we had better attend to it." In that lies its function and its value. Auden's view, though by no means identical with this, is in the same general class, the class of poetic theories which see the distinguishing nature and value of poetry in the way it handles words and the way reality is explored through the exploitation of certain potentialities of language.

The function of irony

Some modern critics have narrowed down their definition of poetry to emphasize the special kind of paradox and double meaning with which a poem expresses a situation. These critics stress the importance of a close and subtle reading of the text of a poem in order to demonstrate the ironical overtones and the paradoxical implications which they see as fundamental to adequate poetic utterance. "A poem, to be good," declared Robert Penn Warren in his lecture on "Pure and Impure Poetry" delivered at Princeton in 1942 and published in *The Kenyon Review*, "must earn itself." And by this he meant that it must not simply state its author's emotional convictions in easy generalities, but must come to terms with all alternatives that threaten those convictions by including them in some way in the poetic statement. "Poetry does not inhere in any particular element but depends upon the set of relationships, the structure, which we call the poem." Mr. Warren proceeds to explain:

Then the question arises: what elements cannot be used in such a structure? I should answer that nothing that is available in human experience is to be legislated out of poetry. This does not mean that anything can be used in *any* poem, or that some materials or elements may not prove more recalcitrant than others, or that it might not be easy to have too much of some things. But it does mean that, granted certain contexts, any sort of material, a chemical formula for instance, might appear functionally in a poem. It also may mean that, other things being equal, the greatness of a poet depends upon the extent of the area of experience which he can master poetically.

Can we make generalizations about the nature of the poetic structure? First, it involves resistances, at various levels. There is the tension between the rhythm of the poem and the rhythm of speech (a tension which is very low at the extreme of free verse and at the extreme of verse such as that of *Ulalume*, which verges toward a walloping doggerel); between the formality of the rhythm and the informality of the language; between the particular and the general, the concrete and the abstract; between the elements of even the simplest metaphor; between the beautiful and the ugly; between ideas . . . ; between the elements involved in irony . . . ; between prosaisms and poeticisms . . . This list is not intended to be exhaustive; it is intended to be merely suggestive. But it may be taken to imply that the poet is like the jiujitsu expert; he wins by utilizing the resistance of his opponent—the materials of the poem.

. . . [Poets] have not only tried to say what they mean, they have tried to prove what they mean. The saint proves his vision by stepping cheerfully into the fires. The poet, somewhat less spectacularly, proves his vision by submitting it to the fires of irony—to the drama of his structure —in the hope that the fires will refine it. In other words, the poet wishes to indicate that his vision has been earned, that it can survive reference to the complexities and contradictions of experience. And irony is one such device of reference.

The emphasis here is on poetic *structure*. The good poem is so organized that the interplay between its elements sets up a complex of meaning in which the poet *wins through* to his final utterance. Irony and paradox are important because they are devices for including or at least for taking account of all attitudes which threaten the one assumed by the poet in the poem. To take an oversimplified example: if the poet can laugh at himself at the same time as he is being seriously passionate in a love poem, he anticipates the possible laughter of others and insures himself against parody. It is a kind of homeopathic treatment. The naive poet, who does not, in his organization of images and his other poetic devices, take account of the waiting parodist or the potential mocker, will write a poem that slides too easily toward its meaning, a poem which will be likely to depend "upon stock materials and stock responses [and so become] simply a toboggan slide, or a fall through space."

Poetry and paradox

Though such a view seems at first sight to be concerned only with lyrical poetry, where ironic tensions can be found in the treatment of rhythms and imagery, it can be expanded to include all imaginative literature. For the devices which make for tension may be in the structure of a novel or a play as well as in that of a poem, in the recurrent images or adjectives with which a character is described, in the way in which description of the natural or social background is related to the presentation of the characters and the action, and so on. But the modern critics who hold this position have preferred on the whole to illustrate it with reference to poems, perhaps because, while it is not difficult to show that these elements exist in other forms of imaginative literature, it is less convincing to suggest that these elements constitute the only significant differentiating qualities of a good play or novel. But it has been more than once argued that these elements do constitute the differentiating qualities of a good poem. Consider, for example, the arguments put forward by Cleanth Brooks in his book *The Well Wrought Urn* (1947):[2]

Few of us are prepared to accept the statement that the language of poetry is the language of paradox. Paradox is the language of sophistry, hard, bright, witty; it is hardly the language of the soul. We are willing to allow that paradox is a permissible weapon which a Chesterton may on occasion exploit. We may permit it in epigram, a special subvariety of poetry; and in satire, which though useful, we are hardly willing to allow to be poetry at all. Our prejudices force us to regard paradox as intellectual rather than emotional, clever rather than profound, rational rather than divinely irrational.

Yet there is a sense in which paradox is the language appropriate and inevitable to poetry. It is the scientist whose truth requires a language purged of every trace of paradox; apparently the truth which the poet utters can be approached only in terms of paradox. I overstate the case, to

[2] From *The Well Wrought Urn*, copyright, 1947, by Cleanth Brooks. Reprinted by permission of Harcourt, Brace and Company, Inc.; and Dennis Dobson Ltd.

be sure; it is possible that the title of this chapter ["The Language of Paradox"] is itself to be treated as merely a paradox. But there are reasons for thinking that the overstatement which I propose may light up some elements in the nature of poetry which tend to be overlooked.

The case of William Wordsworth, for instance, is instructive on this point. His poetry would not appear to promise many examples of the language of paradox. He usually prefers the direct attack. He insists on simplicity; he distrusts whatever seems sophistical. And yet the typical Wordsworth poem is based upon a paradoxical situation. Consider his celebrated

> It is a beauteous evening, calm and free,
> The holy time is quiet as a Nun
> Breathless with adoration. . . .

The poet is filled with worship, but the girl who walks beside him is not worshipping. The implication is that she should respond to the holy time, and become like the evening itself, nunlike; but she seems less worshipful than inanimate nature itself. Yet

> If thou appear untouched by solemn thought,
> Thy nature is not therefore less divine:
> Thou liest in Abraham's bosom all the year;
> And worship'st at the Temple's inner shrine,
> God being with thee when we know it not.

The underlying paradox (of which the enthusiastic reader may well be unconscious) is nevertheless thoroughly necessary, even for that reader. Why does the innocent girl worship more deeply than the self-conscious poet who walks beside her? Because she is filled with an unconscious sympathy for *all* of nature, not merely the grandiose and solemn. One remembers the lines from Wordsworth's friend, Coleridge:

> He prayest best, who loveth best
> All things both great and small.

Her unconscious sympathy is the unconscious worship. She is in communion with nature "all the year," and her devotion is continual whereas that of the poet is sporadic and momentary. But we have not done with the paradox yet. It not only underlies the poem, but something of the paradox informs the poem, though, since this is Wordsworth, rather timidly. The comparison of the evening to the nun actually has more than one dimension. The calm of the evening obviously means "worship," even to the dull-witted and insensitive. It corresponds to the trappings of the nun, visible to everyone. Thus, it suggests not merely holiness, but, in the

total poem, even a hint of Pharasaical holiness, with which the girl's careless innocence, itself a symbol of her continual secret worship, stands
in contrast. . . .

Mr. Brooks then proceeds to demonstrate the paradoxical elements
in Wordsworth's sonnet, "Composed upon Westminster Bridge."

It is not my intention to exaggerate Wordsworth's own consciousness
of the paradox involved. In this poem, he prefers, as is usual with him, the
frontal attack. But the situation is paradoxical here as in so many of his
poems. In his preface to the second edition of the *Lyrical Ballads* Wordsworth stated that his general purpose was "to choose incidents and situations from common life" but so to treat them that "ordinary things should
be presented to the mind in an unusual aspect." Coleridge was to state the
purpose for him later, in terms which make even more evident Wordsworth's exploitation of·the paradoxical: "Mr. Wordsworth . . . was to
propose to himself as his object, to give the charm of novelty to things of
every day . . . by awakening the mind's attention from the lethargy of
custom, and directing it to the loveliness and the wonders of the world before us. . ." Wordsworth, in short, was consciously attempting to show his
audience that the common was really uncommon, the prosaic was
really poetic.

Coleridge's terms, "the charm of novelty to things of every day," "awakening the mind," suggest the Romantic preoccupation with wonder—the
surprise, the revelation which puts the tarnished familiar world in a new
light. This may well be the *raison d'être* of most Romantic paradoxes; and
yet the neo-classic poets use paradox for much the same reason. Consider
Pope's lines from *The Essay on Man:*

> In doubt his Mind or Body to prefer;
> Born but to die, and reas'ning but to err;
> Alike in ignorance, his Reason such,
> Whether he thinks too little, or too much . . .
>
> Created half to rise, and half to fall;
> Great Lord of all things, yet a Prey to all;
> Sole Judge of Truth, in endless Error hurl'd;
> The Glory, Jest, and Riddle of the world!

Here, it is true, the paradoxes insist on the irony, rather than the wonder.
But Pope too might have claimed that he was treating the things of every
day, man himself, and awakening his mind so that he would view himself in
a new and blinding light. Thus, there is a certain awed wonder in Pope
just as there is a certain trace of irony implicit in the Wordsworth son-

nets. There is, of course, no reason why they should not occur together, and they do. Wonder and irony merge in many of the lyrics of Blake; they merge in Coleridge's *Ancient Mariner*. The variations in emphasis are numerous. Gray's *Elegy* uses a typical Wordsworth "situation" with the rural scene and with peasants contemplated in the light of their "betters." But in the *Elegy* the balance is heavily tilted in the direction of irony, the revelation an ironic rather than a startling one:

> Can storied urn or animated bust
> Back to its mansion call the fleeting breath?
> Can Honour's voice provoke the silent dust?
> Or Flatt'ry sooth the dull cold ear of Death?

But I am not here interested in enumerating the possible variations; I am interested rather in our seeing that the paradoxes spring from the very nature of the poet's language: it is a language in which the connotations play as great a part as the denotations. And I do not mean that the connotations are important as supplying some sort of frill or trimming, something external to the real matter in hand. I mean that the poet does not use a notation at all—as the scientist may properly be said to do so. The poet, within limits, has to make up his language as he goes.

T. S. Eliot has commented upon "that perpetual slight alteration of language, words perpetually juxtaposed in new and sudden combinations," which occur in poetry. It *is* perpetual; it cannot be kept out of the poem; it can only be directed and controlled. The tendency of science is necessarily to stabilize terms, to freeze them into strict denotations; the poet's tendency is by contrast disruptive. The terms are continually modifying each other, and thus violating their dictionary meanings. To take a very simple example, consider the adjectives in the first lines of Wordsworth's evening sonnet: *beauteous, calm, free, holy, quiet, breathless.* The juxtapositions are hardly startling; and yet notice this: the evening is like a nun breathless with adoration. The adjective "breathless" suggests tremendous excitement; and yet the evening is not only quiet but *calm.* There is no final contradiction, to be sure: it is *that* kind of calm and *that* kind of excitement, and the two states may well occur together. But the poet has no one term. Even if he had a polysyllabic technical term, the term would not provide the solution for his problem. He must work by contradiction and qualification.

We may approach the problem in this way: the poet has to work by analogies. All of the subtler states of emotion, as I. A. Richards has pointed out, necessarily demand metaphor for their expression. The poet must work by analogies, but the metaphors do not lie in the same plane or fit neatly edge to edge. There is a continuous tilting of the planes; necessary overlappings, discrepancies, contradictions. Even the most direct and simple poet is forced into paradoxes far more often than we think, if we are sufficiently alive to what he is doing.

But in dilating on the difficulties of the poet's task, I do not want to leave the impression that it is a task which necessarily defeats him, or even that with his method he may not win to a fine precision. To use Shakespeare's figure, he can

> . . . with assays of bias
> By indirections find directions out.

Shakespeare had in mind the game of lawnbowls in which the bowl is distorted, a distortion which allows the skillful player to bowl a curve. To elaborate the figure, science makes use of the perfect sphere and its attack can be direct. The method of art can, I believe, never be direct—is always indirect. But that does not mean that the master of the game cannot place the bowl where he wants it. The serious difficulties will only occur when he confuses the game with that of science and mistakes the nature of his appropriate instrument. . . .

I have said that even the apparently simple and straightforward poet is forced into paradoxes by the nature of his instrument. Seeing this, we should not be surprised to find poets who consciously employ it to gain a compression and precision otherwise unobtainable. Such a method, like any other, carries with it its own perils. But the dangers are not overpowering; the poem is not predetermined to a shallow and glittering sophistry. The method is an extension of the normal language of poetry, not a perversion of it. . . .

We notice in this critical position the same insistence on the need to differentiate poetic from scientific discourse that we found in Richards —and in Coleridge. But the method of differentiation is not the same as Richards', though it has points of similarities with it (and Richards was clearly one of the influences which helped to shape Mr. Brooks' theory) and it is even further removed from that of Coleridge. Science says things explicitly, directly, simply, in "notational" language; poetry expresses itself paradoxically, ironically, indirectly, obliquely in language which, far from having a one-for-one correspondence with what it denotes, creates its own meanings as it moves. If on this view poetry becomes simply a special way of using language, it must also be remembered that language used in this way develops and presents attitudes which could not be developed and presented in any other form of discourse. Though Mr. Brooks and those who take his position appear to be concentrating entirely on the poet's linguistic and structural devices, that is because they consider these matters to have received less than their due share of attention rather than because they consider that that is all that poetry is. It is a question of emphasis: you can say that poetry operates in this way, and in doing so achieves and presents certain kinds of insight, or you can say that poetry seeks to achieve and present certain kinds of insight and in order to do so it has to operate in this way. A cognitive theory of poetry—a view of poetry as a special kind of knowledge—is not incompatible with a view of poetry as paradox, though it might reasonably be claimed that to emphasize paradox exclusively and present it as the sole or at least as the major differentiating quality of poetry is not only to concentrate on the means poetry employs rather than on its end (and that is legitimate enough, for it can fairly be urged that the end can only be properly understood in terms of the means) but to oversimplify the whole situation by maintaining that one among several kinds of means is the only one that really matters. But sometimes this kind of overemphasis and oversimplification is necessary if readers are to be roused out of their preconceptions to consider a new point of view.

Metaphor, symbol and myth

Modern interest in the characteristically poetic way of using language, a way which by its devices for setting up whole series of interacting suggestions differs from the simple denotational use of words found in ordinary expository discourse, naturally leads to inquiry into the function of metaphor and symbol in poetic language and to a new interest in the nature of myth. Metaphor is a device for expanding meaning, for saying several things at once, for producing "ambivalence" (to use that favorite term of modern criticism), and demonstration of how metaphorical expression can help to achieve richness and subtlety of implication is a major concern of the contemporary critic. Imagery, too, is a common subject of investigation: Caroline Spurgeon, in her studies of Shakespeare's imagery,[3] showed how recurring images of a certain

---

[3] *Leading Motives in the Imagery of Shakespeare's Tragedies*, Oxford, 1930; *Shakespeare's Imagery and What It Tells Us*, Cambridge, 1935. See also G. Wilson Knight's *The Wheel of Fire*, Oxford, 1930. Knight is concerned to investigate the symbolic imagery of Shakespeare's plays: in his later books (*The Burning Oracle*, 1939; *The Starlit Dome*, 1941) he applies the method to other poets.

kind can give a characteristic tone, and a whole set of echoing meanings, to a play (as *Hamlet* is dominated by images of disease, *Troilus and Cressida* by images of food and digestion, and so on). Critics have become interested in the symbolic aspects of imagery, and the practice of many modern poets, especially of Yeats, with his deliberate use of symbolic images, has encouraged such interest. This links up, too, with psychological interest in why certain images and symbols affect us as they do; Maud Bodkin's *Archetypal Patterns in Poetry* (Oxford, 1934), following in some degree the psychological theories of Carl Jung, explores the significance of recurring images and situations which, by making contact with some primitive and elemental aspect of man, can always be counted on to have an effect.

The ambivalent, suggestive, symbolic aspects of poetic language relate, it is often held, to more primitive ways of knowing and communicating than is represented by ordinary prose discourse (compare Shelley's view of the nature and origin of language), and interest in this relation has led modern criticism into an investigation of the nature of myth. Literary criticism here makes contact with anthropology as well as with psychology, though myth to the modern critic is not so much the myth of folklore and religion as a kind of symbolic situation produced by the proper use of "archetypal" imagery.[4] (Myth in the anthropological sense, however, has been used by modern poets, notably by T. S. Eliot in *The Waste Land*.) Thus the exploration of the way in which the literary artist uses words, and the concern to distinguish that way from the more ordinary forms of communication in language, have led in a number of directions and added some new territory to the area of the critic's inquiry.

[4] See Richard Chase, "Notes on the Study of Myth," *Partisan Review*, XIII (1946), 238-247; Philip Wheelwright, "Poetry, Myth, and Reality," in *The Language of Poetry* (ed. Tate, Princeton University Press, 1942), pp. 3-33. For some searching (but difficult) investigations into the symbolic aspects of language and meaning, see Kenneth Burke, *The Philosophy of Literary Form* (Louisiana State University Press, 1941) and *A Grammar of Motives* (New York, Prentice-Hall, 1945).

PART TWO

Practical Criticism

Introduction

THE DISTINCTION between critical theory and critical practice is in large degree artificial, but it is one which it is often helpful to draw. Few critics have been able to engage in the assessment of individual works of literature without at some point discussing the principles on which they base their judgment, and similarly it is difficult to inquire into the nature and value of literature without occasionally illustrating your theories by concrete examples, as Aristotle does in the *Poetics*. Nevertheless, to ask what literature *is* and to inquire into the merit of a particular work are two different kinds of activity, however intimately related they may be, and to separate them makes for clarity of understanding.

Thus, though the reader will note in the following pages many digressions from practice into theory and back again, he will also, it is hoped, be able to clarify his mind about the kinds of skill required by the practical critic as distinct from the philosophical inquirer into literary value. To follow the practical critic in action and to observe the kinds of information he draws on, the uses he makes of comparison and contrast, the ways in which he makes description contribute to evaluation, give both an awareness of different critical methods and an appreciation of how judgments of particular works can be arrived at and demonstrated, which no amount of purely "ontological" inquiry can yield. Further, while we may take our general view of the nature and value of literature from some philosopher or esthetician who has impressed and convinced us, we are regularly called upon to make our own evaluation of particular works: we can be good readers without an original esthetic, but we cannot be good readers without the ability to judge for ourselves as we read. That ability is best cultivated by observing closely how practical criticism is successfully done.

11

The establishment of a critical scene

IN PART ONE we have considered some different ways in which critics have answered the questions concerning the nature and value of imaginative literature. We have seen how often critics have been led to give their views of what poetry is and what good it is by their desire to defend it against the attacks of those who considered it useless or immoral or in some other way undesirable. In ages when poetry or imaginative literature as such is not subject to attack, when it is produced freely and abundantly for a public which takes it for granted as a natural part of its civilization, philosophical defense tends to give way to practical discussion, to evaluation of particular works, to consideration of ways of writing well, to study of the tricks of the writer's trade and hints to literary aspirants on how to master their art.

The scope of practical criticism

Thus on the very threshold of the greatest phase of Elizabethan literature, just before Shakespeare appeared on the scene and Spenser wrote
his maturer work, Sidney produced his *Apologie for Poetrie,* while a
generation later Ben Jonson was noting down his *Timber, or Discoveries,*[1] a series of observations on literature and writers which concentrated on practical criticism, or at least on questions of more interest
to the practicing writer than to the philosopher. And toward the end
of the seventeenth century in England, when the tremendous Elizabethan achievement lay in the past to be looked back on and compared
with the product of the Jacobean period and with the very different
literature of the Restoration, John Dryden turned to practical criticism
with a zest and a versatility which were only possible in an age which
on the one hand took the production of literature absolutely for
granted and on the other had sufficient different kinds of literature
available to it from its own literary development to be led naturally
to comparisons between the merits of different styles and different
conventions. Dryden is the first great practical critic in English literature; it does not detract in the least from his genius to suggest that
his most impressive critical qualities—his breadth of view, his skill at
comparison, his sense of changing artistic conventions, his readiness to
hear new evidence and if necessary change his mind, his concern with
the practical questions of craftsmanship—could not have emerged at
an earlier period in English literature, for it required the awareness of
a continuous but changing literary tradition operating in almost constant excitement for well over a century to stimulate this kind of
critical activity. And for the man of letters, as distinct from the philosopher, this kind is more interesting than the theorizing of those who
inquire into the nature and value of imaginative literature. Further, the
kinds of question liable to be asked by the critic moving confidently
among works of his own and previous ages, of his own and other
countries, are remarkably varied in extent and in scope. To ask not what
poetry in general *is* but *how good* is this particular poem is to move
from the descriptive to the normative, from the abstract question of
being to the concrete evaluation of particular examples, with all the
comparisons, contrasts, demonstrations, analyses, illustrations, and

[1] First published posthumously in 1641. Ben Jonson lived from 1573 to 1637.

sense of commitment which such a procedure involves; is to leave the
rarefied air of theoretical speculation for the hot arena of day-to-day
literary activity. Once one is there, there is no limit to the number of
questions that can be asked. Not only "How good is this work and
why?" and "How do we differentiate between the good and the less
good?" are the subjects for debate, but such matters are discussed as
the relation between works of literature and other phases of culture,
psychological questions concerning the way the creative writer operates, sociological questions about the way in which his place in society
affects his way of writing, semantic questions about what happens to
language when it is employed in a certain way, historical questions
about the effect of a writer's age on his language, his literary conventions, and his ideas, textual and bibliographical inquiries into the accuracy of the transmitted text, biographical investigation into the relation between a writer's life and his work. None of these is directly
relevant to an assessment of the value of a literary work, but practical
criticism leads to all of them at some point or another and they all have
their indirect relevance to the original question "How good is it?" For
example, before one can fairly ask how good a work is, one must be
sure one knows *what* it is: do we understand it aright?—perhaps words
have changed their meaning since the writer's day, or changed ideas
have led us to read into certain expressions something far removed
from what the author put there. The critic must turn philologist and
historian to solve these problems. Are we sure this is what the author
really wrote? The critic may have to turn bibliographer or paleog-
rapher to answer that. And even in judging a contemporary work
there are many subsidiary questions to which the alert and responsive
critic will be led before he has gone very far.

It is true, as so many modern critics have insisted, that the quality of
a literary work is to be judged on literary grounds alone, and not by a
discussion of the author's life or times; but there are so many peripheral
questions that demand investigation as soon as one has raised the question of quality that no critic of intellectual curiosity or liveliness of
mind—and surely these are qualities appropriate to the literary critic—
can for long refrain from pursuing them. We shall discuss in a later
chapter some of the relationships between simple evaluation (which in
fact is rarely "simple") and other kinds of literary investigation; here
we shall only note that once the critic becomes involved in practical

criticism there is scarcely a limit to the number and the kinds of problems he may feel called upon to inquire into.

Ben Jonson

Ben Jonson's *Timber* contains no systematic practical criticism of the kind we find so often in Dryden, but the random notes which make up this work do illustrate in a very interesting way the diversity of questions with which the practicing man of letters may concern himself. Consider, for example, this jotting on Shakespeare, Jonson's contemporary:

I remember, the Players have often mentioned it as an honour to Shakespeare, that in his writing, (whatsoever he penn'd) hee never blotted out line. My answer hath beene, would he had blotted a thousand. Which they thought a malevolent speech. I had not told posterity this, but for their ignorance, who choose that circumstance to commend their friend by, wherein he most faulted. And to justify mine owne candor, (for I lov'd the man, and doe honour his memory (on this side Idolatry) as much as any.) Hee was (indeed) honest, and of an open, and free nature: had an excellent *Phantsie;* brave notions, and gentle expressions: wherein hee plow'd with that facility, that sometime it was necessary he should be stop'd: *Sufflaminandus erat* [he required restraining]; as *Augustus* said of *Haterius.* His wit was his owne power; would the rule of it had beene so too. Many times hee fell into those things, could not escape laughter: As when hee said in the person of *Caesar,* one speaking to him; *Caesar thou dost me wrong.* Hee replyed: *Caesar did never wrong, but with just cause;* and such like, which were ridiculous. But hee redeemed his vices, with his vertues. There was ever more in him to be praysed, then to be pardoned.

This is as much critical gossip as criticism, and it combines personal recollection of the man with judgment on his work. And the judgment on the work takes the form of criticism of the method of composition. Here is a critic operating amid the free give and take of daily practical literary activity, informally and conversationally, with his esthetic principles taken so completely for granted that they are not explicitly referred to at all. Yet for all its casualness, Jonson's opinion is grounded on principle; he had a well thought out and consistent point of view on all the major critical questions and even his most spontaneous utterances derive ultimately from this point of view. But living in the midst of a tremendously creative age, and himself participating in that creation, he did not feel the need to refer all his practical judgments to fundamental esthetic laws.

Ben Jonson, however, took much less for granted than many later practical critics, and if on occasion he would jot down (or bring out in conversation—as we know from Drummond of Hawthornden's record of Jonson's conversations with him) remarks of the kind quoted above, he also noted down in his *Timber* many general principles which he got from classical writers, notably Quintilian, and from the renaissance humanist critics, notably the Dutch critic Daniel Heinsius. As his criticism of Shakespeare suggests, he was much concerned with order and discipline in writing, and much that the later classical writers had said about the art of the orator—whose task was to use words in such a way that he would *persuade* his readers or *move* them in the way he wished—Jonson transfers to the poet or dramatist. Study, practice, imitation of the best ancient writers, these are necessary, according to Jonson, before even the greatest original genius can properly realize his gifts. In this respect Jonson's critical temper was "classical" rather than "romantic," if we may use those grossly over-worked terms. He was himself a man of considerable scholarship, and was moreover still influenced by that renaissance zeal for classical learning which had so stimulated the earlier humanists and brought about such a notable revival of classical interests and studies in the sixteenth century. His own learning, the influence of renaissance humanism, and his own temperament, which led him, both in his theory and in his practice, to put careful and studious craftsmanship before imaginative boldness, all helped to make him one of the first significant "neo-classic" critics in English. By "neo-classic" we mean simply a critic who endeavors to develop his theory and practice on the basis of the achievement of the great Greek and Latin writers and who tries to systematize classical practice and classical critical ideas into a set of rules for the guidance of modern writers.

For a man to write well, there are required three Necessaries. To read the best Authors, observe the best Speakers: and much exercise of his owne style. In style to consider, what ought to be written: and after what manner: Hee must first thinke, and excogitate his matter; then choose his words, and examine the weight of either. Then take care in placing, and ranking both matter, and words, that the composition be comely; and to doe this with diligence, and often. No matter how slow the style be at first, so it be labour'd, and accurate; seeke the best, and be not glad of the forward conceipts, or first words, that offer themselves to us, but judge of what wee invent; and order what wee approve. Repeat often, what wee have formerly written; which besides, that it helpes the consequence, and makes the juncture better, it quickens the heate of imagination, that often cooles in the time of setting downe, and gives it new strength, as if it grew lustier, by the going back. As wee see in the contention of leaping, they jumpe farthest, that fetch their race largest: or, as in throwing a Dart, or Iavelin, wee force back our armes, to make our loose the stronger. Yet, if we have a faire gale of wind, I forbid not the steering out of our sayle, so the favour of the gale deceive us not. For all that we invent doth please us in the conception, or birth; else we would never set it downe. But the safest is to return to our Judgement, and handle over againe those things, the easinesse of which might make them justly suspected. So did the best Writers in their beginnings; they impos'd upon themselves care, and industry. They did nothing rashly. They obtain'd first to write well, and then custom made it easie, and a habit. By little and little, their matter shew'd it selfe to 'hem more plentifully; their words answer'd, their composition followed; and all, as in a well-order'd family, presented it selfe in the place. So that the summe of all is: Ready writing makes not good writing: but good writing brings on ready writing: Yet when wee thinke wee have got the faculty, it is even then good to resist it: as to give a Horse a check sometimes with bit [the same metaphor that he used when he said of Shakespeare that *sufflaminandus erat*], which doth not so much stop his course, as stirre his mettle. Againe, whether a mans *Genius* is best able to reach thither, it should more and more contend, lift and dilate it selfe, as men of low stature, raise themselves on their toes; and so oft times get even, if not eminent. Besides, as it is fit for grown and able Writers to stand of themselves, and worke with their owne strength, to trust and endeavour by their owne faculties: so it is fit for the beginner, and learner, to study others, and the best. For the mind, and memory are more sharpely exercis'd in comprehending an other man's things than our owne; and such as accustom themselves and are familiar with the best Authors, shall ever and anon find somewhat of them in themselves, and in the expression of their minds, even when they feele it not, be able to utter something like theirs, which hath an Authority above their owne. Nay, sometimes it is the reward of a mans study, the praise of quoting an other man fitly: And though a man be more prone, and able for one kind of writing, then another, yet hee must exercise all. For as in an Instrument, so in style, there must be a Harmonie, and consent of parts.

This informal advice on how to become a writer comes from a man who is much more interested in the practical question of what is good writing than in the definition and defense of literary value. The points which Jonson makes here illustrate his view of the importance of precedent and example, his classical sense of the continuity of letters and the dependence of modern writers on standards set up by the great geniuses of the past. Yet he never maintained that mere study of the great writers of the past could produce great writing:

There is no doctrine will doe good, where nature is wanting. Some wits are swelling, and high; others low and still: Some hot and fiery; others cold and dull: One must have a bridle, the other a spurre.

There be some that are forward, and bold; and these will doe every little thing easily: I meane that is hard by, and next them, which they will utter, unretarded without any shamefastnesse. These never perform much, but quickly. They are, what they are on the sudden; they show presently like *Graine*, that, scatter'd on the top of the ground, shoots up, but takes no root; has a yellow blade, but the eare empty. They are wits of good promise at first, but there is an *Ingeni-stitium* [a standing still of wit]: They stand still at sixteene, they get no higher.

You have others, that labour onely to ostentation; and are ever more busie about the colours, and surface of a worke, then in the matter, and foundation: For that is hid, the other is seene.

Others, that in composition are nothing, but what is rough, and broken. . . . These men erre not by chance, but knowingly, and willingly; they are like men that affect a fashion by themselves, have some singularity in a Ruffe, Cloake, or Hat-band; or their beards, specially cut to provoke beholders, and set a marke upon themselves. . . .

Others there are, that have no composition at all; but a kind of tuneing, and riming fall, in what they write. It runs and slides, and onely makes a sound. . . .

Some that turne over all bookes, and are equally searching in all papers, that write out of what they presently find of meet, without choice; by which means it happens, that what they have discredited, and impugned in one worke, they have before, or after extolled the same in another. Such are all the *Essayists*, even their Master *Mountaigne*. . . .

Some againe, who (after they have got authority, or, which is lesse, opinion, by their writings, to have read much) dare presently to faine whole bookes, and Authors, and lye safely. For what never was, will not easily be found; not by the most *curious*. . . .

But the Wretcheder are the obstinate contemners of all helpes, and Arts: such as presuming on their owne *Naturals* (which perhaps are excellent) dare deride all diligence, and seeme to mock at the termes, when they understand not the things; thinking that way to get off wittily, with their Ignorance. . . .

In these notes, we see Jonson moving from a discussion of the principles of good writing and a consideration of some typical faults that hinder good writing, to some elementary psychological observations concerning the qualities of mind and temperament which lead to certain faults. But the interest in practical craftsmanship is always there, and Jonson never leaves us for long in doubt that he is a practicing man of letters talking about what he knows from experience. It is this which gives the air of sturdy common sense to many of his judgments, even of those from which we would today dissent, as his brusque remark to Drummond of Hawthornden "that Shakespeare wanted art" or his strictures on Marlowe:

> The true Artificer will not run away from nature, as hee were afraid of her; or depart from life, and the likenesse of Truth; but speake to the capacity of his hearers. And though his language differ from the vulgar somewhat; it shall not fly from all humanity, with the *Tamerlanes*, and *Tamer-Chams*, of the late Age, which had nothing in them but the *scenicall* strutting, and furious vociferation, to warrant them then to the ignorant gapers. Hee knowes it is his onely Art, so to carry it, as none but Artificers perceive it. . . .

Or consider the interest in practical craftsmanship that prompted the following observations on diction:

> *Custome* is the most certaine Mistresse of Language, as the publicke stampe makes the current money. But wee must not be too frequent with the mint, every day coyning. Nor fetch words from the extreme and utmost ages; since the chiefe vertue of a style is perspicuitie, and nothing so vitious in it, as to need an Interpreter. Words borrow'd of Antiquity, doe lend a kind of Majesty to style, and are not without their delight sometimes. For they have the Authority of yeares, and out of their intermission doe win to themselves a kind of grace-like newnesse. But the eldest of the present, and newest of the past Language is the best. For what was the ancient Language, which some men so doate upon, but the ancient Custome? Yet when I name Custome, I understand not the vulgar Custome: For that were a precept no lesse dangerous to Language, then life, if wee should speake or live after the manners of the vulgar: But that I call Custome of speech, which is the consent of the Learned; as Custome of life, which is the consent of the good. . . .

Jonson discusses at some length, in *Timber,* the merits and appropriate uses of different kinds of prose style, and here again his interest in

practical craftsmanship is paramount. He points out, for example, that
an elevated style is appropriately "high and lofty" when "declaring
excellent matter," but "becomes vast and tumorous" when "speaking
of petty and inferiour things." And he gives a characteristically homely
illustration: "Would you not laugh, to meet a great Counsellor of state
in a flat cap, with his trunck hose, and a hobby-horse Cloake, his
Gloves under his girdle, and yond Haberdasher in a velvet Gowne,
furr'd with sables?" He adds: "There is a certaine latitude in these
things, by which we find the degrees."

After his discussion of prose style, he proceeds to poetry, beginning
with a definition of a poet which, like Sidney's, reminds us that the
Greeks called him ποιητής, a maker, and then going on to ask "What
meane you by a Poeme?" He replies:

A Poeme is not alone any worke, or composition of the Poets in many, or
few verses; but even one alone verse sometimes makes a perfect Poeme. As,
when *Aeneas* hangs up, and consecrates the Armes of *Abas*, with this
Inscription;

Aeneas haec de Danais victoribus arma.

[These arms Aeneas (places here), taken
from the conquering Greeks]

And calls it a *Poeme*, or *Carmen*. . . .

BUT, HOW DIFFERS A POEME FROM WHAT WEE CALL POESY?

A Poeme, as I have told you is the worke of the Poet; the end, and fruit
of his labour, and studye. *Poesy* is his skill, or Crafte of making: the very
Fiction it selfe, the reason, or forme of the worke. And these three voices
differ, as the thing done, the doing, and the doer; the thing fain'd, the
faining, and the fainer: so the *Poeme*, the *Poesy*, and the *Poet*. Now, the
Poesy is the habit, or the Art: nay, rather the Queene of Arts: which had
her Originall from heaven, received thence from the *'Ebrewes*, and had in
prime estimation with the *Greeks*, transmitted to the *Latines*, and all Nations, that profess'd Civility. . . .

Theoretical remarks of this kind, which show Jonson following the
conventional notions of his age, do not call forth his characteristic
powers, and he hastens on to discuss the requirements of a good poet.

He has made a distinction between a poem and poetry, but it has not the significance of the same distinction made by Coleridge two hundred years later (and discussed in chapter 6). The poem is the product of the poet's labor, while poetry is the kind of skill involved. Both definitions are turned toward practical criticism, and it is with evident relief that Jonson goes on to describe the qualities needed in a successful poet:

> *First*, wee require in our *Poet*, or maker, . . . a goodnes of naturall wit. For, whereas all other Arts consist of Doctrine, and Precepts: the *Poet* must bee able by nature, and instinct, to powre out the Treasure of his minde. . . . To this perfection of Nature in our *Poet*, wee require Exercise of those parts, and frequent. If his wit will not arrive soddainly at the dignitie of the Ancients, let him not yet fall out with it, quarrell, or be over hastily Angry: offer, to turne it away from Study, in a humor; but come to it againe upon better cogitation; try an other time, with labour.

And on he goes, to discuss, with many examples from classical writers, the importance of care and revision. This is practical criticism in rather a different sense from that in which we use the term when we refer to the evaluation of individual works, but it derives from the same habit of mind as that which turns most readily to the assessment of works of literature and is less happy in philosophical discussion of its nature. Of course, there are many critics who have excelled in both (Coleridge, for example), but this need not prevent us from considering the various phases of practical criticism as constituting not only criticism of a different kind from that represented by the philosophical inquiry discussed in Part One but also as linked more directly to the contemporary literary scene, as more involved in the different kinds of practice going on in the literary world.

Dryden

Jonson, with his neo-classic temper, his concern for craftsmanship and polish, and his sense of involvement in the literary scene of his day, foreshadows in some respects both Dryden and Pope. His criticism, however, was sketchy and relatively small in quantity. Dryden, with a more diverse literary tradition behind him and a much greater critical output, remains the true father of English practical criticism. While sharing Jonson's admiration for the classical achievement, he was sensitive to changes in contemporary taste and eager to exploit the potentialities of new movements. In the great debate between those who claimed that the finest writers of Greece and Rome transcended any possible modern achievement and those who believed, on the other hand, that literature, like the other arts and sciences, could progress beyond anything attainable by the ancient world—the controversy was generally known as the debate between the Ancients and the Moderns —Dryden took no extreme position, but on the whole argued moderately and tolerantly on the side of the Moderns. He was more interested in a work's being good of its kind than in its conformity to any preconceived theories about good art. His own changing tastes and interests helped to make him responsive to different kinds of literary skill and of artistic conventions, thus giving him that primary qualification of the good practical critic—the ability to read the work under consideration with full and sympathetic understanding.

Dryden's *Essay on Dramatic Poesie*, from which, in Part One, we quoted Dryden's definition of a play, is a dialogue between four people about the respective merits of ancient drama, modern (Restoration) drama, seventeenth century French neo-classic drama, and the drama of "the last age" (the age of Shakespeare). The very fact that Dryden cast it into the form of a dialogue, where different people, each representing a different point of view, were allowed their full say, is evidence of his tolerant and inquiring mind. And though, as we have seen, theoretical matters are discussed in this dialogue, the center of interest lies in the practical question of which playwrights produce better plays. All four debaters are agreed on the definition of a play quoted earlier ("A just and lively image of human nature, representing its passions and humours, and the changes of fortune to which it is subject, for the delight and instruction of mankind"): they are chiefly interested in the qualities of craftsmanship which make one play better than another, in the *means*, that is, by which the end, concerning which all are in agreement, is achieved. Crites (the characters, who represent real people, are all given classical names: Dryden himself is Neander) begins by defending the ancients—the Greek and Latin dramatists—on the grounds that they "have been faithful imitators and wise observers of that Nature which is so torn and ill represented in our plays; they have handed to us a perfect resemblance of her; which we, like all copiers, neglecting to look on, have rendered monstrous and disfigured." "Nature" here means, of course, human nature, not natural scenery: Crites is maintaining that classical drama is more convincing as representation of human nature than is modern drama.

The dramatic "unities"

It is only after having made this point that he proceeds to talk about rules and the unities:

. . . I must remember you, that all the rules by which we practise the Drama at this day, (either such as relate to the justness and symmetry of the plot, or the episodical ornaments, such as descriptions, narrations, and other beauties, which are not essential to the play,) were delivered to us from the observations which Aristotle made, of those poets, which either lived before him, or were his contemporaries: we have added nothing of our own, except that we have the confidence to say our wit is better; of which none boast in this our age, but such as understand not theirs. Of that book which Aristotle has left us, περὶ τῆς Ποιητικῆς, Horace his *Art of Poetry* is an excellent comment, and, I believe, restores to us that Second Book of his concerning *Comedy,* which is wanting in him.

Out of these two have been extracted the famous Rules, which the French call Des Trois Unitez, or, the Three Unities, which ought to be observed in every regular play; namely, of Time, Place, and Action.

The Unity of Time they comprehend in twenty-four hours, the compass of a natural day, or as near as it can be contrived; and the reason of it is obvious to every one,—that the time of the feigned action, or fable of the play, should be proportioned as near as can be to the duration of that time in which it is represented; since therefore, all plays are acted on the theatre in a space of time much within the compass of twenty-four hours, that play is to be thought the nearest imitation of nature, whose plot or action is confined within that time; and, by the same rule which concludes this general proportion of time, it follows, that all the parts of it are to be equally subdivided; as namely, that one act take not up the supposed time of half a day, which is out of proportion to the rest; since the other four are then to be straitened within the compass of the remaining half: for it is unnatural that one act, which being spoke or written is not longer than the rest, should be supposed longer by the audience; 'tis therefore the poet's duty, to take care that no act should be imagined to exceed the time in which it is represented on the stage; and that the intervals and inequalities of time be supposed to fall out between the acts.

We need not here argue the historical question whether any such view was, in fact, implicit in Aristotle's *Poetics* or pause to explain how the critics of the Renaissance interpreted Aristotle's descriptive remarks about dramatic practice in his day as justifying the extraction of these rules about the three unities (the only unity that was critically important for Aristotle was that of action: the play had to hang together properly). The interest of this passage, regardless of the historical correctness of its appeal to Aristotle, lies in its assumption that human nature can be most adequately represented on the stage when the time which elapses during the actual performance corresponds most closely to the length of time which that action could be supposed to take in real life. The question, in fact, concerns the nature of the dramatic illusion. But before pursuing the implications for practical criticism of the view of dramatic illusion suggested here, let us allow Crites to conclude his discussion of the Unities as allegedly practiced by the Ancients:

For the second Unity, which is that of Place, the Ancients meant by it, that the scene ought to be continued through the play, in the same place where it was laid in the beginning: for the stage on which it is represented being but one and the same place, it is unnatural to conceive it many; and those far distant from one another. I will not deny but, by the variation of painted scenes, the fancy, which in these cases will contribute to its own deceit, may sometimes imagine it several places, with some appearance of probability; yet it still carries the greater likelihood of truth, if those places be supposed so near each other, as in the same town or city; which may all be comprehended under the larger denomination of one place; for a greater distance will bear no proportion to the shortness of time which is allotted in the acting, to pass from one of them to another; for the observation of this, next to the Ancients, the French are to be most commended. They tie themselves so strictly to the Unity of Place, that you never see in any of their plays, a scene changed in the middle of an act; if the act begins in a garden, a street, or a chamber, 'tis ended in the same place; and that you may know it to be the same, the stage is so supplied with persons, that it is never empty all the time: he that enters second, has business with him who was on before; and before the second quits the stage, a third appears who has business with him. This Corneille calls *la liaison des scenes*, the continuity or joining of the scenes; and 'tis a good mark of a well-contrived play, when all the persons are known to each other, and every one of them has some affairs with all the rest.

Here again, the question at issue concerns the nature of the dramatic illusion, the conditions under which we can achieve what Coleridge called "that willing suspension of disbelief for the moment, which constitutes poetic faith." And again the view put forward by Crites is the strict neo-classic position that the less call on the audience's imagination is made in moving people from place to place on the stage, the more persuasive and satisfying the play will be. (Which is to say that we would take more pleasure in a play which showed us the hero moving, between the first and second acts, from Cambridge to London than one which showed him moving from Cambridge to Inverness, while a play where he moved from Cambridge to Bury St. Edmunds, would be better still, and even better if he only moved to Huntingdon.) Crites continues:

As for the third Unity, which is that of Action, the Ancients meant no other by it than what the logicians do by their *finis*, the end or scope of any action; that which is the first in intention, and last in execution; now the poet is to aim at one great and complete action, to the carrying on of which all things in his play, even the very obstacles, are to be subservient; and the reason of this is as evident as any of the former.

For two actions, equally laboured and driven on by the writer, would destroy the unity of the poem: it would be no longer one play, but two: not but that there may be many actions in a play, as Ben Johnson has observed in his *Discoveries;* but they must be all subservient to the great one, which our language happily expresses in the name of *under-plots. . . .*

If by these rules (to omit many other drawn from the precepts and practice of the Ancients) we should judge our modern plays, 'tis probable that few of them would endure the trial: that which should be the business of a day, takes up in some of them an age; instead of one action, they are the epitomes of a man's life; and for one spot of ground (which the stage should represent) we are sometimes in more countries than the map can show us.

The third unity, that of action, goes beyond the question of visual illusion to touch the much more fundamental matter of the nature of esthetic unity—a matter on which both Aristotle and Coleridge, as we saw in Part One—had cogent points to make. But the objection that a play which presents action which could not be imagined as happening in real life in the limited time and space which actual performance in the theater must conform to is necessarily weaker and less well constructed than a play which ignores the physical boundaries of the theater is surely based on a misunderstanding of the nature of convention in art. It is true that even the greatest dramatists have been aware of discrepancies that may exist between the physical realities of stage performance and the imagined action: we remember Shakespeare's prologue to *Henry V:*

>   . . . But pardon, gentles all,
> The flat unraised spirits that hath dar'd
> On this unworthy scaffold to bring forth
> So great an object. Can this cockpit hold
> The vasty fields of France? Or may we cram
> Within this wooden O the very casques
> That did affright the air at Agincourt?
> O, pardon! since a crooked figure may
> Attest in little place a million;
> And let us, ciphers to this great accompt,
> On your imaginary forces work.

Imitation and convention

The impetuous romantic critic is liable to exclaim "Of course let us use our imagination; does not all art depend on the imagination?" and dismiss the whole question. But there is more to it than that. The poet must provide, and the audience must accept, conventions within which the imaginative expansion can take place. People do not normally sing when conversing, yet they do so in opera, and we accept it in opera by accepting the operatic convention. (If we fail to accept the convention, as Tolstoy did in his famous derisive description of a Wagnerian opera, the performance may appear utterly ludicrous to us.) No individual poet can himself create all his own conventions, for conventions must be based on some degree of public assent; yet he must bring them alive in his own way, or they remain mere conventions and not means of bringing imaginative life and scope to a necessarily limited work.

Dryden was very much aware of all this, and in the subsequent development of the dialogue he touches on the whole question of the nature of the dramatic illusion and its relation to dramatic convention in many indirect ways; and he also discusses, toward the end of the dialogue, the question of rhymed tragedies, and the defense of rhyme in tragedy involves Neander in some discussion of the relation between convention and realism, between Art and Nature. For there is a paradox at the heart of any imitative theory of the arts (as Dryden's theory was): for A to imitate B, A must be distinct and different from B. If A and B were identical there would be no point in one imitating or representing the other. Art and Nature are different; but Art imitates or represents Nature in some sense. If a sculptor were chiseling out a statue, with his model opposite him, and with every stroke made his piece of stone more and more like the model whom he was imitating, would it be the perfection of art or the frustration of art if at the moment of the last stroke the statue suddenly turned into the actual model? Such a question illustrates the paradox in which an imitative or representational theory of the arts is involved.

Let us for the moment skip part of the dialogue to see what Dryden does with this question when he comes face to face with it in his defense of rhyme in tragedy:

It has been formerly urged by you, and confessed by me, that since no man spoke any kind of verse *ex tempore*, that which was nearest Nature was to be preferred. I answer you, therefore, by distinguishing betwixt what is nearest to the nature of Comedy, which is the imitation of common persons and ordinary speaking, and what is nearest the nature of a serious play: this last is indeed the representation of Nature, but 'tis Nature wrought up to a higher pitch. The plot, the characters, the wit, the passions, the descriptions, are all exalted above the level of common converse, as high as the imagination of the poet can carry them, with proportion to verisimility. . . . Verse, 'tis true, is not the effect of sudden thought; but this hinders not that sudden thought may be represented in verse, since those thoughts are such as must be higher than Nature can raise them without premeditation, especially to a continuance of them, even out of verse; and consequently you cannot imagine them to have been sudden either in the poet or in the actors. A play, as I have said, to be like Nature, is to be set above it; as statues which are placed on high are made greater than the life, that they may descend to the sight in their just proportion.

" 'Tis Nature wrought up to a higher pitch." "A play, to be like Nature, is to be set above it." This is to suggest, though not to develop, the role of convention in art and to raise, though implicitly, the whole question of *stylization* and the different degrees to which it is appropriate on different occasions. The diction of Milton's *Paradise Lost*, a deliberately elevated poem intended to convey in a grand, symbolic manner some of the profoundest truths about man and his place in the universe, is very properly more stylized than the diction of a modern satiric poet commenting drily on some defects in contemporary civilization. The movements and gestures of Greek actors on the Greek stage were more formal and less realistic than the movements of actors on the modern stage because the Greek theater, a large, open-air amphitheater with an almost cosmic background and an atmosphere of ritual, demanded a larger-than-life scale if the final impression was to be convincing, "as statues which are placed on high are made greater than the life, that they may descend to the sight in their just proportion." The degree of stylization in a Noel Coward comedy is less than in a tragedy of Sophocles—or at least of a very different kind—and the result in each case is the appropriate kind of illusion. It is therefore uncritical to talk of simple correspondence to the conditions of actual life as constituting greater persuasiveness in the presentation. Art is not life; and if it were it could make no claim to illuminate life.

Dr Johnson on the "unities"

But quite apart from the interesting question of art, convention, and reality, and the relation between the three, the charge brought by Crites against the drama of his own day as compared with classical drama could be refuted in a simple, robust argument. A hundred years after the *Essay of Dramatic Poesy* Dr Johnson, in the preface to his edition of Shakespeare, said the last word on the unities of time and place:

The necessity of observing the unities of time and place arises from the supposed necessity of making the drama credible. The criticks hold it impossible, that an action of months or years can be possibly believed to pass in three hours; or that the spectator can suppose himself to sit in the theatre, while ambassadors go and return between distant kings, while armies are levied and towns besieged, while an exile wanders and returns, or till he whom they saw courting his mistress, shall lament the untimely fall of his son. The mind revolts from evident falsehood, and fiction loses its force when it departs from the resemblance of reality.

From the narrow limitation of time necessarily arises the contraction of place. The spectator, who knows that he saw the first act at *Alexandria,* cannot suppose that he sees the next at *Rome,* at a distance to which not the dragons of *Medea* could, in so short a time, have transported him; he knows with certainty that he has not changed his place, and he knows that place cannot change itself; that what was a house cannot become a plain; that what was *Thebes* can never be *Persepolis.*

Such is the triumphant language with which a critick exults over the misery of an irregular poet, and exults commonly without resistance or reply. It is time therefore to tell him by the authority of Shakespeare, that he assumes, as an unquestionable principle, a position, which, while his breath is forming it into words, his understanding pronounces to be false. It is false, that any representation is mistaken for reality; that any dramatick fable in its materiality was ever credible, or, for a single moment, was ever credited.

The objection arising from the impossibility of passing the first hour at *Alexandria,* and the next at *Rome,* supposes, that when the play opens, the spectator really imagines himself at *Alexandria,* and believes that his walk to the theatre has been a voyage to *Egypt,* and that he lives in the days of *Antony* and *Cleopatra.* Surely he that imagines this may imagine more. He that can take the stage at one time for the palace of the *Ptolemies,* may take it in half an hour for the promontory of *Actium.* Delusion, if delusion be admitted, has no certain limitation; if the spectator can be once persuaded, that his old acquaintance are *Alexander* and *Caesar,* that a room illuminated with candles is the plain of *Pharsalia,* or the bank of *Granicus,* he is in a state of elevation beyond the reach of reason, or of truth, and from the heights of empyrean poetry, may despise the circumscriptions of terrestrial nature. There is no reason why a mind thus wandering in extasy should count the clock, or why an hour should not be a century in that calenture of the brains that can make the stage a field.

The truth is, that the spectators are always in their senses, and know, from the first act to the last, that the stage is only a stage, and that the players are only players. They came to hear a certain number of lines recited with just gesture and elegant modulation. The lines relate to some action, and an action must be in some place; but the different actions that compleat a story may be in places very remote from each other; and where is the absurdity of allowing that space to represent first *Athens,* and then *Sicily,* which was always known to be neither *Sicily* nor *Athens,* but a modern theatre?

By supposition, as place is introduced, time may be extended; the time required by the fable elapses for the most part between the acts; for, of so much of the action as is represented, the real and poetical duration is the same. If, in the first act, preparations for war against *Mithradates* are represented to be made in *Rome,* the event of the war may, without absurdity, be represented, in the catastrophe, as happening in *Pontus;* we know that there is neither war, nor preparations for war; we know that we are neither in *Rome* nor *Pontus;* that neither *Mithradates* nor *Lucullus* are before us. The drama exhibits successive imitations of successive actions; and why may not the second imitation represent an action that happened years after the first, if it be so connected with it, that nothing but time can be supposed to intervene? Time is, of all modes of existence, most obsequious to the imagination; a lapse of years is as easily conceived as a passage of hours. In contemplation we easily contract the time of real actions, and therefore willingly permit it to be contracted when we only see their imitation.

It will be asked, how the drama moves, if it is not credited. It is credited with all the credit due to a drama. It is credited, whenever it moves, as a just picture of a real original; as representing to the auditor what he would himself feel, if he were to do or suffer what is there feigned to be suffered or to be done. The reflection that strikes the heart is not, that the evils before us are real evils, but that they are evils to which we ourselves may be exposed. If there be any fallacy, it is not what we fancy the players, but that we fancy ourselves unhappy for a moment; but we rather lament the possibility than suppose the presence of misery, as a mother weeps over her babe, when she remembers that death may take it from her. The delight of tragedy proceeds from our consciousness of fiction; if we thought murders and treasons real, they would please no more.

Imitations produce pain or pleasure, not because they are mistaken for realities, but because they bring realities to mind. . . .

"He that imagines this may imagine more." This to the modern reader is the true argument against enforcing the unities of time and place, and as far as it goes it is unanswerable. Yet we might add that it is the duty of the dramatist to provide the conditions under which the imagination of his audience can most properly operate. Conventions must be made proper use of, and must be employed with tact and consistency, if they are to be accepted without demur by even the most educated audience. To mix levels of stylization—unless a deliberate effect of irony is intended—may be to make imaginative acceptance impossible. The problem, here raised with reference to the drama, is not confined to plays, though the physical conditions of theatrical representation provide a concrete and easily understood example. The controversy about the unities is an extreme case of a kind of difficulty concerning the relation between art and reality which any

imitative or representational theory of the arts is bound to run into
sooner or later.

The case for "progress" in literature

But to return to Dryden: after Crites has praised the ancient writers
for more strictly observing the unities in drama than the moderns
he goes on to maintain that "if we allow the Ancients to have contrived well, we must acknowledge them to have writ better"—that is,
if their *plots* were good, their *style* was even better. Then another
member of the group, Eugenius, takes up the defense of the moderns
against Crites:

> I have observed in your speech, that the former part of it is convincing
> as to what the Moderns have profited by the rules of the Ancients; but in
> the latter you are careful to conceal how much thay have excelled them;
> we own all the helps we have from them, and want neither veneration nor
> gratitude, while we acknowledge that to overcome them we must make
> use of the advantages we have received from them: but to these assistances
> we have joined our own industry; for, had we sat down with a dull imita-
> tion of them, we might then have lost somewhat of the old perfection, but
> never acquired any that was new. We draw not therefore after their lines,
> but those of Nature; and having the life before us, besides the experience
> of all they knew, it is no wonder if we hit some airs and features which
> they have missed. . . .

Here Eugenius makes the simple but effective point that if art is
representational, the artist will profit more from keeping his eye on the
object to be represented than by looking only at previous representations, though of course he will be glad to get technical hints from his
predecessors. Eugenius also implies that the artist can build on the
achievements of his predecessors and that art can therefore progress
as the sciences can. The example of all who went before, together
with your own experience and talent, can surely combine to produce
something more impressive than has yet appeared.

This is an interesting contention, and one that is often made in our
time. (For example, the publisher of a popular story magazine recently
made the remark that any competent journalist today can open a story
better than Walter Scott.) We know that in the physical sciences a
man with much less genius than Sir Isaac Newton can, by standing on
Newton's shoulders, achieve insights and discoveries that were beyond

Newton's ken. But can we stand on Shakespeare's shoulders to produce better plays? Does art progress in such a way that a mediocre talent coming after a genius can, by basing himself on the achievement of the genius, achieve more than the genius could? The notion that it does—which it surely requires little argument to demonstrate as fallacious—is the typical error of those who supported the Modern side of the Ancients-versus-Moderns controversy, just as the notion that the Latin and Greek classics represented permanent and fixed standards of absolute excellence which subsequent works could only approximate was the characteristic error at the other extreme. Dryden does not, in fact, go very deeply into this question of whether and, if they do, how the arts progress—for they do progress in a sense and in certain areas—but in the course of the dialogue he does allow it to come up more than once. He was more interested in the differing potentialities of changing literary conventions than in the abstract question of whether art progresses in a straight line, and if he sometimes seems almost to accept himself the view which he puts into the mouth of Eugenius—as when he has his characters agree that "the sweetness of English verse was never understood or practised by our fathers"—it is always with reference to certain very limited technical developments.

Eugenius' defense of the moderns also includes the argument that they really stick to the rules of the ancient writers better than the ancient writers do themselves; modern literature is not defended here because it is freer and more imaginative and constructs its own forms regardless of the practice of the classics, but because (as a result of building on classical experience and on independent observation of "Nature") it observes such rules as that of the "unities" more strictly than the classical writers did. For, on this view, one of the functions of the rules is to systematize observation of reality and to provide technical hints on how reality, thus systematized, could be represented in literature—

> Those Rules of old discover'd, not devis'd,
> Are Nature still, but Nature methodiz'd,

as Pope was to write some fifty years later.

Literature and novelty

Eugenius also attacks the classical writers for their use of threadbare plots in drama:

. . . It has already been judiciously observed by a late writer, that in their tragedies it was only some tale derived from Thebes or Troy, or at least something that happened in those two ages; which was worn so threadbare by the pens of all the epic poets, and even by tradition itself of the talkative Greeklings, (as Ben Johnson calls them,) that before it came upon the stage, it was already known to all the audience: and the people, as soon as ever they heard the name of Oedipus, knew as well as the poet, that he had killed his father by a mistake, and committed incest with his mother, before the play; that they were now to hear of a great plague, an oracle, and the ghost of Laius: so that they sat with a yawning kind of expectation, till he was to come with his eyes pulled out, and speak a hundred or two of verses in a tragic tone, in complaint of his misfortunes. But one Oedipus, Hercules, or Medea, had been tolerable: poor people, they scaped not so good cheap; they had still the *chapon bouillé* set before them, till their appetites were cloyed with the same dish, and, the novelty being gone, the pleasure vanished; so that one main end of Dramatic Poesy in its definition, which was to cause delight, was of consequence destroyed.

In their comedies, the Romans generally borrowed their plots from the Greek poets; and theirs was commonly a little girl stolen or wandered from her parents, brought back unknown to the same city, there got with child by some lewd young fellow, who . . . cheats his father; and when her time comes, to cry *Juno Lucina, fer opem* ["Juno, goddess of childbirth, bring help"], one or other sees a little box or cabinet which was carried away with her, and so discovers her to her friends, if some god do not prevent it, by coming down in a machine, and take the thanks of it to himself. . . .

These are plots built after the Italian mode of houses; you see through them all at once: the characters are indeed the imitations of Nature, but so narrow, as if they had imitated only an eye or hand, and did not dare to venture on the lines of a body.

The first point made here is one which is well worth some examination. Can interest be aroused in a play or story which deals with events already known, in general outline, to the public? Eugenius implies that it cannot, and that a tragedy based on a known story can only produce boredom in the audience. We might note that if this is true, it can be charged against Shakespeare almost as much as against the classical dramatists. Most of his plays were based on known plots. The history plays were bound, in general outline, by the pattern of events as known to Shakespeare's contemporaries. Many of the others were based on well-known stories, and even *Hamlet* was a rendering of an earlier play by another Elizabethan dramatist on the same subject. No one today would suggest that these facts meant that Shakespeare lacked originality or that his plays lacked interest. Indeed, there must be few people who go to a performance of a Shakespeare play today who are not familiar with the play at least in some degree. Would it not follow, indeed, if Eugenius' assumption were correct, that we could never enjoy the same play twice, for having seen it once we would know the way the action unfolded and so would be bored at any subsequent performance?

The place of the detective story

It is a commonplace of criticism that an old subject newly imagined can be every bit as exciting as a play or story where the plot is wholly original (if a wholly original plot can ever really be produced); the only kind of story which depends entirely for its effect on the reader's not knowing beforehand anything of what happens is the modern detective story, where the sole interest lies in the mystery of "who-dunit," and surprising turns of plot are appreciated, not as incidents deployed in such a way as to bring out subtle kinds of significance that can be more deeply appreciated at each subsequent reading, but simply as devices to keep the reader in suspense until the mystery is solved. And once the mystery is solved the mood of suspense can never be recaptured and the main interest of the story has disappeared. So that a reader coming into a lending library to borrow a detective story will rightly turn down one which he has read before, for such a book will have no interest for him until he has forgotten it again. We can enjoy a detective story a second time once our memory of it has faded, but few would claim that they would go to the theater a second time to see *Hamlet* or *Antony and Cleopatra* only if they had been able to forget what they had seen the first. An art which depends on fading memory for its second appreciation is clearly in a very special category.

That certain kinds of popular writing, whose appeal is limited entirely to a simple kind of suspense, come into this category will be obvious enough. It will be equally obvious, on a moment's reflection, that neither the *Oedipus* of Sophocles nor the *Hamlet* of Shakespeare come into it. Both these plays could, of course, be regarded simply as "whodunits," with Oedipus the great detective who—in a surprise ending to end all surprise endings—finally proves himself to have been the murderer, and Hamlet the amateur sleuth trying to find out whether his uncle really did murder his father. If these plays were both detective dramas, much of their action and even more of their imagery would be redundant: the proper ending of *Hamlet*, for example, would be in the scene immediately following the play-within-a-play scene, where Hamlet has just satisfied himself of his uncle's guilt and the audience are now satisfied of it by overhearing him admit it. But of course the interest of these plays lies less in the detective side than in the exploration of a human situation in dramatic terms which the dramatist's handling of the story allows him to achieve. This is not, in fact, a point which Dryden has any of his characters make in reply to Eugenius, for Dryden, great critic that he was, was too preoccupied with what his age called "the well made plot" to have spent much time meditating on the relation between plot and total significance. The maintaining of interest by devices to achieve suspense, the provision of a consistently "rising" action, the progressive complicating of the situation until it is neatly unraveled by a timely resolution, the provision throughout of excitement and variety—these were the criteria he looked for when he himself criticized a play, as we shall see when we look at his analysis of Ben Jonson's *Silent Woman*. The only reply to Eugenius' charge is that given implicitly by Lisideius later on in the dialogue, when he defends French neo-classic tragedy on the grounds that its plots "are always grounded upon some known history," with the suggestion that this adds gravity and impressiveness to the action. Nobody in the dialogue relates the problem directly to Aristotle's discussion of probability and possibility and the relation of history to poetry.

The place of suspense

One must not deny that suspense is important in a play like *Oedipus*: it is indeed of the very greatest importance. But one must distinguish between the suspense generated by the play and seen in terms of the play and suspense which is genuine worry on the part of the reader or spectator. We might refer again to Dr Johnson on the unities, and stress the fact that we are dealing with an imaginative experience here, not with a series of personal distresses suffered by each member of the audience at the theater. A properly developed work of art provides the means to allow its readers or spectators to participate in the life which it generates, to participate with a rich imaginative fullness, to live for the time being in the universe created by the work, so that, while previous knowledge of the work can be profitably used to increase perception and understanding it certainly cannot spoil appreciation by preventing suspense or destroying mystery. The simple appeal to experience here—is one's second visit to a play of this kind spoilt by one's knowledge of the story, or does one appreciate the play less by having read it beforehand?—is conclusive.

It is typical of Dryden as a critic—and part of his greatness—that if he does not give all the answers, he does raise, in one form or another, almost all the great critical questions. This question of the relation between knowledge and suspense in a play so dependent on ironic developments in the action as *Oedipus* is suggestive and many-sided, and to explore it fully would mean to explore a great many artistic problems. Aristotle, it will be remembered, had said that plot was the "soul" of a tragedy, but he did not mean by this that the mere excitement of the incidents was all that mattered. Eugenius, in attacking ancient tragedy for basing its plots on known myths, was interpreting Aristotle's dictum too narrowly and unimaginatively, and by insisting on novelty and surprise was illustrating how in the latter part of the seventeenth century contrivance and ingenuity had come to be looked on as the most important qualities in a dramatist.

Eugenius' strictures on Latin comedy are more justifiable; for here he is not talking of a new treatment of an ancient myth, such as the Greek tragedians produced, but of stock comic situations with stereotyped characters, used again and again in very much the same way as nineteenth century farce or melodrama used over and over again the same kinds of situation and the same stock characters.

The question of comic relief

The third of the four characters in the dialogue, whom Dryden calls Lisideius, now undertakes to prove that French neo-classic drama of the seventeenth century is superior to all other: the French keep the classical rules better than the classical writers themselves did, their plots are single and unified, the development of the action well contrived, and the relation between exposition—speeches designed to give the audience information about what has happened before the play opens or what happens offstage—and action managed tactfully and persuasively.

If the question had been stated . . . who had writ best, the French or the English, forty years ago, I should have been of your opinion, and adjudged the honour to our own nation; but since that time . . . we have been so long together bad Englishmen, that we had not leisure to be good poets. Beaumont, Fletcher, and Johnson (who were only capable of bringing us to that degree of perfection which we have) were just then leaving the world; as if (in an age of so much horror) wit, and those milder studies of humanity, had no farther business among us. But the Muses, who ever follow peace, went to plant in another country: it was then that the great Cardinal Richelieu began to take them into his protection; and that, by his encouragement, Corneille, and some other Frenchmen, reformed their theatre, which before was as much below ours, as it now surpasses it and the rest of Europe. But because Crites in his discourse for the Ancients has prevented [anticipated] me, by touching upon many rules of the stage which the Moderns have borrowed from them, I shall only, in short, demand of you, whether you are not convinced that of all nations the French have best observed them? [Lisideius here talks about the unities of time, place, and action, and praises the French plays for their conformity to the two former.] . . . The Unity of Action in all plays is yet more conspicuous; for they do not burden them with underplots, as the English do: which is the reason why many scenes of our tragi-comedies carry on a design that is nothing of kin to the main plot; and that we see two distinct webs in a play, like those in ill-wrought stuffs; and two actions, that is, two plays, carried on together, to the confounding of the audience; who, before they are warm in their concernments for one part, are diverted to another; and by that means espouse the interest of neither. From hence likewise it arises, that the one half of our actors are not known to the other. . . . There is no theatre in the world has any thing so absurd as the English tragi-comedy; 'tis a drama of our own invention, and the fashion of it is enough to proclaim it so; here a course of mirth, there another of sadness and passion, a third of honour, and fourth a duel: thus, in two hours and a half, we run through all the fits of Bedlam. The French affords you as much variety on the same day, but they do it not so unseasonably, or *mal à propos* as we: our poets present you the play and the farce together; and our stages still retain somewhat of the original civility of the *Red Bull* [where all kinds of crude farces as well as prizefighting and animal baiting took place] . . . The end of tragedies or serious plays, says Aristotle, is to beget admiration, compassion, or concernment; but are not mirth and compassion things incompatible and is it not evident that the poet must of necessity destroy the former by intermingling of the latter? that is, he must ruin the sole end and object of his tragedy, to introduce somewhat that is forced in, and is not of the body of it. . . .

This is to make a more serious point than to insist on the unities of time and place, and in attacking the English—especially the Elizabethan—practice of including what we now call "comic relief" in tragedies, and in general of mixing comic and tragic scenes together, Lisideius is raising the question not only of unity of action but of unity of *tone*. More recent critics have justified the comic scenes in many of Shakespeare's tragedies by showing how they relieve tension where temporarily relief is necessary and how at the same time they provide, as it were, a symbolic counterpointing to the main tragic action which enriches its significance and sets going new reverberations of meaning. Yet, while few would question the immense effectiveness of such a scene as the knocking at the gate in *Macbeth*, with its arresting movement from murder to casual, everyday bawdry and its fine counterpointing of crisis and routine, there are, even in Shakespeare, less justifiable pieces of comic business in the midst of tragedy, while there is very little of the comic element in the tragedies of Shakespeare's contemporaries which can be properly defended as dramatically appropriate "comic relief." The Elizabethans did, indeed, overdo the "matching of hornpipes and funerals," as Sidney called it, and Lisideius has a point when he complains of the lack of unity of tone in English drama. Violent and unnecessary shifts in tone can destroy the power of a play as effectively as shifts in degree of stylization (from a popular colloquial diction to formal blank verse, for example) or inconsistencies in convention (such as allowing the spoken poetry to create the descriptive setting in one part of the play and in another relying entirely on painted scenery and lighting effects). The question is, of course, whether in a given case the shift is really violent and unnecessary. Modern poetic drama—notably in the work of T. S. Eliot —uses deliberate shift from formal to colloquial speech in order to achieve a certain kind of irony or make one part of the work comment obliquely on another; and Shakespeare moves from rapid prose to formal blank verse more than once in *Hamlet*, to cite only one example. But changes in tone, in degree of stylization, and in convention, if they are to be justified, must be done deliberately and cunningly in order to enrich the meaning of the work in a specific way, as in the contrast in *Henry IV* between the grave and stately verse of the political scenes and the rapid colloquial prose of the Falstaff scenes.

The throwing in of comic scenes, or scenes written in a different idiom, simply in order to divert the audience, is to mar the total effectiveness of the work, as Marlowe's *Doctor Faustus* is marred by the inclusion (probably not by his hand) of scenes of crude clowning between the soaring poetic explorations of the state of Faustus' soul.

These points will be obvious enough, but are worth making in view of the fact that it has long been the custom to regard all attack on tragicomedy or on comic scenes in tragedy as arising from insensitivity or a pedantic application of the rules. The fact is that such mixtures are dangerous in the hands of any but the real expert, and there are many more examples in English literature of bad mixtures than of effective ones. For the reader to be jarred out of the world which has been created for him through the spoken word operating within a certain convention, by a sudden change into a quite different kind of atmosphere created by language used in a different kind of convention, is a painful experience unless that jarring is deliberately managed to shake the audience or reader into a new perception, as a cunningly placed discord can throw new light on the melodic line in a piece of music. Lisideius, then, is raising a serious objection, which requires a profound answer.

Lisideius then goes on to praise the French plays for being "grounded upon some well known history" and the French dramatist because "he so interweaves truth with pleasing fiction, that he puts a pleasing fallacy upon us; mends the intrigues of fate, and dispenses with the severity of history, to reward that virtue which has been rendered to us there unfortunate." (This argument is reminiscent of Sidney.) And then he goes on to what is his principal reason for preferring the French drama to English:

Another thing in which the French differ from us and from the Spaniards, is, that they do not embarrass, or cumber themselves with too much plot; they only represent so much of a story as will constitute one whole and great action sufficient for a play; we, who undertake more, do but multiply adventures; which, not being produced from one another, as effects from causes, but barely following, constitute many actions in the drama, and consequently make it many plays.

But by pursuing close one argument, which is not cloyed with many turns, the French have gained more liberty for verse, in which they write; they have leisure to dwell on a subject which deserves it; and to represent the passions (which we have acknowledged to be the poet's work), without being hurried from one thing to another, as we are in the plays of Calderon, which we have seen lately upon our theatres, under the name of Spanish plots. . . .

But I return again to the French writers, who, as I have said, do not burden themselves too much with plot, which has been reproached to them by an *ingenious person* of our nation as a fault; for, he says, they commonly make but one person considerable in a play; they dwell on him and his concernments, while the rest of the persons are only subservient to set him off. If he intends this by it, that there is one person in the play who is of greater dignity than the rest, he must tax, not only theirs, but those of the Ancients, and which he would be loth to do, the best of ours; for it is impossible but that one person must be more conspicuous in it than any other, and consequently the greatest share in the action must devolve on him. . . .

But, if he would have us to imagine, that in exalting one character the rest of them are neglected, and that all of them have not some share or other in the action of the play, I desire him to produce any of Corneille's tragedies, wherein every person, like so many servants in a well-governed family, has not some employment, and who is not necessary to the carrying on of the plot, or at least to your understanding of it.

There are indeed some protatick persons [characters appearing only in the opening part of the play] in the Ancients, whom they make use of in their plays, either to hear or give the relation [the exposition]; but the French avoid this with great address, making their notions only to, or by such, who are in some way interested in the main design. And now I am speaking of relations, I cannot take a fitter opportunity to add this in favour of the French, that they often use them with better judgment and more *à propos* than the English do. Not that I commend narrations in general,—but there are two sorts of them. One, of those things which are antecedent to the play, and are related to make the conduct of it more clear to us. But 'tis a fault to choose such subjects for the stage as will force us on that rock, because we see they are seldom listened to by the audience, and that is many times the ruin of the play; for, being once let pass without attention, the audience can never recover themselves to understand the plot: and indeed it is somewhat unreasonable that they should be put to so much trouble, as that, to comprehend what passes in their sight, they must have recourse to what was done, perhaps, ten or twenty years ago.

Lisideius is making several interesting points here. "By pursuing close one argument, which is not cloyed with many turns, the French have gained more liberty for verse, in which they write." French neo-

classic tragedy concentrates on the final moment of crisis and by concentrating all attention on that crisis provides scope for formal poetic
speeches of declamation or analysis. The whole thing is done in slow
motion, as it were, compared with a Shakespearean tragedy, and the
spotlight is fixed on the faces of the principal actors as they twist and
turn in the emotional entanglements in which they have become involved. It is not the development of character under the stress of a
whole series of testing circumstances which interests Corneille and
Racine, but rather the emotional struggles of powerful characters
finally trapped in some web of circumstance. The point made by Lisideius is precisely that made by Lytton Strachey in his essay on Racine,
written in 1908:

. . . The true justification for the unities of time and place is to be found
in the conception of drama as the history of a spiritual crisis—the vision,
thrown up, as it were, by a bull's-eye lantern, of the final catastrophic
phases of a long series of events. Very different were the views of the
Elizabethan tragedians, who aimed at representing not only the catastrophe,
but the whole development of circumstances of which it was the effect;
they traced, with elaborate and abounding detail, the rise, the growth, the
decline, and the ruin of great causes and great persons; and the result was
a series of masterpieces unparalleled in the literature of the world. But, for
good or evil, these methods have become obsolete, and to-day our drama
seems to be developing along totally different lines. It is playing the part
more and more consistently, of the bull's-eye lantern; it is concerned with
the crisis; and, in proportion as its field is narrowed and its vision intensi-
fied, the unities of time and place come more and more completely into
play. . . . Racine . . . fixed the whole of his attention upon the spiritual
crisis; to him that alone was of importance; and the conventional classicism
so disheartening to the English reader—the 'unities,' the harangues, the
confidences, the absence of local colour, and the concealment of the
action—was no more than the machinery for enhancing the effect of the
inner tragedy, and for doing away with every side issue and every chance
of distraction. His dramas must be read as one looks at an airy, delicate
statue, supported by artificial props, whose only importance lies in the
fact that without them the statue itself would break in pieces and fall to the
ground. Approached in this light, even the 'salle du palais de Pyrrhus'
begins to have a meaning. We come to realise that, if it is nothing else, it is
at least the meeting-ground of great passions, the invisible framework
for one of those noble conflicts which 'make one little room an everywhere.' It will show us no views, no spectacles, it will give us no sense
of atmosphere or of imaginative romance; but it will allow us to be present

at the climax of a tragedy, to follow the closing struggle of high destinies, and to witness the final agony of human hearts.[1]

Strachey is putting in the terms of his own day the same arguments that Lisideius was advancing in defense of French neo-classic tragedy. The only real difference between them is that Strachey, having learned from several centuries of criticism and of change of taste, does not plead the virtues of the French as reasons for thinking the English, who possess very different virtues, to be inferior. But Lisideius is a character in a dialogue, and Dryden can make the different points of view which he introduces more clear-cut by having his characters for the most part argue against each other.

Techniques of exposition

Lisideius' discussion of the French method of giving the 'relation,' or as we should call it, the exposition, the initial information the audience must be given if it is to understand the opening of the action, shows his awareness of a very real problem. How is the dramatist to put his audience in possession of the necessary introductory facts without holding up the play by some tedious introductory speech or a piece of opening dialogue in which two characters tell each other what both know in order to inform the audience? Late Victorian comedy used such devices as the housemaid coming into the empty room to dust as soon as the curtain rose, and talking to herself about the various members of the family and their problems. Dramatists have used prologues of different kinds, and many other devices: one of the most interesting aspects of the maturing of Shakespeare's art is the increasing skill with which he manages to convey the necessary introductory information within the unfolding of the dramatic action. But even in his later plays, Shakespeare is sometimes careless about exposition; Prospero's long talk to Miranda in the second scene of *The Tempest*, and his subsequent rehearsal of Ariel's early history by way of punishment for Ariel's impatience, are not the happiest expositional devices. Exposition is most effective when nobody is aware that it is exposition —as in *Hamlet* or *Othello*—or where revelation of past incidents becomes itself an important part of the developing plot, as in Sophocles' *Oedipus* or, in a somewhat different way, in Ibsen's *Ghosts;* or again in

[1] Lytton Strachey, *Books and Characters,* 1922. Reprinted by permission of Harcourt, Brace and Company, Inc. and of Chatto and Windus, Ltd.

Hamlet, where the ghost's speech to the prince is both a high dramatic moment and the revelation of a preceding event.

Lisideius praises the French technique of exposition because in French tragedy the necessary information is given in the course of dramatic conversation between principal characters, not by means of a special prologue or through the conversation of minor characters introduced solely for this purpose. (Yet exposition through a speech of a minor character introduced for the purpose can, in expert hands, be immensely effective, as in Philo's opening speech in *Antony and Cleopatra:*

> Nay, but this dotage of our general's
> O'erflows the measure . . .

where in one sentence we get a vivid impression of what Antony was in Rome and what he has become in Egypt.) On the whole Lisideius is right: the French neo-classic dramatists tended to be more careful about exposition than the Elizabethans, for the diversity and rapidity of Elizabethan drama made it easier for them to slip in an extra scene for purely expositional purposes.

But there is another kind of exposition, Lisideius proceeds to say, which concerns not the presentation of events which happened before the opening of the action of the play, but of events which happen during the play—offstage:

But there is another sort of relations, that is, of things happening in the action of the play, and supposed to be done behind the scenes; and this is many times both convenient and beautiful; for by it the French avoid the tumult which we are subject to in England, by representing duels, battles, and the like; which renders our stage too like the theatres where they fight prizes. For what is more ridiculous than to represent an army with a drum and five men behind it; all which the hero of the other side is to drive in before him; or to see a duel fought and one slain with two or three thrusts of the foils, which we know are so blunted, that we might give an hour to kill another in good earnest with them.

I have observed that in all our tragedies, the audience cannot forbear laughing when the actors are to die; it is the most comic part of the whole play. All *passions* may be lively represented on the stage, if to the well-writing of them the actor supplies a good commanded voice, and limbs that move easily, and without stiffness; but there are many *actions* which can never be imitated to a just height: dying especially is a thing which none but a Roman gladiator could naturally perform on the stage, when he did not imitate or represent, but naturally do it; and therefore it is better to omit the representation of it.

The words of a good writer, which describe it lively, will make a deeper impression of belief in us than all the actor can persuade us to, when he seems to fall dead before us; as a poet in the description of a beautiful garden, or a meadow, will please our imagination more than the place itself can please our sight. When we see death represented, we are convinced it is but fiction; but when we hear it related, our eyes, the strongest witnesses, are wanting, which might have undeceived us; and we are all willing to favour the sleight, when the poet does not too grossly impose on us. They therefore who imagine these relations would make no concernment in the audience, are deceived, by confounding them with the other, which are of things antecedent to the play: those [the exposition of events antecedent to the play] are made often in cold blood, as I may say to the audience; but these are warmed with our concernments, which were before awakened in the play. . . . The soul, being already moved with the characters and fortunes of those imaginary persons, continues going of its own accord; and we are no more weary to hear what becomes of them when they are not on the stage, than we are to listen to the news of an absent mistress. But it is objected, that if one part of the play may be related, then why not all? I answer, some parts of the action are more fit to be represented, some to be related. Corneille says judiciously, that the poet is not obliged to expose to view all particular actions which conduce to the principal: he ought to select such of them to be seen, which will appear with the greatest beauty, either by the magnificence of the show, or the vehemence of passions which they produce, or some other charm which they have in them; and let the rest arrive to the audience by narration. 'Tis a great mistake in us to believe the French present no part of the action on the stage; every alteration or crossing of a design, every new-sprung passion, and turn of it, is a part of the action, and much the noblest, except we conceive nothing to be action till they come to blows; as if the painting of the hero's mind were not more properly the poet's work than the strength of his body. . . .

The last remark of Lisideius here—that drama is more properly concerned with internal action than with mere external physical action—is, of course, true, and would have been admitted as readily by Shakespeare as by Corneille. But the Elizabethans preferred to symbolize the inner action by appropriate outward action, to find in terms of the outward action what T. S. Eliot, in another connection, has called the "objective correlative" of the inward development. This is a difference in dramatic convention, not between the good and the bad, and once again the argument put forward by Lisideius really concerns differences between conventions. The showing of violent action of the stage, the bringing on of a few armed men to represent an army —the kind of thing that Shakespeare does in such profusion in the third act of *Antony and Cleopatra*—was perfectly appropriate on the Elizabethan stage, where the setting was symbolic rather than realistic and the audience understood it to be so, but less so on the picture-frame stage which came in at the Restoration and which Lisideius has in mind. Violent action was equally inappropriate on the Greek stage, for the very different reason that the formal and ritualistic movement of Greek acting made it impossible to do acts of violence convincingly, even at the symbolic level; and so the convention in Greek drama came to be that all such violent actions took place offstage and was announced by a messenger, whose speech was often remarkable for detailed descriptive virtuosity. The French neo-classic dramatists followed this mode, and thus developed their own kind of virtuosity in description of offstage occurrences. It was because in the late seventeenth century critics were beginning to forget the conventions of the Elizabethan stage that devices appropriate to that stage were thought to be unconvincing. It has been left to modern critics to re-interpret Shakespeare's theatrical devices in the light of the conventions of his own stage and in doing so to bring out beauties and kinds of effectiveness that had been missed for almost three centuries. Granville-Barker's *Prefaces to Shakespeare* achieve precisely this.

Dramatic conventions

The questions raised by Lisideius, therefore, in his defense of French neo-classic drama, can only be adequately solved through a proper awareness of differing dramatic and theatrical conventions and the devices appropriate to each. Critics always tend to assume that the conventions of their own day, or the ones to which they are most accustomed, are more "real" or more "natural," just as most theatergoers today probably believe that it is more "real" to see action presented in a room from which the fourth wall has been miraculously removed than to have it done on the platform stage of the Elizabethans with no attempt to give a precise visual location to every scene and with much more fluidity and symbolic scope in the movements of the actors. In fact, of course, neither convention is more "real" than the other. All we can demand is that the convention should be effectively used. There is no limit to the demands that can be made on the imagination—as Dr Johnson claimed in the passage from which we quoted—provided that the demands are made with proper tact. So Lisideius' point that "the words of a good writer . . . will make a deeper impression in us than all the actor can persuade us to, when he seems to fall dead before us" is true enough within the conventions of the Greek or the neo-classic stage, but on the Elizabethan and in considerable degree on the modern stage physical action can supplement speech and symbolically portray its meaning if dramatist, actors, and producer all show their appropriate skills. In bringing together defenders of different dramatic modes in this dialogue, Dryden is obliquely calling attention to the place of convention in art.

Dryden and Johnson on tragi-comedy

Dryden himself, in the person of Neander, answers Lisideius' arguments in favor of French neo-classic drama against the English. He grants "that the French contrive their plots more regularly, and observe the laws of comedy, and decorum of the stage . . . with more exactness than the English," and also admits that there are "irregularities" in English plays lacking in the French; but he believes that "neither our faults nor their virtues are considerable enough to place them above us." He reminds Lisideius that the definition of a play to which they all previously agreed contained the phrase "*lively* imitation of Nature," and maintains that excessive regularity and formality destroy the necessary liveliness in a play. (We might add at this point that almost everything said in this dialogue about plays applies, though not always in quite the same way, to other literary ways of handling a story, especially the novel. The problem of exposition is, in its own way, quite as acute for the novelist as for the dramatist, as is also the problem of convention and the question of the relation between events presented and events talked about.) As for "the mingling of mirth with serious plot," Neander does not condemn this in itself, though he condemns the way it is often done. He goes on:

He tells us, we cannot so speedily recollect ourselves after a scene of great passion and concernment, as to pass to another of mirth and humour, and to enjoy it with any relish: but why should he imagine the soul of man more heavy than his senses? Does not the eye pass from an unpleasant object to a pleasant in a much shorter time than is required to this? and does not the unpleasantness of the first command the beauty of the latter? The old rule of logic might have convinced him, that contraries, when placed near, set off each other. A continued gravity keeps the spirit too much bent; we must refresh it sometimes, as we bait in a journey, that we may go on with greater ease. A scene of mirth, mixed with tragedy, has the same effect upon us which our music has between the acts; and that we find a relief to us from the best plots and language of the stage, if the discourses have been long. I must therefore have stronger arguments, ere I am convinced that compassion and mirth in the same subject destroy each other; and in the mean time cannot but conclude, to the honour of our nation, that we have invented, increased, and perfected a more pleasant way of writing for the stage, than was ever known to the ancients or moderns of any nation, which is tragi-comedy.

"Why should he imagine the soul of man more heavy than his senses?" This sentence is worthy to stand beside Dr Johnson's later "He that imagines this may imagine more" as a sturdy assertion of the rights of the imagination, and Dryden is here defending tragi-comedy on similar grounds to those on which Dr Johnson defended Shakespeare for not paying attention to the unities of time and place. But Dryden has a second point: "contraries, when placed near, set off each other." This is perhaps a rudimentary notion of "comic relief," and indeed Dryden uses the word "relief" a few lines farther on. It is, however, only the barest sketch of a theory of comic relief, for he does not proceed to discuss the conditions under which comic scenes in tragedy can enhance rather than destroy the total tragic effect. Comic relief is surely more than the equivalent of incidental music between the acts; properly used, it is an integral part of the action and meaning of the play.

We might put Dryden's defense of tragi-comedy beside that which Dr Johnson was to include in his preface to his edition of Shakespeare. After pointing out that the distinction between tragedy and comedy arose from the accidental fact that some ancient dramatists chose as their subject "the crimes of men, and some their absurdities," he shows how the laws of each were deduced from ancient practice; and then he proceeds:

. . . there is always an appeal open from criticism to nature. The end of writing is to instruct; the end of poetry is to instruct by pleasing. That the mingled drama may convey all the instruction of tragedy or comedy cannot be denied, because it includes both in its alternations of exhibition and approaches nearer than either to the appearance of life, by shewing how great machinations and slender designs may promote or obviate one another, and the high and the low co-operate in the general system by unavoidable concatenation.

It is objected, that by this change of scenes the passions are interrupted in their progression, and that the principal event, being not advanced by a due gradation of preparatory incidents, wants at last the power to move, which constitutes the perfection of dramatick poetry. This reasoning is so specious, that it is received as true even by those who in daily experience feel it to be false. The interchanges of mingled scenes seldom fail to produce the intended vicissitudes of passion. Fiction cannot move so much, but that the attention may be easily transferred; and though it must be allowed that pleasing melancholy be sometimes interrupted by unwelcome levity, yet let it be considered likewise, that melancholy is often not pleasing, and that the disturbance of one man may be the relief of another; that different auditors have different habitudes; and that, upon the whole, all pleasure consists in variety.

Here Dr Johnson accepts Dryden's view of the pleasure to be derived from interspersing tragic scenes with comic, but makes also the further point that tragi-comedy is justified because life is like that. It was on these grounds, it will be remembered, that Dryden defended irregularities of the English drama in general against the cold formality of the French stage: the English method gave a livelier picture of human nature in action. We must remember that both Dryden and Johnson held that the main function of imaginative literature was to instruct the reader in what human nature was really like by proper representation of men in action, so that the "appeal from criticism to nature" was always available. In other words, any study of technique (which was the *means* of adequately presenting "just and lively images of human nature") could be cut short by an appeal to the *end*, the representational effectiveness of the whole. This is made clear by another passage in Johnson's preface, dealing with the same subject:

Shakespeare's plays are not in the rigorous and critical sense either tragedies or comedies, but compositions of a distinct kind; exhibiting the real state of sublunary nature, which partakes of good and evil, joy and sorrow, mingled with endless variety of proportion and innumerable modes of combination; and expressing the course of the world, in which the loss of one is the gain of another; in which, at the same time, the reveller is hastening to his wine, and the mourner burying his dead; in which the malignity of one is sometimes defeated by the frolick of another; and many mischiefs and many benefits are done and hindered without design.

In the controversy between Lisideius and Neander we often get the impression that Lisideius is so concerned with the means, with the details of technique, that he tends to consider them an end in themselves, while Neander has a more flexible sense of the relation between means and ends and glances from one to the other more readily. Lisideius, however, is in this respect more typical of the professional man of letters, for the practicing writer is as a rule more concerned with practical questions of craftsmanship than with the ultimate question of what it is all meant to achieve. The free play between theory and practice which we find in Dryden's criticism is one sign of his superiority to the ordinary professional critic of his or any other time. We return again to the *Essay on Dramatic Poesie*.

Variety and order

Neander next proceeds to defend the complexity of English plots against the singleness of the French:

And this leads me to wonder why Lisideius and many others should cry up the barrenness of the French plots, above the variety and copiousness of the English. Their plots are single; they carry on one design, which is pushed forward by all the actors, every scene in the play contributing and moving towards it. Our plays, besides the main design, have under-plots or by-concernments, of less considerable persons and intrigues, which are carried on with the motion of the main plot: just as they say the orb of the fixed stars, and those of the planets, though they have motions of their own, are whirled about by the motion of the *Primum Mobile*, in which they are contained. That similitude expresses much of the English stage; for if contrary motions may be found in nature to agree; if a planet can go east and west at the same time, one way by virtue of his own motion, the other by the force of the First Mover [an image from the Ptolemaic system of astronomy] it will not be difficult to imagine how the under-plot, which is only different, not contrary to the great design, may naturally be conducted along with it.

Engenius has already shown us, from the confession of the French poets, that the Unity of Action is sufficiently preserved, if all the imperfect actions of the play are conducting to the main design; but when those petty intrigues of a play are so ill ordered, that they have no coherence with the other, I must grant that Lisideius has reason to tax that want of due connexion; for co-ordination[2] in a play is as dangerous and unnatural as in a state. In the mean time he must acknowledge, our variety, if well ordered, will afford a greater pleasure to the audience.

"Variety, if well ordered" is what Dryden defends, and he shows in this argument a full sense of the importance of the one "unity" that must be adhered to if a work of art is to have any coherence and effectiveness of design at all—the unity of action. If subplots contribute to and enlarge the meaning of the main plot, then they are to be welcomed; if they do not, then they are justly condemned. Dryden had both a feeling for form and a feeling for color and richness, and he did not make the mistake of supposing that one was inconsistent with the other.

He applies the same argument to the question of variety of characters:

There is another part of Lisideius his discourse, in which he has rather excused our neighbours, than commended them; that is, for aiming only to make one person considerable in their plays. 'Tis very true what he has urged, that one character in all plays, even without the poet's care, will have advantage of all the others; and that the design of the whole drama will chiefly depend on it. But this hinders not that there may be more shining characters in the play: many persons of a second magnitude, nay, some so very near, so almost equal to the first, that greatness may be opposed to greatness, and all the persons be made considerable, not only by their quality, but their action. [One might think of Brutus and Cassius in Shakespeare's *Julius Caesar*.] 'Tis evident that the more the persons are, the greater will be the variety of the plot. If then the parts are managed so regularly, that the beauty of the whole be kept entire, and that the variety become not a perplexed and confused mass of accidents, you will find it infinitely pleasing to be led in a labyrinth of design, where you see some of your way before you, yet discern not the end till you arrive at it. . . .

So long as the total design remains unified, variety of characters is a virtue in a play rather than a defect. Everything depends on the way the action is handled; the events must be so bound together that the spectator or reader is led forward "in a labyrinth of design" with

---

[2] Either "lack of" has been unintentionally omitted here, or "co-ordination" is used to mean rival orders acting simultaneously.

the interest and the suspense maintained until the final resolution. Dryden and his contemporaries were in the habit of comparing the plot of a play with a "maze" laid out in a formal garden, which had a careful and intricate design, but which could only be seen bit by bit as a person explored it. The "well made play"—to use a favorite phrase of the day—was laid out like a well made garden: in both there was suspense as to what one was going to see next, in both there were unexpectedness and variety, yet both were ordered with meticulous care.

Kinds of artificiality

Dryden then proceeds to take up Lisideius on the subject of "relations" or exposition, and after some discussion concludes that "if we are to be blamed for showing too much of the action, the French are as faulty for discovering too little of it: a mean betwixt both should be observed by every judicious writer, so as the audience may neither be left unsatisfied by not seeing what is beautiful, or shocked by beholding what is either incredible or undecent." He then goes on to point out that a "servile" observation of the unities of time and place and other rules of that sort can result in "dearth of plot" and "narrowness of imagination."

How many beautiful accidents might naturally happen in two or three days, which cannot arrive with any probability in the compass of twenty-four hours? There is time to be allowed also for maturity of design, which, amongst great and prudent persons, such as are often represented in Tragedy, cannot, with any likelihood of truth, be brought to pass at so short a warning. Farther; by tying themselves strictly to the Unity of Place, and unbroken scenes, they are forced many times to omit some beauties which cannot be shown where the act began; but might, if the scene were interrupted, and the stage cleared for the persons to enter in another place; and therefore the French poets are often forced upon absurdities; for if the act begins in a chamber, all the persons in the play must have some business or other to come thither, or else they are not to be shown that act; and sometimes their characters are very unfitting to appear there. As, suppose it were the king's bed-chamber; yet the meanest man in the tragedy must come and dispatch his business there, rather than in the lobby or courtyard (which is fitter for him), for fear the stage should be cleared, and the scenes broken. Many times they fall by it in a greater inconvenience; for they keep their scenes unbroken, and yet change the place; as in one of their newest plays, where the act begins in the street. There a gentleman is to meet his friend; he sees him with his man, coming out from his father's house; they talk together, and the first goes out: the second, who is a lover, has made an appointment with his mistress; she appears at the window, and then we are to imagine the scene lies under it. This gentleman is called away, and leaves his servant with his mistress; presently her father is heard from within; the young lady is afraid the servingman should be discovered, and thrusts him in through a door, which is supposed to be her closet. After this, the father enters to the daughter, and now the scene is in a house; for he is seeking from one room to another for this poor Philipin, or French Diego, who is heard from within, drolling and breaking many a miserable conceit upon his sad condition. In this ridiculous manner the play goes on, the stage being never empty all the while: so that the street, the window, the houses, and the closet, are made to walk about, and the persons to stand still. Now what, I beseech you, is more easy than to write a regular French play, or more difficult than write an irregular English one, like those of Fletcher, or of Shakespeare?

It is a question of convention again. Which artificiality do you prefer: that of having the same place on the stage represent now one place and now a quite different one, or the sticking to the unity of place at the cost of the unrealities noted above by Dryden? On either side we might claim with Dr Johnson that "he who imagines this may imagine more." The important thing is that, whichever convention is employed, it should be employed skilfully and convincingly.

Neander concludes his defense of the English as against the French plays by "boldly affirming" two things of the English drama:

First, that we have many plays of ours as regular as any of theirs, and which, besides, have more variety of plot and characters; and secondly, that in most of the irregular plays of Shakespeare or Fletcher (for Ben Johnson's are for the most part regular) there is a more masculine fancy and greater spirit in the writing, than there is in any of the French. I could produce, even in Shakespeare's and Fletcher's works, some plays which are almost exactly formed; as *The Merry Wives of Windsor*, and *The Scornful Lady:* but because (generally speaking) Shakespeare, who writ first, did not perfectly observe the laws of Comedy, and Fletcher, who came nearer to perfection, yet through carelessness made many faults; I will take the pattern of a perfect play from Ben Johnson, who was a careful and learned observer of the dramatic laws, and from all his comedies I shall select *The Silent Woman;* of which I shall make a short examen, according to those rules which the French observe.

Dryden on Shakespeare, Beaumont and Fletcher, and Ben Jonson

Before he embarks on this "examen"—which is of particular interest as the first sustained piece of detailed practical criticism in English— Neander is asked by the others to give a general critical opinion of Shakespeare, of Beaumont and Fletcher (considered as a single dramatist), and of Ben Jonson. He does so, in the following paragraphs:

To begin, then, with Shakespeare. He was the man who of all modern, and perhaps ancient poets, had the largest and most comprehensive soul. All the images of Nature were still present to him, and he drew them, not laboriously, but luckily; when he describes any thing, you more than see it, you feel it too. Those who accuse him to have wanted learning, give him the greater commendation: he was naturally learned; he needed not the spectacles of books to read Nature; he looked inwards, and found her there. I cannot say he is everywhere alike; were he so, I should do him injury to compare him with the greatest of mankind. He is many times flat, insipid; his comic wit degenerating into clenches [plays on words], his serious swelling into bombast. But he is always great, when some great occasion is presented to him; no man can say he ever had a fit subject for his wit, and did not then raise himself as high above the rest of poets,

Quantum lenta solent inter viburna cupressi.[3]

The consideration of this made Mr. Hales of Eaton say, that there was no subject of which any poet ever writ, but he would produce it much better treated of in Shakespeare; and however others are now generally preferred before him, yet the age wherein he lived, which had contemporaries with him Fletcher and Johnson [Ben Jonson] never equalled them to him in their esteem: and in the last King's court, when Ben's reputation was at highest, Sir John Suckling, and with him the greater part of the courtiers, set our Shakespeare far above him.

Beaumont and Fletcher, of whom I am next to speak, had, with the advantage of Shakespeare's wit, which was their precedent, great natural gifts, improved by study: Beaumont especially being so accurate a judge of plays, that Ben Johnson, while he lived, submitted all his writings to

[3] As the cypresses do among trailing hedgerow shoots. Vergil, *Eclogues*, I, 25.

his censure, and, 'tis thought, used his judgment in correcting, if not contriving, all his plots. What value he had for him, appears by the verses he writ to him; and therefore I need speak no farther of it. The first play that brought Fletcher and him in esteem was their *Philaster:* for before that, they had written two or three very unsuccessfully. . . . Their plots were generally more regular than Shakespeare's, especially those which were made before Beaumont's death; and they understood and imitated the conversation of gentlemen much better; whose wild debaucheries and quickness of wit in repartees, no poet can ever paint as they have done. Humour, which Ben Johnson derives from particular persons, they made it not their business to describe: they represented all the passions very lively, but above all, love. I am apt to believe the English language in them arrived to its highest perfection: what words have since been taken in, are rather superfluous than ornamental. Their plays are now the most pleasant and frequent entertainments of the stage; two of theirs being acted through the year for one of Shakespeare's or Johnson's: the reason is, because there is a certain gaiety in their comedies, and pathos in their more serious plays, which suits generally with all men's humours. Shakespeare's language is likewise a little obsolete, and Ben Johnson's wit comes short of theirs.

As for Johnson, to whose character I am now arrived, if we look upon him while he was himself (for his last plays were but his dotages), I think him the most learned and judicious writer which any theatre ever had. He was a most severe judge of himself, as well as others. One cannot say he wanted wit, but rather that he was frugal of it. In his works you find little to retrench or alter. Wit, and language, and humour also in some measure, we had before him; but something of art was wanting to the Drama, till he came. He managed his strength to more advantage than any who preceded him. You seldom find him making love in any of his scenes, or endeavouring to move the passions; his genius was too sullen and saturnine to do it gracefully, especially when he knew he came after those who had performed both to such an height. Humour was his proper sphere; and in that he delighted most to represent mechanic people. He was deeply conversant in the Ancients, both Greek and Latin, and he borrowed boldly from them: there is scarce a poet or historian among the Roman authors of those times whom he has not translated in *Sejanus* and *Catiline*. But he has done his robberies so openly, that one may see he fears not to be taxed by any law. He invades authors like a monarch; and what would be theft in other poets, is only victory in him. With the spoils of these writers he so represents old Rome to us, in its rites, ceremonies, and customs, that if one of their poets had written either of his tragedies, we had seen less of it than in him. If there was any fault in his language, 'twas that he weaved it too closely and laboriously, in his serious plays: perhaps too, he did a little too much Romanize our tongue, leaving the words which he translated almost as much Latin as he found them: wherein, though he learnedly followed the idiom of their language, he did not enough comply with the idiom of ours. If I would compare him with Shakespeare, I must acknowledge him the more correct poet, but Shakespeare the greater wit. Shakespeare was the Homer, or father of our dramatic poets; Johnson was the Virgil, the pattern of elaborate writing; I admire him, but I love Shakespeare. To conclude of him; as he has given us the most correct plays, so in the precepts which he has laid down in his *Discoveries*, we have as many and profitable rules for perfecting the stage, as any wherewith the French can furnish us.

It will be seen that much of the effectiveness of the critical method employed here arises from the technique of comparison. Dryden has the qualities of all three (or four) dramatists in his mind at once, and illustrates one by comparing and contrasting it with another—which in fact enables him to say something illuminating about both dramatists at once. His distinction between the great natural gifts of Shakespeare, the cultivation of Beaumont and Fletcher, and Ben Jonson's learning is the main thread on which most of his criticism is strung. There is also a notion of *development* from the grand and rugged to the more polished and refined ("Shakespeare was the Homer, or father of our dramatic poets; Johnson was the Virgil, the pattern of elaborate writing"), though Dryden does not seem sufficiently aware that to excel in a contemporary fashion of witty discourse in a way that makes readers of one particular time hail an author as supreme is no necessary indication of development or improvement in any absolute sense. "The conversation of gentlemen," which Beaumont and Fletcher are praised for reproducing so perfectly, is an ephemeral fashion, and to imitate it too closely is to risk being forgotten when the fashion changes. Dryden might have made the point that Shakespeare builds on the wit of his day to produce something far richer and more permanent, while Beaumont and Fletcher tended to be satisfied with contemporary fashion in both wit and sentiment. In other words, Dryden (like all critics) is in some degree bound by his own time, and looking back from the 1660s on the achievement of the Elizabethan and Jacobean dramatists he cannot help reflecting certain movements of taste that occurred throughout the seventeenth century.

Nevertheless, his catholicity of taste and fairness of judgment are remarkable. The judicial balancing of virtues and faults, the sense that each of these writers has his own special gifts and is not necessarily to be censured for lacking qualities which another may have, the ability to summarize the total achievement of a writer, are all marks of a great critic. This, of course, is not practical criticism of individual works but the rather different type of criticism which consists in general assessment of a man. That shifts in taste as well as abundance in production had helped to develop a more mature and more flexible technique in this kind of criticism can be seen at once if we put Dryden's portrait of these dramatists beside Ben Jonson's sketch of Shakespeare. There are many resemblances, both in manner and in point of view, but the fact remains that Jonson's is a far sketchier and less organized performance than Dryden's more polished studies. Dryden's, of course, is a set piece, while Jonson was merely jotting down some random notes about Shakespeare's work and personality, so it is hardly fair to place them side by side. Yet even if we make allowance for this, the greater critical sophistication of Dryden must be acknowledged.

There is an implied contrast between technical perfection and human vitality in both Jonson's and Dryden's remarks, and when Dryden says that he admires Jonson but loves Shakespeare (which reminds us of Jonson's "I loved the man . . .") one would wish to hear more about the basis of this distinction between admiration and love and why those qualities in a writer which can arouse love in another writer are not also to be admired, even from a technical point of view. This is the means-ends problem again, just hinted at and no more.

Dryden on Jonson's Silent Woman

Dryden then proceeds to his analysis of Ben Jonson's play, *The Silent Woman*. It must be remembered that Dryden is here trying to show that, even if we observe the rules which the French dramatists so insist on and judge a play only by those standards, there are English plays which will emerge with full marks. He takes a play of Jonson's to demonstrate this, because Jonson is the most "regular" of the English dramatists. His "examen" of the play is then a technical analysis intended to show the successful integration of the action, the effective handling of the scenes according to the unities of time and place, the proper illustration of varieties of human nature, and the organization of the plot in such a way that interest is kept mounting until the final resolution. The analysis is a long one, but as it is a technical achievement of a high order and probably the first of its kind in English, it is worth quoting in full.

EXAMEN OF THE SILENT WOMAN

To begin first with the length of the action; it is so far from exceeding the compass of a natural day that it takes not up an artificial one. 'Tis all included in the limits of three hours and a half, which is no more than is required for the presentment on the stage: a beauty perhaps not much observed; if it had, we should not have looked on the Spanish translation of *Five Hours* with so much wonder. The scene of it is laid in London; the latitude of place is almost as little as you can imagine; for it lies all within the compass of two houses, and after the first act, in one. The continuity of scenes is observed more than in any of our plays, except his own *Fox* and *Alchemist*. They are not broken above twice or thrice at most in the whole comedy; and in the two best of Corneille's plays, the *Cid* and *Cinna*, they are interrupted once. The action of the play is entirely one; the end or aim of which is the settling Morose's estate on Dauphine. The intrigue of it is the greatest and most noble of any pure unmixed comedy in any language; you see in it many persons of various characters and humours, and all delightful. As first, Morose, or an old man, to whom all noise but his own talking is offensive. Some who would be thought critics, say this humour of his is forced: but to remove that objection, we may consider him first to be naturally of a delicate hearing, as many are, to whom all sharp sounds are unpleasant; and secondly, we may attribute much of it to the peevishness of his age, or the wayward authority of an old man in his own house, where he may make himself obeyed; and to this the poet seems to allude in his name Morose. Besides this, I am assured from divers persons, that Ben Jonson was actually acquainted with such a man, one altogether as ridiculous as he is here represented. Others say, it is not enough to find one man of such an humour; it must be common to more, and the more common the more natural. To prove this, they instance in the best of comical characters, Falstaff. There are many men resembling him; old, fat, merry, cowardly, drunken, amorous, vain, and lying. But to convince these people, I need but tell them that humour is the ridiculous extravagance of conversation, wherein one man differs from all others. If then it be common, or communicated to many, how differs it from other men's? or what indeed causes it to be ridiculous so much as the singularity of it? As for Falstaff, he is not properly one humour, but a miscellany of humours or images, drawn from so many several men: that wherein he is singular is his wit, or those things he says *præter expectatum*, unexpected by the audience; his quick evasions, when you imagine him surprised, which, as they are extremely diverting of themselves, so receive a great addition from his person; for the very sight of such an unwieldy old debauched fellow is a comedy alone. And here, having a place so proper for it, I cannot but enlarge somewhat upon this subject of humour into which I am fallen. The ancients had little of it in their comedies; for the τὸ γελοῖον [the laughable] of the old comedy, of which Aristophanes was chief, was not so much to imitate a man, as to make the people laugh at some odd conceit, which had commonly somewhat of unnatural or obscene in it. Thus, when you see Socrates brought upon the stage, you are not to imagine him made ridiculous by the imitation of his actions, but rather by making him perform something very unlike himself; something so childish and absurd, as by comparing it with the gravity of the true Socrates, makes a ridiculous object for the spectators. In their New Comedy which succeeded, the poets sought indeed to express the ἦθος [character], as in their tragedies the πάθος [emotion] of mankind. But this ἦθος contained only the general characters of men and manners; as old men, lovers, serving-men, courtezans, parasites, and such other persons as we see in their comedies; all which they made alike: that is, one old man or father, one lover, one courtezan, so like another, as if the first of them had begot the rest of every sort: *Ex homine hunc natum dicas* [You would say that one man was born from the other.]. The same custom they observed likewise in their tragedies. As for the French, though they have the word *humeur* among them, yet they have small use of it in their comedies or farces; they being but ill imitations of the *ridiculum,* or that which stirred up laughter in the Old Comedy. But among the English 'tis otherwise: where by humour is meant some extravagant habit, passion, or affection, particular (as I said before) to some one person, by the oddness of which, he is immediately distinguished from the rest of men; which being lively and naturally represented, most frequently begets that malicious pleasure in the audience which is testified by laughter; as all things which are deviations from customs are ever the aptest to produce it: though by the way this laughter is only accidental, as the person represented is fantastic or bizarre; but pleasure is essential to it, as the imitation of what is natural. The description of these humours, drawn from the knowledge and observation of particular persons, was the peculiar genius and talent of Ben Jonson; to whose play I now return.

Besides Morose, there are at least nine or ten different characters and humours in *The Silent Woman;* all which persons have several concernments of their own, yet are all used by the poet, to the conducting of the main design to perfection. I shall not waste time in commending the writing of this play; but I will give you my opinion, that there is more wit and acuteness of fancy in it than in any of Ben Johnson's. Besides, that he has here described the conversation of gentlemen in the persons of True-Wit, and his friends, with more gaiety, air, and freedom, than in the rest of his comedies. For the contrivance of the plot, 'tis extremely elaborate, and yet withal easy; for the λύσις, or untying of it, 'tis so admirable, that when it is done, no one of the audience would think the poet could have missed it;

and yet it was concealed so much before the last scene, that any other way would sooner have entered into your thoughts. But I dare not take upon me to commend the fabric of it, because it is altogether so full of art, that I must unravel every scene in it to commend it as I ought. And this excellent contrivance is still the more to be admired, because 'tis comedy, where the persons are only of common rank, and their business private, not elevated by passions or high concernments, as in serious plays. Here every one is a proper judge of all he sees, nothing is represented but that with which he daily converses: so that by consequence all faults lie open to discovery, and few are pardonable. . . . But our poet who was not ignorant of these difficulties, had prevailed himself of all advantages; as he who designs a large leap takes his rise from the highest ground. One of these advantages is that which Corneille has laid down as the greatest which can arrive to any poem, and which he himself could never compass above thrice in all his plays; viz. the making choice of some signal and long-expected day, whereon the action of the play is to depend. This day was that designed by Dauphine for the settling of his uncle's estate upon him; which to compass, he contrives to marry him. That the marriage had been plotted by him long beforehand, is made evident by what he tells True-Wit in the second act, that in one moment he had destroyed what he had been raising many months.

There is another artifice of the poet, which I cannot here omit, because by the frequent practice of it in his comedies he has left it to us almost as a rule; that is, when he has any character or humour wherein he would show a *coup de Maistre*, or his highest skill, he recommends it to your observation by a pleasant description of it before the person first appears. Thus, in *Bartholomew-Fair* he gives you the pictures of Numps and Cokes, and in this those of Daw, Lafoole, Morose, and the Collegiate Ladies; all which you hear described before you see them. So that before they come upon the stage, you have a longing expectation of them, which prepares you to receive them favourably; and when they are there, even from their first appearance you are so far acquainted with them, that nothing of their humour is lost to you.

I will observe yet one thing further of this admirable plot; the business of it rises in every act. The second is greater than the first; the third than the second; and so forward to the fifth. There too you see, till the very last scene, new difficulties arising to obstruct the action of the play; and when the audience is brought into despair that the business can naturally be effected, then, and not before, the discovery is made. But that the poet might entertain you with more variety all this while, he reserves some new characters to show you, which he opens not till the second and third act; in the second Morose, Daw, the Barber, and Otter; in the third the Collegiate Ladies: all which he moves afterwards in by-walks, or under-plots, as diversions to the main design, lest it should grow tedious, though they are still naturally joined with it, and somewhere or other subservient to it. Thus, like a skilful chess-player, by little and little he draws out his men, and makes his pawns of use to his greater persons.

This is a close and technical discussion of the play, yet even here Dryden allows himself to digress occasionally into a generalization, for example his discussion of humor. Such digressions give us glimpse of some of the critical principles underlying the analysis. For example, when he defends Jonson for his creation of the character of Morose, he appeals for a moment "from criticism to nature" and says that such a man actually existed. This, of course, would be no defense on Aristotle's principles, for, as we have seen, for Aristotle the actual was not necessarily the probable, and imaginative literature dealt with the latter rather than the former. Dryden touches on this point when he goes on to admit that "others say, it is not enough to find one man in such an humour; it must be common to more, and the more common the more natural." But he answers the point by defining "humour" as "the ridiculous extravagance of conversation, wherein one man differs from all others." This definition is part of a general theory of comedy which, however, Dryden does not elaborate. Nor does he enter into a discussion of the relation between extravagance and "just and lively imitation," though it would not be difficult to show that in this kind of comedy extravagance is the method of producing liveliness.

Dryden's main interest is with "the contrivance of the plot," and he shows in some detail how Ben Jonson succeeds in maintaining inter-est. For him the plot is the "intrigue," the cumulative complication and eventual resolution of the action. "The business of it rises in every act," and the resolution, when we are finally presented with it, is at the same time inevitable and unexpected. One might argue that this is to concentrate on the mere mechanics of a play, and to ignore the sources of its real life; that any competent detective story might be said to have the same virtues; and that nothing is said about the quality of Ben Jonson's imagination or the total esthetic achievement represented by the play. This is true enough up to a point, but it should be noted that in his discussion of humor, of the nature of the characterization, of the devices for making the audience interested in a character before he actually appears, Dryden goes beyond mere detective story devices. Further, Jonson's comedies are in fact brilliant exercises in the portrayal of the humor of character within a frame-work of a progressively intriguing action, the action itself deriving from the "humours" of the characters; they are quite different in kind from, say, such a comedy as Shakespeare's *Twelfth Night* and more akin to the eighteenth century comedies of Sheridan. Dryden's analysis goes further to explain the inner workings and the appeal of this kind of play than this kind of analysis would for Shakespeare—or, to take a very different kind of comedy again, for Bernard Shaw. Finally, it must be remembered that competent craftsmanship is the basic prerequisite for any success on the higher imaginative levels, and it is always healthier for a critic to concentrate on technique, and point out with the expert's eye the kinds of cunning employed in the work under discussion, than to concern himself with grandiose generalizations phrased in vague and subjective language. The most profound practical criticism will move freely from demonstrations of craftsmanship to discussions of ultimate effect and value, and, as we have seen, there is something of this movement in Dryden. If we feel that there is not enough, we must remember that Dryden lived in an age of technical consolidation, after almost a century of brilliant but often erratic literary production; technical discipline rather than surging inspiration was the objective of his generation. And Dryden, himself a practicing poet and dramatist of a very high order, was in a unique position to provide it both in theory and in practice.

We must remember, too, that Dryden's method shifts according to the work he is discussing; he was intelligent and sensitive enough as a critic to realize that different kinds of works require different critical approaches. He would never have analyzed Shakespeare the way he analyzed Jonson, for he knew that they were doing different sorts of thing. The greatest temptation for critics is, once they have worked out a method of analysis which applies to some of their favorite works, to stick to it rigidly and apply it inflexibly to works written on a different plan and with different ends in view. The nineteenth century critics who looked down on Pope because he did not write like Shelley were as much at fault here as the rigid neo-classic critics who censured all those who did not observe the "rules" faithfully. As Pope put it in his "Essay on Criticism," expressing (as he does throughout the essay) in a rhyming tag one of the great commonplaces of criticism:

> In ev'ry work regard the writer's end,
> Since none can compass more than they intend.

Of course, one can discriminate between ends, and maintain that the comedy of Jonson is, as a species of writing, less valuable or less interesting than the comedy of Shakespeare or of Aristophanes. But that must not mean that Jonson should be criticized as though he were an Aristophanes who failed.

Dryden himself summed up the matter very neatly in a note he jotted down on the fly-leaf of a book by Thomas Rymer, a rigid neo-classic critic who objected strenuously to everything that did not strictly follow what he deemed to be the rules of classical writing. Rymer produced in 1678 a book called *The Tragedies of the Last Age*, judging Elizabethan and Jacobean drama by classical rules and finding it sorely wanting, and Dryden made some notes for a reply in the copy which Rymer gave to him, but never published them. "It is not enough," he wrote at one point, "that Aristotle has said so, for Aristotle drew his models of tragedy from Sophocles and Euripides: and, if he had seen ours, might have changed his mind."

Rhyme as a convention in drama

The final argument in the *Essay on Dramatic Poesie* concerns the suitability of rhyme for drama. Dryden defends rhyme in drama against the contention that it is unnatural and gives the impression of an intolerable artificiality, by what is essentially an appeal to the conventional nature of all art. If one character speaks one half of a couplet and the other completes it, is this not monstrously unnatural? It might be in comedy, replies Dryden (as Neander), where greater realism is demanded, but in tragedy, which "is indeed the representation of Nature, but . . . Nature wrought up to an higher pitch" it may be perfectly appropriate. "The plot, the characters, the wit, the passions, the descriptions are all exalted above the level of common converse, as high as the imagination of the poet can carry them, with proportion to verisimility." As for the completion of a couplet by a second speaker, which gives the impression of a "confederacy" of two people—

how comes this confederacy to be more displeasing to you, than in a dance which is well contrived? You see there the united design of many persons to make up one figure: after they have separated themselves in many petty divisions, they rejoin one by one into a gross: the confederacy is plain amongst them, for chance could never produce any thing so beautiful; and yet there is nothing in it, that shocks your sight. . . .

In the defense of the *Essay on Dramatic Poesie*, which Dryden prefixed to the second edition of *The Indian Emperor* in 1668, he went further in this direction:

> As for what he urges, that *a play will still be supposed to be a composition of several persons speaking* ex tempore, *and that good verses are the hardest things which can be imagined to be so spoken;* I must crave leave to dissent from his opinion, as to the former part of it: for, if I am not deceived, a play is supposed to be the work of the poet, imitating or representing the conversation of several persons: and this I think to be clear, as he thinks the contrary.
>
> But I will be bolder, and do not doubt to make it good, though a paradox, that one great reason why prose is not to be used in serious plays, is, because it is too near the nature of converse: there may be too great a likeness; as the most skilful painters affirm, that there may be too near a resemblance in a picture. . . .

A play is not people speaking *ex tempore;* it is "the work of the poet." Art is not Nature, and there would be no point to it if it were. Dryden was the first English critic to concern himself with the relation between convention and naturalism (though he did not use those terms) in a representational theory of art.

Dryden on Chaucer

Dryden's critical output was so diverse that one could write a whole manual of criticism illustrating it solely by quotation from him. But we cannot, in a book of this kind, give too much space to any one critic, however stimulating and versatile. One further example of his critical writing, however, must be given. His *Preface to the Fables,* written in the last year of his life, discussed in a mature and relaxed manner some of the authors he had been translating (Homer, Vergil, Ovid, Chaucer, Boccaccio). There is an illuminating comparison between Homer and Vergil, and another between Ovid and Chaucer, but the high point for the reader interested in English literature is the long account of Chaucer which occupies the whole of the second part of the essay. Historical and biographical facts are here mingled with more strictly critical observations, but the central aim—to give the reader a sense of Chaucer's literary character and achievement—is never lost sight of and Dryden succeeds admirably in projecting into the reader's mind his own feeling for Chaucer as well as providing an objective account of his qualities. This is practical criticism really working; it is not written for the specialist or the fellow critic; the language is free from jargon; the movement from literature to life and back again is made effortlessly; a variety of tools are used to build up a picture of both the man and his work, and of the effect of his work on the reader; and the tone is continuously relaxed and almost colloquial. There are some historical errors: Dryden was led by the changes that had occurred in the language between Chaucer's time and his own into believing that Chaucer's verse was less regular than it in fact was. The seventeenth century did not read Chaucer properly, and was thus unable to appreciate fully his metrical skill; it was only after later scholars had investigated Chaucerian pronunciation that full appreciation of Chaucer as a metrist was possible. But apart from this kind of error, which was inevitable in his day, Dryden's remarks on Chaucer are a model of one kind of practical criticism. The discussion is less technical than the analysis of *The Silent Woman* and does not follow any very obvious plan or method. It is, in fact, popular criticism, but in the best sense of the word. It is criticism addressed to the intelligent layman, and is to be distinguished from the more strenuous kind of professional criticism whose value is of a rather different kind. The discussion of Chaucer follows after a comparison between Chaucer and Ovid. He turns now to "Chaucer in particular."

In the first place, as he is the father of English poetry, so I hold him in the same degree of veneration as the Grecians held Homer, or the Romans Virgil. He is a perpetual fountain of good sense; learn'd in all sciences; and, therefore, speaks properly on all subjects. As he knew what to say, so he knows also when to leave off; a continence which is practiced by few writers, and scarcely by any of the ancients, excepting Virgil and Horace. One of our late great poets is sunk in his reputation, because he could never forgive any conceit which came in his way; but swept like a drag-net, great and small. There was plenty enough, but the dishes were ill sorted; whole pyramids of sweetmeats for boys and women, but little of solid meat for men. All this proceeded not from any want of knowledge, but of judgment. Neither did he want that in discerning the beauties and faults of other poets, but only indulged himself in the luxury of writing; and perhaps knew it was a fault, but hoped the reader would not find it. For this reason, tho' he must always be thought a great poet, he is no longer esteemed a good writer; and for ten impressions, which his works have had in so many successive years, yet at present a hundred books are scarcely purchased once a twelve-month; for, as my last Lord Rochester said, tho' somewhat profanely, *Not being of God, he could not stand.*

Chaucer followed Nature everywhere, but was never so bold to go beyond her; and there is a great difference of being *poeta* and *nimis poeta*, if we may believe Catullus, as much as betwixt a modest behaviour and affectation. The verse of Chaucer, I confess, is not harmonious to us; . . . they who lived with him, and some time after him, thought it musical; and it continues so, even in our judgment, if compared with the numbers of Lydgate and Gower, his contemporaries: there is the rude sweetness of a Scotch tune in it, which is natural and pleasing, tho' not perfect. 'Tis true, I cannot go so far as he who published the last edition of him; for he would make us believe the fault is in our ears, and that there were really ten syllables in a verse where we find but nine: but this opinion is not worth confuting; 'tis so gross and obvious an error, that common sense (which is a rule is everything but matters of Faith and Revelation) must convince the reader, that equality of numbers, in every verse which we call *heroic*, was either not known, or not always practiced, in Chaucer's age. It were an easy matter to produce some thousands of his verses, which are lame for want of half a foot, and sometimes a whole one, and which no pronunciation can make otherwise. We can only say, that he lived in the infancy of our poetry, and that nothing is brought to perfection at the first. We must be children before we grow men. There was an Ennius, and in process of time a Lucilius, and a Lucretius, before Virgil and Horace; even after Chaucer there was a Spenser, a Harrington, a Fairfax, before Waller and Denham were in being; and our numbers [versification] were in their nonage till these last appeared. I need say little of his parentage, life, and fortunes; they are to be found at large in all the editions of his works. . . . As for the religion of our poet, he seems to have some little bias towards the opinions of Wicliffe, after John of Ghant [Gaunt] his patron; somewhat of which appears in the tale of *Piers Plowman:* yet I cannot blame him for inveighing so sharply against the vices of the clergy in his age: their pride, their ambition, their pomp, their avarice, their wordly interest, deserved the lashes which he gave them, both in that, and in most of his *Canterbury Tales*. Neither has his contemporary Boccace [Boccaccio] spared them: yet both these poets lived in much esteem with good and holy men in orders; for the scandal which is given by particular priests reflects not on the sacred function. Chaucer's *Monk*, his *Canon*, and his *Friar*, took not from the character of his *Good Parson*. A satirical poet is the check of the laymen on bad priests. We are only to take care, that we involve not the innocent with the guilty in the same condemnation. . . .

He must have been a man of a most wonderful comprehensive nature, because, as it has been truly observed of him, he has taken into the compass of his *Canterbury Tales* the various manners and humours (as we now call them) of the whole English nation, in his age. Not a single character has

escaped him. All his pilgrims are severally distinguished from each other:
and not only in their inclinations, but in their physiognomies and persons.
. . . The matter and manner of their tales, and of their telling, are so suited
to their different educations, humours, and callings, that each of them
would be improper in any other mouth. Even the grave and serious characters are distinguished by their several sorts of gravity: their discourses
are such as belong to their age, their calling, and their breeding; such as
are becoming of them, and of them only. Some of his persons are
vicious, and some virtuous; some are unlearn'd, or (as Chaucer calls them)
lewd, and some are learn'd. Even the ribaldry of the low characters is different: the Reeve, the Miller, and the Cook, are several men, and distinguished from each other as much as the mincing Lady-Prioress and the
broad-speaking, gap-toothed Wife of Bath. But enough of this; there is
such a variety of game springing up before me, that I am distracted in my
choice, and know not which to follow. 'Tis sufficient to say, according to
the proverb, that *here is God's plenty*. We have our forefathers and great-
grand-dames all before us, as they were in Chaucer's days: their general
characters are still remaining in mankind, and even in England, tho' they
are called by other names than those of Monks, and Friars, and Canons, and
Lady Abbesses, and Nuns; for mankind is ever the same, and nothing lost
out of Nature, tho' everything is altered. May I have leave to do myself
the justice (since my enemies will do me none, and are so far from granting
me to be a good poet, that they will not allow me so much as to be a
Christian, or a moral man), may I have leave, I say, to inform my reader,
that I have confined my choice to such tales of Chaucer as savour nothing
of immodesty. If I had desired more to please than to instruct, the *Reeve*,
the *Miller*, the *Shipman*, the *Merchant*, the *Summer*, and, above all, the
Wife of Bath, in the Prologue to her *Tale*, would have procured me as
many friends and readers, as there are *beaux* and ladies of pleasure in the
town. But I will no more offend against good manners: I am sensible as I
ought to be of the scandal I have given by my loose writings; and make
what reparation I am able, by this public acknowledgment. If anything of
this nature, or of profaneness, be crept into these poems, I am so far from
defending it, that I disown it. *Totum hoc indictum volo.* [I wish all of it
unsaid.] Chaucer makes another manner of apology for his broad speaking,
and Boccace makes the like; but I will follow neither of them. Our coun-
tryman, in the end of his *Characters*, before the *Canterbury Tales*, thus
excuses the ribaldry, which is very gross in many of his novels—

> But firste, I pray you, of your courtesy,
> That ye ne arrete it not my villainy,
> Though that I plainly speak in this mattere,
> To tellen you her words, and eke her chere:

Ne though I speak her words properly,
For this ye knowen as well as I,
Who shall tellen a tale after a man,
He mote rehearse as nye as ever he can:
Everich word of it ben in his charge,
All speke he, never so rudely, ne large:
Or else he mote tellen his tale untrue,
Or feine things, or find words new:
He may not spare, altho he were his brother,
He mote as well say o word as another.
Crist spake himself ful broad in holy Writ,
And well I wote no villainy is it,
Eke *Plato* saith, who so can him rede,
The words mote been cousin to the dede.

Yet if a man should have enquired of Boccace or of Chaucer, what need
they had of introducing such characters, where obscene words were
proper in their mouths, but very indecent to be heard; I know not what
answer they could have made; for that reason, such tales shall be left untold
by me. You have here a specimen of Chaucer's language, which is so obsolete, that his sense is scarce to be understood; and you have likewise more
than one example of his unequal numbers, which were mentioned before.
Yet many of his verses consist of ten syllables, and the words not much
behind our present English: as for example, these two lines, in the description of the Carpenter's young wife—

Wincing she was, as is a jolly colt,
Long as a mast, and upright as a bolt.

. . . Chaucer, I confess, is a rough diamond, and must first be polished,
ere he shines. I deny not likewise, that, living in our early days of poetry,
he writes not always of a piece; but sometimes mingles trivial things with
those of greater moment. Sometimes also, though not often, he runs riot,
like Ovid, and knows not when he has said enough. But there are more
great wits beside Chaucer, whose fault is their excess of conceits, and those
ill sorted. An author is not to write all he can, but all he ought. Having observed this redundancy in Chaucer, (as it is an easy matter for a man of
ordinary parts to find a fault in one of greater,) I have not tied myself to a
literal translation; but have often omitted what I judged unnecessary, or
not of dignity enough to appear in the company of better thoughts. I have
presumed further, in some places, and added somewhat of my own where
I thought my author was deficient, and had not given his thoughts their
true lustre, for want of words in the beginning of our language. And to
this I was the more emboldened, because (if I may be permitted to say it
of myself) I found I had a soul congenial to his, and that I had been con-

versant in the same studies. Another poet, in another age, may take the same liberty with my writings; if at least they live long enough to deserve correction. It was also necessary sometimes to restore the sense of Chaucer, which was lost or mangled in the errors of the press. Let this example suffice at present: in the story of *Palamon and Arcite*, where the temple of Diana is described, you find these verses, in all the editions of our author:—

> There saw I *Danè* turned into a tree,
> I mean not the goddess *Diane*
> But *Venus* daughter, which that hight **Danè**.

Which, after a little consideration, I knew was to be reformed into this sense, that *Daphne*, the daughter of Peneus, was turned into a tree. I durst not make this bold with Ovid, lest some future Milbourne should arise, and say, I varied from my author, because I understood him not.

Dryden then goes on to discuss another objection to his rendering Chaucer into modern English—the view that "there is a certain veneration due to his old language; and that it is little less than profanation and sacrilege to alter it." This leads him to make some interesting remarks on changing language:

When an ancient word, for its sound and significancy, deserves to be revived, I have that reasonable veneration for antiquity to restore it. All beyond this is superstition. Words are not like landmarks, so sacred as never to be removed; customs are changed, and even statutes are silently repealed, when the reason ceases for which they were enacted. As for the other part of the argument, that his thoughts will lose of their original beauty by the innovation of words; in the first place, not only their beauty, but their being is lost, where they are no longer understood, which is the present case. I grant that something must be lost in all transfusion, that is, in all translation; but the sense will remain, which would otherwise be lost, or at least be maimed, when it is scarce intelligible, and that but to a few. . . . I think I have just occasion to complain of them, who because they understand Chaucer, would deprive the greater part of their country-men of the same advantage, and hoard him up, as misers do their grandam gold, only to look on it themselves, and hinder others from making use of it. In sum, I seriously protest, that no man ever had, or can have, a greater veneration for Chaucer than myself. I have translated some parts of his works, only that I might perpetuate his memory, amongst my countrymen. If I have altered him anywhere for the better, I must at the same time acknowledge, that I could have done nothing without him. . . .

It will be seen that Dryden moves freely from critical to historical remarks, and that much of his discussion of Chaucer's technique is threaded on to a historical view of the progress of versification from early crudity to modern refinement. This view of the progressive "refinement of our numbers" Dryden shared with his age. The smooth and polished couplets which were coming to be the norm of accepted verse, and which were to remain so until well into the eighteenth century, were the standard on which Dryden judged Chaucer's verse, as he read it. (And, as we have noted, as he read it it appeared less smooth and polished than in fact it was.) We have here, therefore, an interesting use of a critical preference leading to a historical view of progress. The historical view is in many respects justified: if Dryden was wrong in his view of Chaucer's versification he was certainly right in believing that his own age had seen a progressive refinement (in his sense of the term) of verse, and that the couplets of the late seventeenth century were metrically smoother than, say, the poetry of John Donne. Whether that metrical smoothness represented an absolute virtue is another question; but for those who believed that it did it was perfectly logical to hail Denham and Waller (pioneers in this smoother verse) as the refiners of our numbers and to look back on those who appeared not yet to have acquired it as handicapped by the relatively primitive state of the poetry of their time.

That progress in the technique of versification does in fact take place in certain periods can be proved by many examples, notably the development in the late fifteenth and early sixteenth century. In the relatively rapid change from Middle English to modern English which the language had just undergone, with all the ensuing confusion about accent and pronunciation, a stable metric was difficult to achieve, and that it was achieved progressively can be seen by anyone who compares, say, the sonnets of Wyatt with those of Surrey. Criticism often wishes to take cognizance of such development in order to explain and even defend technical deficiencies in an otherwise admirable writer. That Dryden was mistaken in his view of Chaucer's versification need not blind us to the interest and value of his mingling of critical and historical apparatus in this essay.

Not only does Dryden move freely between history and criticism, allowing each to illuminate the other, but he brings in also biography and autobiography. He relates, though not at length or in any systematic way, Chaucer's character to his way of writing, while deducing the character from the way it reflects itself in the writing—not as circular a procedure as might be imagined, for a view of Chaucer's attitude to life derived from one phase of his work could be helpfully applied to another phase in which the reflection of the author's character is not at once apparent. Dryden also relates Chaucer's portrayal of character on the one hand to general truths about human nature and on the other to the historical situation in Chaucer's day, showing how Chaucer was able to be faithful to both, to present the universal through the particular. Here both history and psychology are employed in critical evaluation.

Other considerations, such as the place of obscenity in literature and the propriety of rewriting the works of an old writer in contemporary language, emerge naturally from the conversational character of the essay, and generalizations on a number of related subjects are thrown out, though not always pursued. The autobiographical references to his own activity and attitudes give point and liveliness to some of these generalizations. Dryden, as a man of letters and a poet in his own right, feels no compunction in using his own situation in order to illustrate literary questions. When he protests his own veneration for Chaucer while defending his right to turn Chaucer's work into the language of Dryden's own day, he is using the example of the relation of one poet to another in order to prove his point. Indeed, much of the ease, versatility, and lack of any rigid critical scheme which this essay shows would be defects in the work of a critic who was not himself a distinguished creative writer. Being a creative writer, Dryden can talk about Chaucer in this relaxed and half autobiographical way and at the same time make illuminating comments. A critic who is merely a critic requires a much more systematic approach if he is to avoid the kind of impressionist chatter which may satisfy the writer but has little to offer to any reader.

In Ben Jonson and Dryden we see the creative writer functioning also as practical critic. In Dryden we can see how the existence of a greater variety of literature on which criticism can exercise itself helps to produce maturity and flexibility in the critic. In the multiple comparisons and contrasts which we find in the *Essay on Dramatic Poesie* —between classical drama, French drama, English drama, and between English drama of different periods—we can see illustrated the truth that practical criticism can only come fully into its own after sufficient literature of different kinds has been produced, each good in its own kind. A mere "two term dialectic," whether the terms are Ancient and Modern, Classical and Romantic, disciplined and free, or anything else, will not provide a basis for critical discussion sufficiently discriminating and sufficiently flexible to be sure of seeing what really goes on in different works. The terms must always be more than two, the question more than a simple "either-or" question, if comparisons are to be fruitfully used in order to establish standards whose application will both increase insight and sharpen judgment.

The "unities"

Critics have long since ceased to argue about the unities of time and place, but the practicing playwright is still concerned with them. There are certain kinds of play where any major jump in time is liable to destroy the unity of tone. One could not imagine, for example, the principal characters in Wilde's *The Importance of Being Earnest* or Shaw's *Candida* meeting ten years later and carrying on in the mood set by the early part of the play. It might be argued that tragedy, which needs development and often depends on the passing of time to bring out the full tragic irony of a situation, can more easily dismiss the unity of time than comedy. It is perhaps significant that the more profound Shaw intends his plays to be the longer time they tend to represent: consider the time element in *Candida*, *Saint Joan*, and *Back to Methusaleh*, for example, which are in ascending order of seriousness. Most contemporary comedies, and indeed the greater number of plays that are not comedies, tend to stick roughly to the unity of time, if only because it takes a greater genius to handle a large area of time successfully than to keep the action confined to a relatively short period.

Tragedies like *King Lear* and *Antony and Cleopatra* require both lapse of considerable time and movement in space to achieve their dramatic intention. But Dryden, handling in his *All for Love* the same story as Shakespeare treated in *Antony and Cleopatra*, sticks rigidly to all the neo-classic unities. Dryden, like the French neo-classic dramatists Corneille and Racine, organizes his story so as to make the unities natural and inevitable; he concentrates on the final moments of crisis in a situation, showing the twists and turns of a heroic mind when landed with an inescapable and insoluble problem. This, of course, puts a greater burden on the exposition. The student might compare how background information is revealed to the audience in Shakespeare's *Antony and Cleopatra* with the way Dryden handles the problem of exposition in *All for Love*. Or compare the problem of exposition that Shakespeare faces in *The Tempest* (the one play where he sticks to the unities) with the exposition in *King Lear*. A comparison of Ibsen's *Ghosts* with his *Peer Gynt* on this point would also be fruitful. In his more tightly knit plays, Ibsen is remarkably successful in making information about the past into dramatic revelations which heighten the dramatic tension. Consider, in this connection, not only *Ghosts* but also *A Doll's House*, *The Master Builder*, and *Rosmersholm*.

The modern dramatist, influenced, perhaps, by the motion picture technique, tends to make frequent use of the "flashback," and will move the play back a long time—say, into the hero's childhood—in a later scene. Consider Arthur Miller's technique in *Death of a Salesman*. The deliberate flashback tends to be more artificial than natural revelation of the past in the course of the dramatic action. The motion picture, with its ability not only to move rapidly in place and time but also to fade one scene into another and to indulge in such devices as having a man turn into a child as we look at him, has suggested new ways of handling the problem of exposition.

The question of the unities and their relation to expository devices concerns the novel as well as the drama. James Joyce in *Ulysses* devotes his huge novel to a presentation of a group of characters in a single city during a single day, yet by the end of the book we know the whole past life of the principal characters, as revealed through retrospective reverie on the characters' part. How different this is from Tolstoy's method in *War and Peace*! Different again is a novel such as George Eliot's *Adam Bede*, with its dependence on time to achieve the changes necessary for the life of the novel. Or consider the extraordinary concentration of mood and tone achieved by Hemingway in *The Old Man and the Sea*. At the other extreme from this concentrated kind of novel, which observes the unities strictly, is the *Bildungsroman*, the novel which presents the education of the hero by his experiences from childhood to manhood. Neither Dickens' *Great Expectations* nor Samuel Butler's *The Way of All Flesh* could be conceived of as observing the unities; in each case change and development over a period of time is the very essence of the novel—as it is, in yet a different way, in Evelyn Waugh's *Brideshead Revisited*. Proust, of course, could not even have begun to imagine his great novel sequence in terms of the unity of time; yet, on the other hand, the author is always in the present remembering; he begins by throwing his mind back and ends by coming back to where he started; and it is the reader's continual awareness of the present personality of the narrator as he draws out his story from his memory that helps to give the book unity. Proust does not deal with time as the picaresque novelist deals with space, leaving one thing behind to move to another: the unity of the rememberer binds all together.

These are only a few suggestions of how the problem of the unities is still very much alive in both drama and fiction.

Imitation and convention

With the revival of poetic drama in the present century, critical interest has again concentrated on the kind of question that Dryden raises in the latter part of his *Essay on Dramatic Poesie*. Yeats was much concerned with the problem of stylization in art, and some of his verse dramas are stylized almost to the point of ritual. One might compare his verse play *Calvary* (where the characters either wear masks or have their faces made up to resemble masks) with his *The Words Upon the Window Pane*, with its colloquial prose, and try to determine the different kind of dramatic effect achieved in each case. Or consider the shift in style and tone in the speech of the four knights at the end of Eliot's *Murder in the Cathedral*. Eliot shifts his degree of stylization deliberately in all his plays, moving from a formal poetic utterance to deliberate colloquialism in order to achieve a certain kind of effect. One might consider how far this is comparable to the use of "comic relief" in Elizabethan tragedy.

Shakespeare, as always, provides a host of fruitful examples for study. Not only can we consider the different functions of verse and prose in those of his plays where he uses both—and this is a most interesting study—but we can compare a play such as *Richard II*, which attempts to give the Elizabethan view of a medieval king by a more ritualistic use of language than he employs anywhere else, with, for example, *Henry IV*, where there is both prose and verse used for different purposes but where even the verse is more forthright and "practical" than it is anywhere in *Richard II*. (The reader might consult Dover Wilson's introduction to the New Cambridge edition of *Richard II* on this point, and also Walter Pater's essay on "Shakespeare's English Kings.") An interesting contrast between a stylized, and therefore timeless, and a realistic, colloquial, and therefore dated, handling of the Richard II theme is between Shakespeare's play and Gordon Daviot's *Richard of Bordeaux.* The latter play presents the characters in terms of attitudes and explanations current about 1930, just as Shaw, in, say, *Caesar and Cleopatra,* presents the Egyptians and Romans realistically in terms of their modern equivalents. As fashions in ideas and expression change, this kind of play becomes rapidly dated. Some degree of stylization is necessary to achieve universality. Of course there are many ways of achieving stylization. Oscar Wilde achieves it in his plays by the continuous use of epigram, so that the whole action is lifted into a realm of ideal wit, rather in the manner of restoration comedy.

Suspense

Suspense may be defined as an intensification of interest in what happens next, and is necessary in some degree for all drama and most fiction. In its most significant form, its effect is not lessened by the reader's or the audience's previous knowledge of the outcome, partly because if the play or novel is effectively handled we lose ourselves in the given moment as it comes along and respond in terms of the situation as it is being developed, and partly because true suspense is not dependent on ignorance of the eventual outcome but on waiting for the inevitable to happen. There is a well-known story of the man who always dropped his shoes after taking them off late at night, until one night, after protests from the people who lived below him, he remembered to be quiet about it—but only after he had already taken off one shoe. He took off the second with great care and laid it gently on the ground. An hour or so later the man who lived below came up, pale with anguish, and exclaimed "For God's sake, when are you going to drop the other shoe?" Waiting for the inevitable is more excruciating than waiting in total ignorance of the possible outcome. We know fairly early in *Oedipus the King*—whether we have read it before or not—that Oedipus will eventually reveal himself to be the murderer; we are fascinated in watching him move unconscious toward his doom.

There are, of course, other kinds of suspense, and it would be profitable to consider in detail the different kinds of suspense in *Oedi-*

pus, Hamlet, Ghosts, Murder in the Cathedral, and a contemporary detective story. And there are degrees of suspense. There is more suspense in *Othello* than in *Hamlet,* more in *Murder in the Cathedral* than in *The Family Reunion.* There are kinds of fiction where there is virtually none—a novel by Thomas Love Peacock or, in a very different way, one by Virginia Woolf. If suspense means heightened interest in the progress of the action, it is worth considering in what way interest can be sustained—and what kind of interest it is—in a novel with no suspense. In this connection one might ask: to what kinds of action, either in drama or fiction, is the analytic method employed by Dryden in his "examen" of *The Silent Woman* applicable?

Comic relief

We tend to take for granted now that comic relief in tragedy is a good thing, yet it has been employed comparatively rarely in the history of literature and even more rarely employed with success. Greek drama, of course, never used it; the Elizabethans used it profusely, and of them only Shakespeare with consistent success. What are the conditions for the success of comic relief? They are difficult to define, but at least one can say that for comic relief to be successful the comic scenes must provide both a relief of tension and an oblique commentary—illuminating by the sudden difference of its point of view from that exhibited in the tragic scenes—on the same kind of human world in which the tragic action takes place. True comic relief completes the picture of the tragic world. The grave diggers in *Hamlet,* jesting as they dig the grave which turns out to be for the most innocent of all the victims of the tragic chain of events which the play develops, remind us of the workaday world in terms of which tragedy can be seen as something special, something out of the run of day-to-day routine activities: if the workaday world did not exist, tragedy would not be tragic. If Polonius and Laertes and Ophelia had not been shown earlier as affectionate members of a happy family, their subsequent individual fates would represent a series of misfortunes rather than elements in a complex tragedy. In Shakespearean tragedy, the heroes are not doomed lonely figures who move through life in a world completely isolated from that of ordinary living. There is something of this in Aeschylean and even Sophoclean tragedy (Prometheus and Oedipus, for example, are fated figures from the start, and hardly live in the world of normal human affections), but Shakespeare always completes his tragic world to make it include ordinary daily living, and by thus completing it—often through comic relief, often by other devices— he makes his tragedies less the symbolic ritual of the suffering hero (anthropologically related to the theme of the dying god), which is what so many Greek tragedies tend to suggest, and more a presentation of the complexities of human life and the different levels at which experience can simultaneously develop. In his comedies, he draws, as it were, a magic circle round his picture of experience which forbids us to look beyond into the world of genuine conflict and suffering. That youth must fade, that even lovers must grow old and die, that the moment of golden sunshine in the garden is soon over and that in any case beyond the garden's confines lie crowded realms of suffering and bitterness and destructive conflicts—this we forget for the time being as we read or watch a play like *Twelfth Night*, where all grief is merely emotional self-indulgence and death and danger mere suggestions of pleasing melancholy. We cannot have "tragic relief" in comedy—not, at least, in this kind of comedy—because the essence of comedy is restriction, the deliberate blocking off of overtones suggestive of the transience of life or its insoluble problems. In comedy all problems are soluble; but if we break the magic circle to allow the outside world to enter, we can no longer consider them so. Aldous Huxley in his essay "Tragedy and the Whole Truth" (in the collection *Music at Night*) argues that "wholly truthful art overflows the limits of tragedy" and shows us all the trivial, everyday, ordinary activities in which we engage for most of our lives and which tragedy, by concentrating on the heroic moments, ignores. Homer, he maintains, who shows us in Book XII of the *Odyssey* the appalling death of six of Odysseus' men at the hands of the monster Scylla, and then goes on to tell how the survivors made their evening meal and *then*, after eating, wept for their dead companions before settling down to sleep—Homer tells "the whole truth" as the writer of tragedies does not. But surely the argument is more effective turned the other way round. Tragedy tells the whole truth, because it includes comedy and goes beyond it: it does not stop with the happy ending, the marriage of the lovers, the accession of the king, the apparent solution of the problem, but goes beyond to explore underlying conflicts and frustrations and to bring them out into the open. Were we to go beyond the circle of comedy to inquire whether in fact Bassanio would have made a good husband for Portia or whether the forced conversion of Shylock really represents a solution to the problems raised by his relations with the other characters in the play; if we ask what kind of a married life Beatrice and Benedict can be expected to lead or inquire into the ethical and sociological significance of the relations between married couples in restoration comedy—then we are rending the fabric of the play. But it does not destroy *Hamlet* if we see the Prince of Denmark merry, or learn from the other characters what a charming young man he had been before his father's death and his mother's second marriage. Tragic relief in comedy would destroy the deliberately restricted world in which comedy moves; comic relief in tragedy, if properly handled, fills out the tragic world but does not destroy it. The wider and deeper view of the human situation is bound to be tragic, for human experience is essentially tragic; to look at it from the point of view of comedy—that is, to present human situations on the assumption that all the problems that arise in those situations are soluble—involves drawing the magic circle, beyond which one must not step.

Thomas De Quincey, in his famous essay "On the Knocking at the Gate in 'Macbeth,'" explores the way in which this scene relates the fatal action to the workaday world by emphasizing the difference between them. The relevant passage from the essay is quoted in Chapter 12.

Variety and unity

The discussion of this question in Dryden's essay has many applications. The crowded canvas of a Dickens novel might be contrasted with Emily Brontë's *Wuthering Heights* or Flaubert's *Madame Bovary*. But there are differences even in Dickens' handling of his abundant material, and the picaresque structure of *The Pickwick Papers* is very different from the tightly-knit action of *Great Expectations*. "Here is God's plenty," said Dryden of Chaucer's *Canterbury Tales;* but this is not always and necessarily praise. Certain conditions are necessary if "God's plenty" is to be properly handled. Consider the different ways in which the action is accommodated to the host of characters in Tolstoy's *War and Peace*, Proust's *Remembrance of Things Past*, and a novel of Dickens. The technical problems involved in moving from one group of characters to another are also worth attention. Methods range from the simply utilitarian

Now wol I stynte of Palamon a lite,
And lete hym in his prisoun stille dwelle,
And of Arcita forth I wol yow telle

of Chaucer's "Knight's Tale," to the elaborately contrived coincidence
which constructs a bridge, as it were, from one character or set of
characters to another. The ease with which George Eliot manipulates
her characters and moves from group to group in *Middlemarch* might
be contrasted with the artificial devices she has to employ in *Daniel
Deronda* to bring the titular hero into the same environment as the
heroine. Or consider the technique developed by Dos Passos in *U.S.A.*
for moving from one character to another. A discussion of the way
Virginia Woolf handled this problem will be found in chapter ten of
the author's *The Novel and the Modern World*.

The set characterization of an author

This kind of practical criticism, so ably demonstrated by Dryden in
his essay, has rather gone out of fashion, having given way to the analysis of the individual work. But it is a valuable—and difficult—kind of
critical activity, equally necessary for the literary historian and for the
writer of obituaries. The reader might try his hand with, for example,
Henry James, Joseph Conrad, and Ernest Hemingway, using the general method employed by Dryden in characterizing Shakespeare, Jonson, and Beaumont and Fletcher. Or are these three novelists too different from each other to allow any reference back and forth between
them? Hawthorne, James, and Conrad might be an effective trio. Or
try three very different modern poets: Frost, Eliot, Dylan Thomas.
Look through a number of histories of literature and see how the summing up of authors is done in a context of historical continuity provided by comparison and generalization.

Similarly, the relaxed discussion of a writer and his work of the
kind Dryden devotes to Chaucer in his preface to the Fables is no
longer popular among serious critics. But it represents the way in
which most people—even the most high-powered professional critics
—*talk* about literature, especially contemporary literature, and there
is no reason why occasionally good written criticism should not imitate good conversation (as Dryden's so often does). Interest in the
character of a writer and the way in which that character is reflected

in his writing may represent "impure" criticism to those who insist
that the whole function of criticism is to describe and evaluate particular works of literature (see Chapter 15) but it is a widespread
interest and to indulge it is to increase understanding if not always
to help evaluation. Dryden himself would make a good subject for
an exercise in this kind of criticism. The reader might also try it on
some American writers—say, Benjamin Franklin, Herman Melville and
Carl Sandburg. Dickens would make an excellent subject, too. Certain kinds of writers would lend themselves to this approach more than
others. The reader might consider why this is so, and what qualities
make a writer most responsive to this kind of criticism.

12

Possibilities and limitations of a method

A s we have seen from the example of Dryden, criticism can have as its object both assessment of quality and increase of appreciation. The critic, that is to say, can regard himself as a judge awarding so many marks to each work, or as a mediator between the work and the reader, whose function is to communicate his own relish and enjoyment and so help the reader to enjoy it similarly.

From theory to practice

Dryden could do all these things at once, and act simultaneously as judge, interpreter and—perhaps one might say—as barker. If it is true, as Dr Johnson maintained, that "Dryden may be properly considered as the father of English criticism, as the writer who first taught us to determine upon principles the merit of composition," it is equally true, again in Johnson's words, that his criticism "is the criticism of a poet; not a dull collection of theorems, nor a rude detection of faults, which perhaps the censor was not able to have committed; but a gay and vigorous dissertation, where delight is mingled with instruction, and where the author proves his right of judgement, by his power of performance." Once English criticism had come into its own with Dryden, however, and the new taste for smooth and polished verse had been firmly established (a taste which Dryden helped to establish but which he himself transcended), the critic as judge became more common than the critic as interpreter or advertiser, and his characteristic activity a stern awarding of points. Nowhere is this better illustrated than in the criticism of Dr Johnson, whose clear ideas of what did and what did not constitute literary merit were reflected in his vigorous practical criticism.

Johnson on "Lycidas" and on the metaphysical poets

Dr Johnson, like Dryden, moved freely from grand generalizations about what literature is to practical application of those generalizations, but his general principles were more strictly maintained and his application of them determined by a narrower taste. But always it is strong, clear, and well argued. The critical parts of his *Lives of the Poets* (1779-81) are models of reasoned practical criticism based on a firmly held view of the nature, function and value of poetry. Where we disagree with Johnson—and most of us today would find something in his criticism with which to disagree—we can nevertheless see the criterion and the taste which led Johnson to the judgment from which we differ, and we can dispute him not by attacking the application of his standards but by questioning the standards themselves. For example, in his famous—or notorious—condemnation of Milton's "Lycidas" we can see exactly what has led him to condemn the poem and we must admit that on his own grounds he is justified:

One of the poems on which much praise has been bestowed is *Lycidas;* of which the diction is harsh, the rhymes uncertain, and the numbers unpleasing. What beauty there is, we must therefore seek in the sentiments and images. It is not to be considered as the effusion of real passion; for passion runs not after remote allusions and obscure opinions. Passion plucks no berries from the myrtle and ivy, nor calls upon Arethuse and Mincius, nor tells of rough *satyrs* and *fauns with cloven heel.* Where there is leisure for fiction there is little grief.

In this poem there is no nature, for there is no truth; there is no art, for there is nothing new. Its form is that of a pastoral, easy, vulgar, and therefore disgusting: whatever images it can supply, are long ago exhausted; and its inherent improbability always forces dissatisfaction on the mind. When Cowley tells of Hervey that they studied together, it is easy to suppose how much he must miss the companion of his labours, and the partner of his discoveries; but what image of tenderness can be excited by these lines!

> We drove a field, and both together heard
> What time the grey fly winds her sultry horn,
> Battening our flocks with the fresh dews of night.

We know that they never drove a field, and that they had no flocks to batten; and though it be allowed that the representation may be allegorical, the true meaning is so uncertain and remote, that it is never sought because it cannot be known when it is found.

Among the flocks, and copses, and flowers, appear the heathen deities; Jove and Phoebus, Neptune and Aeolus, with a long train of mythological imagery, such as a College easily supplies. Nothing can less display knowledge, or less exercise invention, than to tell how a shepherd has lost his companion, and must now feed his flocks alone, without any judge of his skill in piping; and how one god asks another god what is become of Lycidas, and how neither god can tell. He who thus grieves will excite no sympathy; he who thus praises will confer no honour.

This poem has a yet grosser fault. With these trifling fictions are mingled the most awful and sacred truths, such as ought never to be polluted with such irreverent combinations. This shepherd likewise is now a feeder of sheep, and afterwards an ecclesiastical pastor, a superintendent of a Christian flock. Such equivocations are always unskilful; but here they are indecent, and at least approach to impiety, of which, however, I believe the writer not to have been conscious.

Such is the power of reputation justly acquired, that its blaze drives away the eye from nice examination. Surely no man can have fancied that he read *Lycidas* with pleasure, had he not known its author.

This criticism is based on a certain view of the relation between art and experience. If we believe with T. S. Eliot that "the more perfect the artist, the more completely separate in him will be the man who suffers and the mind which creates," and that "poetry is not a turning loose of emotion, but an escape from emotion,"[1] then Dr Johnson's remark that "where there is leisure for fiction there is little grief" will be beside the point, for we will not demand that a poem should be the direct expression of personal grief. Similarly, if we regard the pastoral convention as a method of stylizing the treatment of the theme, of rendering it more perfectly into art and so universalizing it, rather than a violation of the literal facts of experience, we take a very different view of the function and value of the pastoral imagery in the poem. Johnson, who was perfectly willing to concede the claims of the imagination (witness his great defense of Shakespeare in the matter of the "unities"), was nevertheless prevented by his representational view of art from conceding the possibilities of certain kinds of convention, certain degrees of stylization. The same limitation in principle combined with brilliance of application can be seen in the remarks on the metaphysical poets which he introduces into his life of Cowley:

The metaphysical poets were men of learning, and to show their learning was their whole endeavour; but unluckily resolving to show it in rhyme, instead of writing poetry, they only wrote verses, and very often such verses as stood the trial of the finger better than of the ear; for the modulation was so imperfect, that they were only found to be verses by counting the syllables.

If the father of criticism has rightly denominated poetry τέχνη μιμητικὴ, *an imitative art,* these writers will, without great wrong, lose their right to the name of poets, for they cannot be said to have imitated anything; they neither copied nature nor life; neither painted the forms of matter, nor represented the operations of intellect.

Those, however, who deny them to be poets, allow them to be wits. Dryden confesses of himself and his contemporaries, that they fall below Donne in wit, but maintains that they surpass him in poetry.

If Wit be well described by Pope, as being "that which has been often thought, but was never before so well expressed," they certainly never attained, nor ever sought it; for they endeavoured to be singular in their thoughts, and were careless of their diction. But Pope's account of wit is undoubtedly erroneous: he depresses it below its natural dignity, and reduces it from strength of thought to happiness of language.

If by a more noble and more adequate conception that be considered as Wit, which is at once natural and new, that which, though not obvious, is, upon its first production, acknowledged to be just; if it be that, which he

[1] "Tradition and the Individual Talent."

that never found it, wonders how he missed; to wit of this kind the meta-physical poets have seldom risen. Their thoughts are often new, but seldom natural; they are not obvious, but neither are they just; and the reader, far from wondering that he missed them, wonders more frequently by what perverseness of industry they were ever found.

But wit, abstracted from its effects upon the hearer, may be more rigor-ously and philosophically considered as a kind of *discordia concors;* a com-bination of dissimilar images, or discovery of occult resemblances in things apparently unlike. Of wit, thus defined, they have more than enough. The most heterogeneous ideas are yoked by violence together; nature and art are ransacked for illustrations, comparisons, and allusions; their learning instructs, and their subtilty surprises; but the reader commonly thinks his improvement dearly bought, and, though he sometimes admires, is sel-dom pleased.

From this account of their compositions it will be readily inferred, that they were not successful in representing or moving the affections. As they were wholly employed on something unexpected and surprising, they had no regard to that uniformity of sentiment which enables us to conceive and to excite the pains and the pleasure of other minds: they never inquired what, on any occasion, they should have said or done; but wrote rather as beholders than partakers of human nature; as beings looking upon good and evil, impassive and at leisure; as Epicurean deities, making remarks on the actions of men, and the vicissitudes of life, without interest and without emotion. Their courtship was void of fondness, and their lamentation of sorrow. Their wish was only to say what they hoped had been never said before.

Nor was the sublime more within their reach than the pathetick; for they never attempted that comprehension and expanse of thought which at once fills the whole mind, and of which the first effect is sudden astonishment, and the second rational admiration. Sublimity is produced by aggregation, and littleness by dispersion. Great thoughts are always general, and consist in positions not limited by exceptions, and in descriptions not descending to minuteness. It is with great propriety that Subtlety, which in its original import means exility of particles, is taken in its metaphorical meaning for nicety of distinction. Those writers who lay on the watch for novelty could have little hope of greatness; for great things cannot have escaped former observation. Their attempts were always analytick; they broke every image into fragments; and could no more represent, by their slender conceits and laboured particularities, the prospects of nature, or the scenes of life, than he, who dissects a sunbeam with a prism, can exhibit the wide effulgence of a summer noon.

What they wanted however of the sublime, they endeavoured to supply by hyperbole; their amplification had no limits; they left not only reason but fancy behind them; and produced combinations of confused magnificence, that not only could not be credited, but could not be imagined.

Yet great labour, directed by great abilities, is never wholly lost: if they frequently threw away their wit upon false conceits, they likewise sometimes struck out unexpected truth; if their conceits were far-fetched, they were often worth the carriage. To write on their plan, it was at least necessary to read and think. No man could be born a metaphysical poet, nor assume the dignity of a writer, by descriptions copied from descriptions, by imitations borrowed from imitations, by traditional imagery, and hereditary similes, by readiness of rhyme, and volubility of syllables.

In perusing the works of this race of authors, the mind is exercised either by recollection or inquiry; either something already learned is to be retrieved, or something new is to be examined. If their greatness seldom elevates, their acuteness often surprises; if the imagination is not always gratified, at least the powers of reflection and comparison are employed; and in the mass of materials which ingenious absurdity has thrown together, genuine wit and useful knowledge may be sometimes found buried, perhaps in grossness of expression, but useful to those who know their value; and such as, when they are expanded to perspicuity, and polished to elegance, may give lustre to works which have more propriety though less copiousness of sentiment. . . .

Wit and imitation

We see here, in the first place, the firmly held imitative principle, asserted toward the beginning of the discussion with reference to the authority of Aristotle, "the father of criticism." Johnson then discusses the function of wit with reference to this imitative function of poetry. This leads him into an argument which moves continuously between deductive and inductive statements—that is, between statements logically deduced from principles already enunciated ("Those writers who lay on the watch for novelty could have little hope of greatness; for great things cannot have escaped former observation," deriving from his view that art should imitate large general principles of human nature) and new generalizations deriving from a number of preceding particular statements ("Great thoughts are always general"). We note, too, the scrupulous fairness, the clear judicious temper of the argument. Faults are listed and referred to their origins, the fact that these qualities are faults being at the same time proved with reference to a general principle concerning what poetry should be; but the same poetic practice which produced the faults can produce certain virtues. "Great labour, directed by great abilities, is never wholly lost: if they frequently threw away their wit upon false conceits, they likewise sometimes struck out unexpected truths: if their conceits were far-fetched, they were often worth the carriage. To write on their plan, it was at least necessary to read and think." And in the last of the quoted paragraphs the balanced sentences reflect a careful weighing of the pros and cons. "If their greatness seldom elevates, their acuteness often surprises . . ."

Johnson follows this general discussion of the metaphysical poets in his life of Cowley with a close examination of selected passages from their works, where he illustrates with concrete instances the general remarks already made. "Critical remarks are not easily understood without examples," he notes by way of preface to this section, and side by side with this we may put an observation he makes in his life of Dryden:

It is not by comparing line with line that the merit of great works is to be estimated, but by their general effects and ultimate result. It is easy to note a weak line, and write one more vigorous in its place; to find a happiness of expression in the original, and transplant it by force into the version: but what is given to the parts, may be subducted from the whole, and the reader may be weary, though the critick may commend. Works of imagination excel by their allurement and delight; by their power of attracting and detaining the attention. That book is good in vain, which the reader throws away. He only is the master, who keeps the mind in pleasing captivity; whose pages are perused with eagerness, and in hope of new pleasure are perused again; and whose conclusion is perceived with an eye of sorrow, such as the traveller casts upon departing day.

The limitations of professional criticism

Dr Johnson was aware of the limitations of detailed practical criticism of the kind he gave to so many passages in his lives of Cowley, of Dryden, and of many others. Every now and again he turns from his more professional or technical critical activity to make a grand concession to the nature of things, to the facts about readers and writers, appealing "from criticism to nature," as he put it in another connection. Thus at the conclusion of his life of Gray, where he praises the "Elegy" after condemning most of Gray's other poems on grounds similar to those which led him to dismiss "Lycidas," he remarks: "In the character of his *Elegy* I rejoice to concur with the common reader; for by the common sense of readers uncorrupted with literary prejudices, after all the refinements of subtilty and the dogmatism of learning, must be finally decided all claim to poetical honours." This is an observation that few great critics could or would have made—one cannot imagine Ben Jonson or Coleridge or T. S. Eliot making it—and represents a kind of healthy pragmatism which mitigated the strictness of his principles. "No man but a blockhead ever wrote except for money," he once said, and there is a large recognition of the facts of life in Johnson's critical writing which prevents him from ever becoming priggish or from moving in an atmosphere too rarefied for non-professionals to breathe. It is that ability to accept the facts of life that distinguishes Johnson from other critics who, like him, have firmly enunciated principles and a clear and logical method.

Criticism and the historical context

Like Dryden, Dr Johnson was aware of the historical background of an earlier writer and in judging a writer he sometimes used history as a plea in mitigation. "The English nation, in the time of Shakespeare, was yet struggling to emerge from barbarity," he remarks in his preface to Shakespeare, and this excuses what to him are certain crudities in Shakespeare's plays.

Nations, like individuals, have their infancy. A people newly awakened to literary curiosity, being yet unacquainted with the true state of things, knows not how to judge of that which is proposed as its resemblance. Whatever is remote from common appearances is always welcome to vulgar, as to childish credulity; and of a country unenlightened by learning, the whole people is the vulgar. The study of those who then aspired to plebeian learning was laid out upon adventures, giants, dragons, and enchantments. *The Death of Arthur* was the favourite volume.

Shakespeare's fondness for marvels is thus explained and excused and his achievement as an interpreter of human nature becomes all the more remarkable when it is seen against a background of marvellous tales of "giants, dragons, and enchantments." Similarly, in his life of Dryden he magnifies the poet's achievement by putting it in its historical context:

To judge rightly of an author, we must transport ourselves to his time, and examine what were the wants of his contemporaries, and what were his means of supplying them. That which is easy at one time was difficult at another. Dryden at least imported his science, and gave his country what it wanted [lacked] before; or rather, he imported only the materials, and manufactured them by his own skill.

The historical argument has its dangers. To say "This was a wonderful achievement for *A*, who lived in a barbarous age, but it would have been nothing out of the ordinary for *B*," may be to make an interesting historical observation, but is it a real literary judgment? If criticism considered as evaluation has as its purpose the assessment of the work as a piece of literature, then it might be urged that any historical consideration is irrelevant. A work of art is either good or bad, and though historical conditions may help to account for its badness (or its goodness) it cannot alter the fact. If *A*'s achievement was simply wonderful for his age but not wonderful in itself, then has the critic, speaking as a critic, any right to call it wonderful at all? Over a hundred years after Dr Johnson, Matthew Arnold addressed himself to this question:

. . . constantly in reading poetry, a sense for the best, the really excellent . . . should be present in our minds and should govern our estimate of what we read. But this real estimate, the only true one, is liable to be superseded, if we are not watchful, by two other kinds of estimate, the historic estimate and the personal estimate, both of which are fallacious. A poet or a poem may count to us historically, they may count to us on grounds personal to ourselves, and they may count to us really. They may count to us historically. The course of development of a nation's language, thought, and poetry, is profoundly interesting; and by regarding a poet's work as a stage in this course of development we may easily bring ourselves to make it of more importance as poetry than in itself it really is, we may come to use a language of quite exaggerated praise in criticising it; in short, to overrate it. . . .[2]

Arnold goes on to castigate a French critic for regarding the *Chanson de Roland* as "a monument of epic genius." He concedes that historically the poem is immensely interesting but insists that intrinsically it is not of the highest order—not comparable with Homer, for example.

Arnold, of course, has a point: the historical estimate and the in-

[2] Introduction to Ward's *English Poets*, 1880.

trinsic estimate are not necessarily identical. But that does not mean that historical insights may not, under certain circumstances, help us to see the intrinsic merit—a question we shall take up in a later chapter. Arnold's argument leaves unsolved the problem whether a greater degree of literary ability in the writer may, under certain historical circumstances, produce a less good work than may be produced with less ability by another writer living in different circumstances, when a long tradition of literary craftsmanship was available to him. If we are judging, not the work, but the degree of genius involved in producing it, may we not say that, for example, Marlowe's *Tamburlaine* is more impressive than Webster's *White Devil?*

These are some of the considerations suggested by Dr Johnson's use of historical material in his criticism. Neither he nor Dryden ever goes so far as to maintain that mere pioneering is evidence of genius (though that is an interesting question), but both do occasionally refer to history in order to explain away faults or to find further evidence for the greatness of a writer already shown to be great on purely literary grounds.

Johnson's use of biography

Johnson's use of biography is less truly relevant to his critical method, though it figures more prominently in much of his critical work, especially his *Lives of the Poets.* Johnson was interested in people's lives quite apart from any critical principles, and in the *Lives of the Poets* he wrote biographies of each of his subjects before proceeding to criticize their works. This is a defensible enough procedure—there is no reason in the world why one should not learn about a man's life and then have a critical account of his work; such a combination satisfies a perfectly proper curiosity. This is different, however, from that approach which seeks to interpret the works with reference to the life and which draws from the psychology of the author clues for the interpretation and appreciation of what he has written. Johnson's *Lives* were in fact in a tradition of biographical catalogues of distinguished men which goes back to the early seventeenth century and earlier, and they have no direct relation to the later "bio-critical" approach which mingles a study of the man with an interpretation of his work. This latter method became established in the nineteenth century; it differs from Johnson's in not keeping the life and the works separate but in using each as a help in interpreting the other. How far valid critical judgments can derive, directly or indirectly, from biographical knowledge of the writer, is a matter for further discussion, but at least it might be said here that for *interpretation* if not *assessment* of a work biographical knowledge is often useful and sometimes most valuable.

The comparative method

We have noted Dryden's comparisons of Shakespeare, Beaumont and Fletcher, and Ben Jonson. Evaluative criticism tends to use the comparative method as a device for establishing degrees of excellence, and indeed it can be maintained that a purely normative criticism, which aims at giving so many marks to each work and placing it in a scale, cannot go very far without having brought together the work in question with other works, showing the same sort of thing better or worse done elsewhere and by showing this helping the reader to see how excellence is attained. Dr Johnson used comparisons in a manner similar to Dryden's. He rarely used them in discussing individual works, but preferred to make a grand comparison between different kinds of genius, as in his celebrated comparison between Dryden and Pope in his life of Pope. Here he even includes biographical data as part of the comparison, unlike his general habit in the *Lives* where, as we have noted, he generally gave the life first and the criticism afterwards. He is concerned here with establishing the literary character of each writer, his habit of mind and the way his genius worked, before going on to talk about his literary achievement; but each illuminates the other. The concern is with the impression made by each poet's work as a whole.

Integrity of understanding and nicety of discernment were not allotted in a less proportion to Dryden than to Pope. The rectitude of Dryden's mind was sufficiently shewn by the dismission of his poetical prejudices, and the rejection of unnatural thoughts and rugged numbers. But Dryden never desired to apply all the judgement that he had. He wrote, and professed to write, merely for the people; and when he pleased others, he contented himself. He spent no time in struggles to rouse latent powers; he never attempted to make that better which was already good, nor often to mend what he must have known to be faulty. He wrote, as he tells us, with very little consideration; when occasion or necessity called upon him, he poured out what the present moment happened to supply, and, when once it had passed the press, ejected it from his mind; for when he had no pecuniary interest, he had no further solicitude.

Pope was not content to satisfy; he desired to excel, and therefore always endeavoured to do his best: he did not court the candour, but dared the judgement of his reader, and, expecting no indulgence from others, he shewed none to himself. He examined lines and words with minute and punctilious observation, and retouched every part with indefatigable diligence, till he had left nothing to be forgiven.

For this reason he kept his pieces very long in his hands, while he considered and reconsidered them. The only poems which can be supposed to have been written with such regard to the times as might hasten their publication, were the two satires of *Thirty-eight;* . . .

His declaration, that his care for his works ceased at their publication, was not strictly true. His parental attention never abandoned them; what he found amiss in the first edition, he silently corrected in those that followed. . . . It will seldom be found that he altered without adding clearness, elegance, or vigour. Pope had perhaps the judgement of Dryden; but Dryden certainly wanted [lacked] the diligence of Pope.

In acquired knowledge, the superiority must be allowed to Dryden, whose education was more scholastick, and who before he became an author had been allowed more time for study, with better means of information. His mind has a larger range, and he collects his images and illustrations from a more extensive circumference of science. Dryden knew more of man in his general nature, and Pope in his local manners. The notions of Dryden were formed by comprehensive speculation, and those of Pope by minute attention. There is more dignity in the knowledge of Dryden, and more certainty in that of Pope.

Poetry was not the sole praise of either; for both excelled likewise in prose; but Pope did not borrow his prose from his predecessor. The style of Dryden is capricious and varied, that of Pope is cautious and uniform; Dryden obeys the motions of his own mind, Pope constrains his mind to his own rules of composition. Dryden is sometimes vehement and rapid; Pope is always smooth, uniform, and gentle. Dryden's page is a natural field, rising into inequalities, and diversified by the varied exuberance of abundant vegetation; Pope's is a velvet lawn, shaven by the scythe, and levelled by the roller.

Of genius, that power which constitutes a poet; that quality without which judgement is cold and knowledge is inert; that energy which collects, combines, amplifies, and animates; the superiority must, with some hesitation, be allowed to Dryden. It is not to be inferred that of this poetical vigour Pope had only a little, because Dryden had more; for every other writer since Milton must give place to Pope; and even of Dryden it must be said, that if he has brighter paragraphs, he has not better poems. Dryden's performances were always hasty, either excited by some external occasion, or extorted by domestick necessity; he composed without consideration, and published without correction. What his mind could supply at call, or gather in one excursion, was all that he sought, and all that he gave. The dilatory caution of Pope enabled him to condense his sentiments, to multiply his images, and to accumulate all that study might produce, or chance might supply. If the flights of Dryden therefore are higher, Pope continues longer on the wing. If of Dryden's fire the blaze is brighter, of Pope's the heat is more regular and constant. Dryden often surpasses expectation, and Pope never falls below it. Dryden is read with frequent astonishment, and Pope with perpetual delight.

Notice how Dr Johnson uses comparison in order to illuminate the characteristic qualities of each writer. Contrasts between the style of the two poets, for example, are not made simply in order to show how different they are; the terms of the contrast draw attention to the individualizing features of each. Dryden's movement is "vehement and rapid" while Pope's is "smooth, uniform, and gentle." Dryden's page is a "natural field;" Pope's is a "velvet lawn." Dryden's flights are higher, but Pope continues longer on the wing. These images are not mere decoration; they are diagnostic and clarifying; they direct our attention to essential qualities of each poet. And though the conclusion is that Dryden comes just a fraction higher in the scale of poetic genius than Pope, the comparisons and contrasts between them are not made at the expense of either but rather to help the reader appreciate both. This passage is, in fact, a model of the comparative method as employed to characterize the general features of two authors.

In the relation between general principles and practical judgment, in the combination of strict method with pragmatic common sense, in the use of historical data to qualify or assist critical judgment, and in the handling of comparison, Dr Johnson provides an illuminating and suggestive example of the practical critic at work.

Wit

Dr Johnson's discussion of wit in his life of Cowley should be put beside Addison's remarks on true and false wit in numbers 58 to 62 of the *Spectator*. Addison begins by distinguishing several different kinds of "false wit." There is the kind of false wit represented by arranging poems in the shapes of physical objects–like an egg, a pair of wings, or an altar, a practice found among the Greeks and imitated by, among others, George Herbert. Then there are tricks with letters, such as leaving out a particular letter of the alphabet: Tryphiodorus is mentioned as having written an Odyssey in twenty-four books, leaving out the letter *alpha* entirely from the first, avoiding *beta* in the second, and so on. Addison then mentions "that ingenious kind of Conceit which the Moderns distinguish by the Name of a *Rebus*, that does not sink a Letter but a whole Word, by substituting a Picture in its place." Anagrams and acrostics provide another category of false wit, as do *bouts rimés* (writing verses to set rhymes) and the kind of humorous double rhymes found in Butler's *Hudibras*. Punning is considered by Addison as another kind of false wit. He defines a pun as "a conceit arising from the use of two words that agree in the sound, but differ in the sense." (From the time of Addison until the present century the pun was regarded a vulgar literary device, to be employed only in comic verses such as those of Thomas Hood. Nineteenth century critics regularly expressed their surprise at Shakespeare's frequent punning, just as Dr Johnson reproved him for this propensity. The rehabilitation of the pun in serious poetry in recent times is bound up with the view of poetry as complex or paradoxical statement discussed in chapters 9 and 10.)

In the *Spectator* number 62 Addison comes to his definition of true wit. He begins by quoting from Locke's *Essay Concerning Human Understanding:*

Mr. *Lock* has an admirable Reflection upon the Difference of Wit and Judgment, whereby he endeavours to shew the Reason why they are not always the Talents of the same Person. His Words are as follow: *And hence, perhaps, may be given some Reason of that common Observation, That Men who have a great deal of Wit and prompt Memories, have not always the clearest Judgment, or deepest Reason. For Wit lying most in the Assemblage of Ideas, and putting those together with Quickness and Variety, wherein can be found any Resemblance or Congruity, thereby to make up pleasant Pictures and agreeable Visions in the Fancy; Judgment, on the contrary, lies quite on the other Side, In separating carefully one from another, Ideas wherein can be found the least Difference, thereby to avoid being mis-led by Similitude, and by Affinity to take one thing for another. This is a Way of proceeding quite contrary to Metaphor and Allusion; wherein, for the most Part, lies that Entertainment and Pleasantry of Wit which strikes so lively on the Fancy, and is therefore so acceptable to all People.*

This is, I think, the best and most philosophical Account that I have ever met with of Wit, which generally, though not always, consists in such a Resemblance and Congruity of Ideas as this Author mentions. I shall only add to it, by way of Explanation, That every Resemblance of Ideas is not that which we call Wit, unless it be such an one that gives *Delight* and *Surprize* to the Reader: These two Properties seem essential to Wit, more particularly the last of them. In order therefore that the Resemblance in the Ideas be Wit, it is necessary that the Ideas should not lie too near one another in the Nature of things; for where the Likeness is obvious, it gives no Surprize. To compare one Man's Singing to that of another, or to represent the Whiteness of any Object by that of Milk and Snow, or the Variety of its Colours by those of the Rainbow, cannot be called Wit, unless, besides this obvious Resemblance, there be some further Congruity discovered in the two Ideas that is capable of giving the Reader some Surprize. Thus when a Poet tells us, the Bosom of his Mistress is as white as Snow, there is no Wit in the Comparison; but when he adds, with a Sigh, that it is as cold too, it then grows into Wit. Every Reader's Memory may supply him with innumerable Instances of the same Nature. For this Reason, the Similitudes in Heroick Poets, who endeavour rather to fill the Mind with great Conceptions, than to divert it with such as are new and surprizing, have seldom anything in them that can be called Wit. . . .

As *true Wit* generally consists in this Resemblance and Congruity of Ideas, *false Wit* chiefly consists in the Resemblance and Congruity sometimes of single Letters, as in Anagrams, Chronograms, Lipograms, and Acrosticks; Sometimes of Syllables, as in Ecchos and Doggerel Rhymes: Sometimes of Words, as in Punns and Quibbles; and sometimes of whole Sentences or Poems, cast into Figures of *Eggs*, *Axes* or *Altars:* Nay, some carry the Notion of Wit so far, as to ascribe it even to external Mimickry; and to look upon a Man as an ingenious Person, that can resemble the Tone, Posture, or Face of another.

Addison then goes on to distinguish a third kind of wit, which he calls "mixt wit":

As *true Wit* consists in the Resemblance of Ideas, and *false Wit* in the Resemblance of Words, according to the foregoing Instances; there is another kind of Wit which consists partly in the Resemblance of Ideas, and partly in the Resemblance of Words; which for Distinction Sake I shall call *mixt Wit.* This Kind of Wit is that which abounds in *Cowley,* more than in any Author that ever wrote. Mr. *Waller* has likewise a great deal of it. Mr. *Dryden* is very sparing in it. *Milton* had a Genius much above it. *Spencer* is in the same class with *Milton.* The *Italians,* even in their Epic Poetry, are full of it. Monsieur *Boileau,* who formed himself upon the

Ancient Poets, has every where rejected it with Scorn. If we look after mixt Wit among the *Greek* Writers, we shall find it no where but in the Epigrammatists. There are indeed some Strokes of it in the little Poem ascribed to *Musaeus*, which by that, as well as many other Marks, betrays itself to be a modern Composition. If we look into the *Latin* Writers, we find none of this mix Wit in *Virgil*, *Lucretius*, or *Catullus*; very little in *Horace*, but a great deal of it in *Ovid*, and scarce any thing else in *Martial*.

Out of the innumerable Branches of *mixt Wit*, I shall chuse one Instance which may be met with in all the Writers of this Class. The Passion of Love in its Nature has been thought to resemble Fire; for which Reason the Words Fire and Flame are made use of to signifie Love. The witty Poets therefore have taken an Advantage from the double Meaning of the Word Fire, to name an infinite Number of Witticisms. *Cowley* observing the cold Regard of his Misstress's Eyes, and at the same Time their Power of producing Love in him, considers them as Burning-Glasses made of Ice; and finding himself able to live in the greatest Extremities of Love, concludes the Torrid Zone to habitable. When his Mistress has read his Letter in Juice of Lemmon by holding it to the Fire, he desires her to read it over a second time by Love's Flames. When she weeps, he wishes it were inward Heat that distilled those Drops from the Limbeck [alembic]. When she is absent he is beyond eighty, that is, thirty Degrees nearer the Pole than when she is with him. His ambitious Love is a Fire that naturally mounts upwards; his happy Love is the Beams of Heaven, and his unhappy Love Flames of Hell. When it does not let him sleep, it is a Flame that sends up no Smoak; when it is opposed by Counsel and Advice, it is a Fire that rages the more by the Wind's blowing upon it. . . .

The Reader may observe in every one of these Instances, that the Poet mixes the Qualities of Fire with those of Love; and in the same Sentence speaking of it both as a Passion, and as Real Fire, surprizes the Reader with those seeming Resemblances or Contradictions that make up all the Wit in this kind of Writing. Mixt Wit is therefore a Composition of Punn and true Wit, and is more or less perfect as the Resemblance lies in the Ideas or in the Words; Its Foundations are laid partly in Falsehood and partly in Truth; Reason puts in her Claim for one Half of it, and Extravagance for the other. The only Province therefore for this kind of Wit, is Epigram, or those little occasional Poems that in their own Nature are nothing else but a Tissue of Epigrams. . . .

Modern criticism has gone much beyond both Addison and Johnson in its analysis of wit, and in its relish of it. (See chapters 9, 10, and 15.) The kind of semantic analysis introduced first by I. A. Richards (chapter 8) led to much profound study of the nature of wit. See, for example, *The Structure of Complex Words*, by William Empson, especially the first four chapters.[3]

Johnson's definition of *"metaphysical" poetry*

Pope defined "wit" as

> nature to advantage dressed,
> What oft was thought but ne'er so well expressed.

To which Johnson (arguing with William Pepys on the subject) replied: "That, sir, is a definition both false and foolish. . . 'What oft was thought' is all the worse for being often thought, because to be wit, it ought to be newly thought." But if for Johnson true wit was not simply neatly versified platitudes, neither was it far-fetched ingenuity. Johnson modified Pope's definition by saying that wit is "at once natural and new," something not obvious but, once expressed, acknowledged to be just (we are reminded that Keats once said in a letter that true poetry should strike the reader as "*almost* a Remembrance"). This kind of wit, as we have seen, he denied to the metaphysical poets; they had the kind of wit he defined as "discordia concors," the violent yoking together of the most heterogeneous ideas. How far, it might be asked, is this notion of a violent yoking together of opposites fruitful in poetic theory? What is its relation to the modern critic's concern with paradox and ambivalence? There are certain musical analogies here (harmony, counterpoint, discord) which might be profitably examined by the critic who has some knowledge of musical theory. It would be worth examining, too, the exact implications of the term "violent," "yoking together," and "heterogeneous" in Johnson's definition. What exactly is violence in poetic terms, and is it necessarily a bad thing? What ways of yoking things together are open to the poet, and are there degrees of yoking together (one could perhaps distinguish between yoking by mere juxtaposition and a subtler kind of yoking)? And are the heterogeneous elements so yoked super-

---

[3] But see also Elder Olson's well reasoned attack on Empson's method: "William Empson, Contemporary Criticism and Poetic Diction," in *Critics and Criticism, Ancient and Modern*, edited by R. S. Crane, University of Chicago Press, 1952.

ficially heterogeneous but fundamentally akin, or the other way
round? Consider Yeats' "Words for Music, Perhaps" (particularly
the Crazy Jane poems) from this point of view.

Johnson's objections to pastoral poetry

It is worth examining carefully exactly what Johnson's objections
to "Lycidas" are, and their implications. "Passion plucks no berries
from the myrtle and ivy," he declares. And again: "We know that
they never drove a field, and that they had no flocks to batten." It
might be said that Johnson is here looking at the poem from the wrong
esthetic distance, that he has the wrong perspective on it. Milton makes
clear by the style and tone of the poem at what distance, as it were, the
reader should stand from it when he reads. How, the reader might ask
himself, does he do this? What kinds of device are open to the poet
that will enable him to establish within the poem the poetic "probability" of such a convention as the pastoral? This question might profitably be related to Wordsworth's objections to eighteenth century
poetic diction. (Wordsworth and Johnson agree more than might be
supposed.) Wordsworth, like Johnson, was not willing to concede the
possibility of many different levels of probability in poetry, and consequently never addressed himself to the question of the ways in which
different levels of probability could be established.

Johnson also objects to Milton's mingling pagan mythology with
Christian ideas. Such a mingling is, however, a commonplace of English poetry. In Spenser's *Faerie Queene* the very texture of the work
is woven out of a combination of pagan and Christian images, and even
Milton's *Paradise Lost* makes use of pagan imagery. There is an important difference, however, between Milton's use of pagan references
and Spenser's; Milton uses his as analogies rather than as symbols, while
Spenser can see a figure from a pagan myth as a symbol as rich in moral
and even religious meaning as his more specifically Christian material.
The Faerie Queene and *Paradise Lost* might be compared from this
point of view. It might also be asked whether the difference between
metaphor and simile is not, from one point of view, a difference between the level of probability at which the image or the reference
operates.

The general and the particular

Dr Johnson, as is well known, objected to the poet's "numbering the streaks of the tulip." "The business of the poet," he maintained, "is to examine, not the individual, but the species; to remark general properties and large appearances." This view was challenged even in the eighteenth century (as by Joseph Warton in his "Essay on the Genius and Writings of Pope," 1756), and most Romantic critics as well as many later ones have taken it for granted that the opposite of Johnson's view is true, and that the poet's imagery should be precise, individual, and detailed. Obviously, different kinds of poetry are involved here. The generalized imagery of much eighteenth century moral and descriptive poetry sometimes achieves an effect of diffuse platitudinousness, while the cataloguing of suggestive eccentricities indulged in by some nineteenth century poets can lead to the sort of thing parodied by Edward Lear:

> And they bought an owl, and a useful cart,
> And a pound of rice, and a cranberry-tart,
>   And a hive of silvery bees;
> And they bought a pig, and some green jackdaws,
> And a lovely monkey with lollipop paws, . . .

The over-generalized image of the eighteenth century poet can be illustrated by this quotation from Thomson's "Seasons":

> Mysterious round! what skill, what force divine,
> Deep-felt, in these appear! a simple train,
> Yet so delightful mix'd, with such kind art,
> Such beauty and beneficence combin'd;
> Shade, unperceiv'd, so softening into shade;
> And all so forming an harmonious whole;
> That, as they still succeed, they ravish still.

In contrast we can put this by Tennyson:

> Once more a downy drift against the brakes,
>   Self-darken'd in the sky, descending slow!
> But gladly see I thro' the wavering flakes
>   Yon blanching apricot like snow in snow.
> These will thine eyes not brook in forest-paths,
>   On their perpetual pine, nor round the beech;
> They fuse themselves to little spicy baths,
>   Solved in the tender blushes of the peach; . . .

There is a third kind of imagery—that which is precise in order to be symbolic. The haunting precision of the images in Yeats' "Byzantium" achieves a much richer poetic meaning than either the generalizations of Thomson or the carefully observed nature images of Tennyson. The reader might consider to what extent and in what circumstances the question of particularity or generality can provide a useful critical tool.[4]

[4] Consider, in this connection, F. R. Leavis' comment on Johnson's style in "The Vanity of Human Wishes." "Johnson's abstractions and generalities are not mere empty explicitnesses substituting for the concrete; they focus a wide range of profoundly representative experience—experience felt by the reader as movingly present." *The Common Pursuit*, p. 102.

13

History, relativism, impressionism

WE HAVE SEEN how both Dryden and Dr Johnson occasionally drew on history in order to explain how writers of genius sometimes fell short of the standard required by modern taste. The assumption here is that modern taste is final, based on fundamental laws of art, and great writers of the past only sinned against it because the age in which they lived was not mature enough to provide them with the proper standards. The same kind of historical explanation can be used, not to mitigate an author's faults, but to show that they were not faults at all. Pope, it will be remembered, had laid down the maxim

> In ev'ry work regard the writer's end,
> Since none can compass more than they intend,

and sometimes we go to history or biography to determine the end. And if a successful achievement of the end is all we demand of an author, then the standard required by modern taste becomes irrelevant in our assessment of his work; we have to study the taste of his day and the ways in which that taste could be properly satisfied.

Hurd on Spenser

Bishop Hurd, in his *Letters on Chivalry and Romance* (1762), saw the full implications of this argument, and endeavored to show the literary value of works written in an earlier tradition not by explaining away the writer's faults on the grounds that at that period of history he could not possibly have known better, but by showing how the writer was fully successful in doing what he set out to do and what his age expected of him.

The *Letters on Chivalry and Romance* are principally concerned with Spenser's *Faerie Queene*. Hurd's argument is that this poem was not written in the classical or neo-classic style but on the "Gothic" model, and, just as a Gothic cathedral must be judged on the principles of Gothic architecture and not regarded as an unsuccessful Greek temple or neo-classic church, so *The Faerie Queene* must be read as a "Gothic" poem. "Under this idea . . . of a Gothic, not classical poem, the *Faery Queen* is to be read and criticized. And on these principles, it would not be difficult to unfold its merit in another way than has been hitherto attempted."

When an architect examines a Gothic structure by Grecian rules, he finds nothing but deformity. But the Gothic architecture has its own rules, by which when it comes to be examined, it is seen to have its merit, as well as the Grecian. The question is not, which of the two is conducted in the simplest or truest taste: but, whether there be not sense and design in both, when scrutinized by the laws on which each is projected.

The same observation holds of the two sorts of poetry. Judge of the *Faery Queen* by the classic models, and you are shocked with its disorder: consider it with an eye to its Gothic original, and you find it regular. The unity and simplicity of the former are more complete: but the latter has that sort of unity and simplicity, which results from its nature.

The *Faery Queen* then, as a Gothic poem, derives its METHOD, as well as the other characters of its composition, from the established modes and ideas of chivalry.

It was usual, in the days of knight-errantry, at the holding of any great feast, for Knights to appear before the Prince, who presided at it, to which the solemnity might give occasion. For it was supposed that, when such a *throng of knights and barons bold,* as Milton speaks of, were got together, the distressed would flock in from all quarters, as to a place where they knew they might find and claim redress for all their grievances.

This was the real practice, in the days of pure and antient chivalry. And on any extraordinary festival or solemnity: of which, if you want an instance, I refer you to the description of a feast made at Lisle in 1453, in the court of Philip the Good, Duke of Burgundy, for a crusade against the Turks: As you may find it given at large in the memoirs of *Matthieu de Conci, Olivier de la Marche,* and *Monstrelet.*

That feast was for *twelve* days: and each day was distinguished by the claim and allowance of some adventure.

Now laying down this practice, as a foundation for the poet's design, you will see how properly the *Faery Queen* is conducted.

—— "I devise, says the poet himself in his Letter to Sir Walter Raleigh, "that the Faery Queen kept her annual feaste xii days: upon which xii sev-"eral days, the occasion of the xii several adventures happened; which being "undertaken by xii several knights, are in these xii books severally handled."

Here you see the poet delivering his own method, and the reason of it. It arose out of the order of his subject. And would you desire a better reason for his choice?

Yes; you will say, a poet's method is not that of his subject. I grant you, as to the order of *time,* in which the recital is made; for here, as Spenser observes (and his own practice agrees to the Rule) lies the main difference between *the poet historical and the historiographer:* The reason of which is drawn from the nature of Epic composition itself, and holds equally, let the subject be what it will, and whatever the system of manners be, on which it is conducted. Gothic or Classic makes no difference in this respect.

But the case is not the same with regard to the general plan of a work, or what may be called the order of *distribution,* which is and must be governed by the subject-matter itself. It was as requisite for the Faery Queen to consist of the adventures of twelve knights, as for the Odyssey to be confined to the adventures of one Hero: Justice had otherwise not been done to his subject.

So that if you will say anything against the poet's method, you must say that he should not have chosen this subject. But this objection arises from your classic ideas of Unity, which have no place here; and are in every view foreign to the purpose, if the poet has found means to give his work, tho' consisting of many parts, the advantage of Unity. For in some reasonable sense or other, it is agreed, every work of art must be *one,* the very idea of a work requiring it.

If you ask then, what is this *Unity* of Spenser's Poem? I say, It consists in the relation of its several adventures to one common *original,* the appointment of the Faery Queen; and to one common *end*, the completion of the Faery Queen's injunctions. The knights issued forth on their adventures on the breaking up of this annual feast; and the next annual feast, we are to suppose, is to bring them together again from the atchievement of their several charges.

This, it is true, is not the classic Unity, which consists in the representation of one entire action: but it is an Unity of another sort, an unity resulting from the respect which a number of related actions have to one common purpose. In other words, It is an unity of *design,* and not of action.

This Gothic method of design in poetry may be, in some sort, illustrated by what is called the Gothic method of design in Gardening. A wood or grove cut out into many separate avenues or glades was amongst the most favourite of the works of art, which our fathers attempted in this species of cultivation. These walks were distinct from each other, had, each, their several destination, and terminated on their own proper objects. Yet the whole was brought together and considered under one view by the relation which these various openings had, not to each other, but to their common and concurrent center. You and I are, perhaps, agreed that this sort of gardening is not of so true a taste as that which *Kent and Nature* have brought us acquainted with; where the supreme art of the Designer consists in disposing his ground and objects into an *entire landskip;* and grouping them, if I may use the term, in so easy a manner, that the careless observer, tho' he be taken with the symmetry of the whole, discovers no art in the combination . . .

This, I say, may be the truest taste in gardening because the simplest: Yet there is a manifest regard to unity in the other method; which has its admirers, as it may have again, and is certainly not without its *design* and beauty.

Hurd here uses references to historical fact ("I refer you to the description of a feast made at Lisle in 1453") and analogies from other arts (architecture and gardening) in order to establish, first, that Spenser's method was based on ways of thought and action in Gothic times, and, secondly, that this method produces its own unity of design. He is concerned that the reader of *The Faerie Queene* should come to the poem without false analogies in mind, see it for what it really is, and appreciate its own proper excellences.

History and the broadening of taste

This kind of criticism flourishes most when the critic is deliberately attempting to enlarge taste, to make his readers aware of the true nature and virtues of something written in a different tradition from that to which they are accustomed. It is commonly used by scholarly critics today when they want to draw our attention, say, to the theories of rhetoric held by seventeenth century poets, or to the eighteenth century poet's view of the function of satire, and thus help us to see the methods and objectives of the poets for what they really are. Whether what they really are is good or bad is, of course, another question; but at least it can be said that one must—in Matthew Arnold's phrase—"see the object in itself as it really is" before one can begin to assess its value.

This approach is different from going to biography or psychology to discover the author's *intention*, for it is less personal intention than artistic tradition that is the real question. Of course, Spenser's intention was to write what Hurd calls a Gothic poem, but he might have had the intention and still not succeeded, and it would then be of little help to the critic to learn from biographical sources what had been intended. Hurd's method is to establish the nature of the tradition within which the poet worked, and then to show, by an analysis of the poem, that the poem is thoroughly successful once we understand the assumptions about the nature of art with which the poet's tradition provided him. Ideally, we could derive these assumptions from the poem; ideally, there is never any need to go to history in order to find out what kind of work an author has produced. But in fact we are often conditioned by our experience to respond only to a work written in one kind of tradition and so to misread a work of another kind—to treat it as we would be treating a Gothic cathedral if we thought of it as a distorted Greek temple.

Once history has provided us the perspective within which we can see the work properly, we are in a position to look at the work and realize that that perspective is really implicit in it, only we had been blinded by exposure too long to other kinds of work and so could not see it until it was shown to us by the historical approach. A work which continues to be dependent for our appreciation of it on historical background—a work, that is, that does not light up in itself, as it were, as soon as our attention has been drawn to the proper way of looking at it—cannot be a successful work of art, and the historical critic who tries to bludgeon us with background material in order to make us "appreciate" a work which never fully comes alive even under the historical spotlight is doing precisely what Matthew Arnold warned against in the passage we quoted in the preceding section.

Hurd's method of approach is a particularly effective device for broadening taste at a time of critical narrowness and complacency, and it can be applied as fruitfully in the criticism of works written in a new tradition as in the appreciation of earlier literature. The critic who wishes to explain *The Waste Land* to readers brought up on Palgrave's *Golden Treasury* will have to use apparatus similar to that used by the critic explaining the seventeenth century metaphysical poets to the same kind of reader—the reader, that is, who has been educated to believe the Tennysonian lyric the highest form of poetry and who does not admit that astringency and wit have a proper place in the greatest art. In either case the critic will have to begin by an appeal to the reader to forget for a moment the style and method of his favorite poets and consider just what it is that Eliot or Donne is trying to achieve in his complex and ironical handling of imagery. This again involves not so much an appeal to personal intention as an investigation of the cultural climate of the poet's time and the explanation and illumination of his poetic intention with reference to that climate.[1]

The dangers of catholicity

There are, of course, dangers in this approach. Catholicity of taste is a virtue in a literary critic, but only up to a point. There is a kind of academic critic who considers it his duty to approve of everything, however inferior, provided it was produced in the past, and who will spend much patient labor editing and historically justifying a bad eighteenth century versifier whereas he would turn with contempt from his modern equivalent. This is not only to fall into the fault we have already noted as having been censured by Matthew Arnold; it is also to mistake antiquarian for historical justification and to assume that any piece of literature is valuable if it can be dug up and talked about. Of course, bad literature of a previous age has its *interest:* it tells us a great deal about the tastes of the time and may be illuminating

---

[1] Simple biographical intention is irrelevant to the judgment of a work, but intention as realized in the work, as an aspect of the work, might be missed through improper reading. Background knowledge may assist the reader to read properly, to see the work as it really is. But a work of art has an independent existence once it has been created, and in the course of this existence three different aspects may emerge: the work as "intended" by the writer; the work as read by a given reader; the "normal" work as read by those readers who take every meaning in it in its normal sense. What is the relation between these three? And how relevant is biographical information in establishing that relation? These are questions that have agitated many modern critics. See the article, "Intention," in *Dictionary of World Literature*, ed. by Joseph T. Shipley, New York, 1943; and W. K. Wimsatt, Jr. and Monroe C. Beardsley, "The Intentional Fallacy," *Sewanee Review*, LIV (1946), pp. 468-488.

sociologically or historically. But there are degrees of interest, and, more important, *interest* is not the same as *value*. George Orwell once wrote a fascinating study of popular English boys' magazines, explaining their nature, conventions, social code, and so on.[2] But he never concealed his opinion that the stories in these magazines were rubbish: he was explaining, not justifying, a phenomenon of modern culture.

There are dangers in excessive catholicity, and there is a peculiar academic delusion that it is incumbent on professors of literature to praise everything ever produced in the past. (This catholicity with reference to past literature often goes hand in hand with extraordinary narrowness of appreciation where contemporary work is concerned: there were critics in the 1920s who relished both the lushness of Swinburne and the neat pleasantries of minor Queen Anne versifiers but who turned in bewildered horror from James Joyce and T. S. Eliot.) But the dangers of catholicity are neither as great nor as obvious as those of complacent narrowness, and the greatest practical critics have always at some point succeeded in enlarging taste as well as in producing greater discrimination. Hurd's approach, for all its liability to abuse, was immensely fruitful, and led to the more adequate reading of many works which had long been misread through the spectacles of contemporary fashion. That there are different kinds of literary virtues, and that the differences do not necessarily represent higher or lower degrees of value, was a notion which had an immensely liberating effect on criticism and produced much that was permanent in Romantic criticism. Consider, for example, these remarks made by William Hazlitt in 1822:[3]

. . . The dispute between the admirers of Homer and Virgil has never been settled, and never will: for there will always be minds to whom the excellences of Virgil will be more congenial, and therefore more objects of admiration, than those of Homer, and *vice versa*. Both are right in preferring what suits them best—the delicacy and selectness of the one, or the fulness and majestic flow of the other. There is the same difference in their tastes that there was in the genius of their two favourites. Neither can the disagreement between the French and English school of tragedy ever be reconciled till the French become English, or the English French. Both are right in what they admire. We see the defects of Racine; they see the faults of Shakespeare probably in an exaggerated point of view. But we may be sure of this, that when we see nothing but grossness and barbarism,

[2] "Boys' Weeklies" (1939), reprinted in *Critical Essays*, London, 1946.
[3] "On Criticism," in *Table-Talk*, vol. II.

or insipidity and verbiage, in a writer that is the God of a nation's idolatry, it is we and not they who want true taste and feeling. The controversy about Pope and the opposite school in our own poetry comes to much the same thing. Pope's correctness, smoothness, &c., are very good things and much to be commended in him. But it is not to be expected, or even desired, that others should have these qualities in the same paramount degree, to the exclusion of everything else. If you like correctness and smoothness of all things in the world, there they are for you in Pope. If you like other things better, such as strength and sublimity, you know where to go for them. Why trouble Pope or any other author for what they have not, and do not profess to give? Those who seem to imply that Pope possessed, besides his own peculiar exquisite merits, all that is to be found in Shakespeare and Milton, are, I should hardly think, in good earnest. But I do not therefore see that, because this was not the case, Pope was no poet. We cannot by a little sophistry confound the qualities of different minds, nor force opposite excellences into a union by all the intolerance in the world. We may pull Pope in pieces as long as we please for not being Shakespeare or Milton, as we may carp at them for not being Pope; but this will not make a poet equal to all three. If we have a taste for some one precise style or manner, we may keep it to ourselves and let others have theirs. If we are more catholic in our notions and want variety of excellence and beauty, it is spread abroad for us to profusion in the variety of books and in the several growth of men's minds, fettered by no capricious or arbitrary rules. Those who would proscribe whatever falls short of a given standard of imaginary perfection do so not from a higher capacity of taste or range of intellect than others, but to destroy, to "crib and cabin in" all enjoyments and opinions but their own.

This was a salutary position to take up in an age when different critical traditions were meeting each other head-on and the tendency was for different schools to make no attempt whatever to read properly each other's products. (Wordsworth on a sonnet of Gray's was as unperceptive and intolerant as Lockhart on Keats and as many contemporary critics on Wordsworth himself.) Yet this passage shows a danger other than that of an undue catholicity which might result in the abandonment of all standards: "if we have a taste for some one precise style or manner, we may keep it to ourselves and let others have theirs" is not very far removed from "I don't know anything about art, but I know what I like." Mere impressionism, the falling back on autobiographical chatter about personal likes and dislikes and the thrill one gets out of this or that work, is fatal to any critical order or critical method, and when it is rampant literature suffers. If literature is valuable, its value must be demonstrable, and if there is good and bad literature there must be some reasonably objective method of distinguishing the one from the other. Or perhaps not? Is known value always demonstrable and can different degrees of worth always be objectively proved? There are many critics in the history of literature who would have answered these questions in the negative.

The place of impressionism

Mere impressionism, the simple setting forth of an autobiographical response to take the place of critical assessment, is certainly not a valuable critical method. But if literature is a form of communication, then testimony as to the effectiveness of that communication by readers with a wide and deep experience of different kinds can be taken to be in some sense evaluation. Can a case be made for the proper exploitation of the critic's reactions to a work as a means of assisting critical evaluation of it? Many modern critics would deny that such a case can be made, and point out that the critic's duty is to show how the work lives, what its form and structure and essential life really are, and show this by pointing to qualities objectively present in the work itself; the critic, they would maintain, is concerned with the *means* rather than with the end, with how the communication is achieved rather than with effect of the achieved communication on the reader. Autobiography on the critic's part, they would urge, is not criticism.

If practical criticism were solely a matter of evaluation, of giving the author so many marks for each aspect of his work, then the case for any impressionist criticism would be weak. But it is also the function of the critic to increase understanding and appreciation, to bring the reader to see and appreciate what the work really is—to teach him to read it, even—and in achieving this kind of end cannot he be allowed a judicious use of impressionist devices, even of autobiographical gestures? The only way of answering this is to pose a further question: has an impressionist approach ever been successfully employed in illuminating and evaluating a work? Critics like Lamb, Hazlitt and De Quincey used this approach fairly frequently and in varying degrees of purity. Such a remark as Hazlitt's "I can take mine ease in mine inn with Signor Orlando Friscobaldo as the oldest acquaintance I have. Ben Jonson, learned Chapman, Master Webster and Master Heywood are there" is certainly not critical in any strict sense of the term, but it does help to show the kind of atmosphere which certain works create and thus to draw the reader's attention to the proper way of reading the work. Lamb on restoration comedy talks similarly:

I confess for myself that (with no great delinquencies to answer for) I am glad for a season to take an airing beyond the diocese of the strict conscience—not to live always in the precincts of the law-courts—but now and then, for a dream-while or so, to imagine a world with no meddling restrictions—to get into recesses, whither the hunter cannot follow me—

> ———— Secret Shades
> Of woody Ida's inmost grove,
> While yet there was no fear of Jove.

I come back to my cage and my restraint the fresher and more healthy for it. I wear my shackles more contentedly for having respired the breath of an imaginary freedom. I do not know how it is with others, but I feel the better always for the perusal of one of Congreve's—nay, why should I not add even of Wycherley's—comedies, I am the gayer at least for it. . . .[4]

This is to make a serious point about the nature of restoration comedy—that it was fundamentally amoral and its conventions wholly unconcerned with the morality of daily life—in an autobiographical manner, and though the particular kind of confessional coyness employed here by Lamb probably offends most modern tastes, it cannot be denied that the point is deftly made. De Quincey, in his famous "On the Knocking at the Gate in Macbeth," combines autobiographical with more objective remarks and illustrates how a composite method can be used in practical criticism, to establish an impressive series of points.

From my boyish days I had always felt a great perplexity on one point in Macbeth: it was this: the knocking at the gate, which succeeds to the murder of Duncan, produced to my feelings an effect for which I never could account: the effect was—that it reflected back upon the murder a peculiar awfulness and a depth of solemnity: yet, however obstinately I endeavoured with my understanding to comprehend this, for many years I never could see *why* it should produce such an effect.——
Here I pause for one moment to exhort the reader never to pay any attention to his understanding when it stands in opposition to any other faculty of his mind. The mere understanding, however useful and indis-

[4] "On the Artificial Comedy of the Last Century" (1822).

pensable, is the meanest faculty in the human mind and the most to be dis-
trusted: and yet the great majority of people trust to nothing else; which
may do for ordinary life, but not for philosophic purposes. Of this, out of
ten thousand instances that I might produce, I will cite one. Ask of any
person whatsoever, who is not previously prepared for the demand by a
knowledge of perspective, to draw in the rudest way the commonest
appearance which depends upon the laws of that science—as for
instance, to represent the effect of two walls standing at right angles to
each other, or the appearance of the houses on each side of a street,
as seen by a person looking down the street from one extremity.
Now in all cases, unless the person has happened to observe in pictures
how it is that artists produce these effects, he will be utterly unable to make
the smallest approximation to it. Yet why?—For he has actually seen the
effect every day of his life. The reason is—that he allows his understanding
to overrule his eyes. His understanding, which includes no intuitive knowledge of the laws of vision, can furnish him with no reason why a line which
is known and can be proved to be a horizontal line, should not *appear* a
horizontal line: a line, that made any angle with the perpendicular less than
a right angle, would seem to him to indicate that his houses were all
tumbling down together. Accordingly he makes the line of his houses a
horizontal line, and fails of course to produce the effect demanded. Here
then is one instance out of many, in which not only the understanding is
allowed to overrule the eyes, but where the understanding is positively
allowed to obliterate the eyes as it were: for not only does the man believe
the evidence of his understanding in opposition to that of his eyes, but
(which is monstrous!) the idiot is not aware that his eyes ever gave such
evidence. He does not know that he has seen (and therefore *quoad* his consciousness has *not* seen) that which he *has* seen every day of his life. But
to return from this digression,—my understanding could furnish no reason
why the knocking at the gate in Macbeth should produce any effect direct
or reflected: in fact, my understanding said positively that it could not
produce any effect. But I knew better: I felt that it did: and I waited and
clung to the problem until further knowledge should enable me to solve it.
—At length, in 1812, Mr Williams made his *début* on the stage of Ratcliffe
Highway, and executed those unparalleled murders which have procured
for him such a brilliant and undying reputation. On which murders, by
the way, I must observe, that in one respect they have had an ill effect, by
making the connoisseur in murder very fastidious in his taste, and dissatis-
fied with any thing that has been since done in that line. All other murders
look pale by the deep crimson of his: and, as an amateur once said to me
in a querulous tone, "There has been absolutely nothing *doing* since his
time, or nothing that's worth speaking of." But this is wrong: for it is unreasonable to expect all men to be great artists, and born with the genius of

Mr Williams.—Now it will be remembered that in the first of these murders (that of the Marrs) the same incident (of a knocking at the door soon after the work of extermination was complete) did actually occur which the genius of Shakespeare had invented: and all good judges and the most eminent dilettanti acknowledged the felicity of Shakespeare's suggestion as soon as it was actually realized. Here then was a fresh proof that I had been right in relying on my own feeling in opposition to my understanding; and again I set myself to study the problem: at length I solved it to my own satisfaction; and my solution is this. Murder in ordinary cases, where the sympathy is wholly directed to the case of the murdered person, is an incident of coarse and vulgar horror; and for this reason— that it flings the interest exclusively upon the natural but ignoble instinct by which we cleave to life; an instinct which, as being indispensable to the primal law of self-preservation, is the same in kind (though different in degree) amongst all living creatures; this instinct therefore, because it annihilates all distinctions, and degrades the greatest of men to the level of "the poor beetle that we tread on," exhibits human nature in its most abject and humiliating attitude. Such an attitude would little suit the purposes of the poet. What then must he do? He must throw the interest on the murderer: our sympathy must be with *him* (of course I mean a sympathy of comprehension, a sympathy by which we enter into his feelings, and are made to understand them,—not a sympathy of pity or approbation:) in the murdered person all strife of thought, all flux and reflux of passion and of purpose, are crushed by one overwhelming panic: the fear of instant death smites him "with its petrific mace." But in the murderer, such a murderer as a poet will condescend to, there must be raging some great storm of passion,—jealousy, ambition, vengeance, hatred,—which will create a hell within him; and into this hell we are to look. In Macbeth, for the sake of gratifying his own enormous and teeming faculty of creation, Shakespeare has introduced two murderers: and, as usual in his hands, they are remarkably discriminated: but though in Macbeth the strife of mind is greater than in his wife, the tiger spirit not so awake, and his feelings caught chiefly by contagion from her,—yet, as both were finally involved in the guilt of murder, the murderous mind of necessity is finally to be presumed in both. This was to be expressed; and on its own account, as well as to make it a more proportionable antagonist to the unoffending nature of their victim, "the gracious Duncan," and adequately to expound "the deep damnation of his taking off," this was to be expressed with peculiar energy. We were to be made to feel that the human nature, *i. e.* the divine nature of love and mercy, spread through the hearts of all creatures, and seldom utterly withdrawn from man,—was gone, vanished, extinct; and that the fiendish nature had taken its place. And, as this effect is marvellously accomplished in the dialogues and soliloquies themselves, so it is finally consummated by the expedient under consideration; and it is to this that I now solicit the reader's attention. If the reader has ever witnessed a wife, daughter, or sister, in a fainting fit, he may chance to have observed that the most affecting moment in such a spectacle, is *that* in which a sigh and a stirring announce the recommencement of suspended life. Or, if the reader has ever been present in a vast metropolis on the day when some great national idol was carried in funeral pomp to his grave, and chancing to walk near to the course through which it passed, has felt powerfully in the silence and desertion of the streets and in the stagnation of ordinary business, the deep interest which at that moment was possessing the heart of man,—if all at once he should hear the death-like stillness broken up by the sound of wheels rattling away from the scene, and making known that the transitory vision was dissolved, he will be aware that at no moment was his sense of the complete suspension and pause in ordinary human concerns so full and affecting as at that moment when the suspension ceases, and the goings-on of human life are suddenly resumed. All action in any direction is best expounded, measured, and made apprehensible, by reaction. Now apply this to the case in Macbeth. Here, as I have said, the retiring of the human heart and the entrance of the fiendish heart was to be expressed and made sensible. Another world has stepped in; and the murderers are taken out of the region of human things, human purposes, human desires. They are transfigured: Lady Macbeth is "unsexed;" Macbeth has forgot that he was born of woman; both are conformed to the image of devils; and the world of devils is suddenly revealed. But how shall this be conveyed and made palpable? In order that a new world may step in, this world must for a time disappear. The murderers, and the murder, must be insulated—cut off by an immeasurable gulph from the ordinary tide and succession of human affairs—locked up and sequestered in some deep recess: we must be made sensible that the world of ordinary life is suddenly arrested—laid asleep—tranced—racked into a dread armistice: time must be annihilated; relation to things without abolished; and all must pass self-withdrawn into a deep syncope and suspension of earthly passion. Hence it is that when the deed is done—when the work of darkness is perfect, then the world of darkness passes away like a pageantry in the clouds: the knocking at the gate is heard; and it makes known audibly that the reaction has commenced: the human has made its reflux upon the fiendish: the pulses of life are beginning to beat again: and the re-establishment of the goings-on of the world in which we live, first makes us profoundly sensible of the awful parenthesis that had suspended them.

Oh! mighty poet!—Thy works are not as those of other men, simply and merely great works of art; but are also like the phenomena of nature, like the sun and the sea, the stars and the flowers,—like frost and snow, rain and dew, hail-storm and thunder, which are to be studied with entire submission of our own faculties, and in the perfect faith that in them there can be no too much or too little, nothing useless or inert—but that, the further we press in our discoveries, the more we shall see proofs of design and self-supporting arrangement where the careless eye had seen nothing but accident!

In this piece of practical criticism the movement from literature to life and back again is continuous, and autobiography is brought in as part of this movement. De Quincey is not content to chat about his own reactions: he moves immediately from them to an explanation of them, and the art of the passage in question is defended on the grounds of its psychological truth and structural appropriateness. The auto-biographical introduction and the apostrophe to the poet at the con-clusion may seem to us romantic extravagance—especially the latter; but in fact De Quincey has here employed a highly complicated critical method with remarkable success. He has demonstrated before the eyes of the reader the fascination, the paradox, and the success of the scene in *Macbeth* which he is discussing, by means of a technique which uses autobiography only as a starting point and which, once it has got really started, relates literal truth and artistic truth by an im-plied theory of how one makes use of the other, and relates structure to both by showing how the placing of this incident at this point in the play helps to emphasize the psychological truth with which it is concerned. And in the emphasis of the psychological truth lies the dramatic effect.

This is therefore a highly sophisticated piece of practical criticism, and neither simple impressionism nor the naive relating of incidents in a literary work to the facts of actual life. Yet impressionism has a role here, as also does a representational theory of art. How the work affects the reader, the relation of the situation presented in the work to real life, the function and significance of form and structure in the work—all these matters are raised; but the critical assessment de-pends on no single one of them. They are all used together to explain each other and explain the effectiveness of the work.

It is a long road from Hurd's appeal that we should judge Spenser on the standards appropriate to his kind of art to De Quincey's justi-fication and explanation of a scene in *Macbeth* on grounds both psy-chological and formal. But there is a connection between the two. Once Hurd made the point that a work of a previous age must be judged not by objective rules derived from the taste of the age that is judging but rather by rules derived from the criticized work itself the way lay open to relativism and impressionism. History, used to explain and then to justify a work written in a forgotten taste, can eventually be used to break down the taste of an age altogether. When that is done, a greater catholicity of taste emerges, and criticism often falls back on purely autobiographical devices equivalent, at their crudest, to saying simply, "Well, *I* get a kick out of it." The defects of such an approach are perhaps more obvious in the middle of the twentieth century than they were half a century or a century ago; but if we prefer a criticism which claims to be more objective and "scientific," we should not forget how an element of impressionism (that is, of criticism through a parade of autobiographical response to the work criticized) can, when used with discretion as part of a complex technique, achieve remarkable results.

The autobiographical or impressionist approach has been discredited eventually by the facility with which it can be employed by critics of no real intellectual capacity or esthetic awareness. If the application of neo-classic "rules" can, at its most extreme, produce rigid and mechanical awarding of marks without any imaginative understanding of the true nature of the work in question, the deliberate avoidance of rules can, at the other extreme, produce offensive gush of no critical value whatever. Which of these extremes we shun most consciously depends on the critical atmosphere of the age in which we live.

Arnold on Pope

It is interesting to see how different schools of thought, each operating on its own assumptions, can produce different views of the same writer or the same work. We might, for example, contrast Hazlitt's view of Pope, based on toleration for all poetic styles, with the well-known and long-popular view expressed by Matthew Arnold in his introductory essay to Thomas Ward's anthology of English poetry. Arnold, too, regards the verse of Dryden and Pope as good of their kind, but he regards the kind as unpoetic:

Are Dryden and Pope poetical classics? Is the historic estimate, which represents them as such, and which has been so long established that it cannot easily give way, the real estimate? Wordsworth and Coleridge, as is well known, denied it; but the authority of Wordsworth and Coleridge does not weigh much with the young generation, and there are many signs to show that the eighteenth century and its judgments are coming into favour again. Are the favourite poets of the eighteenth century classics?

It is impossible within my present limits to discuss the question fully. And what man of letters would not shrink from seeming to dispose dictatorially of the claims of two men who are, at any rate, such masters in letters as Dryden and Pope; two men of such admirable talent, both of them, and one of them, Dryden, a man, on all sides, of such energetic and genial power? And yet, if we are to gain the full benefit from poetry, we must have the real estimate of it. I cast about for some mode of arriving, in the present case, at such an estimate without offence. And perhaps the best way is to begin, as it is easy to begin, with cordial praise.

When we find Chapman, the Elizabethan translator of Homer, expressing himself in his preface thus: "Though truth in her very nakedness sits in so deep a pit, that from Gades to Aurora and Ganges few eyes can sound her, I hope yet those few here will so discover and confirm that, the date being out of her darkness in this morning of our poet, he shall now gird his temples with the sun,"—we pronounce that such a prose is intolerable. When we find Milton writing: "And long it was not after, when I was confirmed in this opinion, that he, who would not be frustrate of his hope to write well hereafter in laudable things, ought himself to be a true poem," —we pronounce that such a prose has its own grandeur, but that it is obsolete and inconvenient. But when we find Dryden telling us: "What Virgil wrote in the vigour of his age, in plenty and at ease, I have undertaken to translate in my declining years; struggling with wants, oppressed with sickness, curbed in my genius, liable to be misconstrued in all I write,"—then we exclaim that here at last we have the true English prose, a prose such as we would all gladly use if we only knew how. Yet Dryden was Milton's contemporary.

But after the Restoration the time had come when our nation felt the imperious need of a fit prose. So, too, the time had likewise come when our nation felt the imperious need of freeing itself from the absorbing preoccupation which religion in the Puritan age had exercised. It was impossible that this freedom should be brought about without some negative excess, without some neglect and impairment of the religious life of the soul; and the spiritual history of the eighteenth century shows us that the freedom was not achieved without them. Still, the freedom was achieved; the preoccupation, an undoubtedly baneful and retarding one if it had continued, was got rid of. And as with religion amongst us at that period, so it was

also with letters. A fit prose was a necessity; but it was impossible that a
fit prose should establish itself amongst us without some touch of frost to
the imaginative life of the soul. The needful qualities for a fit prose are
regularity, uniformity, precision, balance. The men of letters, whose destiny it may be to bring their nation to the attainment of a fit prose, must of
necessity, whether they work in prose or in verse, give a predominating, an
almost exclusive attention to the qualities of regularity, uniformity, precision, balance. But an almost exclusive attention to these qualities involves
some repression and silencing of poetry.

We are to regard Dryden as the puissant and glorious founder, Pope as
the splendid high-priest, of our age of prose and reason, of our excellent
and indispensable eighteenth century. For the purposes of their mission and
destiny their poetry, like their prose, is admirable. Do you ask me whether
Dryden's verse, take it almost where you will, is not good?

> A milk-white Hind, immortal and unchanged,
> Fed on the lawns and in the forest ranged.[5]

I answer: Admirable for the purposes of the inaugurator of an age of prose
and reason. Do you ask me whether Pope's verse, take it almost where you
will, is not good?

> To Hounslow Heath I point, and Banstead Down;
> Thence comes your mutton, and these chicks my own.[6]

I answer: Admirable for the purposes of the high priest of an age of prose
and reason. But do you ask me whether such verse proceeds from men with
an adequate poetic criticism of life, from men whose criticism of life has
a high seriousness, or even, without that high seriousness, has poetic large-
ness, freedom, insight, benignity? Do you ask me whether the application
of ideas to life in the verse of these men, often a powerful application, no
doubt, is a powerful *poetic* application? Do you ask me whether the poetry
of these men has either the matter or the inseparable manner of such an
adequate poetic criticism; whether it has the accent of

> "Absent thee from felicity awhile . . ."[7]

or of

> "And what is else not to be overcome . . ."[8]

[5] Dryden, *The Hind and the Panther*, i, 1-2.
[6] Pope, *The Second Satire of the Second Book of Horace*, 143-144.
[7] *Hamlet*, V, ii, 358. Arnold had earlier quoted lines 357-360 as an example of the
highest poetry.
[8] *Paradise Lost*, I, 109. Arnold had earlier quoted lines 108-109.

or of

"O martyr souded in virginitee!"[9]

I answer: It has not and cannot have them; it is the poetry of the builders of an age of prose and reason. Though they may write in verse, though they may in a certain sense be masters of the art of versification, Dryden and Pope are not classics of our poetry, they are classics of our prose.

Against this one might set F. R. Leavis's defense of Pope as a "metaphysical" poet in his chapter on the poet in his *Revaluation* (1936), or Edith Sitwell's analysis of the various textures of Pope's verse in chapter 18 of her *Alexander Pope* (1930).

Critical relativism

One of the best modern defenses of critical relativism is Frederick A. Pottle's *The Idiom of Poetry* (1946), especially the first two chapters. At the end of his first chapter, Professor Pottle sums up his views as follows:[10]

1) Poetry always expresses the basis of feeling (or sensibility) of the age in which it was written.

2) Critics of the past were as well qualified to apply a subjective test to poetry as we are. ("The presumption that it is we who are more nearly at rest has no serious foundation; it is mere self-flattery.")

3) Poetry is whatever has been called poetry by respectable judges at any time and in any place. ("Respectable" may be thought to beg the question. I mean to include in the term those critics who had the esteem of their own age, as well as those whom we admire.)

4) The poetry of an age never goes wrong. Culture may go wrong, civilization may go wrong, criticism may go wrong, but poetry, in the collective sense, cannot go wrong.

This, of course, is in sharp opposition to the common modern view that something went wrong with the poetic sensibility in the late

9 Chaucer, *The Prioress's Tale*, line 92.
10 Reprinted by permission of Cornell University Press.

seventeenth century which has only recently been put right (see Cleanth Brooks' *Modern Poetry and the Tradition*). It is equally in sharp contrast with the views and critical method of F. R. Leavis, a stern modern opponent of relativism and a critic who believes that it is possible—and desirable—to trace the true tradition of English poetry and English fiction through the few great writers who alone represent it (see, for example, his book on the English novel, significantly called *The Great Tradition*, where the tradition is defined and the elect, who belonged to and perpetuated it, named and discussed). One can of course be, like Leavis, an opponent of relativism and at the same time sensitively aware of shifts in literary style and fashion; to oppose relativism is not necessarily to deny that there are different kinds of good literature and that some kinds flourish more readily in the climate of one age than in that of another, but it *is* to deny Professor Pottle's contention that "poetry is whatever has been called poetry by respectable judges at any time and in any place" and to deny even more strongly that "the poetry of an age never goes wrong."

Professor Pottle's relativist position enables him to see the futility of a critic's attempting to reverse a new tide of taste; the chief function of the critic of contemporary literature, as he sees it, is "to recognize and to define the emergent idiom: to detach it from the background of the moribund but highly respectable idiom which obscures it." He continues:

He should realize that he has little or no power to change its essential character or direction; no more, let us say, than the linguist has to change the development of a language. Nothing is more futile than to scold an O'Neill because he has not written like Aeschylus, or an Eliot for not having written like Tennyson. Jeffrey's criticism of Wordsworth is a classical example of the folly of the judicial method. . . .

Such a pragmatic approach to the problem of evaluation would not satisfy those critics who insist on seeking norms and applying standards which they consider perpetually valid. Such critics might quarrel with Professor Pottle for not distinguishing with any precision between means and ends; they might say that there are many different kinds of style and idiom which a poet might legitimately employ and that sensibility certainly operates differently in different periods, but they would insist that this is a question of means, not of ends, and that what a great work of literature *is* and *does* can always be defined in the same way. There are many implications here, both for theoretical and for practical criticism, and the reader might profitably consider some of them.

14

From appreciation to analysis

To DEFINE a critical approach and discuss its merits and demerits is a relatively easy matter. The great majority of critics, however, have rarely used a single and easily definable method in their practical criticism. The academic critic, in particular, with his various kinds of scholarly information—biographical, historical, textual—is often tempted to combine information, explanation, elucidation, and praise in his remarks on a given work or a given writer.

Critical chat

This eclectic method, as it may be called, is not necessarily muddle-headed: we have already noted some effective examples of criticism which combines elements from different methods, and many more could be cited, particularly from late nineteenth and early twentieth

century academic criticism, where the "bio-critical" approach flour-
ished vigorously and at its best was highly successful in conveying to
the reader a sense of a writer's achievement set against the background
of his life and time. It was an approach which, for obvious reasons, did
better with writers as a whole than with individual works; its greatest
successes lay in giving the reader a total impression of the kind of work
a writer produced, with appraisal of individual works used as an
example to illustrate the generalizations rather than as critical assessment in its own right. Consider, for example, George Saintsbury's remarks on Prior:

I do not know whether the haughty and delicate souls who, in opposition to Mr. Dobson, declare eighteenth century poetry "unreadable," make
any exceptions, even for Pope himself; in the nearly complete ignorance
which, it is to be feared, accompanies their haughtiness and their delicacy,
they seem only too likely not to make any for others. Yet how much are
they to be pitied if they do not know Prior, especially with the recently
discovered fragments of which the most charming but not the only
charming one is on that "Jinny the Just", who—

Read, and accounted, and paid, and abated;
Eat and drank, played and worked, laughed and cried, loved and hated,
As answered the end of her being created.

But these additions, for which we wiser folk so much thank Longleat and
the Marquis of Bath, Cambridge and Mr. Waller, are only a sort of "rere-
supper," a corollary to an abundant previous entertainment. That the great
comic poets have almost if not quite as much idiosyncrasy in their comedy
as the great tragic or serious poets in their other kinds, is a fact not much
likely to be disputed, though it is sometimes left unrecognized; and there
is hardly one who has more of it than Prior. With the eternal and almost
unnecessary exception of Shakespeare, Prior is about the first to bring out
that true English humour which involves sentiment and romance, which
laughs gently at its own tears, and has more than half a tear for its own
laughter. One might not have thought the lover of Cloe (unless, which is
not impossible, Cloe's anecdotographers have maligned her) and the fre-
quenter of pot shops likely to be troubled with "fine fancies," and certainly
he does not force them on us. But how airily they flit, and how delicate
and varicoloured they are, from the early and gay celebration of the little
Dutch chaise with its contents, literary and other, to those epitaphs which
are assuredly neither morbid nor cynical merely! Prior himself may have
written none too happily of Solomon, but he had at least one right to

write; for no one, except Thackeray, has ever entered more thoroughly
into the spirit of *Ecclesiastes*. How different is the sad and yet not in the
least moping or whining morality of the poem to Montagu, a poem with
its singular music infused into apparently quite commonplace metre—

> Our hopes, like towering falcons, aim, etc.,

from the mere "copy-book" so often charged against the century! How
admirable a variant in the same key is furnished by the *Lines written in
Mezeray*, with their strangely haunting close—

> Unwilling to retire, though weary!

And this seasoning and saving "Vanitas Vanitatum" is not absent from
things where it keeps farther in the background—the very "Lines to a Child
of Quality" owing not a little of their savour to it. Yet with this faculty,
which, it may be admitted, does easily turn in other men to morbidness and
cynicism, there is no bad blood in Prior. As we have no wittier so we have
no kindlier poet, though the wit keeps the kindliness from ever turning
mawkish. The *Tales*, though Johnson, unfair to Prior as a whole, granted
them his *imprimatur* as "a lady's book," are rather out of fashion to-day.
They are too naughty for the old-fashioned and not nasty enough for mod-
ernists. But they are thoroughly good-humoured. Some High-and-Mighti-
nesses have dismissed Prior's love poems as not ethereal enough—not so
much suggestive of the way of a superman with a supermaid as of that of
a man of the bag with a maid of the bar. Now half of this is due to the
tittle-tattle of the anecdote-mongers above mentioned; and even in the
other half there is not much justice. The "Cloe" poems certainly do not
suggest Amadis and Oriana, but in the House of Love as elsewhere there
are many mansions. At any rate they are extremely lively, extremely
pretty, and they hit off a partnership of *amare* and *bene velle* which persons who have confidence in their taste enough not to bother about other
people's may find not a little delectable, and no more "nasty" than the "nasty
hard rosebud," which revenged itself by finding such an agreeable resting-
place. Prior cannot be ill-natured. "The English Padlock" on one side is the
very incarnation of sweet and not unwholesome temper, as "My noble
lovely little Peggy" is on another; "Down Hall" on yet a third; others (for
though ill-nature is rather monotonous, good is always surprising when
it is not stupid, as Prior never is) on others yet. There are people—not always bad people—who seem to mistake Cowper's phrase, "easy jingle" as a
suggestion to take Prior lightly. Cowper himself did not mean it so; and it
may be diffidently suggested that if any young gentleman of the latest
block (the term is not used offensively, but is pure Elizabethan for the

fashion of hats), even after inspiring himself by the thought (not quite at first hand) that Tennyson does not exist and that Browning was a well-meant but not wholly successful anticipation of the twentieth century, that Swinburne was a musical-box and Stevenson an ineffectual Christmas toy—if any such will just try to imitate the jingle and the easiness—we shall see. While as for the longer poems, though the whimsical inconsequence of *Alma* is sometimes a little teasing, and though *Solomon* has (rather too obviously) been dismissed as an instance of a clever man trying something for which he was not fitted, it is still lawful to take for the Muse in regard to them Poins's wish for his sister when Scandal gave her to Prince Hal, "May the girl have no worse fortune!"

There is indeed a singular delectableness, partly arising from a certain strangeness and hidden quality in Prior. Some people even think, when they read of those morning walks which Swift and Prior took in the Park, "one to make himself fat and one to make himself thin," that of all that notable set the unquestionably greater could not have chosen a better companion. If he has not Pope's intense craftsmanship, Prior has, as has been hinted, something of the "behind the veil" touch that Pope never even hints at. With more delicacy even than Addison, he has also more passion than Steele and Gay. Arbuthnot and even Berkeley fall, the former into lower and more unequal levels, the latter, despite his greatness, into a specialist and abstract division. Possibly, as the common theory goes, Prior may have to some extent clogged the wings of the spirit with Epicurean living; possibly, as it has been more charitably suggested, the diplomatic work (for which he was in some ways unsuited, but the duties of which he seems to have discharged faithfully enough till they called for actual heroism, which he did not possess) overloaded him. He may even have actually given the best of what was in him, helped by pleasure on the one hand and perhaps even by business as a contrasting influence on the other. But undoubtedly there is, for some tastes at any rate, in Prior a flavour of one sort, an atmosphere of Venus and Cupid and kindly sport and fun, contrasted quintessentially with a "finish" of something quite different. His own short piece on "Democritus and Heraclitus" gives us a key, too much neglected, to his attitude; and he can "give a hand to each" as hardly any one else, except (once more) Thackeray, has done, and in a fashion different from Thackeray's.[1]

Perhaps this is, in a sense, literary chat rather than strictly literary criticism. We observe the relaxed, informal tone, the casual and confident use of quotation, the conversational references to contemporary taste and to the critic's view of it, the quick movement from one work to another with no attempt to give a thorough or systematic account

[1] *The Peace of the Augustans*, 1916. Reprinted by permission of Oxford University Press.

of any one. The critic here is taking for granted that his reader knows something about the subject and recognizes the quotations and the numerous literary references. The critic is also quite unconcerned with method—in fact, one might reasonably argue that this discussion of Prior shows no method at all. What are Saintsbury's criteria of a good poem, as shown in this discussion of Prior's poetry? "Jinny the Just" is described as "charming," and the charm is illustrated by a brief quotation. The kind of entertainment which Prior's poetry provides is illustrated by a great number of analogies which cumulatively suggest a cheerful and wholly healthy Epicureanism. The special quality of his humor is praised as, Shakespeare apart, probably the first true English variety, which is then defined very generally as "sentiment and romance, which laughs gently at its own tears, and has more than half a tear for its own laughter." (No quotation illustrates this very general definition.) Then comes a contrast between the delicacy of Prior's fancy—mentioned as a good quality—and Prior's habits in real life. Prior is next praised for entering more thoroughly into the spirit of *Ecclesiastes* than any other writer except Thackeray, and examples of an *Ecclesiastes*-like sadness are given. "Singular music infused into apparently quite commonplace metre" is cited as a virtue of one poem, but the quality is not analysed; it is, however, illustrated by the "strangely haunting" close of another poem. And so it goes—a personal, unsystematic, eclectic kind of criticism, creating as it moves a highly literary atmosphere, an atmosphere of the study, perhaps, but a study with comfortable leather chairs as well as well-lined bookshelves.

The success of this kind of criticism depends on its author's ability to handle the various elements of which it is composed in such a way as to build up a tone, an atmosphere, which reflects in some way the special qualities of the writer who is being criticized. But the tone is never wholly subdued to its subject: there is always the critic's personality before us, with the critic's preferences and prejudices, his references to pet authors (Thackeray, in Saintsbury's case) and favorite controversies, peppering his comment. As a result, it is not so much the essence of Prior that is distilled for us as we read Saintsbury's discussion of that poet, as a confrontation of essence of Prior with essence of Saintsbury. Out of this confrontation whatever is valuable in the criticism emerges—which is one reason why this kind of criticism is much more successful when the critic is letting himself go about a favorite author than when he is attempting to appraise the work of someone to whom he has no temperamental kinship. Saintsbury's taste was catholic enough, his range of enthusiasms enormous, but he strikes sparks only when his personality is responding to some aspect of a work or writer, when he is least scientific and most relaxed and discursive.

In criticism such as Saintsbury's the severer critical questions are taken for granted. Criticism is not a "discipline," as many modern critics like to regard it, but a civilized exchange of opinion. No attempt is made to demonstrate with analytic precision the presence of any given quality in a work, and whether any given quality represents a fault or a virtue is a question whose answer is assumed rather than debated. It is on the whole a response to the achieved work, not a technical demonstration of how the work is achieved. Such a criticism is likely to appear only after centuries of varied literary production have led not only to a broad view of the total literary scene but also to the establishment of a social tradition of bookish discourse about books. Professor Saintsbury was a great connoisseur of wines as well as a literary scholar and critic, and there does seem to be a relation between the two sides of his activity. His writing has an after-dinner flavor, a note of conversation among gentlemen over the port, and his criticism has a quality of savoring, of wine-tasting. Only a generation secure in its possession of a rich and stable literary tradition can afford to be so relaxed, so much the wine-tasting connoisseur, about its literary criticism. When that security ebbed, the connoisseur gave way to the analyst.

The case for amateurism

Most modern readers would regard the change as unquestionably one for the better. They welcome the increase in precision, in subtlety, in professionalism, that they see in modern criticism when compared with the Saintsbury variety. Yet there is a great deal to be said for the elegant amateurism of the Saintsbury tradition (for in a sense Saintsbury, though a professor and a professional critic and scholar, was the great amateur: his *manner* was amateur). To relegate critical discussion solely to the professional, to regard the critic as a highly specialized technical expert who writes for his fellow experts, has its own dangers. A civilization is judged by its amateurs, by the degree to which intelligent non-experts can discuss with sense and understanding the phenomena of their culture. If the critic becomes too far removed from the reader of literature—not necessarily from the "man in the street," that vague entity, but from the interested and sensitive non-professional—he will tend to develop a technical jargon of his own and to regard himself as a necessary mediator between the creative writer and the ordinary reader. Indeed, in so far as he will be intelligible only to fellow experts, he will not even be a mediator between writer and public, but a barrier indicating the impossibility of non-professional appreciation of good literature. Saintsbury, for all the occasional looseness of his criticism and his deliberate lack of method, or perhaps because of these qualities, always talked to his readers as their fellow-appreciator, not as their technical adviser. If a generation less complacent about its literary tradition and less likely to view after-dinner discussion as the fine flower of civilized discourse has learned to look for a sterner kind of criticism—more analytic, more methodical, and in general more tough minded—we can appreciate its need while at the same time perhaps envying an age which could take its culture more for granted.

It should be added that criticism as philosophical inquiry into the nature and value of imaginative literature—the kind that was discussed in Part One of this book—is almost always practiced by professional critics, for that can never be anything else but a strenuous philosophical activity. It is practical criticism, not philosophical criticism, that is likely to move toward an eclectic amateurism in a period when the man of letters fits comfortably into a long-established social and intellectual tradition. Critics of this kind tend to dismiss the fundamental esthetic questions with an epigram or an "every schoolboy knows" attitude.

For all the charm of the Saintsbury brand of criticism, for all its relaxed confidence, its assurance of the continuity of civilization, it deals competently only with works that grow obviously out of the past and falls silent in the face of any really challenging departure from traditional norms. When, about the time of the first world war, as the result of a long process of disintegration, the relation between tradition and the individual talent had to be fundamentally re-examined and the whole question of what goes on in a work of literary art was re-opened, criticism was forced to leave behind the relaxed air and the amateur tone and become more astringent and more technical.

Eliot on Swinburne: the analytic approach

If we set beside Saintsbury's discussion of Prior one of T. S. Eliot's earlier critical essays—on Marlowe, or Ben Jonson, or Andrew Marvell, for example—we are struck at once with the complete difference in *temper*. Eliot is not concerned to talk with wit and urbanity about literary achievements on which his readers are largely in agreement; Eliot's wit—so different from Saintsbury's—serves the purpose of arresting attention, not of illustrating general knowledge, and his prose deliberately lacks urbanity. Eliot's object is to explore the literary work in order to show what goes on in it; he wishes to surprise the reader into paying proper attention to the true life of the work. Percy Lubbock, in his book *The Craft of Fiction*, first published in 1921, defined this kind of criticism with reference to the novel:

The business of criticism in the matter of fiction seems clear, at any rate. There is nothing more that can usefully be said about a novel until we have fastened upon the question of its making and explored it to some purpose. In all our talk about novels we are hampered and held up by our unfamiliarity with what is called their technical aspect, and that is consequently the aspect to confront. That Jane Austen was an acute observer, that Dickens was a great humourist, that George Eliot had a deep knowledge of provincial character, that our living romancers are so full of life that they are neither to hold nor to bind—we know, we have repeated, we have told each other a thousand times; it is no wonder if attention flags when we hear it all again. It is their books, as well as their talents and attainments, that we aspire to see—their books, which we must recreate for ourselves if we are ever to behold them. And in order to recreate them durably there is the one obvious way—to study the craft, to follow the process, to read constructively. The practice of this method appears to me at this time of day, I confess, the only interest of the criticism of fiction. It seems vain to expect that discourse upon novelists will contain anything new for us until we have really and clearly and accurately seen their books.[2]

"To study the craft, to follow the process, to read constructively" —that might well have been Eliot's motto. At least, it describes accurately what his most characteristic practical criticism has been aimed at. Consider, for example, his essay on Swinburne, written in 1920:

[2] Reprinted by permission of Charles Scribner's Sons, New York; and Jonathan Cape Limited, London.

It is a question of some nicety to decide how much must be read of any particular poet. And it is not a question merely of the size of the poet. There are some poets whose every line has unique value. There are others who can be taken by a few poems universally agreed upon. There are others who need be read only in selections, but what selections are read will not very much matter. Of Swinburne, we should like to have the *Atalanta* entire, and a volume of selections which should certainly contain *The Leper, Laus Veneris,* and *The Triumph of Time*. It ought to contain many more, but there is perhaps no other single poem which it would be an error to omit. A student of Swinburne will want to read one of the Stuart plays and dip into *Trisram of Lyonesse*. But almost no one, today, will wish to read the whole of Swinburne. It is not because Swinburne is voluminous; certain poets, equally voluminous, must be read entire. The necessity and the difficulty of a selection are due to the peculiar nature of Swinburne's contribution, which, it is hardly too much to say, is of a very different kind from that of any other poet of equal reputation.

We may take it as undisputed that Swinburne did make a contribution; that he did something that had not been done before, and that what he did will not turn out to be a fraud. And from that we may proceed to inquire what Swinburne's contribution was, and why, whatever critical solvents we employ to break down the structure of his verse, this contribution remains. The test is this: agreed that we do not (and I think that the present generation does not) greatly enjoy Swinburne, and agreed that (a more serious condemnation) at one period of our lives we did enjoy him and now no longer enjoy him; nevertheless, the words which we use to state our grounds of dislike or indifference cannot be applied to Swinburne as they can to bad poetry. The words of condemnation are words which express his qualities. You may say "diffuse." But the diffuseness is essential; had Swinburne practised greater concentration his verse would be, not better in the same kind, but a different thing. His diffuseness is one of his glories. That so little material as appeared to be employed in *The Triumph of Time* should release such an amazing number of words, requires what there is no reason to call anything but genius. You could not condense *The Triumph of Time*. You could only leave out. And this would destroy the poem; though no one stanza seems essential. Similarly, a considerable quantity—a volume of selections—is necessary to give the quality of Swinburne although there is perhaps no one poem essential in this selection.

If, then, we must be very careful in applying terms of censure, like "diffuse," we must be equally careful of praise. "The beauty of Swinburne's verse is the sound," people say, explaining, "he had little visual imagination." I am inclined to think that the word beauty is hardly to be used in connexion with Swinburne's verse at all; but in any case the beauty or effect of sound is neither that of music nor that of poetry which can be set to music. There is no reason why verse intended to be sung should not present a sharp visual image or convey an important intellectual meaning, for it supplements the music by another means of affecting the feelings. What we get in Swinburne is an expression by sound, which could not possibly associate itself with music. For what he gives is not images and ideas and music, it is one thing with a curious mixture of suggestions of all three.

> Shall I come, if I swim? wide are the waves, you see;
> Shall I come, if I fly, my dear Love, to thee?

This is Campion, and an example of the kind of music that is not to be found in Swinburne. It is an arrangement and choice of words which has a sound-value and at the same time a coherent comprehensible meaning, and the two things—the musical value and meaning—are two things, not one. But in Swinburne there is no *pure* beauty—no pure beauty of sound, or of image, or of idea.

> Music, when soft voices die,
> Vibrates in the memory;
> Odours, when sweet violets sicken,
> Live within the sense they quicken.
>
> Rose leaves, when the rose is dead,
> Are heaped for the beloved's bed;
> And so thy thoughts, when thou art gone,
> Love itself shall slumber on.

I quote from Shelley, because Shelley is supposed to be the master of Swinburne; and because his song, like that of Campion, has what Swinburne has not—a beauty of music and a beauty of content; and because it is clearly and simply expressed, with only two adjectives. Now, in Swinburne the meaning and the sound are one thing. He is concerned with the meaning of the word in a peculiar way: he employs, or rather "works," the word's meaning. And this is connected with an interesting fact about his vocabulary: he uses the most general word, because his emotion is never particular, never in direct line of vision, never focused; it is emotion reinforced, not by intensification, but by expansion.

> There lived a singer in France of old
> By the tideless dolorous midland sea.
> In a land of sand and ruin and gold
> There shone one woman, and none but she.

You see that Provence is the merest point of diffusion here. Swinburne defines the place by the most general word, which has for him its own value. "Gold," "ruin," "dolorous": it is not merely the sound that he wants, but the vague associations of idea that the words give him. He has not his eye on a particular place, as:

> *Li ruscelletti che dei verdi colli*
> *Del Casentin discendon giuso in Arno* . . .
> [The little streams that from the green hills
> Of the Casentino flow down to the Arno . . .
> Dante, *Inferno,* XXX.]

It is, in fact, the word that gives him the thrill, not the object. When you take to pieces any verse of Swinburne, you find always that the object was not there—only the word. Compare

> Snowdrops that plead for pardon
> And pine for fright

with the daffodils that come before the swallow dares. The snowdrop of Swinburne disappears, the daffodil of Shakespeare remains. The swallow of Shakespeare remains in the verse of *Macbeth;* the bird of Wordsworth

> *Breaking the silence of the seas*

remains; the swallow of "Itylus" disappears. Compare, again, a chorus of *Atalanta* with a chorus from Athenian tragedy. The chorus of Swinburne is almost a parody of the Athenian: it is sententious, but it has not even the significance of commonplace.

> *At least we witness of thee ere we die*
> *That these things are not otherwise, but thus.* . . .

> *Before the beginning of years*
> *There came to the making of man*
> *Time with a gift of tears;*
> *Grief with a glass that ran.* . . .

This is not merely "music"; it is effective because it appears to be a tremendous statement, like statements made in our dreams; when we wake up we find that the "glass that ran" would do better for time than for grief, and that the gift of tears would be as appropriately bestowed by grief as by time.

It might seem to be intimated, by what has been said, that the work of Swinburne can be shown to be a sham, just as bad verse is a sham. It would only be so if you could produce or suggest something that it pretends to be and is not. The world of Swinburne does not depend upon some other

world which it simulates: it has the necessary completeness and self-suffi-
ciency for justification and permanence. It is impersonal, and no one else
could have made it. The deductions are true to the postulates. It is indestructible. None of the obvious complaints that were or might have been
brought to bear upon the first *Poems and Ballads* holds good. The poetry
is not morbid, it is not erotic, it is not destructive. These are adjectives
which can be applied to the material, the human feelings, which in Swinburne's case do not exist. The morbidity is not of human feeling but of
language. Language in a healthy state presents the object, is so close to the
object that the two are identified.

They are identified in the verse of Swinburne solely because the object
has ceased to exist, because the meaning is merely the hallucination of
meaning, because language, uprooted, has adapted itself to an independent
life of atmospheric nourishment. In Swinburne, for example, we see the
word "weary" flourishing in this way independent of the particular and
actual weariness of flesh or spirit. The bad poet dwells partly in a world
of objects and partly in a world of words, and he never can get them to
fit. Only a man of genius could dwell so exclusively and consistently among
words as Swinburne. His language is not, like the language of bad poetry,
dead. It is very much alive, with this singular life of its own. But the language which is more important to us is that which is struggling to digest
and express new objects, new feelings, new aspects, as, for instance, the
prose of Mr. James Joyce or the earlier Conrad.[3]

It will be seen that Eliot's interest here is less in the effect of the
poetry than in *what goes on* in it. He has Saintsbury's width of literary
reference and more than Saintsbury's confidence, but he has not
Saintsbury's confidence in his readers. The reader must be startled
from his conventional view of Swinburne into looking at the poetry
again and seeing precisely what happens in it. Eliot is continually
making distinction between, for example, diffuseness as a fault and
diffuseness as an essence, between different kinds of relationship between meaning and sound, between intensification and expansion, and
so on. And when he quotes other poets it is generally in order to draw
our attention to a distinction, a difference, not to cite resemblances
or echoes. The whole approach is basically analytic.

Oliver Elton on Swinburne: academic
generalization

That Eliot is less concerned with the effect of the poem on the
reader than with the kind of life such poetry possesses becomes

[3] From *Selected Essays* 1917-1932 by T. S. Eliot, copyright, 1932, by Harcourt, Brace and Company, Inc. and Faber and Faber Limited.

clear if we put beside his essay on Swinburne a discussion of the poet
by a critic working in the late nineteenth century academic eclectic
tradition. Professor Oliver Elton's *The English Muse*, though it appeared in 1933, is in that older tradition. Here are his remarks on
Swinburne:

. . . Swinburne's language flows from the purest fount. He was nourished
on the ancient classics, on the English classics, and above all on the Author-
ised Version. He had a perfect ear and was a mighty inventor of lyrical
measures; there is no surer or more brilliant instrumentalist in English. Yet
the salvage of his poetry, though not small in itself, is small in proportion
to the mass. For all their skill of conduct the two Greek plays leave, as
tragedies, a faint impression. Even in the famed choruses there is a waste
of words. But this we forgive for the glory of sound and motion, and for
a certain electrical quality that time cannot alter. It comes and goes; but it is
maintained, in *Atalanta*, throughout the splendid interchanges of the
Chorus with Meleager:

> Would God ye could carry me
> Forth of all these;
> Heap sand and bury me
> By the Chersonese,
> Where the thundering Bosphorus answers the thunder of Pontic seas.

'Before the beginning of years' and 'When the hounds of spring' are also
in stanza. Well, after fifty years we may smile at the 'brown bright nightingale amorous' and the Maenad and the Bassarid, nor did we ever take
them too seriously. But 'ah the singing, ah the delight, the passion!',—this
has not vanished; nor the music of the long billowing strophes in *Erec-
theus*. Swinburne's other choric odes, to Athens or to Victor Hugo, sound
mechanical beside them. His sapphics and choriambics have less matter and
meaning than Tennyson's 'experiments' in classical measures; but in glory
of passionate sound they have no equal, among feats of this kind. As to the
song pure and simple, in the *Oblation* ('Ask nothing more of me, sweet')
and in the sixteen lines of 'Love laid his weary head' Swinburne wrote
what may outlive many of his later volumes. Some of these lighter and
briefer lyrics are certainly the most enduring. Many are in short lines,
Anima Anceps, A Match, Ex-Voto. In the first *Poems and Ballads* there is
much about the passing of love, and the call of the poppied sleep. The desire of a youth to die and be extinguished is expressed to perfection in the
Garden of Proserpine; and it is heard, more rhetorically yet in its fullest
force, in *Ilicet*.

Swinburne poured out lavishly his eulogies of the living and memorial
verses to the dead. The lyrics addressed to Landor and Mazzini and the

Adeiux à Mary Stuart are plain, concise, and severe; also the sonnet of Cardinal Newman, a salute of honour from the camp of the pagans. Among the sonnets to the old dramatists the most distinct and happy are those to Beaumont and Fletcher and to John Day. A few verses in the grand style, welcome and articulate amid the whirl of sound, can be picked out from the first ode to Victor Hugo and from the elegy on Baudelaire.

Many of Swinburne's passions may be called literary; but his love for wild English nature and for the sea is personal and physical. The *Forsaken Garden* and *Winter in Northumberland*, though never definite in *drawing*, give the very atmosphere of the place and weather. In the *Lake of Gaube* he records his own raptures as a swimmer. The sea is hymned in the finale of *Tristram of Lyonesse*, as Love is in the still greater overture. The great story, we may fear, is almost washed away in the torrent of words. But in the *Tale of Balen* the 'golden moorland side' and the 'rioting rapids of the Tyne' are the setting for a clear narrative that rides on gallantly; the poet, as he says,

> Reining my rhymes into buoyant order
> Through honied leagues of the northland border.

It rides on, with the shadow cast before it, to the innocent mutual fratricide of Balen and Balan.

I have said nothing of the amorous element in the first *Poems and Ballads* that fluttered the public of the day; of 'Faustine, Fragoletta, Dolores', and of the snake-eyed, sea-green-eyed, and also cat-eyed, Félise. These poems are sincere, headlong, wonderful of course in rhythm, and finally a little absurd; intended, in part, to curdle the blood of the *bourgeois*. In any case, Swinburne put all this behind him, as he tells us in the Prelude to *Songs Before Sunrise*. There is great poetry in that *Prelude*; and also, surely, in the *Pilgrims*, where the 'lady of love' is now humanity itself, marching on to its ideal goal through willing self-sacrifice. The volume is inspired by the political visions of Mazzini and the recent liberation of Italy; and among the Italian poems *A Marching Song* and *Siena* are pre-eminent. *Hertha* is a lofty lyrical celebration, loose enough in its thinking, of the universal life-force: a kind of lay pantheism. *The Hymn of Man* and *Before a Crucifix* are powerful tirades; the lines to *Walt Whitman in America* have some of the rhythm of the Atlantic. Swinburne has no very distinct creed; his early nihilism gives way to a more aspiring and hopeful temper, and the transcendental strain of *Songs Before Sunrise* never entirely leaves him.[4]

The two methods compared

Even if we allow for the fact that Professor Elton's discussion is part of a history of English poetry while Eliot's is an individual essay on

[4] Reprinted by permission of G. Bell & Sons, Ltd.

Swinburne, so that the former had to be more comprehensive in his survey of the poet's work than the latter needed to be, we cannot help being struck by the looser texture of Professor Elton's remarks. He makes many of the same points that Eliot makes, but is content to note them generally, from the point of view of the effect on the reader rather than of what actually goes on in the poetry in order to achieve that effect. Elton notes "a waste of words," while Eliot explains with analytic precision how Swinburne dwelt in a self-contained world of words, not of objects, and by appropriate comparisons and contrasts shows the special nature of Swinburne's case. Elton mentions "a certain electrical quality that time cannot alter," but Eliot avoids such general and abstract descriptions, and after his admission of the effectiveness of certain lines he notes what happens if you transpose the images in them. Elton uses phrases like "a glory of passionate sound," "verses in the grand style," "the desire of a youth to die . . . is expressed to perfection," "there is great poetry in that *Prelude*," and sometimes moves away from assessment of value altogether in such descriptions as "In the *Lake of Gaube* he records his own raptures as a swimmer," or "The sea is hymned in the finale of *Tristram of Lyonesse*," but Eliot sticks throughout to his single task, that of explaining, by a careful analysis illustrated by illuminating contrasts from apparently similar but actually different kinds of poem, exactly what it is that goes on in Swinburne's verse and what kind of achievement it represents. Elton is not uncritical. "The great story, we may fear, is almost washed away in the torrent of words" is a valid point against Swinburne. But Eliot examines carefully the question whether Swinburne's diffuseness is matter for praise or for blame, balancing something of both, showing that while "diffuseness is one of his glories" and of the very essence of his kind of poetry it is nevertheless "the word that gives him the thrill, not the object," and though this is a fault it has nothing to do with the kind of badness of those poets who "dwell partly in a world of objects and partly in a world of words." In short, Eliot illuminates by making multiple distinctions, Elton by talking of the general effect Swinburne's poems have on the reader.

Eliot's method, with its rigorous concern for the literary process, for the devices which go to achieve the literary effect, is symptomatic of an increasing amount of modern criticism from the 1920s onward. The revolt against impressionism, autobiography, general discourse concentrating on the effect of the work on the critic, as well as against the eclectic mingling of scholarship and "appreciation," was one of the features of the second quarter of the present century, and it produced ever more rigorous analytic techniques.

The close critic

The best and most characteristic modern criticism prefers to deal with an individual work rather than with a writer's achievement as a whole, and this helps to explain the difference in tone and method between Elton and Eliot on Swinburne; Eliot, even when he makes generalizations, nearly always has a specific poem in mind. The procedure of the modern close critic has been well defined by F. R. Leavis: "The critic's aim is, first, to realize as sensitively and completely as possible this or that which claims his attention; and a certain valuing is implicit in the realizing. As he matures in experience of the new thing he asks, explicitly and implicitly: 'Where does this come from? How does it stand in relation to . . . ? How relatively important does it seem?' . . . The business of the literary critic is to attain a peculiar completeness of response and to observe a peculiarly strict relevance in developing his response into commentary; he must be on his guard against abstracting improperly from what is in front of him and against any premature or irrelevant generalizing—of it or from it. His first concern is to enter into possession of the given poem (let us say) in its concrete fullness, and his constant concern is never to lose his completeness of possession, but rather to increase it. In making value-judgments (and judgments as to significance) implicitly or explicitly, he does so out of that completeness of possession and with that fullness of response. He doesn't ask, 'How does this accord with these specifications of goodness in poetry?'; he aims to make fully conscious and articulate the immediate sense of value that 'places' the poem." ("Literary Criticism and Philosophy: a Reply." *Scrutiny*, Vol. VI, no. 1, 1937. This was a reply by Leavis to an article by René Wellek which had appeared in the previous number of *Scrutiny*.

15

Analysis in action

W E NOTED, in chapter 10, how many modern critics have been concerned to lay their finger on the uniquely poetic way of handling language, and how as a result they have come to see in complexity, in irony, and in paradox the special qualities of poetic discourse.

Practical results of stressing the uniqueness of poetic use of language

The effects of this view of poetry can be seen clearly in practical criticism (for example, in Cleanth Brooks' discussion of Words-worth's sonnet quoted on page 163): the critic will concentrate on demonstrating the existence of those qualities which for him con-stitute the differentiating qualities of poetry, and in some degree of imaginative literature in general. This reinforces that tendency to substitute for general appreciative criticism a close analytical descrip-tion of a particular work discussed in the previous section. To illustrate the various kinds of analytic closeness with which texts can be read would require a large anthology in itself. Such criticism is inevitably detailed and therefore lengthy. It can concern itself with interrelations of meaning of the most subtle kind, with the minutest elements of structure, with oblique suggestions and overtones which even the reader thoroughly familiar with the work in question may never have noticed—and sometimes which can only be read into the work by ingenious special pleading. Though the charge of over-ingenuity has sometimes been brought against these critics, it can at least be said of their method that it requires intelligence, patience, and thoroughness. As Dr Johnson said of the metaphysical poets: "To write on their plan, it was at least necessary to read and think."

Is analytic criticism normative as well as descriptive?

To what extent, it might be asked, is this close analytic criticism normative as well as descriptive? Does it, that is to say, demonstrate how good a work is, or does it merely tell us what is in the work? To admit that this critical method has provided us with a more rigorous technique of description is far from claiming that it satisfies the modern demand for a more scientific assessment of value. The answer to this question is twofold. First, if complexity, irony, paradox, and the other qualities seen as the differentiating qualities of poetic discourse by such critics as Brooks do represent the criteria of poetry, then the demonstration that irony, paradox, etc., exist in the poem is demonstration that it is true poetry. But does that mean the more irony and paradox, the greater the poem? Or simply that if these qualities are shown to be effectively working in the poem, then the poem is a true poem and questions of greater or lesser are beside the point? The latter is the more widely-held view, and probably the more consistent one. It is therefore not surprising that, while the critics who employ this method can often brilliantly demonstrate whether a work is a true poem or not—an ode of Keats being a true poem, while Joyce Kilmer's "Trees" is not—they tend to deprecate the use of comparison as between good poems and are not inclined to arrange poems into a "good, better, and best" order. A poem (and the same goes for other kinds of literature) is either admitted into the canon, as it were, or it is not. Those admitted have all an equal status and are not likely to be arranged in an order of merit. It would not be true to say that all modern analytic critics take this position, but the practice of the majority of them does seem to conform to it.[1]

The second answer to the question whether this criticism can be normative as well as descriptive is that a work susceptible of this kind of treatment must be a true work of literature. The careful probing of meanings, the picking out of suggestions and countersuggestions playing against each other to weave a rich complex of meaning, can only be applied to an effective work. Value is demonstrated by the degree to which the work lends itself to this kind of treatment. Whether this means that the critic must have made up his mind about the quality of a work before he proceeds to demonstrate it, or even that he must feel that it is good before he tries to find out whether it is good, is arguable. It might be claimed that with sufficient ingenuity, complexity and paradox can be read into anything (W. H. Auden has seen rich profundities in "The Hunting of the Snark" and an ironic commentary on a theory of Kirkegaard in Lear's limerick, "There was an old man of Whitehaven"), and that therefore their discovery cannot in itself mean anything very much; the critic must first know that they are objectively discoverable. This is perhaps to press a point too far. The modern analytic critic is generally content to describe the work under consideration with more minute accuracy, with greater subtlety and penetration, than those critics who prefer to discuss the work in general terms of its effect on themselves; they leave it to the reader to make up his mind about the degree of merit, their own concern being to make sure that the reader first reads it properly.

Empson and multiple meaning

One of the pioneers in this close analytic criticism, with special reference to the possibilities of the meaning of words, is William Empson, a pupil of I. A. Richards who developed Richards' concern with meaning into a special kind of descriptive technique, which has had great influence both in Britain and America. His *Seven Types of Ambiguity* (1930) explored different kinds of multiple meanings, and his *Some Versions of Pastoral* (1935; reprinted in America as *English Pastoral Poetry*, 1938) applied this concern with multiple meaning in critical

[1] Perhaps another factor enters into these critics' reluctance to make comparative judgments, namely the awareness that it is form which makes a work poetry, though more than form which makes it greater or lesser poetry. Their tools are suited for the determination of the first, not the second.

discussion of a number of different works. Consider the following extract from his discussion of Andrew Marvell's poem "The Garden":

The chief point of the poem is to contrast and reconcile conscious and unconscious states, intuitive and intellectual modes of apprehension; and yet that distinction is never made, perhaps could not have been made; his thought is implied by his metaphors. . . . The Oxford edition notes bring out a crucial double meaning (so that this at least is not my own fancy) in the most analytic statement of the poem, about the Mind—

> Annihilating all that's made
> To a green thought in a green shade.

Either "reducing the whole material world to nothing material, *i.e.* to a green thought," or "considering the material world as of no value compared to a green thought"; either contemplating everything or shutting everything out. This combines the idea of the conscious mind, including everything because understanding it, and that of the unconscious animal nature, including everything because in harmony with it. Evidently the object of such a fundamental contradiction (seen in the etymology: turning all *ad nihil, to* nothing, and *to* a thought) is to deny its reality; the point is not that these two are essentially different but that they must cease to be different so far as either is to be known. So far as he has achieved his state of ecstasy he combines them, he is "neither conscious nor not conscious," like the seventh Buddhist state of enlightenment. This gives its point, I think, to the other ambiguity, clear from the context, as to whether the *all* considered was *made* in the mind of the author or the Creator; to so peculiarly "creative" a knower there is little difference between the two. Here as usual with "profound" remarks the strength of the thing is to combine unusually intellectual with unusually primitive ideas; thought about the conditions of knowledge with a magical idea that the adept controls the external world by thought. . . .

Nature when terrible is no theme of Marvell's, and he gets this note of triumph rather from using nature when peaceful to control the world of man.

> How safe, methinks, and strong, behind
> These Trees have I encamp'd my Mind;
> Where Beauty, aiming at the Heart,
> Bends in some Tree its useless Dart;
> And where the World no certain Shot
> Can make, or me it toucheth not.
> But I on it securely play,
> And gaul its Horsemen all the Day.

The masculine energy of the last couplet is balanced immediately by an acceptance of Nature more masochist than passive, in which he becomes Christ with both the nails and the thorns. (*Appleton House,* lxxvi.)

> Bind me ye *Woodbines* in your 'twines,
> Curle me about ye gadding *Vines*,
> And Oh so close your Circles lace,
> That I may never leave this Place:
> But, lest your fetters prove too weak,
> Ere I your Silken Bondage break,
> Do you, *O Brambles,* chain me too,
> And courteous *Briars* nail me through.

He does not deify himself more actively, and in any case the theme of the *Garden* is a repose.

> How vainly men themselves amaze
> To win the Palm, or Oke, or Bayes;
> And their uncessant Labours see
> Crown'd from some single Herb or Tree.
> Whose short and narrow verged Shade
> Does prudently their Toyles upbraid;
> While all Flow'rs and all Trees do close
> To weave the Garlands of repose.

This first verse comes nearest to stating what seems the essential distinction, with that between powers inherent and power worked out in practice, being a general and feeling one could be; in this ideal case, so the wit of the thing claims, the power to have been a general is already satisfied in the garden. "Unemployment" is too painful and normal even in the fullest life for such a theme to be trivial. But self-knowledge is possible in such a state so far as the unruly impulses are digested, ordered, made transparent, not by their being known, at the time, as unruly. Consciousness no longer makes an important distinction; the impulses, since they must be balanced already, neither need it to put them right nor are put wrong by the way it forces across their boundaries. They let themselves be known because they are not altered by being known, because their principle of indeterminacy no longer acts. This idea is important for all the versions of pastoral, for the pastoral figure is always ready to be the critic; he not only includes everything but may in some unexpected way know it.

Another range of his knowledge might be mentioned here. I am not sure what arrangement of flower-beds is described in the last verse, but it seems clear that the sun goes through the "zodiac" of flowers in one day, and that the bees too, in going from one bed to another, reminding us of the labours of the first verse, pass all summer in a day. They compute their time as well as we in that though their lives are shorter they too contract all experience into it, and this makes the poet watch over large periods of time as well as space. So far he becomes Nature, he becomes permanent. It is a graceful finale to the all-in-one theme, but not, I think, very important; the crisis of the poem is in the middle.

Once you accept the Oxford edition's note you may as well apply it to the whole verse.

> Meanwhile the Mind, from pleasure less,
> Withdraws into its happiness;
> The Mind, that Ocean where each kind
> Does streight its own resemblance find;
> Yet it creates, transcending these,
> Far other worlds, and other Seas,
> Annihilating . . .

From pleasure less. Either "from the lessening of pleasure"—"we are quiet in the country, but our dulness gives a sober and self-knowing happiness, more intellectual than that of the overstimulated pleasures of the town" or "made less by this pleasure"—"The pleasures of the country give a repose and intellectual release which make me less intellectual, make my mind less worrying and introspective." This is the same puzzle as to the consciousness of the thought; the ambiguity gives two meanings to pleasure, corresponding to his Puritan ambivalence about it, and to the opposition between pleasure and happiness. *Happiness,* again, names a conscious state, and yet involves the idea of things falling right, happening so, no being ordered by an anxiety of the conscious reason. (So that as a rule it is a weak word; it is by seeming to look at it hard and bring out its implications that the verse here makes it act as a strong one.)

The same doubt gives all their grandeur to the next lines. The sea if calm reflects everything near it; the mind as knower is a conscious mirror. Somewhere in the sea are sea-lions and -horses and everything else, though they are different from land ones; the unconsciousness is unplumbed and pathless, and there is no instinct so strange among the beasts that it lacks its fantastic echo in the mind. In the first version thoughts are shadows, in the second (like the *green thought*) they are as solid as what they image; and yet they still correspond to something in the outer world, so that the poet's intuition is comparable to pure knowledge. This metaphor may reflect back so that *withdraws* means the tide going down; the *mind* is *less* now, but will return, and it is now that one can see the rock-pools. On the Freudian view of an Ocean, *withdraws* would make this repose in Nature a return to the womb; anyway it may mean either "withdraws into self-contemplation" or "withdraws altogether, into its mysterious processes of digestion." *Streight* may mean "packed together," in the microcosm, or "at once"; the beasts see their reflection (perhaps the root idea of the metaphor) as soon as they look for it; the calm of Nature gives the poet an immediate self-knowledge. But we have already had two entrancingly witty verses about the sublimation of sexual desire into a taste for Nature (I should not say that this theme was the main emotional drive behind the poem, but it takes up a large part of its overt thought), and the *kinds* look for their *resemblance*, in practice, out of a desire for *creation;* in the mind, at this fertile time for the poet, they can *find* it "at once," being "packed together." The transition from the beast and its reflection to the two pairing beasts implies a transition from the correspondences of thought with fact to those of thought with thought, to find which is to be creative; there is necessarily here a suggestion of rising from one "level" of thought to another; and in the next couplet not only does the mind transcend the world it mirrors, but a sea, to which it is parallel, transcends both land and sea too, which implies self-consciousness and all the antinomies of philosophy. Whether or not you give *transcendent* the technical sense "predicable of all categories" makes no great difference; in including everything in itself the mind includes as a detail itself and all its inclusions. And it is true that the sea reflects the *other worlds* of the stars; Donne's metaphor of the globe is in the background. Yet even here the double meaning is not lost; all land-beasts have their sea-beasts, but the sea also has the kraken; in the depths as well as the transcendence of the mind are things stranger than all the kinds of the world.

Miss M. C. Bradbrook has pointed out to me that the next verse, while less triumphant, gives the process a more firmly religious interpretation.

> Here at the Fountains sliding foot,
> Or by some Fruit-trees mossy root,
> Casting the Bodies Vest aside,
> My Soul into the boughs does glide;
> There like a Bird it sits, and sings,
> Then whets, and combs its silver Wings;
> And, till prepar'd for longer flight,
> Waves in its Plumes the various Light.

The bird is the dove of the Holy Spirit and carries a suggestion of the rainbow of the covenant. By becoming inherent in everything he becomes a soul not pantheist but clearly above and apart from the world even while still living in it. Yet the paradoxes are still firmly maintained here, and the soul is as solid as the green thought. The next verse returns naturally and still with exultation to the jokes in favour of solitude against women.

Green takes on great weight here, as Miss Sackville West pointed out, because it has been a pet word of Marvell's before. . . .

Grass indeed comes to be taken for granted as the symbol of pastoral humility:

Unhappy Birds! what does it boot
To build below the Grasses' Root;
When Lowness is unsafe as Hight,
And Chance o'er takes what scapeth Spight?

It is a humility of Nature from which she is still higher than man, so that
the grasshoppers preach to him from their pinnacles:

And now to the Abyss I pass
Of that unfathomable Grass,
Where men like Grashoppers appear,
But Grashoppers are Gyants there;
They, in there squeking Laugh, contemn
Us as we walk more low than them:
And, from the Precipices tall
Of the green spire's, to us do call.

It seems also to be an obscure merit of grass that it produces "hay," which
was the name of a country dance, so that humility is gaiety.

With this the golden fleece I shear
Of all these Closes ev'ry Year,
And though in Wool more poor than they,
Yet I am richer far in Hay.

To nineteenth century taste the only really poetical verse of the poem is
the central fifth of the nine; I have been discussing the sixth, whose dramatic position is an illustration of its very penetrating theory. The first
four are a crescendo of wit, on the themes "success or failure is not important, only on the repose that follows the exercise of one's powers" and
"women, I am pleased to say, are no longer interesting to me, because nature is more beautiful." One effect of the wit is to admit, and so make
charming, the impertinence of the second of these, which indeed the first
puts in its place; it is only for a time, and after effort among human beings,
that he can enjoy solitude. The value of these moments made it fitting to
pretend they were eternal; and yet the lightness of his expression of their
sense of power is more intelligent, and so more convincing, than Wordsworth's solemnity on the same theme, because it does not forget the
opposing forces.

When we have run our Passions heat,
Love hither makes his best retreat.
The *Gods*, that mortal beauty chase,
Still in a Tree did end their race.
Apollo hunted *Daphne* so,
Only that she might Laurel grow,

> And *Pan* did after *Syrinx* speed,
> Not as a Nymph, but for a Reed.

The energy and delight of the conceit has been sharpened or keyed up here till it seems to burst and transform itself; it dissolves in the next verse into the style of Keats. So his observation of the garden might mount to an ecstasy which disregarded it; he seems in this next verse to imitate the process he has described, to enjoy in a receptive state the exhilaration which an exercise of wit has achieved. But striking as the change of style is, it is unfair to empty the verse of thought and treat it as random description; what happens is that he steps back from overt classical conceits to a rich and intuitive use of Christian imagery. When people treat it as the one good "bit" of the poem one does not know whether they have recognised that the Alpha and Omega of the verse are the Apple and the Fall.

> What wond'rous Life in this I lead!
> Ripe Apples drop about my head;
> The Luscious Clusters of the Vine
> Upon my Mouth do crush their Wine;
> The Nectaren, and curious Peach,
> Into my hands themselves do reach;
> Stumbling on Melons, as I pass,
> Insnar'd with Flow'rs, I fall on Grass.

Melon, again, is the Greek for apple; "all flesh is *grass*" and its own *flowers* here are the snakes in it that stopped Eurydice. Mere grapes are at once the primitive and the innocent wine; the *nectar* of Eden, and yet the blood of sacrifice. *Curious* could mean "rich and strange" (Nature), "improved by care" (art) or "inquisitive" (feeling towards me, since nature is a mirror, as I do towards her). All these eatable beauties give themselves so as to lose themselves, like a lover, with a forceful generosity; like a lover they *ensnare* him. It is the triumph of the attempt to impose a sexual interest upon nature; there need be no more Puritanism in this use of sacrificial ideas than is already inherent in the praise of solitude; and it is because his repose in the orchard hints at such a variety of emotions that he is contemplating *all that's made*. Sensibility here repeats what wit said in the verse before; he tosses into the fantastic treasure-chest of the poem's thought all the pathos and dignity that Milton was to feel in his more celebrated Garden; and it is while this is going on, we are told in the next verse, that the mind performs its ambiguous and memorable *withdrawal*. For each of the three central verses he gives a twist to the screw of the microscope and is living in another world. . . .[2]

---

[2] Reprinted by permission of W. W. Norton & Company, Inc. and Chatto and Windus Ltd.

This is probing meaning very deeply, and the reader cannot hope to make much of such criticism unless he has the text of the original poem by him and refers to it constantly. The significance of what Saintsbury or Professor Elton had to say comes across to the reader quite satisfactorily without any such reference to the text of the original. Modern analytic criticism directs the reader to the text at every point, and whether the reader agrees with the critic's interpretation or not he has at least to read the text with the greatest care in order to follow the discussion, and he cannot disagree without having formed a closely reasoned opinion of his own.

The analytic critic and the historical background

It will be noted, too, that Empson does not depend on the historical context for the elucidation of this seventeenth century poem, though the precise meaning, and many of the overtones of meaning, may in many cases derive from some seventeenth century point of view about man or nature or God, or the relation between these, which has since gone completely out of fashion. Critics like Rosamond Tuve have taken issue with Empson on this point and shown how seventeenth century poets have drawn on a rich tradition of theological and other ideas and rhetorical devices, and unless we make ourselves familiar with these no amount of subtle analysis will bring out what is really in the poem. Ideally, of course, it is true that every poem, as a self-contained work of art, should be regarded as though it were contemporary and anonymous; but language is far too unstable a medium for us to be able to do this in practice. Language, the medium of poetry, is itself subject to the processes of history, it is a convention based on agreement, like other conventions, and as the convention changes shifts occur in the meaning, sometimes major and obvious shifts, sometimes delicate minor ones (the delicate shifts often being the more important in poetic expression). We have noted in preceding sections that an awareness of the conventions in which a particular work of art is written is necessary for its proper appreciation—is necessary, indeed, before we even know how to read it—and we sometimes have to turn to historical scholarship before we can know those conventions. When we realize that language itself is one of the conventions, and that, far from being an absolute and wholly objective medium whose precise shades of meaning and suggestion can be discovered by probing the work sufficiently deeply, it is a medium some of whose aspects can on occasion only be fully discovered by looking beyond the work to the historical context in which it was produced, we realize one phase of the relationship between scholarship and criticism (a matter which is more fully taken up in a later chapter). This is not to say that Empson's technique is not immensely fruitful, or that the sensitive analysis of the pattern of meaning in a work without regard to historical shifts in meaning is not a valuable critical activity; but it does mean that this activity can often be usefully supplemented by, or effectively employed in conjunction with, historical inquiry into systems of thought which help to give richer or more precise implication to the significance of words used by the poet. Of course, in the case of contemporary works, this question does not arise, or at least it does not arise in precisely that form. Clearly, historical scholarship is not going to aid the analytic critic in discussing a work produced by a poet of his own time. But there can be differences of convention and tradition even among contemporaries, and the critic who wishes to see the full meaning of the religious overtones in, say, T. S. Eliot's *Ash Wednesday* requires background information very different from that which is needed to appreciate adequately the religious terminology of Dylan Thomas.

Scope of the analytic method

It is perhaps a mistake to talk about the analytic method as though it were a single critical method; it is an approach, rather than a method, and though it is especially common among contemporary critics, who are still reacting against the relaxed eclectic criticism of an earlier generation, it is to be found in other periods as well. Aristotle, when he discusses particular examples of Greek plays in his *Poetics*, does so with analytic precision; Dryden's critique of *The Silent Woman* is in its way analytic; Dr Johnson, in his life of Cowley (in the *Lives of the Poets*) analyzes some passages of Donne and others in great detail; Coleridge is thoroughly analytic in much of his practical criticism, notably in his lectures and notes on Shakespeare; and many other examples could be given. It is perhaps unfair, too, to single out Empson as the one critic from whom to illustrate this approach.[3] But Empson

[3] And, it may be added, unfair to quote one of his more vulnerable pieces of criticism. But no other is so self-contained and suitable for quotation.

deserves the distinction because of his pioneer work in popularizing this way of approaching a text and because of the thoroughness with which he employs it. Other modern critics have produced other varieties of analytic criticism, sometimes using and sometimes ignoring the aids to the discovery of shades of meaning which history can provide. For all these critics the individual work is the thing, not facts about the author's life or about their own reactions, and their objective is to discover and demonstrate its complexity and richness of meaning and the esthetic completeness of its pattern. The relation of literature to life they tend to take for granted; of course a work of literary art is a kind of illumination of experience, but *qua* work of art its special features are its "structure and texture," its way of organizing meaning into a satisfying complex unity.

With such an objective, it is natural that these critics should concentrate on those literary works where paradoxical handling of ideas, the unification of opposites, the deliberate play with irony and double meaning, are clearly present, as in the metaphysical poets of the seventeenth century and those modern poets who have been influenced by them. The change of taste which began to take place just before the first world war, a change which ousted the "soft" romantic poetry of the nineteenth century in favor of the more intellectual and complicated poetry of Donne and Gerard Manley Hopkins, a change which is seen so dramatically in the contrast between the early and the later poems of W. B. Yeats and which has influenced in some degree all modern poetry—this change was felt equally in criticism and in creation. As poets cultivated complexity, irony, paradox, critics came to look for these qualities in all poetry which could claim to be properly regarded as such. Modern critical practice is closely related to the techniques of modern poetry.

PART THREE

Literary Criticism and Related Disciplines

Introduction

     THIS SECTION, LIKE PART TWO, deals with practical criticism, but instead of dealing with methods of assessing the value of particular works it concerns itself with the relation between critical evaluation and certain kinds of knowledge which have no direct bearing on critical judgment but which nevertheless the practical critic often has to employ. To criticize a work we have to know it: to what degree, and under what circumstances, is non-literary knowledge necessary before we can fully "know" a literary work? We must of course know the language in which it is written—and this in itself involves more than mere philological knowledge, as we shall see; we must know what the work *is*, in the sense that we must have a proper text of it before us, not a text marred by misprints or deliberate tampering. If the work was written in an earlier age, do we require to know anything of its historical context? Do we need to know anything about the life of the author? Do we need to know the books he read, the kind of society he lived in, the philosophical assumptions he took for granted? Can the practical critic always do his job with only critical tools, such as an understanding of structure, imagery, verse forms, and similar matters? And if he needs other tools, what kind of tools are they, when does he need them, and how are they to be employed in the process of making a purely literary judgment? These are not easy questions to answer, and there is wide divergence among modern critics as to what the right answers should be. In taking a sample of these problems and illustrating how different critics have handled them while at the same time trying to draw some general conclusions, we hope to help to clear the air on this whole question of the relation between criticism and background knowledge.

16

Criticism and scholarship

H ISTORICAL SCHOLARSHIP can be used to discover
the tradition within which a work of literature is written and the
standard on which it is to be judged, as we have seen. That is how
Bishop Hurd approached Spenser's *The Faerie Queene* and how many
later critics have approached the products of an earlier age. We have
noted, too, how history can be used to make allowances for an early
writer, explaining his faults as deriving from the conditions under
which he wrote, from the rudimentary state of craftsmanship in his age
or something of that sort, and we have discussed the implications of
such a view, that literature, at least in some of its aspects, progresses
and advances in a way comparable to that of the sciences. But what
exactly is the relation between scholarship and critical evaluation?

Periods and movements

The answer to this question has been in some degree confused in our time by modern reaction against certain confusions and abuses. The slow patterning of English literature into movements, with their precursors and successors, the isolation of separate periods, each with its own characteristics, the plotting of the rise and fall of movements—Elizabethan and Jacobean; the reaction against the metaphysical poets and the movement toward Dryden and Pope; pre-Romantics pointing forward to Romantics who are in turn followed by Victorians—all this had been going on steadily in the work of a host of scholars and critics and historians, until by the end of nineteenth century the "history of English literature" (or of any national literature, for that matter) was a fairly stereotyped affair of movements and periods, each illustrated by its own "characteristic" group of writers. The stages by which this patterning was established go back at least to Dryden, with his view of Chaucer as the peak of medieval English literature, followed by a slope down and then the ascent through the Tudor poets to the glories of the Elizabethan age, followed by another valley and then the ascent to the "refinement of our numbers" in Dryden's own time. This "peaks and valleys" view of literary history—which it is easy to laugh at but extremely difficult to replace—was modified and developed throughout the eighteenth and nineteenth centuries, the common Victorian attitude being that, after Shakespeare, the highest peak of all was that represented by the Romantic movement, which was a great soaring upward from the valley of eighteenth century artificiality. Even the striking change in taste which started in the second decade of the present century, decrying romantics like Shelley and Victorians like Tennyson and restoring to favor such poets as Donne and the hitherto virtually unknown Hopkins, did not at once destroy this historical patterning, but turned it inside out, as it were, so that, in biblical phrase, every valley was exalted and every mountain and hill made low. Eventually critics came to protest against this division of literature into periods and movements at the expense of individual works of literary art, and in so protesting they naturally tended to minimize the claims of history in favor of "pure" criticism.

The survey course

It was not only the historical patterning into movements and influences that annoyed these critics; it was also the anecdotal use of the mass of biographical information about writers which generations of scholars had by now built up. Literature, as taught in schools and colleges, was far too often a confused mixture of movements and anecdotes, with the real individual qualities of the literary works—surely the most important thing of all—never seriously considered. In colleges the "survey course" in literature tended to consist of general remarks about the characteristics of periods spiced with scraps of information about the lives of authors, the whole cemented with lists of adjectives proper to be applied in specific instances. The problem of "teaching" literature—and with the increasing popularity of courses in literature the problem became ever more pressing—resulted in the brewing of a mixture which any reasonably competent teacher could handle. Facts about movements and periods, qualities to be ascribed to individual authors as illustrating the movements and periods of which they were a part, and some biographical anecdotes; perhaps some plot summaries put in at intervals to enable students to write about some works as though they had read them—this became the standard mixture, and it was not conducive to any real view of literature. In rebelling against it, many modern critics understandably attacked the whole idea of a survey course and pleaded strongly for concentration on particular authors and on particular works.

Rebellion against the survey course

The rebellion was understandable enough. We may not agree that a survey course in itself is a bad thing; we may recognize the value of general notions about the climate of opinion in a given period and the relation of writers to their age; but most of us will agree that the run-of-the-mill survey course was an uninspired hodgepodge of no real value to anybody. Literature is one of the most difficult of subjects to teach, and a lowest common denominator of courses (which is what the typical survey course came to be) is not likely to be inspiring. So the revolt against the survey course, with its nondescript use of history and biography, led in some sort to a revolt against history and biography, or at least to the view that these were not necessary tools for the critic, whose principal function was to describe individual works minutely and evaluate them on the basis of his description.

Effect of the rebellion on critical theory and practice

The pedagogical result of this revolt (which include the substitution of "author courses" for "period courses" at so many colleges and universities and concentration on the analysis of one work isolated from any context instead of the chronological survey of an age) are not so much our concern here as its effect on critical theory and practice. Do descriptive and evaluative criticism suffer by ignoring history and biography? The answer would seem to be that we need neither biographical nor historical information in order to assess the written work as it exists, an independent and self-existent work of art, but we may need such information in order to see the work properly before we begin to assess it. The argument is less strong with reference to biography. Though an author's biography is of the greatest interest and importance for an understanding of how he came to write, for a study of the psychology of literary creation (which may loosely be included in the term *criticism* but is clearly not descriptive or evaluative criticism), it rarely helps us to see better the work as it objectively is:

Even when a work of art contains elements which can be surely identified as biographical, these elements will be so re-arranged and transformed in a work that they lose all their specifically personal meaning and become simply concrete human material, integral elements of a work. . . .

The whole view that art is self-expression pure and simple, the transcript of personal feeling and experiences, is demonstrably false. Even where there is a close relationship between the work of art and the life of an author, this must never be construed as meaning that the work of art is a mere copy of life. The biographical approach forgets that a work of art is not simply the embodiment of experience but always the latest work of art in a series of such works; it is drama, a novel, a poem "determined," so far as it is determined at all, by literary tradition and convention. The biographical approach actually obscures a proper comprehension of the literary process, since it breaks up the order of literary tradition to substitute the life cycle of an individual. The biographical approach ignores also quite simple psychological facts. A work of art may rather embody the "dream" of an author than his actual life, or it may be the "mask," the "anti-self" behind which his real person is hiding, or it may be a picture of the life from which the author wants to escape. Furthermore, we must not forget that the artist may "experience" life differently in terms of his art: actual experiences are seen with a view to their use in literature and come to him already partially shaped by artistic traditions and preconceptions.

We must conclude that the biographical interpretation and use of every work of art needs careful scrutiny and examination in each case, since the work of art is not a document for biography. We must seriously question Miss Wade's *Life of Traherne*, which takes every statement of his poems as literal biographical truth, or the many books about the lives of the Brontës which simply lift whole passages from *Jane Eyre* or *Villette*. There is *The Life and Eager Death of Emily Brontë* by Virginia Moore, who thinks that Emily must have experienced the passions of Heathcliff; and there are others who have argued that a woman could not have written *Wuthering Heights* and that the brother, Patrick, must have been the real author. This is the type of argument which has led people to argue that Shakespeare must have visited Italy, must have been a lawyer, a soldier, a teacher, a farmer. Ellen Terry gave the crushing reply to all this when she argued that, by the same criteria, Shakespeare must have been a woman.

But, it will be said, such instances of pretentious folly do not dispose of the problem of personality in literature. We read Dante or Goethe or Tolstoy and know that there is a person behind the work. There is an indubitable physiognomical similarity between the writings of one author. The question might be asked, however, whether it would not be better to distinguish sharply between the empirical person and the work, which can be called "personal" only in a metaphorical sense. There is a quality which we may call "Miltonic" or "Keatsian" in the work of their authors. But this quality can be determined on the basis of the works themselves, while it may not be ascertainable upon purely biographical evidence. We know what is "Virgilian" or "Shakespearean" without having any really definite biographical knowledge of the two great poets.

Still, there are connecting links, parallelisms, oblique resemblances, topsy-turvy mirrors. The poet's work may be a mask, a dramatized conventionalization, but it is frequently a conventionalization of his own experiences, his own life. If used with a sense of these distinctions, there is use in biographical study. First, no doubt, it has exegetical value: it may explain a great many allusions or even words in an author's work. The biographical framework will also help us in studying the most obvious of all strictly developmental problems in the history of literature—the growth, maturing, and possible decline of an author's art. Biography also accumulates the materials for other questions of literary history such as the reading of the poet, his personal associations with literary men, his travels, the landscape and cities he saw and lived in: all of them questions which may throw light on literary history, i.e., the tradition in which the poet was placed, the influences by which he was shaped, the materials on which he drew.

Whatever the importance of biography in these respects, however, it seems dangerous to ascribe to it any real critical importance. No biographical evidence can change or influence critical evaluation. The frequently adduced criterion of "sincerity" is thoroughly false if it judges literature in terms of biographical truthfulness, correspondence to the author's experience or feelings as they are attested by outside evidence. Byron's "Fare Thee Well . . ." is neither a worse nor a better poem because it dramatizes the poet's actual relations with his wife, nor "is it a pity," as Paul Elmer More thinks, that the MS shows no traces of the tears which, according to Thomas Moore's *Memoranda*, fell on it. The poem exists; the tears shed or unshed, the personal emotions, are gone and cannot be reconstructed, nor need they be.[1]

The place of biography and history

This is a moderate statement of a position with which most modern critics would probably agree. Biography is of little help in evaluating a literary work. But it must be emphasized that this does not mean that biography of great writers is of itself of little value. Biography may not help us to assess a work, but it is an interesting and illuminating study in its own right. Intellectual curiosity is always fruitful, and curiosity about the "lives of great men" especially so. To the serious inquirer into literature, no knowledge comes amiss—but that does not mean that no knowledge is irrelevant to evaluation. Only very special kinds of knowledge are relevant to the critical assessment of a work of art.

What, then, about history? We observed in an earlier section that language itself is a phenomenon that manifests itself in history, not something wholly stable and objective, so that it is often necessary to study the ideas and traditions of an author's age if we are to see the work he wrote as it really is. This is not committing what some modern critics call the "intentional fallacy," of judging the work by what the

[1] From *Theory of Literature* by René Wellek and Austin Warren, copyright, 1942, 1947, 1949, by Harcourt, Brace and Company, Inc. and Jonathon Cape Ltd.

author intended it to mean; it is simply realizing the undoubted truth that language, as a convention, depends for its proper understanding on our knowledge of that convention. If the word "homely" means "cosily domestic" in England and "ugly" in America, English readers seeing the word in an American poem, and American readers seeing it in an English poem, will misunderstand the poem completely without this background information. This is a simple and obvious example of the kind of scholarship necessary before one can see a work for what it is—and one must see it for what it is before one can hope to be able to evaluate it. To someone with no knowledge of Greek, a Greek poem is simply a series of marks on the paper, whose only "meaning" would derive from the physical pattern in which the marks were set out.

But linguistic knowledge is not historical knowledge, it may be argued. Everybody admits that you must know the language in which the work is written before you can understand it. It is a question of degree, however. The difference between Shakespeare's English and our own speech is not as great as that between Chaucer's language and ours, and there are any number of intermediate stages. Further, language is not merely the dictionary meaning of words, but their whole host of associations and overtones deriving from preconceptions of all kinds, systems of thought, rhetorical traditions, and other things which change in time, sometimes much more rapidly than we realize. A work of art, Wellek and Warren point out in the passage quoted above, "is drama, a novel, a poem" 'determined,' so far as it is determined at all, by literary tradition and convention." And literary tradition and convention are often only recoverable by historical study. If we saw a picture that was meant to be part of a massive series of wall decorations in a church and wrongly thought that it was supposed to hang by itself in a frame on a drawing-room wall, our evaluation of it would be quite wrong, and what were really its virtues might be seen by us as faults and vice versa. If we had no knowledge whatever of the conventions of Greek tragedy and approached Sophocles' *Oedipus the King* as though it were a witty farce about sex, we should be in no position to assess it properly. Much historical knowledge about the conventions in which earlier works were written is now taken for granted among educated people, so that they make use of this knowledge without realizing it and often imagine they are making a "pure" evaluation of an objectively existing work, without reference to any background information, whereas in fact they are unconsciously drawing on a considerable amount of such information.

An unreal controversy

The modern controversy between what used to be called the "new criticism"—which insists on regarding the literary work as an independent, self-existent, work of art, to be described, analyzed, and evaluated without regard to its author's intention or to any other extrinsic consideration—and historical criticism thus centers on the question of emphasis and proportion. Arguments such as that between Professor A. S. P. Woodhouse and Professor Cleanth Brooks[2] never really meet: one insists that to see what the work really is we pay attention to the tradition in which it was written, the other says that what the work really is can only be properly evaluated in terms appropriate to a work of literary art. One must surely agree with both. Yet one cannot resolve the argument by maintaining that all historical criticism concerns the recovery of the proper shape and meaning of the work with reference to elements in its historical context which alone make that shape and meaning recognizable, while "pure" criticism, having been helped by historical criticism to see the work as it really is, takes over and makes an analysis and an assessment of it. To regard the historical critic as engaged in a necessary "pre-criticism," after which he hands over to the "pure" critic to find the esthetic verdict, is to be guilty of a gross oversimplification in theory and a misstatement of critical practice. For the insights of the historical critic are often so intimately bound up with the nature and significance of the work as a piece of literary art that they cannot but be presented and developed in a normative context. Practical criticism is more flexible and more complex in method than any theoretical statement about it is likely to be. The most fruitful and illuminating kind of criticism of earlier works often moves freely between historical and purely esthetic insights, as it does between descriptive and normative comments, and though these can be sorted out and classified if necessary, the sorting is more important for the student of methodology than for the student of literature. Whenever we deal with the product of a previous age the sense of the past is always with us, if we are literate at all, and we cannot help drawing on it and utilizing it. The critical implications of this have been expressed by Lionel Trilling:

We are creatures of time, we are creatures of the historical sense, not only as men have always been but in a new way since the time of Walter

[2] In *P.M.L.A.*, December 1951.

Scott. Possibly this may be for the worse; we would perhaps be stronger if we believed that Now contained all things, and that we in our barbarian moment were all that ever had been. Without the sense of the past we might be more certain, less weighed down and apprehensive. We might also be less generous, and certainly we would be less aware. In any case, we have the sense of the past and must live with it, and by it.

And we must read our literature by it. Try as we will, we cannot be like Partridge at the play, wholly without the historical sense. The leap of the imagination which an audience makes when it responds to *Hamlet* is enormous, and it requires a comprehensive, although not necessarily a highly instructed, sense of the past. . . .

In the New Critics' refusal to take critical account of the historicity of a work there is, one understands, the impulse to make the work of the past more immediate and more real, to deny that between Now and Then there is any essential difference, the spirit of man being one and continuous. But it is only if we are aware of the reality of the past that we can feel it as alive and present. If, for example, we try to make Shakespeare literally contemporaneous, we make him monstrous. He is contemporaneous only if we know how much a man of his own age he was; he is relevant to us only if we see his distance from us. Or to take a poet closer to us in actual time, Wordsworth's Immortality Ode is acceptable to us only when it is understood to have been written at a certain past moment; if it had appeared much later than it did, if it were offered to us now as a contemporary work, we would not admire it; and the same is true of *The Prelude*, which of all works of the Romantic Movement is closest to our present interest. In the pastness of these works lies the assurance of their validity and relevance.[3]

The sense of the past

Not all modern critics would agree with this. Some would maintain that a work which we would not admire "if it were offered to us now as a contemporary work" could not in any real sense be a good work at all. Some would go so far as to deny that "the spirit of man being one and continuous" is a relevant notion at all, the important thing about a work of art being its structure of ideas and images, the complex unity the creative writer achieves out of his expression of them, their relation to the facts of human experience being incidental. But this latter is an extreme position which does not fit the facts of literary appreciation in any age, for there are few readers and critics who would not agree that in some way and at some point the devices employed by the

[3] "The Sense of the Past," in *The Liberal Imagination*, copyright, 1950, by The Viking Press, Inc.

creator of a work of literary art reflect upon human experience. As to whether we make Shakespeare "monstrous" if we try to make him "literally contemporaneous," that would depend on what we mean by the latter phrase. How can we make a writer of a previous age "literally contemporaneous"? By regarding his work as though it were written by a contemporary? It would then be more likely to appear obscure or extravagant or in some way unsuccessful—or all these things at once—rather than monstrous. When Harley Granville-Barker, in his *Prefaces to Shakespeare*, drew our attention to the theatrical conventions of Shakespeare's day, in the light of which many apparently unsuccessful dramatic devices could be seen to be brilliantly successful, he was using history to remove obscurity, to clarify vision, rather than to correct monstrosity, and the same can be said of those scholars who have labored to set Shakespeare's dramatic patterns against the pattern of ideas in his day. Again, it can be conceded that the duty of the artist is to objectify his material in terms of his medium, so that everything exists in the work he has created and we can find it all out by examining the work; but again it must be emphasized that language is not itself a wholly objective or stable medium, and the subtle and complex relationships that can exist between language and thought are in some degree determined by transient conventions and traditions.

Nevertheless, Trilling's point, that the pastness of a work is often part of its meaning and value, is an interesting one. The kinds of life which a work of art takes on in time are themselves part of its meaning, and these accumulated meanings can never be ignored by the informed reader, whatever critical method he is employing. They often condition his response to a work to a much greater degree than he imagines, certainly to a greater degree than is likely to be made explicit in his criticism.

Bibliography and criticism

Not all literary scholarship is biographical and historical, and the question of the relation of criticism to scholarship concerns also such matters as bibliography and textual criticism, the study of an author's sources, the establishment of the chronology of his work, to mention only a few. Here it can more confidently be said that these activities are pre-critical rather than critical; they are likely to concern the establishment of the author's text, a necessary preliminary to any critical evaluation of it. What is the use of making a careful critical analysis of, say, *Hamlet* if the text of the play which we are using contains alterations, additions, omissions, misprints, and other features for which Shakespeare was not responsible? It is not unknown for critics to have spent much ingenuity proving the aptness and brilliance of a phrase which a scholar has later conclusively shown to have been a misprint. Clearly, the establishment of the text is a pre-condition for critical analysis and evaluation, and the studies of bibliography, paleography and textual criticism, which have developed enormously in the present century, are essential servants of criticism. Critics may differ as to whether concern with an author's intention is legitimate or not, but all would agree that the discovery of what the author wrote, rather than the perpetuation of inaccurate or even seriously corrupt texts, is of the first importance.

This is not the place to go into those modern studies which have contributed so much to the recovery of the text which the author actually wrote. But the critic, and the student of criticism, must have some awareness of their nature and their importance. The textual criticism of Shakespeare is well worth study, not only because of the intrinsic literary value of Shakespeare's plays, but also because Shakespeare himself did not supervise the publication of his plays and the printed texts we have are often at a considerable remove from Shakespeare's autograph. From the eighteenth century on, scholars have attempted to restore the true reading in passages that appear to be corrupt, and only gradually did it come to be realized that a knowledge of Elizabethan handwriting, a detailed familiarity with Elizabethan and Jacobean printing-house methods, and a technical understanding of contemporary bookmaking are necessary before any emendation can be made with confidence. One must be able to explain, in terms of handwriting, the state of the manuscript used as printer's copy, the printer's methods, or some other aspect of the putting of the written word onto the printed page, exactly how that kind of error could have been made and why the suggested emendation is plausible. Early textual critics (such as Pope, in his edition of Shakespeare) who simply changed the reading to one which sounded better to their ear, without making any attempt to show how the error could have arisen and what the physical conditions were which led to this particular misprint, produced a host of emendations not now accepted, and those of them which are now accepted have in many cases later been accounted for in bibliographical terms.

The direct relevance of all this to textual criticism can be seen if we cite the example of one of the most famous of all Shakespearean emendations. In Act I, scene iii of *Henry V* the hostess described the death of Falstaff, and her description includes the often quoted phrase " 'a babbled of green fields," over which critic after critic has waxed enthusiastic. But in the text of the First Folio of 1623 (the first collected edition of Shakespeare's plays, and the only real authority for the text of this play) the phrase appears as "a Table of greene fields," which makes no sense at all. This was emended by Lewis Theobald in his edition of 1733 to read " 'a babbled of green fields," which every subsequent edition has followed. Yet it was only a happy guess, and though modern scholarship can show how the words "a babbled of greene fields" written in Shakespeare's handwriting might well have been read by the printer as "a Table of greene fields," this emendation is not as certainly demonstrated to be correct as many less well-known ones.

Bibliography (the study of the processes by which a work is transferred from manuscript to the printed book, and of the whole procedure of printing and bookmaking) and textual criticism, which so often depends on bibliographical knowledge, are today highly technical studies equipped to solve in a rigorous and scientific manner a great number of problems about the text of literary works. Where, as so often happens, we have the printed text but not the author's manuscript or even the transcript of the author's manuscript from which the text was printed (and we have neither one nor the other in Shakespeare's case) the bibliographer has to try to get behind the printed text to the manuscript which the printer had before him when he set up the type. And then he must try to determine the relation between that manuscript and the author's autograph text. If printers were always one hundred per cent accurate, the first of these problems would not exist; but they never have been, and in Elizabethan and Jacobean times especially, the printers of plays were not distinguished by any great skill or accuracy.

The problem faces us in modern works as well. In the first one-volume American edition of the collected poems of W. B. Yeats there are at least half a dozen misprints which completely change the meaning of the passages in which they occur, and in some cases critics have actually analyzed the misprinted poems unaware of the errors, and have justified and even praised the mistaken words. The printing of "he" as "she" at the end of the second stanza of "Crazy Jane on the Day of Judgment" changes the meaning of the whole poem, for the poem is a dialogue and the misprint transfers a key statement to the wrong speaker. The second line of "Cuchulain's Fight with the Sea," by some extraordinary slip, has dropped out and in its stead the sixth line is printed: this poem is also in dialogue form and the result of this misprint—apart from making nonsense of the first stanza—is to throw every one of the speeches out of gear, giving each to the wrong speaker. Fortunately, these errors can be discovered by the simple process of comparing this edition with other editions; but there are other cases where readings differ and where it is difficult to tell whether one is wrong and the other right (and if so, which is wrong, for both may be plausible) or whether the author himself changed the poem in a later edition.

Thus even in modern works it is not enough for the critic to take the text in front of him and proceed to analyze and evaluate it. At the very least, he must compare texts in different editions, and in some cases he is wholly dependent on the careful researches of the expert bibliographer to tell him which is in fact his author's text. Sometimes it is of prime importance to know which of several editions is the first. In the case of Shakespeare and other playwrights of the sixteenth and seventeenth centuries there was sometimes more than one edition published in the same year. If one of these was printed from the other, then any features of the second one must derive not from the author but from the proofreader in the printing house or from the compositor himself. But it is often extremely difficult to tell which was the first. Here the bibliographer can help. For example, W. W. Greg showed which was the earlier of two editions of Beaumont and Fletcher's play, *The Elder Brother*, though both editions were dated 1637, by noting that in one edition there was a mark produced by an improperly adjusted space-lead before the word *young*, while in the other the word *young* was printed with a meaningless apostrophe before it, *'young*. This single piece of evidence was all that was necessary to prove the priority of the edition with the mark made by the improperly adjusted space-lead: this mark had been read as an apostrophe by the compositor (that is, the man who actually set the type) of the second edition. There is no other explanation of the facts. A meaningless apostrophe could not have been read in such a way as to produce the mark of an improperly adjusted space-lead! One tiny clue thus provided all the evidence needed to show which was the earlier edition (and therefore the edition closer to the author's autograph), but only a trained bibliographer would have noticed it. With his knowledge of which was the earlier edition, derived from the bibliographer, the critic can confidently ignore any variations in the text which appear only in the second.

A more obvious case is Marlowe's *Dr. Faustus*. Are the feeble comic scenes a part of Marlowe's play, to be evaluated as Marlowe's attempt at comic relief? Or are they additions by a later hand? The critic must know, if he is to make a proper evaluation of Marlowe's achievement. The answer to this particular problem is not to be found wholly in bibliography: a variety of scholarly resources must be brought to bear before even a tentative solution can be suggested. Similar problems of whether portions of a play are really part of the original work or later additions by another hand occur with reference to several of Shakespeare's plays—*Macbeth*, for example. And here again the critic must await the verdict of the scholar.

Critical significance of chronology

The question of which edition came first is important enough, but the question of which work was produced first is even more important, though in a different way. If we had no idea at all of the chronology of Shakespeare's plays, for example, and imagined that *The Tempest* and *The Comedy of Errors* were written about the same time, we should have a very different view of Shakespeare's genius than we now have. We would not judge the plays differently, perhaps, but we would judge its author differently. To compare, as earlier critics have done, *The Tempest* with *A Midsummer Night's Dream* as Shakespeare's two "fairy plays," ignoring the fact that *The Tempest* was his last work and *A Midsummer Night's Dream* a fairly early one, is to misconceive completely how Shakespeare's genius developed. A Shakespeare who could produce the *Dream*—still more so a Shakespeare who could produce the *Comedy of Errors*—in the final period of his maturity must have possessed an instability of genius and an uncertainty of taste quite unusual among great writers. Further, if we thought of these works as contemporary—or even as only possibly contemporary—we would read them differently, as indeed critics did before the chronology of Shakespeare's plays was more or less established. The kind of scholarship required to discover, even approximately, the order in which Shakespeare wrote his plays is complex indeed. Such an investigation requires an adroit use of both internal and external evidence—that is, of references to the plays in works of known date, and of references in the plays to events of known date, and the following-up of tentative conclusions so reached by plotting changes in style which appear to have occurred between such works as can now be proved to be early and late, until a tentative curve is established on which other plays can be placed. Historical, bibliographical, biographical, stylistic, philosophical—these are some of the kinds of evidence that have to be employed in establishing the chronology of a writer such as Shakespeare, and here, as in so many other exercises of scholarship, the critical faculty, the sensitive ear, and the response to subtle changes in pattern and attitude are also required, to supplement and confirm the more objective findings.

Requirements of an editor

The sum total of all scholarship which is relevant to the literary critic is also relevant to the production of a really good edition of an earlier work. As Professor F. P. Wilson has said of editing an Elizabethan play: "Of course bibliography is not enough. To no aspect of Elizabethan literature, language, or life can an editor afford to be indifferent, and the ideal editor is at once bibliographer and critic, historian and antiquary, palaeographer, philologist and philosopher."[4] It is in the production of a definitive edition that the true relationship between criticism and scholarship appears. The critic, of course, needs a good edition, a proper, well-established text, if he is to be sure that he is really examining the work he thinks he is examining. But more than that: the critic is needed in the actual preparation of the edition, for there is hardly a scholarly question, however scientific or technical, to whose solution esthetic awareness does not contribute something. Theobald's emendation of "a Table of greene fields" won acceptance because it sounds so *right* before it was shown to be plausible in terms of the kind of misprints printers of the period were likely to make with handwriting of the period, and though taste alone is far too variable and unsure a ground for making any emendation, taste, or, if we prefer a less subjective term, sound literary judgment, must confirm an emendation made on purely bibliographical grounds. If an emenda-

---

[4] "Shakespeare and the new Bibliography," *The Bibliographical Society 1892-1942, Studies in Retrospect*, London, 1945, page 135.

tion makes nonsense, if it produces something utterly out of keeping with the genius of the author concerned, then the bibliographer must think again. And the bibliographer himself must be the literary critic whose judgment provides this safeguard. In spite of the specialization of function that has been going on in literary scholarship in the present century, and in spite of the fact that some distinguished modern bibliographers consider themselves scientific bibliographers and nothing else, the fact remains that the bibliographer, like other literary scholars, uses his purely critical judgment more often than he sometimes thinks. And the great pioneers of modern bibliography—A. W. Pollard, R. W. McKerrow, W. W. Greg—were literary critics of taste and sensibility as well as scholars, to the advantage of both their criticism and their scholarship.

17

Criticism and psychology

I N EXPLAINING the nature of a work of literary art, the critic is often led into psychology, into a discussion of the state of mind out of which literary creation arises.

How psychology comes into criticism

Psychology comes into criticism in two ways, in this investigation of the act of creation and in the psychological study of particular authors to show the relation between their attitudes and states of mind and the special qualities of their work. The first, and more general, use of psychology in criticism is the older and the more widespread. Few critics have gone far in an investigation of imaginative literature as an

activity without having to deal with psychological factors. The critic
who considers literature as a series of works rather than as an activity
on the part of the authors of those works will not, of course, be led
so readily to psychology: Aristotle, for example, is less concerned with
how men come to write tragedies than with what tragedies are. But
Plato, in his *Ion,* is in a sense giving a psychological account of literary
creation. The Romantic critics were particularly interested in this
aspect of criticism.

This aspect belongs to the descriptive and not to the normative side
of criticism. No amount of psychological investigation, either of the
creative process in general or of the problems of individual authors,
can tell us whether a work is good or bad, though the psychological
investigation of individual authors can sometimes help us to see why
those authors displayed certain characteristic qualities in their work
(whether those qualities are good or bad can only be decided on a
proper theory of literary value adequately applied to the works
concerned).

Wordsworth as psychological critic

The use of psychology in criticism is, like the use of sociology, *genetic:*
it helps us to explain how literature comes into being. Naturally, the
conditions of origin of an art have a direct bearing on its nature, and to
many critics the proper definition of literature can only be given by
providing an account of its psychological origins. Thus we find
Wordsworth, in his preface to the 1800 edition of *Lyrical Ballads,*
beginning his inquiry into the nature of poetry by asking how the
poet operates:

Taking up the subject, then, upon general grounds, let me ask, what is
meant by the word Poet? What is a Poet? To whom does he address himself? And what language is to be expected from him?—He is a man speaking to men: a man, it is true, endowed with more lively sensibility, more
enthusiasm and tenderness, who has a greater knowledge of human nature,
and a more comprehensive soul, than are supposed to be common among
mankind; a man pleased with his own passions and volitions, and who rejoices more than other men in the spirit of life that is in him; delighted to
contemplate similar volitions and passions as manifested in the goings-on of
the Universe, and habitually impelled to create them where he does not
find them. To these qualities he has added a disposition to be affected more

than other men by absent things as if they were present; an ability of con-
juring up in himself passions, which are indeed far from being the same as
those produced by real events, yet (especially in those parts of the general
sympathy which are pleasing and delightful) do more nearly resemble the
passions produced by real events, than anything which, from the motions
of their own minds merely, other men are accustomed to feel in themselves:
—whence, and from practice, he has acquired a greater readiness and power
in expressing what he thinks and feels, and especially those thoughts and
feelings which, by his own choice, or from the structure of his own mind,
arise in him without immediate external excitement.

For Wordsworth, the poet differs in degree and not in kind from
other men; he has "more lively sensibility, more enthusiasm and tenderness" and "a greater knowledge of human nature and a more comprehensive soul" than his fellows, and the recollection of former
experiences can move him as though they were still actually present.
From this description of the poet's state of mind, of his special psychological qualifications, Wordsworth proceeds to derive his theory
of poetic diction. Since the poet is a man speaking to men, responding,
though in a more sensitive way, to common human experiences, his
language should not differ substantially from that of real men under-
going real experiences. "The poet thinks and feels in the spirit of
human passions. How, then, can his language differ in any material
degree from that of all other men who feel vividly and see clearly?"
One need not accept the argument here—indeed, it is curiously naive,
and ignores the fact that the poet, unlike the ordinary man, is using
language as a medium of artistic expression; the subject matter of an
art does not condition its medium in this simple and literal way—but
one can see that Wordsworth is trying to derive a normative notion
from a psychological description of the way the poet works. And
though psychological description cannot itself be normative, as we
have noted, it can be used as the basis for a normative superstructure,
as it were—as I. A. Richards used it, though he employed a very different kind of psychology.

Later on in his essay, when Wordsworth is endeavoring to reconcile
his view that poetry should be written in the real language of men
with his having written in rhyme and meter, he is led again to a description of the process of poetic creation, as a preliminary to his justification of rhyme and meter:

I have said that poetry is the spontaneous overflow of powerful feelings:

it takes its origin from emotion recollected in tranquillity: the emotion is contemplated till, by a species of reaction, the tranquillity gradually disappears, and an emotion, kindred to that which was before the subject of contemplation, is gradually produced, and does itself actually exist in the mind. In this mood successful composition generally begins, and in a mood similar to this it is carried on; but the emotion, of whatever kind, and in whatever degree, from various causes, is qualified by various pleasures, so that in describing any passions whatsoever, which are voluntarily described, the mind will, upon the whole, be in a state of enjoyment.

Wordsworth goes on to justify the use of rhyme and meter in poetry as helping to achieve that "overbalance of pleasure" which is a characteristic of the actual poetic experience. We see here, therefore, psychology used to provide a genetic explanation of poetry—an explanation of how it arises in the mind of the poet—and that genetic explanation in turn used to justify a certain kind of poetry. There is a tendency here—common among the Romantics—to define poetry in terms of the process of poetic creation. To write good poetry one must be in such-and-such a state of mind; such-and-such a kind of poetry is the most adequate reflection of this state of mind; therefore that kind of poetry is the most poetic and the best. The argument might appear at first sight to be circular, and in a sense it is; but the interesting thing about it is that it is an attempt to derive normative judgments from psychological description, and such attempts have been common in criticism ever since. (The reader should compare with Wordsworth's argument the arguments of I. A. Richards as described on pages 135-142.)

Art and neurosis

Various schools of modern psychology have each had something to say about the psychological conditions out of which art arises. The Freudians have their view of the relation between art and neurosis, the Jungians have found in works of literary art archetypal images and echoes of basic and recurring myths, and there have been any number of modifications and additions to both kinds of theory. The notion that the artist is neurotic, sick, maladjusted, that art is somehow a by-product of this sickness and maladjustment, has become immensely popular during the last hundred and fifty years, and modern psychology seems to have justified it. Edmund Wilson, in his essay "The Wound and the Bow" takes Sophocles' play *Philoctetes* as an allegory of the artist: Philoctetes was marooned on an island because he suffered from an evil-smelling wound, yet his fellow Greeks sought him out because they needed his magic bow for the Trojan war. The artist pays for his creative vision by his sickness, and though society rejects him it nevertheless needs him because of the healing power of his art. This view does not derive inevitably from modern psychology, and social at least as much as psychological factors account for its rise and popularity. The best reply to it is Lionel Trilling's essay on "Art and Neurosis." Trilling points out that writers are more available to psychoanalytic explanation than others because they are more articulate about themselves; but if we are to use the abundant material about themselves which they provide for us to prove that their art derives from their being in some way mentally sick, we must make the same assumption about all other kinds of intellectual activity.

It is the basic assumption of psychoanalysis that the acts of *every* person are influenced by the forces of the unconscious. Scientists, bankers, lawyers, or surgeons, by reason of the traditions of their professions, practice concealment and conformity: but it is difficult to believe that an investigation according to psychoanalytical principles would fail to show that the strains and imbalances of their psyche are not of the same frequency as those of writers, and of similar kind. I do not mean that everybody has the same troubles and identical psyches, but only that there is no special category for writers.

If this is so, and if we still want to relate the writer's power to his neurosis, we must be willing to relate all intellectual power to neurosis. We must find the roots of Newton's power in his emotional extravagances, and the roots of Darwin's power in his sorely neurotic temperament, and the roots of Pascal's mathematical genius in the impulses which drove him to extreme religious masochism—I choose but the classic examples. If we make the neurosis-power equivalence at all, we must make it in every field of endeavor. Logician, economist, botanist, physicist, theologian—no profession may be so respectable or so remote or so rational as to be exempt from the psychological interpretation.[1]

Trilling goes on to argue that not only intellectual success but also failure and limitation should logically be attributed to neurosis, and since this gives us success, failure, and mediocrity accounted for by neurosis, "we have most of society involved." Society may well be in-

[1] Lionel Trilling, *op. cit.*

volved. "But with neurosis accounting for so much, it cannot be made exclusively to account for one man's literary power."

Criticism as analysis of the author

Perhaps more fruitful than general psychological and psychoanalytic theories of the origin of art are the particular applications to particular cases. True, the older "bio-critical" approach had discussed the psychology of the author concerned and related it to the special features of his work (one can see this in almost any volume of the "English Men of Letters" series, produced for the most part in the latter part of the nineteenth century), but in a common sense and unsystematic way. The new psychological systems made possible much more methodical approaches. One could analyze a particular work and draw from the analysis inferences about the psychology of its author; one could take the whole body of an author's writing and derive from it general conclusions about his state of mind which could then be applied to elucidate particular works. One could take the biography of a writer, as illustrated by the external events of his life and by such things as letters and other confessional documents, and construct out of these a theory of the writer's personality—his conflicts, frustrations, traumatic experiences, neuroses, or whatever they happened to be—and use this theory in order to illuminate each one of his works. Or one can work back and forth between the life and the work, illuminating each by the other, noting from the biography certain crises reflected in the works, and seeing from the way they are reflected in the works what their real biographical meaning was. This is often dangerous, if highly stimulating, theorizing, and its relation to critical evaluation is, at most, very tenuous. But if this kind of psychological inquiry does not help us to assess the value of a work, it often helps us to see more clearly what literary works are as products of the human imagination working in certain ways under certain conditions.

Edmund Wilson as psychological critic

One can illustrate Plato's view of literature by a quotation of half a dozen pages, but to illustrate the kind of modern criticism which begins with a study of the elements in a writer's biography that

helped to condition his kind of imagination and proceeds to apply this
to each one of his works, clearly cannot be done in such brief compass. One of the most effective critical essays of this kind, Edmund
Wilson's "Dickens: The Two Scrooges,"[2] is over a hundred pages
long and it is far from comprehensive. No brief selection from this
essay would illustrate the method, for the very essence of it consists
in first laying out the relevant biographical facts, then drawing conclusions from them about the author's psychology, and then applying
these conclusions to the individual works. To quote any of these
three parts without the others would be to give a wrong picture of the
method. The reader, therefore, must go to these essays himself—to
Wilson's essays on Housman (in *The Triple Thinkers*, 1938), Dickens, and Kipling especially.

Wilson uses what might be called a common-sense mixture of
psychology and sociology in his endeavors to demonstrate the conditions which explain the special nature of a writer's work. His awareness of social factors is not derived from any rigid system, as is that
of the Marxists, but is freely related to the psychological elements in
studies of a writer's feeling about his class, the effect on him of early
economic struggles, the kinds of friction which social conventions
made for him, and so on. Dickens' father's imprisonment for debt and
Dickens' having to go to work in a blacking factory are presented by
Wilson as key factors in determining the set of his imagination, and
he traces their influence in the books. He points out the humiliation
which Dickens suffered, his bitter indignation with his mother for
having wanted to keep him working at the blacking warehouse, the
social dubiety of his origins. "All these circumstances are worth
knowing and bearing in mind, because they help us to understand
what Dickens was trying to say," Wilson comments. A purely
analytic critic might object to this: he would argue that what the
writer is *trying* to say is not of interest to the critic, who is concerned
with what he *succeeds* in saying, with what he puts objectively into
art, and if we need to go to biography to find out what is really being
said by a work of art then the work cannot be successful.[3] But
Wilson sees the writer as (to use Wordsworth's phrase) "a man
speaking to men" and is most interested in the human implications
of the work of literary art, its origins in human hopes and fears and
desires and frustrations. The function of the literary critic, as he sees

[2] In *The Wound and the Bow*, New York, 1941. The essay on Kipling is also in
this volume.
[3] See above, p. 266, footnote 1.

it, is to enlarge the unit observed by the reader until it includes not merely the text of a work, or even a group of such texts, but the whole pattern of influence and causation, of action and reaction, of psychological and sociological forces, of which the given work is the center. But this enlargement is conceived not simply as a contribution to history; it is also intended as a contribution to esthetic understanding and appreciation. If we arrive late at a concert at which the first item played is a set of variations on a theme, and we take our seat as the third variation is being played, *imagining it to be the theme*, we shall have got the wrong perspective on the whole piece of music, we shall be hearing the wrong pattern, however keen our ear. But if we are familiar enough with the music to be able to supply the main theme mentally as we hear the further variations, or if someone puts a score of the main theme into our hand, this error will be corrected and we shall be able to get the proper significance out of the music.

In some sense, it might be said that for Edmund Wilson and those modern critics who employ his kind of critical approach the literature produced by any writer can best be understood as variations on a theme. The theme is the writer's life and circumstances, in the most complete sense, and we can only be sure of seeing the right pattern in the particular works if we are able to relate them to the theme on which they are unconscious variations. Yet it is not always (as Wilson would admit) quite as simple as that. We cannot always be sure which is the air and which the variations: sometimes the relationship between the writer's life and his work is so complex and subtle that it would be false to regard the latter simply as variations on the former; each throws light on the other, the man puts the work into its right perspective, but perhaps as a key signature helps us in reading a piece of music or as a frame brings out the proper relationship between the parts and the whole in a picture. At all events, on this view of criticism the critic has a duty to discover and present interpretations of works of art based on an understanding of the artist's nature and purposes. Such activity might not provide us with standards on which to decide what is good literature and what bad, but it might help us to discover how literature becomes what it is. "It is necessary to see him as a man in order to appreciate him as an artist." "The work of Dickens' whole career was an attempt to digest these early shocks and hardships, to explain them to himself, to justify himself in relation to them. . . ." These are typical quotations from Wilson's essay on

Dickens. Or consider the question he asks himself at the beginning of his essay on Kipling: "But who *was* Kipling?"

Wilson works, on the whole, from the writer's life to his work, explaining the latter with reference to the former. More technical psychological criticism often works from the work to the writer, using the work as the equivalent of the confession on the psychiatrist's couch and proceeding to draw conclusions about the writer's life and state of mind. This is more dangerous, because it does not sufficiently allow for the formal element in art and too often naively assumes that the artist works with complete emotional spontaneity. To argue from *Hamlet* about Shakespeare's life and character is a highly dubious procedure: in *Hamlet* Shakespeare was dealing with a traditional plot and consciously working it into a formal piece of dramatic art to fit the theatrical conventions of his time. If we knew beyond dispute the facts of Shakespeare's life, and had letters and memoirs of his to draw on, then we could perhaps profitably look into his plays for reflections of his personal problems, however indirect, and see things in them which we do not see now. To use the work as a means of psychoanalyzing the author, without any further evidence, is possible only in very special cases. But in any case, such a procedure is hardly literary criticism in any sense of the term.

Psychoanalytic study of the characters in a literary work

The professional psychologist need not, however, confine his interest in literature to attempts to psychoanalyze the author through his works. He can use his knowledge of psychological problems and situations to interpret a work of literature without any reference to its author's biography. We can look at the behavior of characters in a novel or a play in the light of modern psychological knowledge and, if their behavior confirms what we know about the subtleties of the human mind, we can use modern theories as a means of elucidating and interpreting the work. If Hamlet behaves according to a pattern which, say, Freud discovered to be characteristic of certain kinds of individuals acting in certain kinds of circumstances, this does not mean that Shakespeare knew Freud's theories, but it does confirm Shakespeare's remarkable insight into human nature. Such a use of psychology is therefore appropriate to critics who believe with Dryden that the function of literature is to provide "a just and lively image of human nature" or at least who agree on the general proposition that the end of literature is some kind of illumination of the human situation (and of course even the most formal of critics can agree on this end, while concentrating their attention as critics on the technical means by which it is achieved).

Sometimes works which are difficult and apparently confused can be seen more clearly in the light of the psychologist's demonstration of what is actually going on among the characters. For example, the so-called "problem plays" or "bitter comedies" of Shakespeare (which include *Measure for Measure*, *All's Well that Ends Well* and *Troilus and Cressida*) have long puzzled critics by the apparent strangeness of their tone, and many attempts have been made to elucidate them. One of the most interesting attempts at elucidation is the psychoanalytic study of *Measure for Measure* by Dr Hanns Sachs. After detailing some of the difficulties of the play, Dr Sachs comes to the character of Angelo:[4]

The outstanding trait in his [Angelo's] character, constellating his attitude in all matters, small or great, is cruelty. To his subordinates he is gruff and unfriendly, always ready with a rebuke or a threat. He snubs the simple constable ("Elbow is your name? Why dost thou not speak, Elbow?") as well as the kind Provost ("Do your office, or give up your place, and you shall well be spared"). The unhappy Juliet is to him simply a "fornicatrix." To sit as a judge in court inspires him with the same philanthropic sentiment towards the silly but evidently harmless witness as toward the offender: "hoping you'll find good cause to whip them all." His cruelty is best demonstrated by the fact that he selects Claudio as the victim for the renewed enforcement of the laws against profligacy. In this Vienna of bawds and brothels it would have been easy to find a culprit whose transgressions were of a darker hue than those of Claudio. He seems to be singled out by Angelo just because he was the most innocent offender who came within the scope of the law; his betrothal gave him, according to custom, the right of a legitimate husband, especially since these things happened some time before the revival of the strict law. Indeed, this way of enforcing the old statute does nothing to give it renewed authority, but discredits it by making it appear fantastic and impossible. It is not justice or morality which Angelo tries to establish—though he may persuade himself that these are his aims—but terror, wrath and cruelty.

[4] From "The Measure in 'Measure for Measure'" in *The Creative Unconscious* (2d ed., revised and enlarged by A. A. Roback, 1951), copyright, 1942, by Sci-Art Publishers.

This tendency toward cruelty shapes Angelo's life in two ways: first, negatively, by making the ordinary and normal forms of sensuality unattractive to him, or even repulsive. This may be one of the reasons why he pursues them with this cold hate. As the Duke puts it, he

> "scarce confesses
> That his blood flows or that his appetite
> Is more to bread than stone—"

in other words to a free and impartial observer his rigidity seems exaggerated and, therefore, a bit suspicious.

The other, positive, influence is manifested in his bias for meting out punishment, for making others suffer. He loves to wield the sword of justice and to feel entitled in defending a higher cause, to be severe and uncharitable, so long as his own life remains blameless; in this way he satisfies his cravings in a quasi-legitimate way. Through his office he finds an outlet for his dark desire in the form of a social function which has his own approval as well as that of society; in short, he shows what psychoanalysis calls a sublimation, although by no means a perfectly successful one, since his original nature looks through the rents in his gown. This sublimation breaks down with a sudden crash when he meets Isabella. The splendor of her purity, outshining everything to which he has been accustomed, together with the situation which delivers her into his hands, is too much for him.

> "Can it be
> That modesty may more betray our senses
> Than woman's lightness? Having waste ground enough,
> Shall we desire to raze the sanctuary,
> And pitch our evils there?"

Thus stimulated and exposed to the storm of desire, his cruelty loses every aspect of sublimation and falls back, regressively, to its original source, revealing its primeval, sensual form. How near these two have dwelled together in Angelo's mind is illustrated by the identity he sees in murder and the sexual sin: "'tis all as easy Falsely to take away a true life made As to put metal in restrained means To make a false one." The new temptation, against which Angelo fights in vain, is that of sadism. This psychological picture, the conflict caused by the regression to the sadistic stage of sensuality, would to us moderns who are concerned with the psychic processes in their immediate and intimate appearance, constitute an obsessional neurotic. Shakespeare who, as the true son of the Renaissance, projected his psychological intuition into the facts and forms of the world outside, made him a judge.

This diagnosis of Angelo's over-strict sense of justice as the sublimation of his cruelty, a sublimation which breaks down and turns to sadism before Isabella's combination of beauty and purity (thus also illustrating the relation between sensuality and sadism) is not just a matter of giving technical psychoanalytic terms to the obvious; it makes a pattern out of Angelo's behavior which is not otherwise apparent, a pattern which, once pointed out, we feel to be justified in a rereading of the play. But Dr Sachs is not content to diagnose Angelo's character: he relates his diagnosis to his interpretation of the play as a whole.

Judge—this is in one word the problem of *Measure for Measure* from which all the rest proceeds. As it often happens with Shakespeare, it looks at first as if he presented only an ephemeral, accidental side of the problem: the evil judge who misuses his power for his own ends, the judge without mercy whose justice is but cruelty. The deeper meaning is not emphasized or advertised to impress the beholder with its profundity, but rather kept in the background and, especially in the comedies, disguised by jokes and scurrility, like a cliff overgrown with grass and shrubs. . . .

The theme that is harped on constantly in *Measure for Measure* and carried through every possible variation, some straightforward to the point of brutality, some abstract and remote, is this: What happens to justice if the austere judge could commit, would commit, has committed the same crime for which he condemns the offender? What if Angelo is not different from Claudio and deserves to be put in his place—"an Angelo for Claudio?" The question is discussed first in a strictly judicial reasoning at the beginning of Act II by Angelo himself. . . .

Dr Sachs then traces the theme through the play and shows how the idle talk of Lucio and the dialogue of the minor characters represent "the same melody in counterpoint." He proceeds:

. . . Our play shows, at first glance, how in the judicial mind self-restraint for the sake of gaining the respect of others and self-respect break down when temptation takes the form of the suppressed sadistic wishes. The judge, by this resurrection of his primitive, unsublimated sensuality, is driven to repeating the act which he has censured, and thus changes place with the offender. But the scope of the problem grows under the creating hand of the poet and becomes much wider than that of the story. If these possibilities exist generally, if unconscious wishes and drives are not only in existence, but active in the mind of everyone, if they are kept from coming to life only by the special grace of destiny, then it follows that every man who dares to be a judge, is a potential Angelo. It means, if we take it in its full and true sense and set aside as mere accidents the actual temptation and the outward shapes of our acts and our conscious thoughts, that no judge can disclaim his identity in guilt with the criminal before him. In the guise of a comedy *Measure for Measure* unfolds one of the tragic conflicts which disturb the peace of mind and the good conscience of mankind since the first foundations of social life have been laid. The identity of the man who judges and the man who is judged, the subject of Shakespeare's comedy, was used two thousand years earlier as the basis of a tragedy which became the everlasting symbol of human guilt.

Dr Sachs then goes on to point out the similarities between *Measure for Measure* and the *Oedipus the King* of Sophocles. He also discusses the play by Heinrich von Kleist, *Der zerbrochene Krug* ("The Broken Jug"), where a similar theme is treated as high comedy, and proceeds to discuss the ways in which this theme can be made either tragic or comic. "In the tragedy the dreadful crimes are really performed, although unintentionally; in the comedies there is any amount of bad intentions, but nothing happens."

Shakespeare, when he decided to write *Measure for Measure* as a comedy, although his mind was far removed from the humor and sprightliness of his earlier play, respected this fundamental rule by sheer intuition. Whetstone [Shakespeare's source] . . . had already eliminated the unjust execution, but the other crime had to be relegated to the realm of mere intentions as well. The trick by which a legitimate spouse is substituted so that the rape becomes the consummation of marriage, had been used by Shakespeare in *All's Well that Ends Well*. It came in handy here and for this purpose a lady who had been betrothed to Angelo and deserted by him was incorporated into the play. In this manner the original, sinister and bloody story was turned inside out. Angelo's character was much involved in these alterations. . . . It would have been easy to go the whole length with him, to make him the funny, stupid dupe who gets tripped up at every step. The usual way to make him ridiculous would have been to bring him together with the disguised Duke in such a manner that the unrecognized master is slandered in his face by the deceived deceiver. Lucio, who is the shadow without the substance of Angelo's wickedness, is put in this situation instead. The meeting between the Duke and Angelo is not avoided out of regard for the probability that Angelo would see through the disguise, since Escalus actually speaks to him (III/2). Besides, no comedy worth its salt ever respected this sort of improbability. What makes such a comic meeting impossible is Angelo's character. Shakespeare eliminated all the dreadfulness of the crimes by having none of them committed actually, but he retained, he even deepened, their appalling effect as far as Angelo's mind is concerned. He was unwilling to sacrifice the character problem to the comedy.

Angelo obtains his pardon in the end, this is a foregone conclusion. All that happens to him is to be found out and exposed; his pride is turned into humility. He had been tormented not only by the fear of detection, but also by the cruel pangs of his guilty conscience:

> "Would yet he had lived!
> Alack, when once our grace we have forgot,
> Nothing goes right,—we would and we would not."

This wish, that Claudio might still live, is fulfilled. Indeed, the pangs of his conscience must have been greatly alleviated when he learns that he, with all his villainy and cunning, has done no wrong at all. Isabella with her clear and unerring intellect grasps here, as she always does, the true merit of the situation and presents it with her usual lucidity. . . . So Angelo the mighty demon has been, in fact, a perfectly harmless creature. In his sin he saw himself as Lucifer and felt the pride of Lucifer, so that this relief of his guilt-feeling is, at the same time, his deepest humiliation. This shame is for the proud man a worse punishment than "immediate sentence then, and sequent death" for which he begs as a grace. His sins turn out to be of the same low order as those of Lucio: idle words and bad intentions, and he is punished in exactly the same way as Lucio, by being constrained to marry a woman whom he can neither love nor esteem.

Dr Sachs goes on to discuss the relevance of all this to the Gospel admonition "Judge not that ye be not judged" and the contradiction between human justice and sinfulness. He compares Dostoyevski's handling of this theme in *The Brothers Karamazov*, where the final answer to the question Ivan puts to Alyosha—"Can you find forgiveness in your heart for all crimes? Can you forgive wanton cruelty, the torturing and killing of innocent children?"—is given by the Staretz Sossima:

We can forgive the worst sin, the most hideous crime, we can even ask the sinner to forgive us (as Sossima kneels before Dmitri), when we are aware that we ourselves are guilty of his crime and responsible for it. The identity between judge and criminal is reaffirmed in a new sense. For Dostoyevsky this new sense became the cornerstone of his mystical religiosity, yet it can be conceived in a purely human, untranscendental way, and then it coincides to a great extent with the disclosures, made many years later, by Freud. With him it rests on the experience that our entire personality comprehends not only what we want to know about ourselves, but our Unconscious as well. Since unconscious, repressed desires and wishes are essentially the same everywhere, we are all linked together by the bond of common guilt, and it matters little whether we call it by its Christian name of Original Sin or by the psychoanalytic term: Oedipus-Complex. . . .

This is one of the few occasions on which the paths of the two men who knew more about the human mind than all the rest of us, approached each other. They both look at the problem of universal guilt, shared by judge and criminal alike, but the Russian of the nineteenth century is swept away into mysticism, whereas the Elizabethan, although he approaches the abyss, never gets out of touch with the realities of life. He takes it for granted that human society has to go on and will continue even if it be found that justice is, of necessity, bound to be a failure. . . .

The moral is: they are all sinners. Even the highest and purest judge is not better than the villain whom he judges. But what of that? If this world is so full of horrors, if life is a thing without real value, what does it matter if a man tries to take away his brother's life? Even if he succeeds, he cannot succeed in robbing him of anything that is worth while. We are sinners all, but impotent sinners, deceivers deceived by our own passions. Condemning each other, we are "like an angry ape."

Not justice, only mercy, may bring some rays of light into the abysmal darkness while it "will breathe within your lips."

If this measure is applied, the pardon of Angelo which seems such a flagrant injustice, is not irony but really and truly "Measure for Measure."

The argument from psychoanalysis is here directed towards helping us to read the play aright. That it does so help us is confirmed by the similarity of the interpretation it yields to that yielded by the careful application of historical scholarship. Elizabeth Pope, in her essay on "The Renaissance Background of *Measure for Measure*,"[5] inquired into the doctrines of equity and forgiveness that were actually taught to the Elizabethan layman, and also (though from a very different point of view from that of Dr Sachs) found the play to be a commentary on the Gospel text "Judge not, and ye shall not be judged" (Luke 6:37, Geneva version). Miss Pope is concerned solely with explaining certain aspects of the play's meaning in terms of Elizabethan assumptions, with which Shakespeare worked and which he took for granted; Dr Sachs is concerned with applying psychoanalytic knowledge about the nature of the mind to an elucidation of the behavior of the charac-

[5] In *Shakespeare Survey*, 2, Cambridge, 1949.

ters in the play. Though the conclusions certainly do not duplicate each other, they point in a similar direction and they supplement each other.

Psychology, therefore, comes into literary criticism in several ways. It can help to explain the creative process in general, it can provide a means of illuminating a writer's work with reference to his life and vice versa, and it can help to elucidate the true meaning of a given text. In none of these aspects is it directly normative, though in the third it can be indirectly so, for, as the example quoted will illustrate, it can demonstrate that a work superficially baffling and even confused is in truth a profound study of certain aspects of human character.

Archetypal patterns in literature

In addition to considering the psychology of the author as revealed in his work and the psychology of the characters in a play or novel, the psychological critic can consider the degree to which the images and symbols in a work of literature derive their full meaning from some deep psychological source, some perennial aspect of the human mind. The poet, it has been maintained, is more closely in touch with these deep sources of meaning, being, as T. S. Eliot put it, "more primitive, as well as more civilized, than his contemporaries." The psychologist Carl Jung believed in the "collective unconscious" lying behind the individual conscious and unconscious mind, not readily accessible to the ordinary adult. Maud Bodkin, in her *Archetypal Patterns in Poetry* (1934), applied this view to poetry, discovering in certain recurring poetic images, symbols, and situations echoes of this deep-seated primitive sense of meaning. Some poets, notably W. B. Yeats with his view of the "Great Memory," held similar views. G. Wilson Knight's interpretations of Shakespeare, referred to in the last section of the previous chapter, owe something to this view.

Perhaps the most striking modern approach to literature in what might be called the archetypal tradition is that of Northrop Frye, whose *Anatomy of Criticism* (1957) has taken its place as a classic re-definition of the nature both of literature and of criticism. Frye's archetypal approach is bound up with his radically new approach to these questions.

Criticism for Frye is knowledge and not opinion; it has nothing to do with taste and seems to have little to do with evaluation:

Art, like nature, has to be distinguished from the systematic study of it, which is criticism. It is therefore impossible to "learn literature": one learns about it in a certain way, but what one learns, transitively, is the criticism of literature. Similarly, the difficulty often felt in "teaching literature" arises from the fact that it cannot be done: the criticism of literature is all that can be directly taught. . . . Criticism . . . is to art what history is to action and philosophy to wisdom: a verbal imitation of a human productive power which in itself does not speak.

The critic needs his own conceptual universe in which, qua critic, he ought to dwell. This universe can be built up progressively; criticism progresses in the way science progresses; indeed, criticism, Frye insists, *is* a science. The whole approach here is strenuously Aristotelian. "A theory of criticism whose principles apply to the whole of literature and account for every type of valid critical procedure is what I think Aristotle meant by poetics."

Frye's method is to reduce literature to elements out of which any given kind of literature can be built up. Criticism becomes a technique of description by categorization and (though Frye would not admit this) reduction. Different kinds of literature differ in the kind, proportion, combination and manner of employment of their different elements. Frye is fascinating in his categorization of the elements and his classifications of their permutations and combinations. Ultimately, however, such a method is bound to be reductive, subsuming different works in a class, defining by showing the *kind* (as in neo-classic criticism, but in a very different way), not the *quiddity*; always pointing to what a given work has in common with others rather than revealing its special differentiating qualities. Thus criticism is comparative not in the sense that it is concerned with comparing some works with others and saying that *this* is better or worse than *that*, but in the sense that it places a given work in a context, by defining its mode, its kind and its degree of symbolization, the kind of archetypal themes and images it employs, the way it handles words with respect to a real or implied audience or to the writer's relationship to his material. This inevitably makes it 'like' other works (and, of course, unlike still other works), and in the demonstration of this likeness lies the critical act.

The earliest European comedy, Aristophanes' *The Acharnians*, contains the *miles gloriosus* or military braggart who is still going strong in Chaplin's *Great Dictator*; the Joxer Daly of O'Casey's *Juno and the Paycock* has the same character and dramatic function of the parasites of twenty-five hundred years ago, and the audiences of vaudeville, comic strips and television programs still laugh at the jokes that were declared to be outworn at the opening of *The Frogs*.

Frye is continually defining categories and then dividing them into phases, each with its archetypal association. Thus the first three phases of "the *mythos* of winter: irony and satire" are phases of satire which correspond to the first three or ironic phases of comedy and in the second three phases irony takes over from satire and the link is with tragedy rather than comedy. Here is a characteristic definition, referring to the sixth phase of "the *mythos* of winter":

The sixth phase presents human life in terms of largely unrelieved bondage. Its settings feature prisons, madhouses, lynching mobs, and places of execution, and it differs from a pure inferno mainly in the fact that in human experience suffering has an end in death. . . . The human figures of this phase are, of course, *desdichado* figures of misery or madness, often parodies of romantic roles. Thus the romantic theme of the helpful servant giant is parodied in *The Hairy Ape* and *Of Mice and Men*, and the romantic presenter or Prospero figure is parodied in the Benjy of *The Sound and the Fury* whose idiot mind contains, without comprehending, the whole action of the novel. Sinister parental figures naturally abound, for this is the world of the ogre and the witch, of Baudelaire's black giantess and Pope's goddess Dullness. . . .

But Frye makes distinctions as well; indeed, his whole schematic procedure is based on distinctions, the establishment of modes and kinds within which each work is fitted. The first of the four essays that make up the bulk of his book is devoted to a "theory of modes". Fictions are classified by the hero's power of action, which may be greater than, less than, or the same as, ours. The divine hero, superior in *kind* to other men, is the hero of a *myth*; the typical hero of *romance* is superior in *degree* to other men and to his environment; the leader, superior in degree to other men but not to his natural environment, is the hero of the "high mimetic" mode, of most epic and tragedy; the hero who is not superior to other men or to his environment, who is one of us, belongs to the "low mimetic" mode, of most comedy and of realistic fiction. The inferior hero whom we look down on belongs to the ironic mode. This is a genuinely helpful schematization with a clear historical correlation, and Frye applies it to European literature as a whole. Here is a characteristic passage:

Tragedy in the central or high mimetic sense, the fiction of the fall of a leader (he has to fall because that is the only way in which a leader can be isolated from his society), mingles the heroic with the ironic. In elegiac romance the hero's mortality is a natural fact, the sign of his humanity; in high mimetic tragedy it is also a social and moral fact. We said that the ironic fiction-writer is influenced by no considerations except craftsmanship, and the thematic poet in the ironic age thinks of himself more as a craftsman than as a creator or 'unacknowledged legislator'. That is, he makes the minimum claim for his personality and the maximum for his art–a contrast which underlies Yeats's theory of the poetic mask.

The second essay, "Theory of Symbols", in Frye's book distinguishes between *signs*, which point outward to things beyond them, and *motifs*, verbal elements which are understood inwardly as parts of a verbal structure. In all literature there is both an outward direction (which is the final direction of descriptive and assertive writing) and an inward; in literature proper the final direction is always inward, with the outward drives secondary.

Wherever we have an autonomous verbal structure . . . we have literature. In literature, questions of fact or truth are subordinated to the primary literary aim of producing a structure of words for its own sake, and the sign-values of symbols are subordinated to their importance as a structure of interconnected motifs.

We need some elaboration here of the phrase "for its own sake", but it is clear that Frye is outlining a view of literature which goes beyond such distinctions as that between emotive and referential meaning made by the early Richards. Frye's own elaborations, qualifications, subdivisions and illustrative examples are needed if the argument is to be seen in its true persuasiveness. "Within the boundaries of literature we find a kind of sliding scale, ranging from the most explicitly allegorical consistent to being literature at all, at one extreme, to the most elusive, anti-explicit and anti-allegorical at the other."

The third essay in *Anatomy of Criticism*, "Archetypal Criticism: Theory of Myths", takes us into the heart of Frye's critical interests. Here we see more clearly the total cylical pattern of his critical scheme, with the last of a series of categories making contact again with the first. In discussing archetypal meaning, he constructs a scheme which enables him to distinguish between apocalyptic imagery (representing "the categories of reality in the forms of human desire, as indicated by the forms they assume under the work of human civilization"), demonic imagery ("the presentation of the world that desire totally rejects"), and analogical imagery which mediates between these. He finds also archetypal seasonal analogues for comedy (the mythos of spring), romance (summer), tragedy (autumn), and irony and satire (winter).

In his "Tentative Conclusion" Frye explains that, in the necessary process of breaking down barriers between methods, archetypal criticism has a central role:

> One element in our cultural tradition which is usually regarded as fantastic nonsense is the allegorical explanations of myths which bulk so large in mediaeval and Renaissance criticism and continue sporadically (e.g., Ruskin's *Queen of the Air*) to our own time. The allegorization of myth is hampered by the assumption that the explanation "is" what the myth "means". A myth being a centripetal structure of meaning, it can be made to mean an infinite number of things, and it is more fruitful to study what in fact myths have been made to mean.

> The term myth may have, and obviously does have, different meanings in different subjects. These meanings are doubtless reconcilable in the long run, but the task of reconciling them lies in the future. In literary criticism myth means ultimately *mythos*, a structural organizing principle of literary form. Commentary, we remember, is allegorization and any great work of literature may carry an infinite amount of commentary. This fact often depresses the critic and makes him feel that everything to be said about *Hamlet*, for instance, must already have been said many times. To what has occurred to the learned and astute minds of A and B in reading *Hamlet* is added what occurs to the learned and astute minds of C, D, E, and so on, until out of sheer self-preservation most of it is left unread, or (much the same thing culturally) is assigned to specialists. Commentary which has no sense of the archetypal shape of literature as a whole, then, continues the tradition of allegorized myth, and inherits its characteristic of brilliance, ingenuity, and futility.

> The only cure for this situation is the supplementing of allegorical with archetypical criticism. Things become more hopeful as soon as there is a feeling, however dim, that criticism has an end in the structure of literature as a total form, as well as a beginning in the text studied. It is not sufficient to use the text as a check on commentary, like a string tied to a kite, for one may develop a primary body of commentary around the obvious meaning, then a secondary body around the unconscious meaning, then a third body around the conventions and external relations of the poem, and so on indefinitely. This practice is not confined to modern critics, for the interpretation of Virgil's Fourth Eclogue as Messianic also assumed that Virgil was "unconsciously" prophesying the Messiah. But the poet unconsciously meant the whole corpus of his possible commentary, and it is simpler merely to say that Virgil and Isaiah use the same type of imagery dealing with the myth of the hero's birth, and that because of this similarity the Nativity Ode, for instance, is able to use both. This procedure helps to distribute the commentary, and prevents each poem from becoming a separate centre of isolated scholarship.

Criticism and Psychology

349

In spite of his strenuous efforts, Frye is unable to avoid an element of reductiveness in his archetypal categorizations: works are illuminated by being placed in a class, and Aristophanes and Charlie Chaplin (or even a Greek tragedy and a children's skipping rhyme) are seen as doing the same sort of thing. But of course there *are* elements of similarity and even unity that connect and mutually illuminate works of literature. To pinpoint these is not to provide a normative criticism (an aim Frye disclaims) but it can help to show what literature is and how it works.

18

Criticism and sociology

IN MODERN CRITICISM, investigation of a writer's social origins and of the effect which social factors had on his work, has been at least as common as psychological studies of a writer's state of mind, and the two have often gone together.

A genetic approach

As we have seen, critics such as Edmund Wilson have inquired into the social factors affecting the attitude of Dickens, for example, or Kipling, thus seeking sociological causes of psychological phenomena, the psychological phenomena themselves being then used to explain or, genetically, to account for the characteristics of the writer's work.

The problems which arise in any discussion of the relation between sociology and criticism are similar to, and in some respects identical with, those posed by the relation between criticism and psychology. In each case a genetic approach is involved, a consideration of the work in terms of its origins, whether individual or social or both. Three preliminary questions suggest themselves. First: Are the sciences (or pseudo-sciences), in terms of which these origins are explained, themselves normative or are they merely descriptive—do they enable us to pass relative judgments of worth and value, or do they merely tell us what goes on? Second: If they are normative—if we have criteria on which to form value judgments about states of mind and kinds of society—can judgments which are made about the conditions of origin of a literary work be transferred to the literary work itself? Third: If they are not normative, what kind of value can data concerning the psychological or sociological origin of a work possess for the literary *critic* as distinct from the literary *historian*? Let us consider these questions with reference to sociology.

What is sociology?

Is sociology a normative science? To put the question in this way is to assume that it is at least a science, and though this can be debated, and the term "science" itself is not unambiguous in such a context, we can leave that point for the sociologists to wrangle over. We may at least agree that inquiry into the structure of society at any given period of history, and into the modes of behavior that result from that structure, does take place and does yield genuine knowledge. Does the knowledge thus made available provide automatic criteria of social sickness and health? Can the sociologist, in his capacity as sociologist, tell us what forms of social organization are better than others and what particular kinds of social behavior are more and less good? The sociologists themselves would probably be inclined to answer this question in the negative: they would prefer to think of their actions as purely descriptive and not in any degree normative. But though sociology may not in itself be a normative science, it can provide us with knowledge towards which we, as rational and intelligent persons, may adopt a normative attitude. As far as the intelligent layman is concerned, sociology *is* normative, because the intelligent layman is concerned with more than just man as a social animal—he takes all aspects of man into his purview and brings political, ethical, and other notions to bear on the information with which the sociologist provides him. He is the non-specialist humanist, and as such is concerned with relating the specialized studies of the sociologist to man's status and needs as man. He may, for example, interpret sociological data ethically and approve of those social institutions which turn aggressive instincts into other channels or which help to increase the sense of responsibility shown by members of a community to each other while disapproving of institutions serving a contrary function. His criteria will not be drawn from sociology—he will be bringing to bear independently conceived standards of what is good and bad in human behavior—but sociology *will* have provided him with data immediately capable of such treatment. We might go further and say that the data provided by the sociologist cry out for such treatment. Sociology, then, though not in itself a normative science, demands immediate normative treatment as soon as it emerges from the hands of the specialist. We immediately want to ask, when hearing of different kinds of social structure and social convention, which is better, which is more conducive to the good life as we understand it.

Sociological knowledge and the literary critic

Suppose, then, that the experts tell us something about the structure of early eighteenth century society in England, and we—representing as far as sociology is concerned the intelligent layman—make up our minds about the value and significance of that structure: how are we going to apply this to, say, a criticism of the *Spectator* essays? We can, of course, easily relate this information to such questions as the social purpose of the periodical essay, and the reason why such a literary form should arise at this time rather than at any other; we could throw a good deal of light on the tone and choice of subjects of these essays by pointing out that they represent some of the first works of literature addressed specifically to that middle class whose rise in status and influence was symbolized by the revolution of 1689 and who were now faced with the problem of taking over an aristocratic function without an aristocratic tradition. We can use the data provided by the social historian in examining the reasons for reading which prevailed among the class which most eagerly bought the *Spectator* essays; this again will show an interesting correlation between what they read and why they read. These and similar points will be found most helpful by the literary historian in giving an account of the origins and nature of the eighteenth century periodical essay. But how will they help the critic? Can he say that because these essays performed a good social function effectively they are therefore good essays? Clearly, this would be an impossible oversimplification which would result in our treating all literature as rhetoric, the art of persuasion, and judging the rhetoric at least in some degree in accordance with the social worthiness of its objective. Such a view would certainly put *Uncle Tom's Cabin* above *Hamlet* (at least in the eyes of Northern critics).

Let us take another example. Suppose we are interested in the social origins of the "art for art's sake" theories that prevailed at the end of the last century. It would not be difficult (indeed, it has often been done) to relate these theories to the artist's feeling of maladjustment which in turn was produced by the development of industrial society in the nineteenth century and the resulting social attitude of the dominant middle class. These are illuminating facts, and no man of letters would wish to be without them. They advance understanding—but exactly how are they to be used by the critic? If we value art we are bound to take a poor view of a social organization which removes the artist further and further away from his fellow men and leaves him the position either of licensed clown or despised eccentric. Must the critic, then, assume that any new literary forms or devices introduced by writers at this time as a result of the operation of such factors are to be deplored?

As a final example, consider the breakdown of community belief, and the consequent development of private worlds, in modern society; this breakdown derives at least in part from social and economic causes, and it has certainly had an incalculable effect on literary techniques. It has meant, among other things, a remarkable enlargement of the scope of the novel through the writer's being forced to rely on a personal sense of insight rather than on a social sense of value. This has affected style, plot, vocabulary, subject matter—every aspect of the art of fiction. Or consider the modern poet's problem in trying to find a language of symbols to replace those communally held myths which for the first time in many centuries are now no longer tenable even without literal belief. Sociology can help us to see why Joyce wrote as he did, why so much of the most sensitive modern poetry is obscure—but what can it tell us about the value of

Joyce's way of writing or of obscurity in poetry? Are we to disapprove of the enlargement of the scope of the novel because it has social origins which, on any reasonable standard of health in society, most of us would deplore? To take an analogy from medicine: if it could be shown (and the attempt has been made) that Keats' genius flowered as and when it did because he suffered from tuberculosis, are we to conclude that Keats' poetry is therefore bad—or that tuberculosis is therefore good?

Sociological value and literary value

The answer to the second question posed above—can we transfer value judgments about kinds of society to the literary works produced by those kinds of society?—must thus be a tentative negative. We certainly cannot do so in any direct or simple way. Of course, if we believe that if the cause is undesirable the effect must automatically be so, then we shall return a clear affirmative answer to this question. If we believe that because a flood disaster is a bad thing any example of human courage which it provokes must also be bad; if we believe that value in the cause can be transferred unchanged to the effect and that any literary development that arises out of social conditions of which we disapprove must itself be worthy of disapproval—then we have a simple unicellular approach to life and all its problems and need not concern ourselves at all with literary value as distinct from other kinds of value. The more popular type of Marxist critic who is often extremely illuminating when he points to causes (for example, explaining the attitude of Defoe in his novels as arising from his economic and class interests) has nothing to say as a *critic*, as someone appraising literary works on literary grounds, for he simply carries over his view of the social cause to his evaluation of the effect. Thus, believing that the social conditions that helped to produce the esthetic attitude of, say, James Joyce, were undesirable conditions, he might assume that *Ulysses* is therefore an undesirable work. Similarly, a work which arises out of good social conditions, or good social attitudes, would be a good work. Many non-Marxists might agree that the social factors which helped to make Joyce look at life the way he did were factors we should like to eliminate, but they might at the same time recognize the literary interest and value of what these social factors led Joyce to do. More serious and responsible Marxists have, however, found a way of relating their analysis of history to a normative view of the literary work, as the discussion of Georg Lukács below illustrates.

If we believe in literary criticism at all—as distinct from literary history and from mere explanation and description—we must believe that there are criteria of literary excellence derived from the nature of literature itself. We know what a good table is, a good radio, a good loaf of bread. Now we may hold that an individual craftsman working with a pride in his own skill can turn out a better table than a man working in a mass production factory. We may make such a judgment because we know what we want in a table and we discover on inspection that a table made under the former conditions is a better table, according to our ideas of what a table should be, than that made under the latter. We may go on to show *why* mass production is a feature of modern civilization and why it is economically or socially impossible for us today to have our tables made by individual craftsmen: we may, that is to say, explain the conditions under which good and bad tables come to be made: but this explanation only adds to understanding because we started with an independent criterion of what a good table is. We cannot say that a table's badness consists in its being mass produced: we can say (if that is what we believe) that it is bad because of its design, because its shape, size, decoration or some other of its qualities as a table is of *this* kind rather than of *that*, and add the new knowledge that this kind of badness is liable to result when tables are made under modern conditions of manufacture. We have not gone outside our theory of tables in order to discover what a bad table is, but we *have* gone outside it in order to explain, at least partially, how this table came to be bad in this way.

The critic of tables who immediately sees a table as bad when told that it is made under conditions of which he disapproves either means that it is bad not as a table but as a social product—it is made possible by conditions that are socially undesirable—and that is not judging the table as a table at all; or, if he really thinks he is judging the table as a table, he is simply confused. And it is not only the Marxists who have fallen into one or other of these categories: the art criticism of John Ruskin continually falls into the confusion of a man who is sensitive to esthetic values as such yet keeps insisting that good art is only that which is produced by good social and ethical conditions.

The point might be illustrated by another analogy. In the years after Hitler became the political leader of Germany, many people in America and elsewhere refused to buy, for example, Rhine wine because they did not want to give economic support to a régime they detested. They refused to buy wine from Germany because they thoroughly disapproved of the social and political conditions prevailing in Germany at the time. But they remained fond of Rhine wine, and few believed that the Liebfraumilch produced under Hitler was any worse than that produced under the Weimar Republic.

It is true that this is not a very accurate analogy, because a work of literary art often bears the stamp of its social origin in its very texture in a way that a table or a bottle of wine does not. We often, in fact, require the assistance of the social historian to explain to us what a work of art really is, as we have noted in discussing the relation to criticism of historical scholarship. Before we can evaluate anything we must know what it truly is, and that is one of the links between history (and sociology) and criticism and between the genetic and the evaluative approach. Sometimes (though by no means always) if we see how a thing has come to be what it is we are in a better position to appreciate what it really is and thus to evaluate it for what it is. Is a painting meant to hang in a gallery or to decorate the walls of a particular church? Is a lyric meant to be sung to the lute, read aloud, or meditated in the study? Is *Gulliver's Travels* a child's adventure story or a satire on mankind? If the first object of the critic is to see the work in itself as it really is, the sociologist, like the historian, can often help him. But once he has seen what it is, he must apply a criterion suitable to the nature of what he sees.

Descriptive function of sociological criticism

Sociological criticism can, then, help us to avoid making mistakes about the nature of the work of literature we have before us, by throwing light on its function or on the conventions with reference to which certain aspects of it are to be understood. It has therefore an important *descriptive* function, and as accurate description must precede evaluation it can be called a handmaid of criticism. And a very important handmaid it often is. If we read Chaucer's *Troilus and Criseyde* with a knowledge of the courtly love tradition in the light of which so much of its action is developed, we can see the work more clearly, we know better what we are dealing with, and we can proceed to evaluate it with all the more confidence.

Sociological explanation of the characteristics of an age

But sociological criticism has perhaps a more important function than this. It can greatly advance knowledge by helping the reader to see why some faults are characteristic of works of a certain period—can even help to explain the nature of such faults, though the discovery that they are faults is made with reference to purely literary standards. One does not go to the social historian to discover that certain kinds of sentimentality—such as that which mars the ending of Barrie's *The Little Minister*—represent a literary fault; the social historian, however, by drawing our attention to the social causes of sentimentality, can assist us to a deeper understanding of what sentimentality really is. If we are puzzled by the difference in tone between the first part of the *Romance of the Rose*, written by Guillaume de Lorris, and its continuation by Jean de Meun, the social historian can help us by showing the tone of the first part as characteristic of a certain social class at a certain period and that of the second as deriving from an author whose mode of thought was to some extent conditioned by the mental habits of a new and rising class. This helps to explain what has been going on in the work, and in turn helps us to see it more clearly. The critic notes a quality (as fault or as virtue or as neutral); the social historian, like the psychologist, can help to explain why this particular quality can be found in that writer.

The sociological critic in action

Studies of the social background of an author's work, and of the influence of that background on that work, are of necessity of some length, for they involve first the description of that background and then the investigation of individual works with that description in mind. It is not easy, therefore, to do justice to this critical approach in a fairly brief quotation. *The Dickens World*, by Humphry House,[1]

---

[1] Oxford University Press, 1941.

an admirable example of sociological criticism, makes its points by alternating between sections giving accounts of the changing historical scene in Dickens' day and illustrations of the reflection of this changing scene in Dickens' novels. The author's statement of his purpose shows clearly what this kind of study hopes to achieve:

This book will attempt to show in a broad and simple way the connexion between what Dickens wrote and the times in which he wrote it, between his reformism and some of the things he wanted reformed, between the attitude to life shown in his books and the society in which he lived. It will be concerned a good deal with facts, and illustrated with quotations from miscellaneous sources; for it is only in such details that a writer's environment can be seen and his purposes understood; the exact language of contemporaries alone can have the authentic tone and idiom necessary to conviction. With an author so variously and intricately wound into the history of his time the workings of his imagination can often best be seen from others' views of the events with which he started. . . .

Some notion of the sociological critic in action can be got from the following quotation from the sixth chapter ("The Changing Scene") of House's book:

Dickens lived through the years which saw the making of modern England, and of the middle-class oligarchy which is its government. His boyhood ended with the struggles for Catholic Emancipation and the Reform Bill: his writing life coincided almost exactly with the rule of the Ten-Pound Householders. Middle-class government then meant middle-class reform—the assault on obsolete privileges and procedure [Mr. House, in another chapter, discusses how such assaults enter into the very fabric of Dickens' novels], the abolition of restraints on trade, industry, and acquisitiveness, and the painful construction of a legal and administrative system adapted to the conditions which gave the middle classes their power.

The technical achievements of the years between 1812 and 1870 had a far greater effect on those who saw them than any such achievements since: railways altered the whole pattern of the country's life more deeply than cars or aeroplanes. For us, accustomed to ever-accelerating change, it is difficult to recover the mood of mixed utilitarian satisfaction and emotional excitement with which railway, telegraph, and submarine cable were greeted. Our grandfathers were enthralled by such books as Lardner's on the steam-engine and his *Museum of Science and Art* 'illustrated by engravings on wood.' The cuts of cranks and valves provoked them to something like aesthetic enthusiasm; the titbits of astronomy and geology made them think seriously, and often with disastrous result, about the Creation of the World; the chapters on cables and telegraphs urged them irresistibly to quote the boast of Puck. The more thoughtful perhaps shared something of Carlyle's apprehension, first voiced in 1829, that mechanization of external life might mean a baleful mechanization of the mind. But all alike, after a first hesitation or resistance, were compelled to accept the new world and the social changes that it brought: all were part of it, and there was no more escape for Dickens than for anybody else.

Some measure of the changes can be made if we compare *Pickwick* with *Our Mutual Friend*. The books are plainly by the same author; but when all allowances have been made for the obvious differences of form, theme, mood, and setting, for the influence of Dickens's private life upon his art, for developments in his art itself, it still remains clear that the two books are the product of different climates. It is sometimes said in discussions of Dickens's technique as a novelist that any of his great characters could step out of one book into another without materially disturbing the arrangement of either. But if we try to imagine Sam Weller in *Our Mutual Friend* the limitations of this formal criticism are at once plain. The physique, features, and complexion of the characters have changed between the two books almost as much as their clothes: the grimaces of villains have conformed to a new fashion; manners are so altered that one would as little expect that Boffin should get drunk as that John Harmon should fight a duel. We feel that people use knives and forks in a different style. Everybody is more restrained. The eccentrics and monsters in the earlier books walk through a crowd without exciting particular attention: in the latter they are likely to be pointed at in the streets, and are forced into bitter seclusion; social conformity has taken on a new meaning. Silas Wegg and Mr. Venus are at odds and ends with their world as Daniel Quilp was not. The middle classes are more self-important, the lower less self-assured. London, though vastly bigger in extent, is smaller in mystery: it has been opened up by the police. The whole scene seems narrower, more crowded, and, in a peculiar way, more stuffy. The very air seems to have changed in quality, and to tax the powers of Sanitary Reform to the uttermost. In *Pickwick* a bad smell was a bad smell; in *Our Mutual Friend* it is a problem.

These changes cannot be attributed to machinery only, nor to any one cause: but the cumulative effect of difference is so striking that it is impossible to understand Dickens without following in some detail the impact of external changes on his work. . . . [Mr. House then quotes from contemporary accounts of these external changes.]

The general chronology of *Dombey and Son* works out quite well if we assume that the book's plot ended with the writing of it in 1848. Florence was then the mother of a son old enough to talk intelligently about his 'poor little uncle': supposing she was then twenty-one or two, Paul would have been born about 1833 and died 1840-1. This fits some of the main episodes that can be dated by historical events. The journey of Dombey and the Major to Leamington happened soon after Paul's death: the London and Birmingham Railway, by which they travelled, was fully opened in September 1838, and the Royal Hotel, Leamington, at which they stayed, was pulled down about 1841-2. In describing the Leamington scenes Dickens was obviously drawing on memories of a holiday he had there with Hablot Browne in the autumn of 1838; and Browne was their illustrator. Mr. Carker's death at Paddock Wood station was only possible after 1844, when the branch line was opened from there to Maidstone. The book and the period thus hang together without any serious problems of anachronism. In it there is still a lot from the 1820's. Sol Gills with his decaying, out-of-date business, and even the Dombey firm itself, living on the worn maxim, ill-observed, of a pushing eighteenth-century merchant, are intended to appear as survivals from another age. On the whole the book shows an emotional as well as a practical "consciousness of living in a world of change," an apprehension of what the changes meant in detail every day, the new quality of life they brought. *Dombey*, more than any other of his major works, shows how quickly and surely Dickens could sense the mood of his time, and incorporate new sensations in imaginative literature.

The new mood and atmosphere are very largely caused by the railways: the publication of the book coincided with the railway mania of the middle 'forties. It would be hard to exaggerate the effect of those years on English social life. Practically the whole country was money-mad; the public attitude to investment was quite altered, and it then first became clear that Joint Stock companies, however imperfectly managed, were certain to become a permanent and influential feature of finance. Railway works helped to absorb the unemployed and so to remove the fear of revolution. The growth of home consumption was enormously accelerated by improved transport: diet, furniture, fireplaces, and all the physical appurtenances of life changed character more rapidly; the very landscape was given a new aesthetic character—even perhaps a new standard—by embankments, cuttings, and viaducts. But, above all, the scope and tempo of individual living were revolutionized, even for a workman and his family, on a Parliamentary train.

Mr. House then goes on to note the impact of these changes on Dickens' novels, emphasizing particularly the effects he got by contrasting the new world of railways with the dying world of stagecoaches. He shows, too, how, by describing the changing countryside as viewed by a passenger sitting in a train and looking out of the window, he can give a panoramic picture of the new industrial England and point the contrast between living conditions in the congested factory areas and the spacious dwelling of the country landowners.

Against this detailed social background, Mr. House then discusses a number of the novels, which emerge with some of their features more clearly visible than they would be to the reader who has not had his attention drawn to the social and economic factors at work on their author's attitude. For example:

Great Expectations is the perfect expression of a phase of English society: it is a statement, to be taken as it stands, of what money can do, good and bad; of how it can change and make distinctions of class; how it can pervert virtue, sweeten manners, open up new fields of enjoyment and suspicion. The mood of the book belongs not to the imaginary date of its plot, but to the time in which it was written; for the unquestioned assumptions that Pip can be transformed by money and the minor graces it can buy, and that the loss of one fortune can be repaired on the strength of incidental gains in voice and friends, were only possible in a country secure in its internal economy, with expanding markets abroad: this could be hardly be said of England in the 'twenties and 'thirties [when the action was supposed to have taken place].

Pip's acquired "culture" was an entirely bourgeois thing: it came to little more than accent, table manners, and clothes. In these respects a country gentleman with an estate in a remoter part of England would probably have been, even at Queen Victoria's accession, more like the neighbouring farmers than like Mr. Dombey. The process of diffusing standard "educated," London and Home Counties, speech as the norm expected of a gentleman was by no means complete: its rapid continuance through the Dickens period was an essential part of the increasing social uniformity between the middle and upper classes, helped on by the development of the "public" schools.

We are told that Pip "read" a great deal, and that he enjoyed it; but we do not know what he read, or how it affected his mind, or what kind of pleasures he got from it. He knew enough about Shakespeare and acting to realize that Mr. Wopsle turned Waldengarver was ridiculous; but what other delights he found in theatre-going in his prosperous days we are left to judge for ourselves; painting and music certainly had no large part in his life. People like Pip, Herbert Pocket, and Traddles have no culture but domestic comfort and moral decency. They are sensitive, lovable, and intelligent, but their normal activities are entirely limited to a profession and a fireside. When one of their kind extends his activities beyond this range it is in the direction of "social work," and even that is likely to be governed by his profession, as Allan Woodcourt is a good doctor, and Mr. Milvey a good parson. David Copperfield's other activity is to write novels like *Great Expectations* and *David Copperfield:* so we come full circle. . . .

Here the sociological critic has illuminated certain features of literary works by drawing our attention to the way in which social changes and other social factors are mirrored in them. He is not assessing value; he is throwing searchlights from new angles and, like the historical scholar and the psychological critic, spotlights aspects of the works he discusses by explaining how they came to be what they are. The pattern that emerges under this searchlight is not the "true" or the "complete" pattern of the work—no single pattern is. But it is a pattern which, if we bear it in mind when looking at the work from other points of view, can add its share to increased perception and enjoyment. For works of literary art are multiple things, with many meanings growing out of each other, and no one critic or school of critics can exhaust their significance.

With what kinds of work is sociological criticism most helpful?

It can be argued that sociological criticism is most usefully applied to certain kinds of prose works, and less usefully to lyric poetry. The prose novel in English has, until fairly recent times, been largely a public instrument, dependent for its pattern of meaning on agreement between the writer and his public about the significance of human action and the nature of morality, while the lyric poet tends to communicate a more private vision of reality. Robinson Crusoe, on finding himself alone on his island, did not seek to exploit his loneliness by meditation on the relation between the individual and the universe: his task was to recreate in this distant isolation the skeleton at least of the civilization he had left behind him—complete with umbrella. For the English novel depended on society, and on public agreement about what, among the multifarious details of daily life, was worth picking out as significant. What was significant was what altered a social relationship—love and marriage, quarreling and reconciliation, gain or loss of money or of social status. You could, of course, criticize society, but you did it by showing how social convention did not in fact lead to that generally-approved practical morality which it professed to foster. You could explore the relation between spontaneity of feeling and social convention, as Jane Austen did, or the relation between gentility and morality, as Thackeray did, or the effect of industrial society on private character, as Dickens did, or investigate the possibilities of self-knowledge and vocation in a context of society at work, as George Eliot did, but in every case the plot would be carried forward by public symbols. And in every case society is *there*, to be taken account of and accepted as a basic fact about human life even when the author wishes to attack it or alter it. The eighteenth and nineteenth century novel is therefore a particularly happy hunting ground for the sociological critic, and the student might ask himself what sociological questions can profitably be asked about, for example, the novels of Richardson, Jane Austen, Dickens, Thackeray and George Eliot. But with such a novelist as Emily Brontë, who worked with a poet's kind of imagination, the sociological approach is perhaps less fruitful. Similarly, with the twentieth century novel, we can perhaps profitably ask sociological questions about Wells, Galsworthy, Dos Passos, even (though in his own way he operates as a poet) Faulkner, but what about Virginia Woolf, D. H. Lawrence, and Hemingway? (Hemingway, though he apparently deals with man in society, is, in his best novels, constructing heroic myths which derive from an essentially poetic sensibility. Lawrence's social origins can be usefully investigated by those interested in his psychology, but the relevance of such investigation to an understanding of the way in which his imagination works in his novels is surely dubious.) These are distinctions which the reader would do well to consider, whatever the conclusions he may reach.

On the other hand, a sociological approach has been brought to bear on poetry, not only by the Marxists (who endeavor to explain works of literature by relating them to their origins in the individual's response to the class situation in which he finds himself) but by such a critic as F. W. Bateson, in his *English Poetry: A Critical Introduction* (1950). Bateson's tenth chapter is a discussion of Gray's "Elegy" which contrasts sharply in method with Cleanth Brooks' analysis of the poem in *The Well Wrought Urn*. Bateson starts from the fact that the "Elegy" was composed in two installments, the second (which contains the last fifty-six lines) inferior to the first. The second part of the "Elegy," Bateson argues, is an unsuccessful attempt to depersonalize it after a brilliant first section in which the plangent contrast between "the natural, almost animal life of the village" and "the futile artificial life of the 'Proud' " presents the Gray of 1742 (friendless and dependent) arraigning the Gray of 1741 (before the death of his only intimate friend, Richard West). After an interesting analysis of the way in which symbolic images operate in the poem, Bateson concludes: "The *Elegy*, in addition to all the other things that it is, was a tract for the times. It was a plea for decentralization, recalling the over-urbanized ruling class to its roots in a rural society based upon the benevolent despotism of the manor-house."

Bateson divides the history of English poetry into six consecutive schools—Anglo-French, Chaucerian, Renaissance, Augustan, Romantic, and Modern, and distinguishes six consecutive social orders to which they correspond—the Period of Lawyers' Feudalism, the Local Democracy of the Yeomanry, the Centralized Absolutism of the Prince's Servants, the Oligarchy of the Landed Interests, the Plutocracy of Business, and the Managerial State. Then he proceeds to relate particular poems to the social organization of their period, showing how attitude, image, state of mind, are in each case related to the poet's response to the social world of which he was a part. The titles of his chapters are instructive: "The Yeoman Democracy and Chaucer's 'Miller's Tale,' " "The Money-Lender's Son: 'L'Allegro' and 'Il Penseroso,' " "The Quickest Way out of Manchester: Four Romantic Odes," and so on. Brief quotation does serious injustice to the cogency and closeness of Bateson's reasoning, but perhaps this conclusion to his essay on Waller will help to illustrate his method:

This central contradiction is the ultimate explanation of the pretentiousness and the emptiness of much Augustan poetry. With no mystical or traditional basis of authority on the one hand, and no rational basis on the other, except in the single field of agricultural improvement [Bateson has previously discussed in some detail the agricultural improvements of the period], the ruling class could only justify its privileges in the eyes of the nation by being an *aristocracy*, living in the best houses, eating the best food, reading the best books and patronizing the best poets. Hence their "ritual of conspicuous waste"—Palladian mansions that were too large to live in, Pindaric odes that were too dull to read. None of the Augustan poets entirely resolves the contradiction, and there is therefore no Augustan poem that can quite be called great, but the better poets succeed in mitigating it. Waller's "Panegyric to my Lord Protector," Dryden's "Secular Masque," Rochester's "Satyr against Mankind," Pope's portrait of Lord Timon (in the fourth "Moral Essay"), and Gray's brilliant "On Lord Holland's Seat near Margate" go some way at any rate to salving the period's social conscience.[2]

Another important recent work which endeavors to explain the

2 Reprinted by permission of Longmans, Green & Co., Ltd.

tone of works of literature with reference to the social context and to enable us to see their literary qualities more clearly by showing us how they reflect the writer looking at his world is *Poets on Fortune's Hill*, by John F. Danby (1952). The following quotation from Danby's introductory chapter will make clear his point of view:[3]

> The picture of the Hill of Fortune, and of literature bound to the patronage of either Great House or Public Theatre, already makes the Elizabethan-Jacobean scene less monolithic than it is sometimes imagined. Taking the image further, increasing complications become evident. The Hill has different levels and different sides. Movements up and down, and around and about, or movements combining both these, are possible. Different views are to be expected from different positions on the Hill. Elizabethan society is as highly differentiated as any other. Literature is what happens "in" a man, certainly. What can happen "in" him, however, will be partly conditioned by what has happened "to" him in virtue of his place and behaviour on the Hill. Finally, literature is addressed by a man from his place to those of his contemporaries (on the same Hill) who are in a position to listen to him. . . . Literature has a three-dimensional setting. Very often it is reduced in the study to something as two-dimensional as the paper it is written on.
>
> Some of the differences between specific works might best be accounted for in terms of social placing. The *Arcadia* is Great House literature, and Sidney the interpreter of the *ethos* of the Great House. Shakespeare's plays belong to the open town, the open Elizabethan country, and the unroofed commercial theatre. Beaumont and Fletcher are curious hybrids: second-generation scions of the Elizabethan *élite*, and second-generation exploiters of a theatre now no longer, possibly, open to the sky. . . .
>
> A recognition of the social placing of the writers concerned helps, I think, towards a clearer view of how matters stand between them on these questions [of influence and impact and changes in style]. And not only that. The question of "influences" ceases to be academic, eccentrically driving away from the text. When "influences" are seen in relation to social placing, and when social place is seen to imply a whole *ethos*, intellectual, temperamental, and spiritual, the question of "influence" takes on a new significance. It is brought into relation with the essential quality of the work itself, as written by a man from his place. It is, in other words, made relevant to a just appreciation of what the work under consideration *is*, and not merely what it is "derived" from.

The pure formalist might say that Danby's investigations might show us "what the work under consideration *is*" but not what it is *qua*

[3] Reprinted by permission of Faber and Faber Limited.

work of literary art. But there can be little doubt that this method, properly used, does help us to see why certain poets and dramatists wrote as they did, and what the moral pattern of their work really is. It also illuminates differences between contemporary poets. Consider, for example, this statement:

Sidney is on the top of Fortune's hill, whereas Spenser is not. Spenser's poetry must win him preferment, and then maintain him in place in the body of the world. For Sidney poetry is the private devotion to truth. For Spenser it must also be the public vindication of his claim to recognition as a poet, a proof that the poet as such is engaged on work of national importance. There is therefore in Spenser a professional earnestness, an earnestness not only about "truth" but also an earnestness to display his command over all the poetic crafts. His poetry requires the external occasion, the prescriptions of theory and form, the suggested topic; and in its most ambitious assay of skill it will load story with allegory, and allegory with morality, and morality with platonism, to form a massive assembly of all the by-products of renaissance learning and art. . . .

Such an approach, used in a discussion of Sidney's *Arcadia* as "the Great House Romance," of the relation between Sidney's work and the late-Shakespearean romance, and of other aspects of Shakespeare and of Beaumont and Fletcher, can not only explain the reasons for certain features of their work which we already know; it can also draw our attention to literary qualities in their work which we had not before clearly seen. Thus sociological criticism can help to increase literary perception as well as to explain origins.

Marxist Criticism: Georg Lukács

The thoughtful Marxist critic who prides himself on the "dialectical" nature of his insights into both society and history will not be content with any genetic explanation of the origins or the characteristics of a literary work. Believing as he does that Marxism provides a uniquely "correct" insight into social structures and historical forces and their cultural super-structure, he can, with Georg Lukács, dismiss as practitioners of "vulgar sociology" critics who are content to discuss social factors and correlations in a merely descriptive manner and instead endeavor to show how a writer's stature depends on his insights into the realities of social and historical forces (realities as "correctly" understood by a Marxist analysis) which he depicts with power and conviction often in spite of his political beliefs. The Hungarian Marxist Georg Lukács has written especially well on Walter Scott (and the historical novel in general) and on Balzac (and "European realism" in general) precisely because he sees them as rendering profound insights into social and political reality, vividly particularized in individual examples, in spite of being conservative in their conscious political views. Balzac was a Catholic royalist and Zola was a left-wing reformer, but Lukács sees the former as the greater writer because he saw the significant truth about what was happening in society however wrongly he may have interpreted then in his own personal political views.

The central intellectual problem of realism is the adequate presentation of the complete human personality. But as in every profound philosophy of art, here, too, the consistent following-up to the end of the aesthetic viewpoint leads us beyond pure aesthetics: for art, precisely if taken in its most perfect purity, is saturated with social and moral humanistic problems. The demand for a realistic creation of types is in opposition both to the trends in which the biological being of man, the physiological aspects of self-preservation and procreation are dominant (Zola and his disciples) and to the trends which sublimate man into purely mental, psychological processes. But such an attitude, if it remained within the sphere of formal aesthetic judgments, would doubtless be quite arbitrary, for there is no reason why, regarded merely from the point of view of good writing, erotic conflict with its attendant moral and social conflicts should be rated higher than the elemental spontaneity of pure sex. Only if we accept the concept of the complete human personality as the social and historical task humanity has to solve; only if we regard it as the vocation of art to depict the most important turning-points of this process with all the wealth of the factors affecting it; only if aesthetics assign to art the role of explorer and guide, can the content of life be systematically divided up into spheres of greater and lesser importance; into spheres that throw light on types and paths and spheres that remain in darkness. Only then does it become evident that any description of mere biological processes—be these the sexual act or pain and sufferings, however detailed and from the literary point of view perfect it may be—results in a levelling-down of the social, historical and moral being of men and is not a means but an obstacle to such essential artistic expression as illuminating human conflicts in all their complexity and completeness. It is for this reason that the new contents and new media of expression contributed by naturalism have led not to an enrichment but to an impoverishment and narrowing-down of literature. . . .

An unbiased investigation of life and the setting aside of these false traditions of modern literature leads easily enough to the uncovering of the true circumstances, to the discovery which had long been made by the great realists of the beginning and middle of the nineteenth century and which Gottfried Keller expressed thus: "Everything is politics." The great Swiss writer did not intend this to mean that everything was immediately tied up with politics: on the contrary, in his view–as in Balzac's and Tolstoy's–every action, thought and emotion of human beings is inseparably bound up with the life and struggles of the community, i.e., with politics; whether the humans themselves are conscious of this, unconscious of it or even trying to escape from it, objectively their actions, thoughts and emotions nevertheless spring from and run into politics.

The true great realists not only realized and depicted this situation–they did more than that, they set it up as a demand to be made on men. They knew that this distortion of objective reality (although, of course, due to social causes), this division of the complete human personality into a public and a private sector was a mutilation of the essence of man. Hence they protested not only as painters of reality, but also as humanists, against this fiction of capitalist society however unavoidable this spontaneously formed superficial appearance. If as writers, they delved deeper in order to uncover the true types of man, they had inevitably to unearth and expose to the eyes of modern society the great tragedy of the complete human personality.

In the works of such great realists as Balzac we can again find a third solution opposed to both false extremes of modern literature, exposing as an abstraction, as a vitiation of the true poesy of life, both the feeble commonplaces of the well-intentioned and honest propagandist novels and the spurious richness of a preoccupation with the details of private life.

This brings us face to face with the question of the topicality today of the great realist writers. Every great historical period is a period of transition, a contradictory unity of crisis and renewal, of destruction and rebirth; a new social order and a new type of man always come into being in the course of a unified though contradictory process. In such critical, transitional periods the tasks and responsibility of literature are exceptionally great. But only truly great realism can cope with such responsibilities; the accustomed, the fashionable media of expression, tend more and more to hamper literature in fulfilling the tasks imposed by history. It might more legitimately surprise many that these studies express a sharp opposition to Zola and Zolaism.

Such surprise may be due in the main to the fact that Zola was a writer of the left and his literary methods were dominant chiefly, though by no means exclusively, in left-wing literature. It might appear, therefore, that we are involving ourselves in a serious contradiction, demanding on the one hand the politization of literature and on the other hand attacking insidiously the most vigorous and militant section of left-wing literature. But this contradiction is merely apparent. It is, however, well suited to throw light on the true connection between literature and *Weltanschauung*.

The problem was first raised (apart from the Russian democratic literary critics) by Engels, when he drew a comparison between Balzac and Zola. Engels showed that Balzac, although his political creed was legitimist royalism, nevertheless inexorably exposed the vices and weakness of royalist feudal France and described its death agony with magnificent poetic vigour. This phenomenon, references to which the reader will find more than once in these pages, may at the first glance again–and mistakenly–appear contradictory. It might appear that the *Weltanschauung* and political attitude of serious great realists are a matter of no consequence. To a certain extent this is true. For from the point of view of the self-recognition of the present and from the point of view of history and posterity, what matters is the picture conveyed by the work; the question to what extent this picture conforms to the views of the authors is a secondary consideration.

This, of course, brings us to a serious problem of aesthetics. Engels, in writing about Balzac, called it "the triumph of realism"; it is a problem that goes down to the very roots of realist artistic creation. It touches the essence of true realism: the great writer's thirst for truth, his fanatic striving for reality–or expressed in terms of ethics: the writer's sincerity and probity. A great realist such as Balzac, if the intrinsic artistic development of situations and characters he has created comes into conflict with his most cherished prejudices or even his most sacred convictions, will, without an instant's hesitation, set aside these his own prejudices and convictions and describe what he really sees, not what he would prefer to see. This ruthlessness towards their own subjective world-picture is the hall-mark of all great realists, in sharp contrast to the second-raters, who nearly always succeed in bringing their own *Weltanschauung* into "harmony" with reality, that is forcing a falsified or distorted picture of reality into the shape of their own world-view. This difference in the ethical attitude of the greater and lesser writers is closely linked with the difference between genuine and spurious creation. The characters created by the great realists, once conceived in the vision of their creator, live an independent life of their own: their comings and goings, their development, their destiny is dictated by the inner dialectic of their social and individual existence. No writer is a true realist–or even a truly good writer, if he can direct the evolution of his own characters at will. . . .

The greatness of Balzac's art rests, says Marx, "on a deep understanding of real conditions," i.e., of the conditions governing the development of French capitalism. We have shown how faithfully Balzac depicted the specific traits of the three warring factions and how well he understood the peculiarities in the development of all classes of society in France since the revolution of 1789. But such a statement would be incomplete if it disregarded the other side of the dialectic of class evolution i.e., the continuity of the evolutionary trends from the French revolution onwards, or rather from the emergence of a *bourgeois* class in France and the beginning of the struggle between feudalism and absolute monarchy. The deep comprehension of this continuity of development was the foundation on which the great edifice of the *Human Comedy* was built. Revolution, Empire, restoration and July monarchy were in Balzac's eyes merely stages in the great, continuous and contradictory process in which the irresistible and the atrocious are inseparably linked together. . . .

This overall conception of the process of capitalist evolution enabled Balzac to uncover the great social and economic forces which govern historical development, although he never does so in direct fashion.

In Balzac's writings social forces never appear as romantic and fantastic monsters, as superhuman symbols (as e.g. later in Zola). On the contrary Balzac dissolves all social relationships into a network of personal clashes of interests, objective conflicts between individuals, webs of intrigue, etc. He never, for instance, depicts justice or the courts of law as institutions independent of society and standing above it. Only certain petty bourgeois characters in his novels imagine the law courts to be that. A law court is always presented by Balzac as consisting of individual judges whose social origins, ambitions and prospects the author describes in great detail. Every participant in the proceedings is shown enmeshed in the real conflicts of interest around which the lawsuit in question is being fought every position taken up by any member of the judiciary depends on the position he occupies in this jungle of conflicting interests. An instance of this are the judicial intrigues in *The Harlot's Progress* or in the *Cabinet of Antiques*.

It is against such a background that Balzac shows the workings of all the great social forces. Each participant in these conflicts of interest is, inseparably from his own purely personal interests, the representative of a certain class, but it is in these purely personal interests and indivisibly from them, that the social cause, the class basis, of these interests find expression. Thus, precisely by stripping the social institutions of their apparent objectivity and seemingly dissolving them into personal relationships, the author contrives to express what is truly objective in them, what is really their social *raison d'être* : their functions as bearers of class interests and as the instruments of enforcing them. The essence of Balzac's realism is that he always reveals social beings as the basis of social consciousness, precisely through and in the contradictions between social being and social consciousness which must necessarily manifest themselves in every class of society. . . .

It is this quality of Balzacian realism, the fact that it is solidly based on a correctly interpreted social existence, that makes Balzac an unsurpassed master in depicting the great intellectual and spiritual forces which form all human ideologies. He does so by tracing them back to their social origins and making them function in the direction determined by these social origins.[1]

"Solidly based on a correctly interpreted social existence." Provided the writer renders the social scene in a way that is consistent with a "correct" Marxist analysis of it, he is both a truth-teller and is to be admired. He may be "correct" in spite of himself, as both Scott and Balzac were in Lukács's view. There is no simple correlation here

[1]George Lukács, *Studies in European Realism*, London, 1972.

between a writer's political views and his merits as an artist. His merits as an artist will depend on the degree to which his renderings of human and social reality are, in themselves and independent of conscious intention, consistent with what a Marxist analysis sees as the "correct" interpretation.

This is normative Marxist criticism, seeking to explain literary phenomena as a preliminary to evaluating them. It is to be distinguished from the cruder kinds of Marxist criticism which gives points to writers in accordance with their degree of sympathy with the workers or the degree to which they reflect reactionary or progressive elements in the society of their time. It is also to be distinguished from those Marxist or quasi-Marxist discussions of cultural phenomena seen as an inevitable part of the whole super-structure of ethical, religious, aesthetic and other values that are the inevitable by-product of underlying economic factors. Lukács would not deny this relationship—indeed as a Marxist he stresses it—but he sees that a recognition of it does not in itself constitute literary criticism.

19

Criticism, linguistics and anthropology

Enlarging the Context

THE THREE subjects listed in the title of this chapter may seem a surprising combination. But in fact one of the most interesting developments in twentieth-century criticism has been the attempt to link the study of the nature and structure of works of literature with both the nature and structure of language and the patterns discussed by the anthropologist in the culture of primitive societies. The man whose work is most associated with this attempt is the French social anthropologist Claude Lévi-Strauss, whose works, in particular *La Pensée Sauvage* (1962 ; English version *The Savage Mind*, 1966) and the three volumes of *Mythlogiques* (1964–68), bring together a variety of insights from different disciplines to explore ways in which man has ordered and interpreted the sensory evidence provided by his environment to transform Nature (the "raw")into Culture (the "cooked"). Such a brief summary of his aims is of course inadequate, and Lévi-Strauss himself writes in such an opaque style that even experts in the French language and in the various disciplines which he calls upon often find themselves at a loss to know his precise meaning. Nevertheless, his work is stimulating and suggestive and has influenced literary critics in a variety of ways.

The starting point for this approach can be said to be the apprehension of the ways in which the human mind transforms Nature into Culture by organizing perceptions into two categories which in information theory are called codes (i.e. the elements of a system that can be used in constructing communicative patterns) and messages (i.e., the use of that system to transmit meaning). Although communication here embraces communication by all sorts of cultural means as well as language, these two categories correspond to a distinction made by the French linguist Ferdinand de Saussure (1857–1913), one of the pioneers of modern linguistics, between *langue* (language) and *parole* (speech). *Langue* is the system of linguistic conventions (e.g. the English language) that is drawn upon in any verbal communication; *parole* is the specific communication in which the speaker uses the conventions provided by the system to construct a particular combination of words (using *these* words in *this* order) in order to communicate meaning. Language is thus one example of a code of signs that can be drawn on to send specific messages. All cultural activities–not only myths but also patterns of social behaviour including sexual and marriage customs, eating habits, conventions of dress, attitudes to animals, etc–represent patterns of signs that, according to Lévi-Strauss, can be studied most directly in the activities of primitive societies to whom the concept of historical change is unknown and who see their own way of life as timeless.

Structuralism

On this view, man's perception of the external world is mediated by a system of ordering and categorizing determined in the final analysis by the nature of our sense organs and the structure of our brain. (Edmund Leach, in his book on Lévi-Strauss, takes as an example our recognition of colour, which derives from the mind's selecting separate single colours from a physically constituted continuum and the use we make of those colours in e.g. traffic lights.) Nature itself is subject to a prior ordering before we can make sense of our perceptions of it, while Culture is built up of a complex pattern of relations of signs which derive ultimately from the way we apprehend Nature. It is by examining the structure of these sign-patterns that we can see what is involved in cultural phenomena, of which literature is one example. Hence arises the critical technique known as "structuralism", developed by another French critic Roland Barthes (*Elements of Semiology*, 1967) whose distinction between what he calls *system* (in language, clothes, food, furniture, etc.) and *syntagm* corresponds in some degree to the distinction between code and message. In all cultural behaviour there is a structured use of signs (verbal or non-verbal) which provides meaning. Structuralism is thus applicable to many more activities than literature, and it is related to the modern science of "semiology", the study of signs and symbols. As applied to literature, it is the study of the underlying patterns and directions (often unconscious until probed by the structuralist critic) implied by the way language is used in a given literary work. Thus structuralism provides not only a theory of literature but also a mode of practical criticism. How this works is best seen by an example. A particularly lucid one is provided by Jonathan Culler in his essay "Structuralism and Literature" (in *Contemporary Approaches to English Studies*, edited by Hilda Schiff, 1977), of which the following is an extract.

The task of structural analysis, we may then say, is to formulate the underlying systems of convention which enable cultural objects to have meaning for us. In this sense structuralism is not hermeneutic: it is not a method for producing new and startling interpretations of literary works (although in another sense which I shall mention below it *is* hermeneutic). It asks, rather, how the meanings of literary works are possible. . . .

The best way to ease oneself into this structuralist perspective is to take linguistics as a model and to think of the relationship between an utterance and the speaker/hearer. A sentence which I utter comes to you as a series of physical events, a sequence of sounds which we might represent by a phonetic transcription. You hear this sequence of sounds and give it a meaning. The question linguistics asks is how is this possible, and the answer, of course, is that you bring to the act of communication an immense amount of implicit, subconscious knowledge. You have assimilated the phonological system of English which enables you to relate these physical sounds to the abstract and relational phonemes of English; you have assimilated a grammatical system, so complex that we are only beginning to understand it, which enables you to assign a structural description to the sentence, to ascertain the relations among its parts, and to recognize it as grammatically well-formed, even though you have never heard it before; and finally, your knowledge of the semantic component of the language enables you to assign an interpretation to this string of sounds. Now we may say, if we wish, that the phonological and syntactic structure and the meaning are *properties* of the utterance, so long as we remember that they are properties of the utterance only with respect to the complex grammar which speakers of English have assimilated. Without the complex knowledge brought to the communicative act, they have none of these properties.

Moving from language to literature, we find an analogous situation. Imagine someone who knows English but has no knowledge of literature and indeed no acquaintance with the concept of literature. If presented with a poem he would be quite baffled. He would understand words and sentences, certainly, but he would not know what this strange thing was; he would not, quite literally, know what to do with this curious linguistic construction. What he lacks is a complex system of knowledge that experienced readers have acquired, a system of conventions and norms which we might call 'literary competence'. And we can say that just as the task of linguistics is to make explicit the system of a language which makes linguistic communication possible, so in the case of literature a structuralist poetics must enquire what knowledge must be postulated to account for our ability to read and understand literary works.

Lest you be sceptical about the importance of this implicit knowledge that we bring to the act of reading poetry, let me offer a simple and crude example. Take a perfectly ordinary sentence, such as 'Yesterday I went into town and bought a lamp', and set it down on a page as a poem:

> Yesterday I
> Went into town and bought
> A lamp.

The words remain the same, and if meanings change it is because we approach the poem with different expectations and interpretative operations. What sort of thing happens? First of all, 'Yesterday' takes on a different force: it no longer refers to a particular day but to the set of possible yesterdays and serves primarily to set up a temporal opposition within the poem (between present and recent past). This is due to our conventions about the relationship of poems to the moment of utterance. Secondly, we expect the lyric to capture a moment of some significance, to be thematically viable; and we thus apply to 'lamp' and 'bought' conventions of symbolic extrapolation. The traditional associations of *lamp* are obvious; *buying* we can take as one mode of acquisition as opposed to others; and we thus acquire potential thematic material. Thirdly, we expect a poem to be a unified whole and thus we must attempt to interpret the fact that this poem ends so swiftly and inconclusively. The silence at the end can be read as a kind of ironic comment, a blank, and we can set up an opposition between the action of buying a lamp, the attempt to acquire light, and the failure to tell of any positive benefits which result from yesterday's action. This general structure can, of course, support a variety of paraphrases, but any interpretation of the poem is likely to make use of these three elementary operations enshrined in the institution of poetry. The conventions of the lyric create the possibility of new and supplementary meanings.

Note also, and this is important, that though in one sense these meanings are in the poem–they are public, can be argued about, and do not depend upon individual subjective associations–in another sense, which is more important given the current critical climate, they are not *in* the poem. They depend on operations performed by readers (and assumed by poets). . . .

Structuralism leads us to think of the poem not as a self-contained organism but as a sequence which has meaning only in relation to a literary system, or rather, to the 'institution' of literature which guides the reader. The sense of a poem's completeness is a function of the totality of the interpretive process, the result of the way we have been taught to read poems. And to avoid misunderstanding I should perhaps emphasize that, though it is preferable to talk about reading rather than writing, we are dealing with conventions which are assumed by the writer. He is not just setting words down on paper but writing a poem. Even when he is in revolt against the tradition, he still knows what is involved in reading and writing poems; and when he chooses among alternative words or phrases, he does so as a master of reading. . . .

A structuralist approach starts by stressing the artificiality of literature, the fact that though literature may be written in the language of information it is not used in the 'language-game' of giving information. It is obvious, for example, that by convention the relationship of speaker to utterance is different when we are dealing with a poem and with another speech act. The poet does not stand in the same relation to a lyric as to a letter he has written, even if the poem be Ben Jonson's 'Inviting a Friend to Supper'. This initial strangeness, this artifice, is the primary fact with which we have to deal, and we can say that the techniques of reading are ways of simultaneously cherishing and overcoming this strangeness–ways of 'naturalizing' the text and making it something of a communication. To naturalize a text–I use this word in preference to what some of the French theorists call *vraisemblablisation*–is to transform it so that it can be assimilated to an order of *vraisemblance*. This is absolutely basic to the reading of literature, and a simple example would be the interpretation of metaphor. When Shelley writes 'my soul in an enchanted boat' we must, in order to 'understand' this, naturalize the figure; we must perform a semantic transformation on 'enchanted boat' so as to bring it under a particular order of *vraisemblance*, which here we might call 'possible characteristics of the soul'. Of course, the fact that understanding involves more than translation of this kind must be stressed: we must preserve the distance traversed in the act of translation as a sign in its own right. Here, for example, we have a sign of a particular lyric posture, of the poetical character, of the inadequacy of ordinary discourse, and so on.

Now there are various levels at which we can naturalize, various sets of conventions which can be brought into play. And of course these change with the institution of literature itself, so that once a style or mode of discourse becomes established it is possible to naturalize a poem as a comment upon this literary mode. When we read Lewis Carroll's 'A-Sitting on a Gate' as a parody of Wordsworth's 'Resolution and Independence' we naturalize the former and make its strange features intelligible as commentary upon the latter.

The conventions of literature guide the process of naturalization and provide alternatives to what might be called 'premature naturalization'. This is a direct move from poem to utterance which ignores the former's specifically literary characteristics, as if we were to naturalize Donne's 'The Good Morrow' by saying: the poet was in bed with his mistress one morning when the sun rose and, being still befuddled with drink, he uttered this statement in the hope that the sun would go away and shine elsewhere. If one had no knowledge of the institution of literature this is what one might be tempted to do, but even the least advanced student knows that this is an inappropriate step, that he must naturalize at another level which takes into account some of the conventions of literature. The protest to the sun is itself a figure the situation of the utterance of a poem is a fiction which must be incorporated in our interpretation. We are likely to naturalize 'The Good Morrow' as a love poem which uses this situation as an image of energy and annoyance, and hence as a figure for a strong, self-sufficient passion.

This ought at least to indicate what I mean by naturalization: it is the process of making something intelligible by relating it to what is already known and accepted as *vraisemblable*. We are guided in this process by various codes of expectations which we ought to try to make explicit. . . .

The symbolic code is one of the oddest and most difficult to discuss. It is also the code with which students have the greatest difficulty, and both students and teachers ought to attempt to gain clearer notions of what it involves than we have at present. What governs the perception and interpretation of symbols? There are obviously a few symbols, consecrated by tradition, which seem to bear an intrinsic meaning, but most potential symbols are defined by complex relations with a context. The rose, for example, can lead in a variety of directions, and within each of these semantic fields (religion, love, nature) its significance will depend on its place in an oppositional structure. Sun and moon can signify almost anything, provided the opposition between them is preserved. Although, as I say, this code is poorly understood, it seems clear that symbolic extrapolation is a teleological process with a set of goals which limit the range of plausible interpretations and specify what kind of meanings serve as adequate *termini ad quem*. For example, there is a rule of generalization: to be told that in a phrase like 'shine on my bowed head, O moon' the moon symbolizes 'the quarterly production quota set by the district manager' is bathetic. We quickly learn that there is a set of semantic oppositions, such as life and death, simplicity and complexity, harmony and strife, reality and appearance, body and soul, certainty and doubt, imagination and intellect, which are culturally marked as in some way 'ultimate' and hence as goals in the process of symbolic extrapolation. But we ought to be able to say a good deal more about this process which we expect students to master.

After these sketchy indications of the problems involved, I should like to turn by way of example to the kind of fundamental expectations concerning poetry which govern the operation of codes and the process of naturalization. We might start with a short poem by William Carlos Williams:

> This Just to Say
> I have eaten
> the plums
> that were in
> the icebox
>
> and which
> you were probably
> saving
> for breakfast
>
> Forgive me
> they were delicious
> so sweet
> so cold

The fact that this is printed on a page as a poem brings into play our expectations concerning poetry (as sentences in a novel it would, of course, be read differently), the first of which we might call the convention of distance and impersonality. Although at one level the sentences are presented as a note asking forgiveness for eating plums, since poetry is by convention detached from immediate circumstances of utterance we deprive it of this pragmatic function, retaining simply the reference to a context as an implicit statement that this kind of experience is important, worthy of poetry. By doing this we avoid the premature naturalization which says, 'the poet ate the plums and left this note on the table for his wife, writing it as verse because he was a poet'.

Starting then with the assumption that this is not a pragmatic utterance but a lyric in which a fictional 'I' speaks of eating plums, we are faced with the question of what to do with this object, how to structure it. We expect poems to be organic wholes and we possess a variety of models of wholeness: the simplest is the binary opposition which is given a temporal dimension (not X but Y); another is the unresolved opposition (neither X nor Y but both simultaneously); next there is the dialectical resolution of a binary opposition; and finally, remaining with simple models of wholeness, the four-term homology (X is to Y as A is to B) or the series closed and summed up by a transcendent final term. In studying this poem we need to apply a model of completeness so as to secure an opening up of the poem and to establish a thematic structure into which we can fit its elements, which thus become sets of features subject to thematic expansion. Our elementary model of the opposition can here take the thematic form of rule and transgression: the plums were to be saved for breakfast but they have been eaten. We can then group various features on one side or the other: on the side of 'eating' we have 'delicious', 'sweet' and 'cold', stressed by their final position (this is a conventional rule) and implying that eating plums was indeed worth it; on the other side we have the assumed priority of domestic rules about eating (one recognizes them and asks for forgiveness), the reference to 'breakfast', the orderly life represented by the hypostatization of meal-times. The process of thematic interpretation requires us to move from facts towards values, so we can develop each thematic complex, retaining the opposition between them. Thus we have the valuing of immediate sensuous experience, as against an economy of order and saving, which is also valued, though transgressed.

Then, presumably, the question we must ask ourselves is whether this structure is complete: whether the opposition is a simple one, a move from X to Y, or whether the attitude of the poem is in fact more complex and requires us to call upon other models. And here we can take account of what we earlier set aside–the fact that the poem masquerades as a note asking forgiveness. We can say that the poem itself acts as a mediating force, recognizing the priority of conventions (by the fact of writing a note) but also seeking absolution. We can also give a function at this level to the deictics, the 'I' and 'you' which we had set aside, taking the relationship as a figure of intimacy, and say that the note tries to bring this realm of immediate sensuous experience into the realm of interpersonal relations, where there will be tension, certainly, but where (as the abrupt ending of the poem implies) there is hope that intimacy and understanding will resolve the tension.

Although I have been naming and paraphrasing, what I am producing is, of course, a thematic structure which could be stated in various ways. The claim is simply that in interpreting a poem like this we are implicitly relying on assumptions about poetry and structural models without which we could not proceed: that our readings of the poem (which will, of course, differ) depend upon some common interpretive operations.

Interpretation might generally stop here, but if we think about the fact that these sentences are presented as a poem we can go a step further by asking 'why?'. Why should this sort of banal statement be a poem? And here, by an elementary reversal which is crucial to the reading of modern poetry, we can take banality of statement as a statement about banality and say that the world of notes and breakfast is also the world of language, which must try to make a place for this kind of immediate experience which sounds banal and whose value can only be hinted at. This, we could go on to say, is why the poem must be so sparse and apparently incomplete. It must produce, as it were, a felt absence, a sense of missing intensity and profundity, so that in our desire to read the poem and to make it complete we will supply what the poem itself dare not claim: the sense of significance.

Let me turn now to a poem of a rather different kind, one which is usually read as a political statement and act of engagement, Blake's 'London'.

> I wander through each chartered street,
> Near where the chartered Thames does flow,
> And mark in every face I meet
> Marks of weakness, marks of woe.
>
> In every cry of every Man,
> In every Infant's cry of fear,
> In every voice, in every ban,
> The mind-forged manacles I hear.
>
> How the Chimney-sweeper's cry
> Every black'ning Church appalls;
> And the hapless Soldier's sigh
> Runs in blood down Palace walls.
>
> But most thro' midnight streets I hear
> How the youthful Harlot's curse
> Blasts the new-born Infant's tear,
> And blights with plagues the Marriage hearse.

I don't want to suggest that this isn't a political poem, but I would like to impress upon you how much work we must do in order to make it a political statement and what a variety of extremely artificial conventions we must call upon in order to read it in this way.

The poem is organized as a list of things seen and heard: I mark marks; I hear manacles; I hear how. . . . And it is obvious from the outset that the things heard or seen are bad (marks of weakness, marks of woe, manacles, blasts and blights). This gives us our initial opposition between the perceiving subject and the objects of perception and provides a thematic centre which helps us to organize details. We may start with the assumption, based on the convention of unity, that we have a series which will cohere at some level (the second stanza with its repetitions of 'every' is ample warrant for that). But it is quite difficult to produce this coherence. In the third stanza we can try to collate the two propositions in order to discover their common subject: I hear how the cry of the sweep and the sigh of the soldier act upon the church or palace. This gives us a sound (which fits into the series of 'marks' which the 'I' perceives), an actor (who, our cultural model tells us, counts among the oppressed), and an institution which they affect. The opposition between institution and oppressed is one whose parameter we know: the possibilities are those of protest and submission, the results the indifference or guilt of the institution. And in fact the structure which Blake has established is ambiguous enough to preclude our really knowing which to choose here. One critic, citing historical evidence, argues that the sigh of the soldier is the murmur of possible rebellion and that the visionary can already see the blood on palace walls in a native version of the French Revolution. But we can also say, in an alternative naturalization, that the palace is bloody because it is responsible for the blood of soldiers whom it commands. Both readings, of course, are at some distance from the 'sigh running in blood', but we are sufficiently accustomed to such interpretive operations for this not to worry us.

What, though, of the chimney-sweep? One might assume that the Church is horrified ('appalled') at the conditions of child labour, but the convention of coherence invariably leads critics to reject this reading and to emphasize that 'appall' means to make pale or (since by convention puns are permitted when relevant) to cast a pall over and to weaken the Church's moral authority. The 'black'ning' church either becomes black, with guilt as well as soot, or makes things black by its indifference and hypocrisy; and the cry of the sweep changes its colour either by making it pale or by casting a pall of metaphorical soot over it. Our ability to perform these acts of semantic transference, moving 'black' and 'soot' around from sweep to church to its moral character, works as a kind of proof of the poem, a demonstration that there is a rich logical coherence and semantic solidarity here. The point, however, is that the lines do not carry an obvious meaning; they cannot be naturalized as an intimation of oppression without the help of a considerable amount of condensation and displacement.

The last stanza too has an initial strangeness which is difficult to naturalize. The speakers hears how a harlot's curse blasts a tear. We could, of course, read this as a harlot cursing at the fact that her own baby is crying, but since this is to be the climax of the poem we are constrained to reject this interpretation as premature naturalization. Indeed, such is the force of conventional expectations that no commentary I have read cites this reading, though it is the most obvious. To produce unity we must discover mind-forged manacles, and the best candidate for manacling is the infant. If we are to allow his tear to be blasted we must perform semantic operations on it: the tear can be an expression of protest and feeling, of innocence also perhaps, which is cursed and manacled not so much by the curse of the harlot (and again we become involved in semantic transfers) as by her existence. Her curse becomes her sign or mark and thus fits into the series of sounds which the narrator hears. By another transfer we can say that the infant himself is cursed, as he becomes an inhabitant of this world of harlots and charters. Similarly, in the last line we can transfer epithets to say that it is marriage itself which is blighted, so that the wedding carriage becomes a hearse, through the existence of the harlot. We could, of course, work out a casual relationship here (marriage is weakened if husbands visit harlots), but the level of generality at which the poem operates suggests that this will make coherence difficult. 'London' is not after all a description of specific social evils, and that, if we read the poem as a protest, is a fact with which we must now contend.

We must ask, in other words, what we are to say about the fact that the poem goes some way towards defeating our expectations: the cries are not cries of misery only but every cry of every man, even the shouts of street vendors. What are we to make, shall we say, of this odd semiotic procedure and of the interpretive requirements which the poem imposes upon us? There is a great distance which the reader must traverse in order to get from the language of the text to political protest. What does this signify? And the answer is, I think, that here, in the kind of reading which the poem requires, we have a representation of the problems of the visionary state. The distance between every cry and mind-forged manacles is great, so great that there is a possible ambiguity about whose mind is manacled. The speaker 'marks marks'; is it because he is 'marking' that he sees marks? He perceives, after all, the same thing in every street cry, in every face. In order to make sense of this we must construct an identity for the 'I' of the poem; we must postulate the figure of a visionary who sees what no one else sees, who can traverse these distances and read signs whose meaning is obscure to other observers. The city is not itself aware of its problems, its grief. The gap between appearance and awareness is presented, we can say, as the greatest terror of London. The true misery of manacles forged in the mind lies in the fact that they restrict the perception of misery and that no one else, not even the reader until the poem has forced him to exercise his symbolic imagination, can see the blood run down palace walls.

This has been a laboured account of what seems required if we are to read the poem as we do. It is not a structuralist interpretation for it agrees, except for the last paragraph, with customary readings of the poem. If it seems different, that is because it tries to make explicit some of the operations which we are accustomed to taking for granted. Some of these operations are highly conventional; they involve a special logic of literary interpretation, and it is not at all strange that critics prefer to take them for granted. But I think that if we are concerned with the nature of literature itself, or with dispelling the popular notion of the interpretation of literary texts as involving a complex guessing game, it is important to think more explicitly about the operations which our interpretations presuppose.

As Culler himself points out, the interpretation of a poem that emerges from a structuralist analysis may not be significantly different from what is revealed by a more conventional kind of analysis. The difference is that it makes explicit processes we tend to take for granted. Or at least that is the claim and the intention.

20

Criticism and the cultural context

A TYPE OF CRITICISM which is related both to historical and to sociological criticism is that which concerns itself with the whole complex of cultural activities of which the production of literature is only one fragment.

The cultural scene

The critic looks at the whole cultural scene and tries to assess its healthfulness for the literary artist. He considers questions of popular taste, the function of reviews and periodicals, the relation between "highbrows" and "lowbrows," the effect of religious, moral and political ideas on literary judgment, the relation between writers and publishers and the significance of such phenomena as the "best seller," and the kind and degree of responsiveness to artistic activities that can be found among different sections of the community. Here again the critic is not in the first instance making a value judgment of particular works; his first concern is to describe how the cultural climate of a period affects the production and appreciation of literature.

Arnold on middle class culture

One of the first important English critics to discuss literature from this point of view was Matthew Arnold, who felt that the solid middle classes of Victorian England, with their worship of material progress, were not the proper guardians of a literary heritage or the most satisfactory audience for imaginative literature, while the stern evangelical religion which so many of them professed produced an insensitivity to esthetic values. What happens to culture, he asked, in such an environment, and what is the message which true culture has to bring to such people?

. . . Every one must have observed the strange language current during the late discussions as to the possible failure of our supply of coal. Our coal, thousands of people were saying, is the real basis of our national greatness; if our coal runs short, there is an end of the greatness of England. But what *is* greatness?—culture makes us ask. Greatness is a spiritual condition worthy to excite love, interest, and admiration. If England were swallowed up by the sea to-morrow, which of the two, a hundred years hence, would most excite the love, interest, and admiration of mankind,—would most, therefore, show the evidences of having possessed greatness,—the England of the last twenty years, or the England of Elizabeth, of a time of splendid spiritual effort, but when our coal, and our industrial operations depending on coal, were very little developed? . . .

Wealth, again, that end to which our prodigious works for material advantage are directed,—the commonest of commonplaces tells us how men are always apt to regard wealth as a precious end in itself; and certainly they have never been so apt thus to regard it as they are in England at the present time. Never did people believe anything more firmly, than nine Englishmen out of ten at the present day believe that our greatness and welfare are proved by our being so very rich. Now, the use of culture is that it helps us, by means of its spiritual standard of perfection, to regard wealth as but machinery, and not only to say as a matter of words that we regard wealth as but machinery, but really to perceive and feel that it is so.

If it were not for this purging effect wrought upon our minds by culture, the whole world, the future as well as the present, would inevitably belong to the Philistines. The people who believe most that our greatness and welfare are proved by our being very rich, and who most give their lives and thoughts to becoming rich, are just the very people whom we call Philistines. Culture says: "Consider these people, then, their way of life, their habits, their manners, the very tones of their voice; look at them attentively; observe the literature they read, the things which give them pleasure, the words which come forth out of their mouths, the thoughts which make the furniture of their minds; would any amount of wealth be worth having with the condition that one was to become just like these people by having it?" And thus culture begets a dissatisfaction which is of the highest possible value in stemming the common tide of men's thoughts in a wealthy and industrial community, and which saves the future, as one may hope, from being vulgarised, even if it cannot save the present. . . .

Every one with anything like an adequate idea of human perfection has distinctly marked [the] subordination to higher and spiritual ends of the cultivation of bodily vigour and activity. "Bodily exercise profiteth little; but godliness is profitable unto all things," says the author of the Epistle to Timothy. And the utilitarian Franklin says just as explicitly:—"Eat and drink such an exact quantity as suits the constitution of thy body, *in reference to the services of the mind.*" But the point of view of culture, keeping the mark of human perfection simply and broadly in view, and not assigning to this perfection, as religion or utilitarianism assign to it, a special and limited character—this point of view, I say, of culture, is best given by these words of Epictetus:—"It is a sign of ἀφυΐα," says he,—that is, of a nature not finely tempered,—"to give yourselves up to things which relate to the body; to make, for instance, a great fuss about exercise, a great fuss about eating, a great fuss about drinking, a great fuss about walking, a great fuss about riding. All these things ought to be done merely by the way: the formation of the spirit and character must be our real concern." This is admirable; and, indeed, the Greek word εὐφυΐα, a finely tempered nature, gives exactly the notion of perfection as culture brings us to conceive it: a harmonious perfection, a perfection in which the characters of beauty and intelligence are both present, which unites "the two noblest of things," —as Swift, who of one of the two, at any rate, had himself all too little, most happily calls them in his *Battle of the Books,*—"the two noblest of things, *sweetness and light.*" The εὐφυής is the man who tends towards sweetness and light; the ἀφυής, on the other hand, is our Philistine. The immense spiritual significance of the Greeks is due to their having been inspired with this central and happy idea of the essential character of human perfection . . .

In thus making sweetness and light to be characters of perfection, culture

386 Literary Criticism and Related Disciplines

is of like spirit with poetry, follows one law with poetry. Far more than on our freedom, our population, and our industrialism, many amongst us rely upon our religious organisations to save us. I have called religion a yet more important manifestation of human nature than poetry, because it has worked on a broader scale for perfection, and with greater masses of men. But the idea of beauty and of a human nature perfect on all its sides, which is the dominant idea of poetry, is a true and invaluable idea, though it has not yet had the success that the idea of conquering the obvious faults of our animality, and of a human nature perfect on the moral side,—which is the dominant idea of religion,—has been enabled to have; and it is destined, adding to itself the religious idea of a devout energy, to transform and govern the other. . . .

The impulse of the English race towards moral development and self-conquest has nowhere so powerfully manifested itself as in Puritanism. Nowhere has Puritanism found so adequate an expression as in the religious organisation of the Independents. The modern Independents have a newspaper, the *Noncomformist*, written with great sincerity and ability. The motto, the standard, the profession of faith which this organ of theirs carries aloft, is "The Dissidence of Dissent and the Protestantism of the Protestant religion." There is sweetness and light, and an ideal of complete harmonious human perfection! One need not go to culture and poetry to find language to judge it. . . . Men have got such a habit of giving to the language of religion a special application, of making it a mere jargon, that for the condemnation which religion itself passes on the shortcomings of their religious organisations they have no ear; they are sure to cheat themselves and to explain this condemnation away. They can only be reached by the criticism which culture, like poetry, speaking a language not to be sophisticated, and resolutely testing these organisations by the ideal of a human perfection complete on all sides, applies to them.

But men of culture and poetry, it will be said, are again and again failing, and failing conspicuously, in the necessary first stage to a harmonious perfection, in the subduing of the great obvious faults of our animality, which it is the glory of these religious organizations to have helped us to subdue. True, they do often so fail. They have often been without the virtues as well as the faults of the Puritan; it has been one of their dangers that they so felt the Puritan's faults that they too much neglected the practice of his virtues. I will not, however, exculpate them at the Puritan's expense. They have often failed in morality, and morality is indispensable. And they have been punished for their failure, as the Puritan has been rewarded for his performance. They have been punished wherein they erred; but their ideal of beauty, of sweetness and light, and a human nature complete on all its sides, remains the true ideal of perfection still; just as the Puritan's ideal of perfection remains narrow and inadequate, although for what he did well he has been richly rewarded. Notwithstanding the mighty results of the Pilgrim Fathers' voyage, they and their standard of perfection are rightly judged when we figure to ourselves Shakespeare or Virgil,—souls in whom sweetness and light, and all that in human nature is most humane, were eminent,—accompanying them on their voyage, and think what intolerable company Shakespeare and Virgil would have found them! In the same way let us judge the religious organizations which we see all around us. Do not let us deny the good and the happiness which they have accomplished; but do not let us fail to see clearly that their idea of human perfection is narrow and inadequate, and that the Dissidence of Dissent and the Protestantism of the Protestant religion will never bring humanity to its true goal. As I said with regard to wealth; Let us look at the life of those who live in and for it,—so I say with regard to the religious organizations. Look at the life imaged in such a newspaper as the *Nonconformist*—a life of jealousy of the Establishment, disputes, tea-meetings, openings of chapels, sermons; and then think of it as an ideal of a human life completing itself on all sides, and aspiring with all its organs after sweetness, light, and perfection!

Another newspaper, representing, like the *Nonconformist*, one of the religious organizations of this country, was a short time ago giving an account of the crowd at Epsom on the Derby day, and of all the vice and hideousness which was to be seen in that crowd; and then the writer turned suddenly round upon Professor Huxley, and asked him how he proposed to cure all this vice and hideousness without religion. I confess I felt disposed to ask the asker this question: and how do you propose to cure it with such a religion as yours? How is the ideal of a life so unlovely, so unattractive, so incomplete, so narrow, so far removed from a true and satisfying ideal of human perfection, as is the life of your religious organization as you yourself reflect it, to conquer and transform all this vice and hideousness? . . .

Arnold then quotes some examples of middle-class self-congratulation on material achievements, and continues:

But teaching the democracy to put its trust in achievements of this kind is merely training them to be Philistines to take the place of the Philistines whom they are superseding; and they too, like the middle class, will be encouraged to sit down at the banquet of the future without having on a wedding garment, and nothing excellent can then come from them. Those who know their besetting faults, those who have watched them and listened to them, or those who will read the instructive account recently given of them by one of themselves, the *Journeyman Engineer*, will agree that the idea which culture sets before us of perfection,—an increased spiritual activity, having for its characters increased sweetness, increased

388 *Literary Criticism and Related Disciplines*

light, increased life, increased sympathy,—is an idea which the new democracy needs far more than the idea of the blessedness of the franchise,
or the wonderfulness of its own industrial performances. . . .

The pursuit of perfection, then, is the pursuit of sweetness and light. He
who works for sweetness and light, works to make reason and the will of
God prevail. He who works for machinery, he who works for hatred,
works only for confusion. Culture looks beyond machinery, culture hates
hatred; culture has one great passion, the passion for sweetness and light. It
has one even yet greater!—the passion for making them *prevail*. It is not
satisfied till we *all* come to a perfect man; it knows that the sweetness and
light of the few must be imperfect until the raw and unkindled masses of
humanity are touched with sweetness and light. If I have not shrunk from
saying that we must work for sweetness and light, so neither have I shrunk
from saying that we must have a broad basis, must have sweetness and light
for as many as possible. Again and again I have insisted how those are the
happy moments of humanity, how those are the marking epochs of a people's life, how those are the flowering times for literature and art and all the
creative power of genius, when there is a *national* glow of life and thought,
when the whole of society is in the fullest measure permeated by thought,
sensible to beauty, intelligent and alive. Only it must be *real* thought and
real beauty; *real* sweetness and *real* light. Plenty of people will try to give
the masses, as they call them, an intellectual food prepared and adapted in
the way they think proper for the actual condition of the masses. The ordinary popular literature is an example of this way of working on the masses.
Plenty of people will try to indoctrinate the masses with the set of ideas
and judgments constituting the creed of their own profession or party.
Our religious and political organizations give an example of this way of
working on the masses. I condemn neither way: but culture works differently. It does not try to teach down to the level of inferior classes; it does
not try to win them for this or that sect of its own, with ready-made judgments and watchwords. It seeks to do away with classes; to make the best
that has been thought and known in the world current everywhere; to
make all men live in an atmosphere of sweetness and light, where they may
use ideas, as it uses them itself, freely—nourished, and not bound by them.

This is the *social idea;* and the men of culture are the true apostles of
equality. The great men of culture are those who have had a passion for diffusing, for making prevail, for carrying from one end of society to the
other, the best knowledge, the best ideas of their time; who have labored
to divest knowledge of all that was harsh, uncouth, difficult, abstract, professional, exclusive; to humanize it, to make it efficient outside the clique of
the cultivated and learned, yet still remaining the *best* knowledge and
thought of the time, and a true source, therefore, of sweetness and light.
Such a man was Abelard in the Middle Ages, in spite of all his imperfec-

tions; and thence the boundless emotion and enthusiasm which Abelard
excited. Such were Lessing and Herder in Germany, at the end of the last
century; and their services to Germany were in this way inestimably
precious. Generations will pass, and literary monuments will accumulate,
and works far more perfect than the works of Lessing and Herder will be
produced in Germany; and yet the names of these two men will fill a German with a reverence and enthusiasm such as the names of the most gifted
masters will hardly awaken. And why? Because they *humanized* knowledge; because they broadened the basis of life and intelligence; because
they worked powerfully to diffuse sweetness and light, to make reason and
the will of God prevail.[1]

At first sight this kind of lay preaching might seem very far removed from literary criticism; Arnold himself called *Culture and
Anarchy* "an essay in political and social criticism." But the concern
with the nature and quality of culture which Arnold exhibits here is
very relevant to the criticism of literature, though it is not in itself
literary criticism. Not only has literature a function in helping to
remedy the state of affairs which Arnold was deploring; that state
of affairs has its own effect on the kind of literature which is produced and enjoyed. In his essay on "The Function of Criticism at
the Present Time," written in 1864,[2] Arnold made clear that he
was concerned with the state of civilization, the whole pattern of a
people's culture, and that in discussing literary criticism one must
take into account the cultural situation in which it operates. The
trouble with literary criticism in his day, he maintains in this essay,
is that it was not sufficiently disinterested, and in explaining this lack
of disinterestedness he is led into an attack on the whole middle class
way of thinking:

. . . And how is it to be disinterested? By keeping aloof from practice;
by resolutely following the law of its own nature, which is to be a free
play of the mind on all subjects which it touches; by steadily refusing to
lend itself to any of those ulterior, political, practical considerations about
ideas, which plenty of people will be sure to attach to them, which perhaps
ought often to be attached to them, which in this country at any rate are
certain to be attached to them quite sufficiently, but which criticism has
really nothing to do with. Its business is, as I have said, simply to know the
best that is known and thought in the world, and by in its turn making this
known, to create a current of true and fresh ideas. Its business is to do this

1 "Sweetness and Light," in *Culture and Anarchy*, 1869.
2 Published in *Essays in Criticism*, 1865.

with inflexible honesty, with due ability; but its business is to do no more, and to leave alone all questions of practical consequences and applications, questions which will never fail to have due prominence given to them. Else criticism, besides being really false to its own nature, merely continues in the old rut which it has hitherto followed in this country, and will certainly miss the chance now given to it. For what is at present the bane of criticism in this country? It is that practical considerations cling to it and stifle it; it subserves interests not its own; our organs of criticism are organs of men and parties having practical ends to serve, and with them those practical ends are the first thing and the play of mind the second; so much play of mind as is compatible with the prosecution of those practical ends is all that is wanted. An organ like the *Revue des Deux Mondes,* having for its main function to understand and utter the best that is known and thought in the world, existing, it may be said, as just an organ for a free play of the mind, we have not; but we have the *Edinburgh Review,* existing as an organ of the old Whigs, and for as much play of the mind as may suit its being that; we have the *Quarterly Review,* existing as an organ of the Tories, and for as much play of mind as may suit its being that; we have the *British Quarterly Review,* existing as an organ of the political Dissenters, and for as much play of mind as may suit its being that; we have the *Times,* existing as an organ of the common, satisfied, well-to-do Englishman, and for as much play of mind as may suit its being that. And so on through all the various fractions, political and religious, of our society; every fraction has, as such, its organ of criticism, but the notion of combining all fractions in the common pleasure of a free disinterested play of mind meets with no favour. Directly this play of mind wants to have more scope, and to forget the pressure of practical considerations a little, it is checked, it is made to feel the chain. . . .

It is because criticism has so little kept in the pure intellectual sphere, has so little detached itself from practice, has been so directly polemical and controversial, that it has so ill accomplished, in this country, its best spiritual work; which is to keep man from a self-satisfaction which is retarding and vulgarizing, to lead him towards perfection, by making his mind dwell upon what is excellent in itself, and the absolute beauty and fitness of things. A polemical practical criticism makes men blind even to the ideal imperfection of their practice, makes them willingly assert its ideal perfection, in order the better to secure it against attack: and clearly this is narrowing and baneful for them. If they were reassured on the practical side, speculative considerations of ideal perfection they might be brought to entertain, and their spiritual horizon would thus gradually widen. Sir Charles Adderley says to the Warwickshire farmers:

"Talk of the improvement of breed! Why, the race we ourselves represent, the men and women, the old Anglo-Saxon race, are the best breed in the whole world. . . . The absence of a too enervating climate, too un-clouded skies, and a too luxurious nature, has produced so vigorous a race of people, and has rendered us so superior to all the world."

Mr. Roebuck says to the Sheffield cutlers:

"I look around me and ask what is the state of England? Is not property safe? Is not every man able to say what he likes? Can you not walk from one end of England to the other in perfect security? I ask you whether, the world over or in past history, there is anything like it? Nothing. I pray that our unrivalled happiness may last."

Now obviously there is a peril for poor human nature in words and thoughts of such exuberant self-satisfaction, until we find ourselves safe in the streets of the Celestial City. . . .

But neither Sir Charles Adderley nor Mr. Roebuck is by nature in-accessible to considerations of this sort. They only lose sight of them owing to the controversial life we all lead, and the practical form which all speculation takes with us. They have in view opponents whose aim is not ideal, but practical; and in their zeal to uphold their own practice against these innovators, they go so far as even to attribute to this practice an ideal perfection. Somebody has been wanting to introduce a six-pound franchise, or to abolish church rates, or to collect agricultural statistics by force, or to diminish local self-government. How natural, in reply to such proposals, very likely improper or ill-timed, to go a little beyond the mark and to say stoutly, "Such a race of people as we stand, so superior to all the world! The old Anglo-Saxon race, the best breed in the whole world! I pray that our unrivalled happiness may last! I ask you whether, the world over or in past history, there is anything like it?" And so long as criticism answers this dithyramb by insisting that the old Anglo-Saxon race would be still more superior to all others if it had no church rates, or that our unrivalled happiness would last yet longer with a six-pound franchise, so long will the strain, "The best breed in the whole world!" swell louder and louder, everything ideal and refining will be lost out of sight, and both the assailed and their critics will remain in a sphere, to say the truth, perfectly unvital, a sphere in which spiritual progression is im-possible. But let criticism leave church rates and the franchise alone, and in the most candid spirit, without a single lurking thought of practical inno-vation, confront with our dithyramb this paragraph on which I stumbled in a newspaper immediately after reading Mr. Roebuck:—

"A shocking child murder has just been committed at Nottingham. A girl named Wragg left the workhouse there on Saturday morning with her young illegitimate child. The child was soon afterwards found dead on Mapperly Hills, having been strangled. Wragg is in custody."

Nothing but that; but, in juxtaposition with the absolute eulogies of Sir

Charles Adderley and Mr. Roebuck, how eloquent, how suggestive are those few lines! "Our old Anglo-Saxon breed, the best in the whole world!"—how much that is harsh and ill-favoured there is in this best! *Wragg!* If we are to talk of ideal perfection, of "the best in the whole world," has anyone reflected what a touch of grossness in our race, what an original shortcoming in the more delicate spiritual perceptions, is shown by the natural growth among us of such hideous names—Higginbottom, Stiggins, Bugg! In Ionia and Attica they were luckier in this respect than "the best race in the world"; by the Ilissus there was no Wragg, poor thing! And "our unrivalled happiness"—what an element of grimness, bareness, and hideousness mixes with it and blurs it; the workhouse, the dismal Mapperly Hills,—how dismal those who have seen them will re- member—the gloom, the smoke, the cold, the strangled illegitimate child! "I ask you whether, the world over or in past history, there is anything like it?" Perhaps not, one is inclined to answer; but at any rate, in that case, the world is very much to be pitied. And the final touch—short, bleak and inhuman: *Wragg is in custody.* The sex lost in the confusion of our unrivalled happiness; or (shall I say?) the superfluous Christian name lopped off by the straightforward vigour of our old Anglo-Saxon breed! There is profit for the spirit in such contrasts as this; criticism serves the cause of perfection by establishing them. By eluding sterile conflict, by refusing to remain in the sphere where alone narrow and relative concep- tions have any worth and validity, criticism may diminish its momentary importance, but only in this way has it a chance of gaining admittance for those wider and more perfect conceptions to which all its duty is really owed. Mr. Roebuck will have a poor opinion of an adversary who replies to his defiant songs of triumph only by murmuring under his breath, *Wragg is in custody;* but in no other way will these songs of triumph be induced gradually to moderate themselves, to get rid in what in them is excessive and offensive, and to fall into a softer and truer key.

Arnold is here turning an esthetic eye on social behavior, and finding it ugly. And so long as the whole pattern of civilization is shot through with ugliness, true literary criticism cannot be practiced and the greatest literature can neither be produced nor appreciated. Arnold is perfectly aware of the apparent irrelevance of his remarks to liter- ary study, and he follows the passage just quoted by a defense of their relevance:

It will be said that it is a very subtle and indirect action which I am thus prescribing for criticism, and that, by embracing in this manner the Indian virtue of detachment and abandoning the sphere of practical life, it condemns itself to a slow and obscure work. Slow and obscure it may be, but it is the only proper work of criticism . . .

It may seem a paradox that Arnold relates literature to the context of the civilization of which it is a part in order to preach distinterestedness and detachment; but it is by showing how the squalor and dullness of practical life is affecting literary controversies that he can best demonstrate the need for disinterestedness. And literary criticism, if practiced disinterestedly, can then return and help to improve the atmosphere of civilization, bringing "sweetness and light" into the complacent darkness of industrial England and thus setting the stage for a new efflorescence of creative writing.

Literature in an industrial civilization

The effects of the Industrial Revolution on the literary imagination and on critical ideas disturbed other critics besides Arnold—Ruskin and William Morris, for example. The new urban classes, free popular education with its resulting mass literacy, the growth of popular literature and a popular press to appeal to that mass literacy and the resulting split of literary audiences into "highbrow" and "lowbrow" are problems that have been much discussed since Arnold's day. Writers like Lewis Mumford have been concerned with what might be called the esthetics of our civilization, and quality of our living, building, working, reading, and entertaining. Such a book as *Culture and Environment* by F. R. Leavis and Denys Thompson (London, 1933) studies the effect of modern industrial conditions, of advertising, mass production, and standardization, on the way in which people live and think and the nature of their response to literature and the arts. And there are many other critics in our time continuing the Arnold tradition, setting literature in the wider context of contemporary culture and seeking to improve the one by improving the other. The critics who carry on this kind of activity do not, as a rule, profess to be impartial—they are not historical or sociological critics simply investigating the relationship between environment and art, though their activity sometimes overlaps with that of these critics; they tend to be active missionaries, concerned about standards, concerned about the improvement of critical awareness, concerned about the plight of the arts in an industrial civilization. Arnold pioneered in showing this kind of concern, and his successors find themselves unable to avoid it at some point. In a world of pulp magazines and little reviews, of best sellers and complex metaphysical poetry, of "classics and commercials," the literary critic cannot help asking himself what makes these differences and whether they are healthy. And to ask such questions is to become a critic not only of literature but also of civilization.

The writer and his cultural context

The critic concerned with the cultural context within which an author operates need not confine his interest to the problems raised by middle class Philistinism and similar phenomena. He may wish simply to see how the quality and tone of literature is related to the kind of culture of which the author was a part. This interest overlaps with that of the sociological critic, discussed in the previous chapter. One might distinguish between courtly literature, "Great House" literature, literature produced under the patronage system, the literature of Grub Street, literature produced by writers working for commercial publishers in the modern sense, literature produced serially in magazines, railway literature, and so on, and in each case relate the qualities of the works under consideration to the context within which they were written. One can distinguish a difference in tone between those of Shakespeare's plays that were written for the public theater and those that were written for the private theater: the cultural context was different in each case. The difference between Shakespeare, Ben Jonson, and Beaumont and Fletcher can be considered as a difference between the social context within which each moved. (This is the approach used in J. F. Danby's *Poets on Fortune's Hill*, referred to in Chapter 18.) The difference between the writer as a gentleman writing to please himself and his friends and the writer as a professional reflects a more deep-seated difference between the kinds of culture in which each flourishes. This kind of criticism is not evaluative; its aim is to help to account for differences in tone, style, and method between writers by showing how those differences are related to shifts in the cultural context. Although Matthew Arnold and his successors linked the question of the production of good literature to the question of the health of society, thus making value judgments about both society and literature, it is possible–and profitable–for a more historically-minded critic to look at literature in its cultural context without any normative intention, but simply in order to add to understanding.

Epilogue

THERE IS NO single 'right' method of handling literary problems, no single approach to works of literary art that will yield all the significant truths about them. Works of literature have been produced in enormous variety over a very long period of human history; and—though the differentiating qualities of literary art can be isolated and discussed by the philosophic critic—generalizations applicable to all examples of that art are more interesting to the metaphysician than to the man of letters. While the scrutinizing of literary theories is a valuable philosophical activity that can not only throw light on the nature of literature but also help us read individual works with greater understanding and appreciation, the active appreciation of literature is not always dependent on such theorizing.

It would be absurd to maintain that no Greek appreciated Sophocles until Aristotle had written the *Poetics* or that English playgoers had to wait for A. C. Bradley or Professor Heilman before they could appreciate and enjoy *King Lear*. Appreciation can be independent of critical theory, although the development and application of critical theory can help to clarify, focus, and increase appreciation.

Art is greater than its interpreters, and it should be clear from the preceding pages that not even the greatest critic has been able to pin down all its kinds of significance and value. All criticism is tentative, partial, oblique. This is not by any means to say that there are no standards of value, that we must fall back on personal taste, or vague impressionism, or mere gush. We do, however, mean that no critical statement about a work of literary art can be a complete statement of what it is and whether or not it is good. On the level of critical theory, it may be possible to construct a set of valid general principles; as far as practical criticism is concerned—criticism designed to demonstrate the nature and quality of a work and so to increase understanding and appreciation—it must always be fragmentary, indirect, approximate. It can never be a complete and wholly satisfactory description of what takes place in the work of art.

It is not difficult to see why this should be so. A work of literature —a poem, for example—is an immense complex of meaning which is nevertheless often simple and immediate in its impact, and it is impossible (or at least difficult) to describe that complex and simultaneously to account for its impact. To resolve a poem into mere complexity by analytic discussion is often useful and helpful, but such a procedure does not necessarily explain the reasons for the poem's total impact on the reader. Nor does it necessarily increase appreciation for the inexperienced. Something is left over, which the critic has to try to show his reader by his tactful handling of analogies and suggestions. Literary criticism remains an art, not a science, and the critic who tries to reduce his practice to the following of a rigid scientific method runs the risk of letting the true vitality of the work of literature elude him and his readers. The truth that the critic can know about a work, and precisely communicate, is part of the larger truth he can only suggest. And a literary critic without a fully developed technique of suggestion is like a music critic trained only in acoustics.

Further, criticism, as T. S. Eliot once remarked, is not "autotelic"; it is not an end in itself, but a means to the greater understanding and appreciation of literary works. It should always be tested by its success in achieving that end. The tendency of professional critics is to establish a method, which can be taught to disciples, and to set more store by the right handling of the method than by the increased perception, understanding, and appreciation it yields. The study of literary criticism is properly the study of techniques of illumination; if it becomes the study of different kinds of specialized vocabulary or different kinds of professional tricks merely, the student is wasting his time. There are more techniques of illumination than can be comprised in the examination of different formal approaches. Whatever enables a reader to see further into the manifold life of a literary work is effective criticism. There are some who can be brought to enter into the rich vitality of a work more effectively by having it read aloud slowly, with proper phrasing and emphasis, than by the most careful analysis of its structure. Art is meant to be experienced, and in the last analysis the function of criticism is to assist that experience.

All this may seem obvious, but it perhaps needs saying after much discussion of critical methods and approaches. Criticism has its own fascination—from the philosophical appeal of the theoretical inquiry into the nature of literary art to the historical scholar's excitement in seeing new meanings in a phrase or an image by setting it in the intellectual context of its time. To civilized man, no knowledge comes amiss, and knowledge about works of literature—their organization, their meaning, their psychological and sociological causes, their relation to the civilization that produced them—can be welcomed as knowledge without being needed to increase appreciation. But such knowledge, simply regarded as knowledge, however exciting to pursue, is no better and no worse than the pursuit of any other kind of knowledge. Only when it is put at the service of understanding, discrimination, and appreciation can it claim a place in liberal education.

To enjoy with discrimination, to discern value, to recognize and reject the spurious, to respond maturely to the genuine, never to be fooled by the shabby and the second-hand—that is the civilized approach to the arts. We turn to criticism to develop and strengthen that approach; and, as we have seen, criticism can come to this task directly or indirectly, through a frontal attack on individual literary works, through theoretical discussion of the nature of literary value, through investigation of origin and growth and causation. Every effective literary critic sees some facet of literary art and develops our awareness with respect to it; but the total vision, or something approximating it, comes only to those who learn how to blend the insights yielded by many critical approaches.

Index